LANDSCAPES

GROUNDWORK FOR COLLEGE READING

CHRISTINE EVANS CARTER

ST. LOUIS COMMUNITY COLLEGE—MERAMEC

WADSWORTH
CENGAGE Learning·

Australia • Brazil • Japan • Korea • Mexico • Singapore • Spain • United Kingdom • United States

WADSWORTH
CENGAGE Learning·

Landscapes: Groundwork for College Reading
Christine Evans Carter

Senior Publisher: Lyn Uhl

Director of Developmental Studies: Annie Todd

Executive Editor: Shani Fisher

Development Editor: Marita Sermolins

Assistant Editor: Elizabeth Rice

Editorial Assistant: Matt Conte

Media Editor: Amy Gibbons

Marketing Coordinator: Brittany Blais

Marketing Communications Manager: Linda Yip

Content Project Manager: Corinna Dibble

Senior Art Director: Cate Rickard Barr

Manufacturing Planner: Betsy Donaghey

Rights Acquisition Specialist: Don Schlotman

Production Service and Composition: MPS Limited, a Macmillan Company

Text and Cover Designer: Dare Porter

Cover Image: *Countryside in Val d'Orcia.*

Credit: Flirt/SuperStock.

For product information and technology assistance, contact us at **Cengage Learning Customer & Sales Support, 1-800-354-9706**

For permission to use material from this text or product, submit all requests online at **www.cengage.com/permissions.** Further permissions questions can be emailed to **permissionrequest@cengage.com.**

Library of Congress Control Number: 2011937590

Student Edition:

ISBN-13: 978-0-495-91316-0

ISBN-10: 0-495-91316-2

Wadsworth
20 Channel Center Street
Boston, MA 02210
USA

Cengage Learning is a leading provider of customized learning solutions with office locations around the globe, including Singapore, the United Kingdom, Australia, Mexico, Brazil and Japan. Locate your local office at **international.cengage.com/region**

Cengage Learning products are represented in Canada by Nelson Education, Ltd.

For your course and learning solutions, visit **www.cengage.com.**

Purchase any of our products at your local college store or at our preferred online store **www.cengagebrain.com.**

Instructors: Please visit **login.cengage.com** and log in to access instructor-specific resources.

Printed in China
2 3 4 5 6 7 18 17 16 15

TABLE OF
CONTENTS

iii

UNIT
2

MAIN
IDEAS

PinkTag/iStockphoto.com

UNIT 3

RELATIONSHIPS BETWEEN IDEAS

Subbotina Anna/Shutterstock.com

CHAPTER 5: PATTERNS OF ORGANIZATION   320
Theme: Sleep and Dreams

CHAPTER 6: SUPPORTING DETAILS   396
Theme: The World of Work

UNIT
4

CRITICAL
THINKING

Josie Lepe/San Jose Mercury News/MCT

CHAPTER 7: CRITICAL READING   472
Theme: Issues in the Modern World

FOREWORD TO STUDENTS:
THE *LANDSCAPES* APPROACH

Put a check mark after each statement that could apply to you.

- I often read an assignment for school and then cannot remember what I've read. ___
- I read and think I understand a passage, but I cannot figure out what the author's main point is. ___
- I read assigned material for my college classes, but I have trouble identifying what to study. ___
- I read assigned material for my college classes, but I have trouble identifying the meanings of complicated words and phrases. ___

These are very common problems for college students. *Landscapes: Groundwork for College Reading* will help you improve your reading so you can increase your success in college-level courses.

This book is titled *Landscapes* because the readings, skills, and strategies you will learn about comprehension, vocabulary, and study skills will set the foundation and lay your groundwork for college success. Learning with this book, you can use your wealth of experience to your advantage in becoming a better reader if you connect what an author has written to that background knowledge.

Another type of groundwork that you will do is learning how to enhance what you already know with specific skills and strategies that are proven to improve reading. Also, you set your groundwork by reading about themes and topics that are common in college classes, which will put you a step ahead.

Reading improvement involves using both skills and strategies to aid comprehension. A skill is an ability that is developed through practice. Skills, when learned, become automatic and require little thought in their application. For new skills to become habits, you must practice them so they do become automatic. A strategy is a plan or method used to achieve a specific result. Strategies are battle plans for learning that let you use a series of skills to their best advantage.

Many students come to college not knowing very much about college-level course content. But you know more than you think you know, and you can use this to help you understand what you read. At the start of each chapter, you will think through what you already know so your brain is primed to learn and remember information. Also, you will be able to "think through" each skill and strategy in each of the chapters with the step-by-step explanations provided in the Thinking It Through sections. Afterward, you can try your hand at applying the skills and strategies in the On Your Own sections. Sometimes, however, practice really does make perfect. Therefore, *Landscapes* provides you with many practice exercises for you to complete to make sure that you can apply each skill and strategy. The exercises following the application readings will strengthen fundamental comprehension and vocabulary skills that you will need to succeed in college reading.

You will also build your general knowledge stores from the *Landscapes* readings, drawn from popular subjects common in college courses. By learning about related topics in each chapter, you will build your background knowledge. This, in turn, will make future college work easier for you, as background knowledge and comprehension of a reading are closely linked. In addition, you will apply what you learn to actual college textbook chapters from popular introductory courses. The exercises and questions in the text are not repetitive, but the practice of skills and strategies is recursive, meaning you will build on what you learn in each chapter as you progress through the book.

As you interact with *Landscapes*, you will learn how to work with your brain to process information more effectively. You will learn how to overcome the problems commonly encountered in reading at the college level—and what you read will begin to make better sense. A smart student can use the *Landscapes* approach to become a more effective, efficient, and successful learner.

ACKNOWLEDGMENTS

Like the creation of *Mindscapes: Critical Reading Skills and Strategies*, **Landscapes: Groundwork for College Reading** has been a stimulating and very rewarding undertaking, involving much time, dedication, and effort. All of this would be impossible without the help of so many talented and helpful professionals.

To Annie Todd, Director of Developmental English at Cengage Learning: Thank you for your enthusiasm, support and encouragement in writing this second text. Marita Sermolins, Development Editor: thank you for your tremendous help and expertise in making this process a smooth one. Thanks also to Shani Fisher, Executive Editor, College Success and Developmental Reading and Corinna Dibble and Jane Lee, Content Product Managers. Ed Dionne and the production team were consummate professionals—thanks to all of you. Also, Elizabeth Rice, Assistant Editor, did excellent work handling the supplements for Landscapes.

Thanks to the many reviewers who provided insightful and creative suggestions for improving this book through its stages.

Sandra Albers, Leeward Community College
James Andersen, Springfield Technical Community College
Tamera Ardrey, North Lake College
Bernadette Austin, Mott College
Susan Banach, South Suburban College
Kathleen Barlow, Martin University
Doralee Brooks, Community College of Allegheny County
Kathleen Carlson, Brevard Community College
Helen Ceraldi, North Lake Community College
Cynthia Crable, Allegany College of Maryland
Beverly Dile, Elizabethtown Community and Technical College
Sherry Dilley, Minneapolis Community and Technical College
La Tonya Dyett, Community College of Baltimore County—Catonsville
Mindy Flowers, Midland College
Marty Frailey, Pima Community College
Polly Green, Arkansas State University
Patricia Hill-Miller, Central Piedmont Community College
Judith Isonhood, Hinds Community College
Brandi Jackson, South Plains College
Julie Kelly, St. Johns River Community College
Sunita Lank, Hartnell College
Marilyn Leahy, Virginia Commonwealth University
Mary S. Leonard, Wytheville Community College

Tina Luffman, Yavapai College

Lara Messersmith-Glavin, Portland Community College

Lisa Mizes, St. Louis Community College at Meramec

Meridith Nelson, Des Moines Area Community College

Judy Parks, Macon State College

Ann Perez, Miami Dade College

Tracey Rhodes, Des Moines Area Community College

Craig E. Sasser, Northeast Mississippi Community College

Margaret Seymour, South Plains College

Marjorie Sussman, Miami Dade College

Michelle Van de Sande, Arapahoe Community College

Shari Waldrop, Navarro College

Helen Woodman, Ferris State University

Also, many thanks to the following people:

My students at St. Louis Community College at Meramec over the past twelve years

My colleagues at St. Louis Community College

My family: for you, once again

APPROACHING COLLEGE READING

UNIT
1

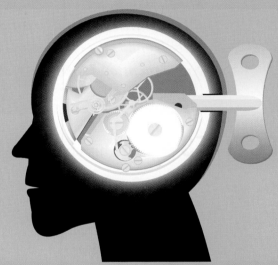

Ivan Gusev/iStockphoto.com

ACTIVE READING AND PREVIEWING

THEME *Success in College—Your Attitude*

"The function of education is to teach one to think intensively and to think critically.... Intelligence plus character—that is the goal of true education." — MARTIN LUTHER KING, JR.

OBJECTIVES

In this chapter, you will focus on:

COMPREHENSION SKILLS

Learn how to find information in a reading with

- Active reading
- Previewing
- Predicting

LEARNING HOW TO FIND INFORMATION

READING STUDY SKILLS

Learn how to find information in a reading through the reading process

VOCABULARY SKILLS

Learn how to find information from context clues to determine the meaning of unknown words using

- Definition clues
- Synonym clues

© Cengage Learning 2013

WHY DO YOU NEED TO KNOW THIS?

Problem: Cassandra is 24 and new to college. She is smart and motivated, but she is unsure about how to best approach the pages upon pages of reading she is assigned for all her classes. She feels overwhelmed and stressed with the pressure of going back to school along with the demands of her full-time job. Cassandra tries to get all of the reading done for each class but often struggles with these questions: "What is the important information I need to learn from each chapter? How do I focus on my reading without drifting off and thinking about something else?"

Lichtmeister/Shutterstock.com

WHAT ADVICE WOULD YOU OFFER TO CASSANDRA?

_____

_____

_____

_____

Solution: Cassandra, like many students, is unaware that there are effective methods of reading and learning for college success. Reading actually begins with thinking and investigating *before* you start reading a passage from start to finish. The first step to being a successful college student is to learn how to approach and begin a reading assignment. When you understand how your brain processes information and learns effectively, you can apply that step-by-step process to reading. This chapter introduces you to fundamental skills and strategies to jump-start your college reading and learning experience.

WHAT DO YOU ALREADY KNOW?

Fill in the first two columns, K and W, of the KWL chart here. When you reach the end of this chapter, come back and fill out the L column.

K: WHAT I <u>KNOW</u>	W: WHAT I <u>WANT</u> TO LEARN	L: WHAT I <u>LEARNED</u>
What do you already know about being successful in college?	What do you want to learn about being successful in college?	What have you learned about being successful in college?

PRE-ASSESSMENT

This pre-assessment will help you measure what you already know and what you need to learn about the reading skills and strategies explored in this chapter. Your results will help you understand your strengths and weaknesses. Read the article, and then answer the Comprehension Check questions that follow.

College Survival Tips: Making the Transition

1   The jump to college can be stressful. You're leaving behind your school, friends, family, and home, and going off to explore a new place, make new friends, learn new things, and set your own priorities.

2   Many students overlook the stress involved in making so many big changes in such a brief period of time. The more prepared you are for college when you get there, the more ready you'll be to confront any new pressures. Here are some realities to consider and a few commonsense ways to help you handle them:

The Work is Harder

3   Courses are at a higher level than high school classes, and the material is presented at a faster pace. Plus, professors are likely to assign more reading, writing, and problem sets than you may be used to.

Your Strategy

4   All first-year college students contend with this bend in the <u>learning curve</u>, so don't think having to struggle to keep up is somehow a failing on your part. Give yourself an opportunity to adjust gradually to the new academic demands. Choose a course load that includes some challenging classes and others that will be less intense.

You Make the Schedule

5   You are responsible for managing your time in college. If you cut classes and don't do assignments, no one will nag you. You may wish they had if it comes time for the final and you don't know the material.

Your Strategy

6   Buy a calendar and make sure you write down when and where your classes meet, when assignments are due, and when tests will take place. Give yourself ample time to study rather than waiting until the last minute and pulling an all-nighter.

More Independence—and Responsibility

7   You may not have the same day-to-day support system as you do now. For example, how will you manage your money and debt, especially when credit card companies are bombarding you with offers? Who is around to make sure you're not getting sick or rundown? Factors like stress, late-night parties, and generally pushing yourself too hard can take a toll.

Your Strategy

8   Don't always do what's easiest at the time. Make smart decisions. For example, when it comes to your money, stick to a budget and use credit cards wisely. When it comes to your health, get enough sleep, eat well, and pay attention to what your body tells you. You'll need energy to enjoy all that college has to offer.

A New Social Scene

9   New social opportunities (and pressures) abound. Suddenly, you can re-create yourself in any way you want.

Your Strategy

10   While forming new friendships can be <u>exhilarating</u>, true friendships are formed slowly, and the beginning of college can consequently be a lonely time. If you're unsure about participating in certain social scenes or activities, don't hesitate to seek guidance about the best ways to resist these pressures. Talk to parents, trusted friends from high school, and college counselors.

Reach Out to Resources

11   College is full of resources—professors, tutors, counselors, and often resident advisors. In college, it is up to you to initiate getting help. The good news is that once you do adjust to college life, it opens new doors to all sorts of learning—and living.

"College Survival Tips: Making the Transition" adapted from http://www.collegeboard.com/student/plan/college-success/963.html © 2010

COMPREHENSION CHECK

Circle the best answer to the questions based on information in the reading.

1   **Based on the first and second paragraph, the author will**

A. Discuss both the stresses and provide solutions.

B. Discuss the reasons for stresses.

C. Discuss the solutions for stresses.

(Continued)

2   **What is the topic of this reading?**

A. College costs
B. College survival
C. College requirements

3   **Which of the following is not a major supporting point in this reading?**

A. College work is harder.
B. College is costly.
C. In college, you bear more responsibility for managing your time.

4   **Based on the last paragraph, the author feels you can**

A. Succeed in college despite the cost.
B. Succeed in college if you make use of financial aid.
C. Succeed in college if you take advantage of the resources for help and support.

5   **The work in college is harder because**

A. There is more reading.
B. The level of the reading is more complicated.
C. There is more reading and the level of the reading is more complicated.

6   **Who is responsible for your study schedule?**

A. The instructor
B. The student
C. The learning curve

7   **What is meant by the phrase *learning curve* in paragraph 4?**

A. The complex reading, assignments, and demands.
B. There is a grading curve.
C. There are resources to help you with academic problems.

8   **In paragraph 8, the author discusses smart decisions. Which of the following is not discussed?**

A. Financial decisions
B. Health decisions
C. Social decisions

9   **What do you figure the word *exhilarating* means in paragraph 10?**

A. Overwhelming
B. Exciting
C. Slow moving

10 **What do you think is the main point of this reading?**

A. College is stressful.
B. College can make you more mature.
C. College is stressful, but you can be successful if you follow helpful strategies.

FOCUS ON READING STUDY SKILLS
The Reading Process

The reading process is a series of steps that help you understand reading by following **before, during,** and **after reading strategies.** Being an active reader means interacting with a reading and thinking about what the author is communicating. An active reader predicts what an author will say next. When you follow this reading process, you increase your understanding of what you are reading, and it helps you focus. You are in control of your reading and learning—you know what to do to get the most out of any reading task. To use the reading process, you will apply reading strategies before you read, while you read, and after you read. You'll be introduced to the strategies in this chapter, but the rest of this book will break down each of these steps in more detail to help you practice the strategies.

TABLE 1.1 THE READING PROCESS

BEFORE	DURING	AFTER
• Activate background knowledge.	• Predict what the author will discuss next to follow his or her thoughts.	• Rewrite notes to solidify ideas and learn.
• Set your purpose for reading.	• Monitor your comprehension.	• Organize information.
• Preview.	• Pose questions and find answers to guide reading.	• Use spaced practice to absorb ideas fully.
	• Mark text and take notes.	• Predict test questions and practice answering them.

© Cengage Learning 2013

BEFORE YOU READ

Many students start a reading assignment by beginning with the title and reading through to the end. Is this what you typically do? This is one way to approach a college reading assignment, but it is not always the *best* way to handle academic reading. Practice these steps before you read to help you understand what you are going to read:

1. **Activate background knowledge.** Activating **background knowledge** means thinking about what you already know about a topic before reading. Ask

FOCUS ON READING STUDY SKILLS: The Reading Process

yourself, "What do I already know about the topic?" Your brain understands and memorizes information better if you work with what you already know about a topic. So take a few moments to think about what you have already learned or what you already know from life experience about the subject of the reading. If you do not know anything about the topic of the reading, do some basic research. Read the summary, if available, or ask your instructor for some basic information about the topic first. Do a Web search to familiarize yourself with the topic. This way, the new information will make more sense and you can learn it more easily.

2. **Determine your purpose for reading the assignment.** Ask yourself, "What is my purpose in reading this assignment?" Your **purpose for reading** involves determining how much information you need to learn, how much understanding is required, and how long the activity will take so you can plan effectively. Think about what you want to learn—set a purpose or goal for your reading. Think about what you need to learn from the reading based on your assignment, questions you will have to answer, or what your instructor wants you to do after you read the passage.

    There is a difference between reading for enjoyment, such as reading a magazine, and reading for study, such as reading a textbook. Reading for study involves more concentration and understanding of the key points in a reading; when you read for enjoyment, you decide how much concentration and detail you need. Reading for fun means you can read quickly. Reading for school means you may have to slow down and really think about the reading. For academics, your assignment may be to learn details from a reading or just to gain an overview of a topic—you need to know what is expected of you from the outset. When you set a goal for your reading, you are more focused on the task. You also become more aware of what you should get out of a reading when you reach the end—if you haven't reached your goal by the end of your reading, you know that you'll need to go back to read more carefully. You need to consider how much time this activity will take you and prepare to set aside sufficient time to complete your assignment. If a lot of concentration and understanding are required, you will need to read slowly and carefully. If a general overview of the reading is required, you can read quickly and focus on the general ideas.

3. **Preview the reading.** When you **preview** a reading, you look the entire reading over quickly before reading it all the way through the first time. You scan for words that are repeated and get a sense of the structure or layout of the reading. Previewing allows you to see how the reading is set up, how long it will take you to read, and what is included in the reading. Previewing helps you establish your

purpose for reading and activate your background knowledge, both essential for working with how your brain learns best.

This approach may seem forced or unnatural when you first begin to use it, but it will greatly improve your comprehension and make pulling out key points easier with practice.

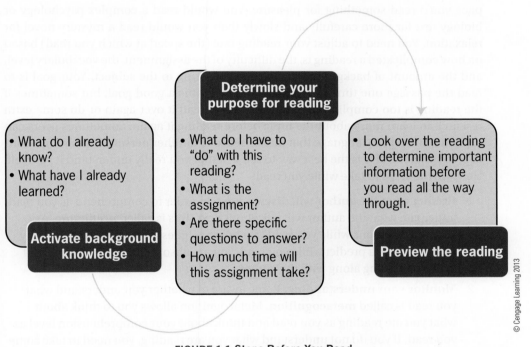

- What do I already know?
- What have I already learned?

Activate background knowledge

Determine your purpose for reading

- What do I have to "do" with this reading?
- What is the assignment?
- Are there specific questions to answer?
- How much time will this assignment take?

- Look over the reading to determine important information before you read all the way through.

Preview the reading

© Cengage Learning 2013

FIGURE 1.1 Steps Before You Read

WHILE YOU READ

When you read, you are trying to understand what you are reading. Sometimes this can be a challenge, depending on how much background knowledge you have about the topic. Understanding a reading can also be challenging if the ideas are complicated. For example, if you are reading about a topic about which you have no background knowledge or you cannot follow the author's train of thought, comprehension

FOCUS ON READING STUDY SKILLS: The Reading Process

problems are likely. Without a foundation in, let's say, psychology, reading a psychology textbook can be challenging because there are so many new ideas to absorb. Also, if the vocabulary used in the reading is challenging, your comprehension can be affected. If you are reading about biological science and you don't know the meaning of the scientific terms, you might struggle with the meaning of the passage. For example, if you are reading about health science and come across the word *lipid* and do not know what that word means, you may not understand the rest of the passage.

Not all college reading can be read at the same pace, and especially not at the same pace you'd read something for pleasure. You would read a complex psychology or biology text far more carefully and slowly than you would read a mystery novel for relaxation. You need to adjust your reading rate (the speed at which you read) based on how complicated a reading is, the difficulty of the assignment, the vocabulary level, and the amount of background knowledge you bring to the subject. Your goal is to read the passage one time and understand it. That is a good goal, but sometimes if the reading is too complicated, you will need to read it over again or do some extra research to learn more about the topic before reading it again. Sometimes peers can explain a concept in language that makes sense to another person. Explaining a concept to someone else is the best way to see whether you really understand it yourself. Here are the steps to take while you read:

1. **Predict what the author will discuss next.** In order to comprehend as you read, anticipate what the author will talk about next. This is called **predicting.** Ask yourself questions while you read that help you guess what the author will say next. When you predict while you read, you are absorbed in your reading and actively thinking along with the author.

2. **Monitor your understanding.** Being aware of whether you understand what you read is called **metacognition.** Metacognition allows you to think about what you are reading as you read and think about your comprehension level as you read. If you do not understand what you are reading, you need to take some action! An active reader is aware of whether he or she really understands what is being read. Sometimes, no matter how well you follow the reading process, you may still have trouble understanding a reading.

3. **Read to answer assigned questions or make up questions to guide your reading.** Often an instructor will provide questions for you to answer after you read. Similarly, many readings are followed by comprehension or discussion questions. Read questions first and then read to answer them. If you are not provided with questions to answer, try to make up your own by using the title or headings of the reading. You will learn more about this technique in Chapter 2.

4. **Take notes on the reading.** Write down important information while you read. Write down the key points of the reading, focusing on answering comprehension questions. You will learn more about taking notes in later chapters, but for now, write down what seems important.

QUICK TIPS WHAT YOU CAN DO IF YOU DON'T UNDERSTAND A READING

1. Research the basic topic so you have background knowledge.

2. Read or create questions to focus your reading on finding the important points.

3. If it's a textbook, read the summary, outline, and introduction.

4. Slow down.

5. Reread the passage and take it section by section.

6. Read aloud so you can hear the words.

7. Work on vocabulary—figure out the words from the surrounding information, or look up difficult words in the dictionary.

8. Review your notes or the instructor's outline.

9. Get help from your instructor, a learning resource, or a peer.

10. Write the passage in your own words.

AFTER YOU READ

Once you have completed your reading, your task is to *learn* the information in the reading and complete the assignment you've been given. This is the time when you evaluate whether you've reached your goal of your reading. If your goal was to gain an overview of a reading, can you state what the key points are? If your goal was to learn the details in a reading, can you list them and put them in your own words? The only way to learn new information is to review it. This is called **rehearsal.** Just as an actor has to rehearse his lines over and over again, a student needs to rehearse new information to learn it.

FOCUS ON READING STUDY SKILLS: The Reading Process

The simple fact is that learning or studying is repetition or rehearsal. Information must be learned over time to be retained. Here are the steps to take after reading:

1. **Rewrite important information.** Go back to the text and rewrite important information or the answers to the assigned questions.

2. **Make sure notes are clear and organized.** Your brain works best with organized information, so notes that are clear will help you remember the material.

3. **Learn information through review and rehearsal.** It is best to go over new information every day for several days until you are sure you understand and have learned it. Studying material for half an hour each day helps you learn information most effectively. This is called **spaced practice.** Spaced practice involves learning over time to help you remember what you read and help you build on what you know. Cramming for tests does not result in long-term learning.

4. **Predict test questions and make sure you can answer them.** You can predict test questions based on the questions provided by the instructor, questions following the reading, or questions you made up based on the title or headings.

QUICK TIPS   QUESTIONS TO ASK YOURSELF AFTER YOU READ

- ■ What questions will be asked about this information?
- ■ What are the key points in each section?
- ■ Can I explain these points in simple terms?
- ■ Can I explain these points to someone else who is not familiar with the subject?
- ■ How does this information relate to the course objectives or course topic?
- ■ Did my strategies before and during reading help me understand this information?

On Your Own UNDERSTANDING THE READING PROCESS

For the following reading and learning steps, indicate if the step is part of a before reading, while reading, or after reading strategy by putting an *X* in the appropriate column.

Step	Before Reading	While Reading	After Reading
1. Predict what the author will talk about next.			
2. Ask yourself what you need to get out of reading the passage.			
3. Rewrite your notes.			
4. Think about what you already know about the topic.			
5. Determine your purpose for doing the assignment.			
6. Write down the important information.			
7. Be aware if the reading makes sense.			
8. Organize your notes.			
9. Rehearse information.			
10. Avoid cramming.			

© Cengage Learning 2013

FOCUS ON COMPREHENSION

Active Reading, Previewing, and Predicting

Reading in college can be overwhelming. College courses require so much assigned reading, as well as other assignments and activities to complete. Time is in short supply for today's busy student. And college reading is harder and more time consuming than reading you did in high school. You need more strategies to be the best student you can be. Active reading strategies will jump-start your understanding of a reading. An **active reading strategy** is a strategy that makes you interact with the text so you can control your understanding, increase your concentration, and improve your learning. Being an active learner and an active reader involves using the reading process to increase your understanding of what you read for college classes.

ACTIVE LEARNING

To understand new information, you need to become an active learner. **Active learning** involves more than being on top of your course assignments; active learning involves working with your brain to maximize your success. An active learner

- Takes responsibility for learning.

- Knows what to do if a reading doesn't make sense.

- Does all the reading and takes selective notes.

- Does not rely on or blame the instructor if something is not clear; makes note of questions; and asks the instructor to clarify before, during, or after class.

- Asks questions, rereads the text, and uses the college support services for help when stuck.

- Forms a study group with other students so they can help each other clarify the important points covered in class or in-class reading assignments.

Active learning is the opposite of **passive learning.** If you are a passive learner, learning is done *to* you rather than *by* you. This type of learner does not actively interact with the text and does not learn to the best of his or her ability. Look at the bulleted list of characteristics of an active learner. Imagine the opposite is true of a passive learner. You can see that this kind of student is not setting him- or herself up for success.

ACTIVE READING

Being an active reader requires that you work with your brain to learn best. Like active learning, **active reading** involves taking responsibility and using available resources and techniques to improve and increase your understanding of a reading. Active reading also involves using reading strategies before, during, and after reading, collectively known as the **reading process.** Passive reading results from not using the reading process to improve your understanding of a reading. The first step to reading actively is to be aware of how your brain processes information and using that knowledge to improve your reading comprehension.

On Your Own UNDERSTANDING ACTIVE LEARNING

Write an *A* next to statements that indicate active learning and a *P* next to statements that indicate passive learning. Be prepared to explain your answers.

_____ 1. Read parts of the text only the night before a test.

_____ 2. Read the text as assigned before the class in which it's being discussed.

_____ 3. Ask questions if anything is unclear.

_____ 4. Do not ask questions and explain, "I didn't understand the material," after the test.

_____ 5. Join with others in the class to study for the test.

_____ 6. Leave class to study later, if at all.

_____ 7. Understand and use college learning resources to improve.

_____ 8. Do not know what resources are available and do not ask.

_____ 9. Use the reading process.

_____10. Use before, during, and after reading strategies.

(Continued)

FOCUS ON COMPREHENSION: Active Reading, Previewing, and Predicting

Which active learning strategies do you already use? Which strategies will you try today to improve your learning? Fill in this chart, focusing on what you already do and what you will try. Share your responses with a peer or in a small group.

Active Learning Strategies I Use	Active Learning Strategies I Will Try

© Cengage Learning 2013

MEMORY AND HOW THE BRAIN PROCESSES INFORMATION

To be both an active reader and an active learner, you need to ask yourself, "What is the best way to learn in harmony with how my brain works? How does my brain remember?" There has been a lot of research on how people learn and remember. Researchers agree that memory involves three processes in the brain: the sensory memory, the working memory, and the long-term memory. Each part of this system plays a crucial role in learning. And the more you know about the way memory works, the more you can improve your learning and maximize how you process information so it's easier for your brain.

Memory Flow Chart

Data adapted from: http://static.howstuffworks.com/gif/amnesia-2a.gif

Sensory Memory

Your brain receives information through your five senses—sight, hearing, taste, touch, smell—and is the reason that this part of the memory system is named **sensory memory** (pertaining to the senses). Sensory memory holds information for a brief time, during which your brain decides to accept or reject the incoming stimuli. For example, if you are very busy and absorbed by a task, you may not hear your dog barking outside. However, if you are distracted, bored, or not paying full attention to your work, you will hear your dog barking outside. If you are consciously aware of the incoming stimuli, like hearing the dog barking, then it is moved to your working memory to be further processed. If you do not hear the dog barking within a few seconds, it doesn't register at all in your conscious mind. Similarly, when you read, the content initially enters your sensory memory.

FOCUS ON COMPREHENSION: Active Reading, Previewing, and Predicting

Working Memory

The **working memory**, sometimes called *short-term memory,* is the part of the memory system that actively organizes and processes information. If incoming sensory information is identified or accepted, it is now in your working memory. For example, if you hear your dog barking, you are thinking about the sound and the implications for you to respond. The sensory input (the bark) has now registered in your working memory. Similarly, when you think about the visual cues in the form of words as you read, this new information is being processed in your working memory. The same goes for hearing text being read or feeling text with your fingers if you are reading Braille. Your working memory is, essentially, your mind: what you are thinking about at any given time. The working memory is where you start the process of learning information and studying. Imagine this part of your brain as a small surface onto which you can place just seven to nine pieces of information at one time. If you try to cram more information onto this limited space, something you were thinking about will get bumped from your thoughts. Working memory can only hold or remember information for a limited time without forgetting before it gets transferred to long-term memory.

There are things you can do to keep your working memory from forgetting. The information you are studying needs to be as organized as possible. Your brain likes organized information because it can more easily be stored for later recall. The process of organizing information is called **encoding.** When information is organized, you brain has an easier time remembering it and committing it to long-term memory.

Long-Term Memory

If you learn the information you have read, this new information is stored in your long-term memory. The **long-term memory** is the storage component of the memory system. Similarly, you learn to recognize your dog's particular bark because your brain stores this information for you. Unlike your working memory, your long-term memory has an unlimited capacity. In other words, if it were possible to study 24 hours a day for the rest of your life, you would never run out of storage space for your learned information. In fact, the *more you learn, the more you are capable of remembering* because the connections between your background knowledge and new knowledge are strengthened. This related information is called **schema** (singular: *schemata*). The more you associate new information you are learning to information you have already learned that is related to the topic, the easier it will be to remember. The readings in each chapter of this book are thematically linked—they all concern a related topic. This approach will help you build schema that you will use throughout your college education and in your life, as well as help you remember key points about each chapter. You should always think about what you know about a subject before trying to learn more about that topic in order to help you remember the new information later. You did this in the beginning of this chapter in the What Do You Already Know feature.

Forgetting

Forgetting information can occur anywhere along the memory process—from the initial sensory memory stage up to the long-term memory stage. Most forgetting has to do with the lack of repeated review of the information. To learn information successfully, you must study over time and go over information repeatedly. You may forget information you have studied for a few reasons:

- You were not focused as you read, so the information was bumped from your working memory.

- Your new information was not organized effectively enough to be stored and retrieved.

- You did not repeat your review of the information enough times so it was not retained.

Figure 1.2 (based on a research by Hermann Ebbinghaus, a German psychologist who pioneered research on memory) demonstrates how quickly you forget information that is not rehearsed or studied over time as represented by the blue line. In addition, you can see the positive effect that studying or rehearsal of information over time has on your ability to recall or remember information, as represented by the orange line.

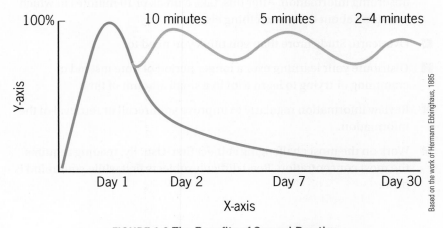

FIGURE 1.2 The Benefits of Spaced Practice

FOCUS ON COMPREHENSION: Active Reading, Previewing, and Predicting

Look back at Figure 1.2 more closely. The vertical line on the left of the graph is called the *y* axis. This line represents the amount or percentage of information that is recalled after a study session. The horizontal line at the bottom is called the *x* axis. This line shows the passage of time from the first day of study, to the second, seventh, and, last, thirtieth day after study. The blue line represents how much you remember of what you study. During the first day, right away, you can remember most if not all of what you just studied. However, notice the steep drop in the blue line by the second day—you only remember a small fraction of what you studied the day before. A week later, the information that you thought you had learned is almost gone from your mind. By the end of the month, you remember very little and could certainly not pass a test on the material. The orange line represents how your memory of learned information improves when the information is reviewed on a regular and frequent basis. Notice that if you study for 10 minutes on day 2, you will recall the learned information that you first studied on day 1. A week later, you will need to spend less time reviewing the information to remember it all over again. This type of studying is called **spaced practice.** Learning happens over time in order to work with how the brain learns and remembers. The opposite of spaced practice is **cramming,** or when you study in one session. If you do this, you are less likely to remember the information as time passes. If you space your learning over a month at regular intervals, you will be more likely to remember what you have studied and will more effectively learn the material.

QUICK TIPS COMBATING PROBLEMS WITH FORGETTING

■ Space your studying. Spaced practice means that you study in chunks. Thirty- to 60-minute chunks are optimal for concentrating and absorbing information. After this, take a break of 10 minutes in which you think about or do something else.

■ Overlearn. Study more than you think you need to.

■ Distribute your learning over a longer period of time instead of cramming or trying to learn a lot in a small amount of time.

■ Review information regularly to improve your recall or retrieval of the information.

■ Work on the most challenging subject first. Usually, reading requires the most concentration. Read difficult subjects first while your mind is fresh.

PREVIEWING

When you **preview** a reading, you aren't reading the whole passage from beginning to end. Instead, you scan the reading by focusing only on the important parts of the reading: the title, the first paragraph, the headings (if there are any), the first sentence of body paragraphs, and the concluding paragraph. Why should you preview a reading beforehand? Previewing is important because it

- Activates your background knowledge.
- Primes your brain to receive new information.
- Allows you to make predictions about what the passage will be about.
- Helps you see how the author arranges the information.
- Reveals what important points the author will discuss.

Take these steps to preview a reading:

1. **Read the title.**

   Why read the title? The title can tell you who or what the passage is about. You want to consider the topic or subject in order to activate your background knowledge to prime your brain to learn and understand new information.

2. **Read the first paragraph.**

   Why read the first paragraph? The first paragraph usually contains the author's key points or what the author plans to cover in the entire reading.

3. **Read the headings, if there are any.**

   Why read the headings? The headings tell you what each section will cover.

4. **Read the first sentence of each body paragraph.**

   Why read the first sentence of each body paragraph? The first sentence

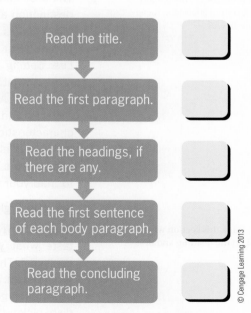

© Cengage Learning 2013

FIGURE 1.3 How to Preview a Reading
Use this checklist to make sure you complete each step when you preview a reading. Check off the boxes to the right as you complete each step.

FOCUS ON COMPREHENSION: Active Reading, Previewing, and Predicting

of each body paragraph is likely to include the major point about that paragraph, so they are also important for understanding the overall structure of the reading.

5. **Read the concluding paragraph.**

   Why read the concluding paragraph? If the author's key points are not clearly stated in the introduction, then they may be stated in the concluding paragraph.

Thinking It Through   PREVIEWING A READING

Here is a reading by Dianne Hales from *An Invitation to Health*, a textbook for an introductory college health course. Follow the steps to previewing a reading, and read only the highlighted sections of the passage. Then read the questions about the reading in the margins. Try to answer these questions. Afterward, read answers to the questions that follow the reading.

Who or what will the reading be about?

What do you think the author's main point is about setting goals to achieve what you want in life?

Going for Your Goals

1   Think of goals as road maps that give you both a destination and a planned itinerary for getting there. "To set goals means to set a course for your life," says psychologist James Fadiman, author of *Unlimit Your Life: Setting and Getting Goals.* "Without goals, you remain what you were. With goals, you become what you wish." As studies of performance in students, athletes, and employees have shown, the one single characteristic that separates high- and low-achievers is having a clear, specific goal. The following sections describe the most effective strategies for using goals to map your way to the life you want.

Set Your Sights on a Destination or Target

What do you think this section will be about, based on the heading and first sentence?

2   The more vividly that you can see, feel, touch, and taste what you want, the more likely you are to achieve it. The reason, explains psychologist Kenneth W. Christian, author of *Your Own Worst Enemy,* is that a destination goal transforms your brain into a satellite dish picking up the signals that are most relevant to your quest. "You begin to see possibilities that pull you closer to your goal. You meet people who can help you. It can seem magical, but it's not. Your

unconscious mind is working on your goal while you go on with your life."

Take a Step and a Stretch

3   With your target goal in sight, set "step-and-stretch" goals. Think of them like stair steps that lift you out of your comfort zone and keep you moving forward. It doesn't matter how many there are. In some instances, it may be six; in others, sixty. Every goal should be a reach from where you are that will bring you to the next level.

What do you think this section will be about?

4   Break down each step goal into projects and every project into tasks. Ask yourself the following questions, and write down the answers.

- What skills do I need to achieve this?
- What information and knowledge must I acquire?
- What help, assistance, or resources do I need?
- What can block my progress? (For each potential barrier, list solutions.)
- Whom can I turn to for support?
- Who or what is likely to get in my way?
- How am I most likely to sabotage myself?

Use an Affirmation

5   Once you've pictured your goal in detail, express it in an **affirmation**, a single positive sentence. As decades of psychological research have shown, affirmations serve as powerful tools for behavioral change. Make sure to use the present tense. For example, tell yourself "I am not a smoker" daily—even though you may still light up occasionally.

What do you think this section will be about?

6   Once you've polished your affirmation, put it on paper. By putting it in writing, you become more committed to making your words come true. Some people post their affirmations on their computers and night stands or carry them in their wallets. Wherever you jot yours, look at your affirmation often—ideally at least once a day.

(Continued)

FOCUS ON COMPREHENSION: Active Reading, Previewing, and Predicting

Go All the Way

What do you think this section will be about?

7   Despite good intentions and considerable progress, many people give up their goals just before the rainbow's end and congratulate themselves for getting that far. "Would you ever board a plane for Chicago and say, 'Well, we got three-quarters of the way there!' as if that were good?" asks psychologist Christian, who urges goal-seekers to persist, persevere, and "not settle for almost-there." If you stall on the final stretch, do a quick reality check. May be you need to add some smaller-step goals, seek more support, or simply allow yourself more time.

What new information is suggested in the conclusion?

8   Whenever you achieve a goal, acknowledge it, tell a friend, or just raise your hands above your head like a runner crossing the finish line. This is what builds your sense of, "I can do it. I AM doing it. Look how far I've come!"

From HALES. *An Invitation to Health, Brief Edition (with Personal Health Self Assessments)*, 6E. © 2010 Brooks/Cole, a part of Cengage Learning, Inc. By permission.

1. **Based on the title, who or what will the reading be about?** The reading will be about setting goals. Use this information to think about your background knowledge about setting goals: What do you already know about setting goals that may help you understand the most important points in this reading?

2. **Based on the introductory paragraph, what will the author discuss in this reading?** The author says there are strategies you can follow to set effective goals to achieve what you want in life. So, by reading the introduction, you know what the rest of the reading will be about, and you can predict that the rest of the reading will outline and explain the strategies to set effective goals.

3. **What does each heading and the first sentence of each body paragraph reveal about the reading?**

   - **Heading 1: "Set Your Sights on a Destination or Target."** This section will be about seeing a goal or target. The clearer your goal, the more likely you will attain it.
   - **Heading 2: "Take a Step and a Stretch."** This section discusses how goals are incremental. Once you meet a small goal, strive for the next logical step as you reach for the larger goal.

- **Heading 3: "Use an Affirmation."** This section advises you to solidify and focus your goal into one written sentence.
- **Heading 4: "Go All the Way."** This section urges you to make sure to follow your goal until it's achieved.

4. **What new information is suggested in the concluding paragraph?** The conclusion suggests that once a goal is achieved, you celebrate your success.

From previewing, you can learn a great deal about the structure of a passage and the key points. Look at all the information you just learned about this reading, and you haven't even read it all the way through! An active reader uses previewing for all reading assignments to get a head start in understanding the reading. Previewing will make reading the whole passage much easier since you already have a firm grasp of the major points.

On Your Own PREVIEWING A READING

Choose a reading that is assigned in another class, and follow the steps for previewing. Ask the following questions of yourself about this reading.

1. Based on the title, who or what will the reading be about?

2. Based on the introductory paragraph, what will the author discuss in this reading?

3. What does each heading and the first sentence of each body paragraph reveal about the reading?

4. What new information is suggested in the concluding paragraph?

5. Now, reflect on your experience with previewing. How has using previewing helped you understand your reading assignment better?

_____

_____

_____

_____

FOCUS ON COMPREHENSION: Active Reading, Previewing, and Predicting

MAKING PREDICTIONS

An active reader thinks along with the author. One effective way to focus on the author's train of thought is to predict what will be discussed in a reading and what will be covered next. **Predicting** means that you anticipate what will happen before it happens. If you focus on predicting what will come next, you are less likely to mentally wander off while reading and more likely to focus on and comprehend the content. Consider the following sentence from *Going for Your Goals* on page 22.

> The more vividly that you can see, feel, touch, and taste what you want, the more likely you are to achieve it.

What is the author likely to discuss next?

_____

_____

_____

If you think the author will provide reasons for this statement—why being able to pinpoint and internalize goals may lead to a greater likelihood of achieving them—you are correct. Go back and read the section "Set Your Sights on a Destination or Target" from *Going for Your Goals,* and you'll see this is exactly what the author discusses. Try this next sentence.

> Once you've polished your affirmation, put it on paper.

What do you think the author will discuss next?

_____

_____

_____

If you think the author will explain why writing goals down has an impact on attaining them, you are correct.

On Your Own PREVIEWING A READING AND MAKING PREDICTIONS

Apply prereading strategies to the following article by answering these questions.

1. Based on the title of this reading, what do you think this reading is about? _____

_____

2. Activate your background knowledge. What do you already know about this topic?

_____

_____

Now, preview the reading following these steps. Use a highlighter or a pen to underline the parts of the reading you read when previewing.

- Read the title.
- Read the first paragraph.
- Read the headings, if there are any.
- Read the first sentence of each body paragraph.
- Read the concluding paragraph.

Now read the article all the way through. Predict what the author will discuss, using the while-reading strategy of making predictions. Write your predictions in the space provided in the margins as you read.

Campus Resources: You Paid For 'Em, So Use 'Em

1   Think about all the services and resources that your tuition money buys: academic advising to help you choose classes and select a major; access to the student health center and counseling services; a career planning office that you can visit even after you graduate; athletic, arts, and entertainment events at a central location; and much more.

What do you predict the author will discuss next?

2   If you live on campus, you also get a place to stay with meals provided, all for less than the cost of an average hotel room.

What do you predict the author will discuss next?

3   And, by the way, you get to attend classes.

4   Following are a few examples of services available on many campuses. Check your school's catalog for even more.

What do you predict the author will discuss next?

(Continued)

FOCUS ON COMPREHENSION: Active Reading, Previewing, and Predicting

5   ***Academic advisors*** can help you with selecting courses, choosing majors, career planning, and adjusting in general to the culture of higher education.

6   ***Alumni organizations*** can be good sources of information about the pitfalls and benefits of being a student at your school.

7   ***Athletic centers*** and gymnasiums often open weight rooms, swimming pools, indoor tracks, and athletic courts for students.

8   ***Childcare*** is sometimes provided at a reasonable cost through the early-childhood education department.

What do you predict the author will discuss next?

9   ***Computer labs,*** where students can go 24 hours a day to work on projects and use the Internet, are often free.

10   ***Counseling centers*** help students deal with the emotional pressures of school life, usually for free or at low cost.

11   ***Financial aid*** offices help students with loans, scholarships, grants, and work-study programs.

12   ***Job placement and career-planning*** offices can help you find part-time employment while you are in school and a job after you graduate.

13   ***Libraries*** are a treasure on campus and employ people who are happy to help you locate information.

14   ***Newspapers*** published on campus list events and services that are free or inexpensive.

15   ***Registrars*** handle information about transcripts, grades, changing majors, transferring credits, and dropping or adding classes.

16   ***School media***—including campus newspapers, radio stations, Websites, and instructional television services—provide information about school policies and activities.

17   ***School security*** employees provide information about parking, bicycle regulations, and traffic rules. Some school security agencies provide safe escort at night for students.

18   ***Student government*** can assist you in developing skills in leadership and teamwork. Many employers value this kind of experience.

19   **Student organizations** offer you an opportunity to explore fraternities, sororities, service clubs, veterans' organizations, religious groups, sports clubs, political groups, and programs for special populations. The latter include women's centers, multicultural student centers, and organizations for international students, disabled students, and gay and lesbian students.

20   **Student unions** are hubs for social activities, special programs, and free entertainment.

21   **Tutoring programs** can help even if you think you are hopelessly stuck in a course—usually for free. Student athletes and those who speak English as a second language can often get help here.

22   **Note:** Community resources—those located off-campus—can range from credit counseling and chemical dependency treatment to public health clinics and churches. Check the city Website.

> What do you predict the author will discuss next?

From MASTER STUDENT. Book Block for Ellis' *BAMS: The Essential Guide to Becoming a Master Student,* 1E. © 2010 Wadsworth, a part of Cengage Learning, Inc. By permission.

3. Do you feel that you had a good idea of the contents of this reading from your preview? Why or why not? _____

_____

_____

_____

4. Were your predictions accurate? Why or why not? _____

_____

_____

_____

FOCUS ON VOCABULARY
Definition and Synonym Context Clues

As a new college student, one goal you should have is improving your vocabulary because it will help your reading comprehension. Research has shown that vocabulary level is linked with a higher income and a better job: people with bigger vocabularies make more money than those who have less developed vocabularies. And, most of you probably have goals of making more money and obtaining a better job. You can start moving toward that goal by focusing on improving your vocabulary. Part of being an active reader is paying attention to words you don't know, learning or figuring out their meanings, and making use of the words so that you remember them.

What do you do when you encounter words that you don't know? Textbooks sometimes define a word or key term in the text, the margin, or a glossary. But sometimes you encounter a word you do not know that is not defined. Context clues are always your first strategy when unlocking the meaning of an unknown word. A vocabulary **context clue** is the surrounding information in the text that gives hints to the reader about the meaning of an unknown word.

College texts are full of mysterious words that affect your understanding of a reading. However, there is a way to unlock the meaning of an unknown word without having to resort to a dictionary each time, interrupting your train of thought. The surrounding information, or context, may be within the sentence that contains the unknown word, or in sentences around the sentence containing the unknown word. There are four types of context clues: definition clues, synonym clues, antonym clues,

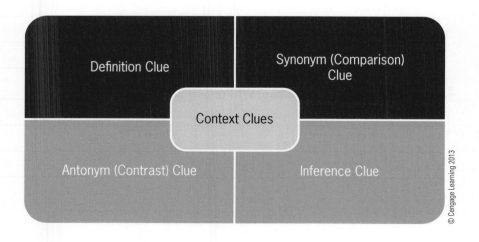

Definition Clue

Synonym (Comparison) Clue

Context Clues

Antonym (Contrast) Clue

Inference Clue

© Cengage Learning 2013

Zelenskaya/Shutterstock.com

and inference clues. Here, you will focus on the first two types of context clues. In Chapter 2, you will learn about the second two types of clues.

TRANSITION WORDS

One way to recognize context clues is by being alert to transition words that offer clues to an author's thought process. What do you already know about transition words? They are not complicated words, and you have definitely encountered these words in other reading you have done, but you probably never considered before how important they are to notice. **Transition words**, sometimes also called *signal words*, are words or phrases writers use to link ideas in a logical progression from one to the other. Transition words are used frequently in writing to make ideas flow together and to indicate important points. (You will learn more about transition words in Chapter 5.) Here are some common transition words and phrases with which you may be familiar from reading and writing: *like, similarly, in other words, in contrast, on the other hand, but, instead of, consequently, therefore, first, second,* and *finally*. As you learn about the different context clues, you will also learn about the different transition words that signal a clue.

DEFINITION CLUE

A **definition clue** is used when an author directly defines a word in a phrase or sentence. This type of clue is helpful because the information you need—what the unknown word means—is obvious because it is directly stated. Many college 100-level classes use textbooks that include definition clues since these courses are geared toward building your awareness of the vocabulary of a discipline. Definition clues can often have the unknown word in bold print or italics, so it stands out, like a key word. Sometimes, transition words or phrases like *means, is defined as*, or *is* follows the word you do not know. Definition clues can also be recognized through punctuation, such as a colon (:) or a dash (—) followed by the definition. Study Table 1.2, paying close attention to the transition words or phrases that indicate a definition clue.

FOCUS ON VOCABULARY: Definition and Synonym Context Clues

TABLE 1.2 TRANSITION WORDS OR PUNCTUATION THAT INDICATE DEFINITION CLUES

TYPE OF CONTEXT CLUE	TRANSITION WORDS OR PUNCTUATION	EXAMPLE (WITH DEFINITION OF BOLDED TERM UNDERLINED)
DEFINITION CLUE	**TRANSITION WORDS OR PHRASES**	
A definition (phrase) of a term, often in boldface or italics	• *is* • *is defined as* • *means* • *refers to*	**Long-term memory** is the part of the mind that holds all memories from past experience in a network of organized ideas.
	PUNCTUATION/FORMATTING	
	• Colon (:) followed by definition • Dash (—) followed by definition • Comma (,) followed by definition • **Boldface** • *Italics* • Definition offset by parentheses () or brackets []	**Mnemonic devices**—memory aids that facilitate learning information—are useful for studying and learning.

© Cengage Learning 2013

Take a look at these examples of definition context clues.

> Before you can apply any study strategy to become the best learner you can be, and before you can achieve any of the goals you have set, you must first be motivated to succeed. Motivation is defined as wanting something badly enough to work for it. Motivation pushes you to succeed in a task and is especially important in college learning.

Notice in this example how the term *motivation* is followed by the phrase *is defined as* and then its definition.

> Feelings of self-worth are important. When we feel good about our achievements and what we have earned, we also tend to value and feel good about ourselves. **Self-esteem,** our positive or negative evaluation of our self-concept or sense of personal worth, is important because it both nurtures and feeds success.
>
> —Contacts Interpersonal Communication in Theory, Practice, and Context, by Teri Kwal Gamble and Michael W. Gamble, Houghton-Mifflin

Notice in this example how the definition of self-esteem is offset by commas and directly follows the key term or phrase to be defined.

> **Reading comprehension**—understanding what you read while you are reading—is a complex cognitive process.

Notice in this example how the definition is offset by dashes following the term *reading comprehension*. The important thing to remember about definition clues is that the definition is clearly stated and directly follows or precedes the word in question.

On Your Own RECOGNIZING DEFINITION CONTEXT CLUES

For the following boldfaced words, underline the definition provided in the surrounding sentence or sentences. Circle the transition word or phrase or the punctuation that helps you find the definition.

1. **Motivation** is the frame of mind that activates your behavior and gives you direction.
2. **External motivation** is defined as something outside of yourself that makes you want to succeed, such as family pressure, or a need for more money, or to keep a good job.
3. **Internal motivation:** something within yourself that makes you want to succeed, like wanting to show yourself that you can do a good job at college, the pride that comes from receiving a good grade, or simply because you enjoy learning.
4. **Long-term goals**—life goals that help you see where you are now in relation to where you want to end up in the future—are vital to success in college.
5. Unlike short-term goals, **intermediate goals** are goals that span 2 to 5 years.
6. **Short-term goals** (which are sometimes called *objectives*) are the goals you set for yourself to accomplish in day-to-day activities that lead you to your intermediate and long-term goals.
7. **An active reading strategy** is a strategy that makes you interact with the text so you can control your understanding, increase your concentration, and improve your learning.

(Continued)

FOCUS ON VOCABULARY: Definition and Synonym Context Clues

8. **Active learning,** being in control of your learning, is the opposite of **passive learning,** which is not being in control of your learning.

9. The process of organizing information is called **encoding.** When information is organized, you brain has an easier time remembering it and committing it to long-term memory.

10. Being aware of whether you understand as you read is called **metacognition.**

SYNONYM CLUE

A **synonym** is a word that means the same as another word, in this case, the word with which you are not familiar. *Syn* means "same" or "with," and *nym* refers to a word or name. A synonym for the unknown word can appear next to it, offset by commas, or with the word *or* clarifying that the words are synonyms. **Synonym clues** are similar to definition clues but instead of being a direct definition or longer phrase, a synonym clue is usually a word or a couple of words. Synonyms for an unknown word may not just be within that same sentence, however. A synonym for an unknown word can be in the sentence before or after it appears, or even a few sentences before or after it appears. Study Table 1.3, paying close attention to the transition words or phrases that indicate a synonym clue.

Take a look at these examples of synonym context clues.

> **Self-esteem,** or sense of personal worth, is important because it both nurtures and feeds success.

Notice in this example how the term *self-esteem* is followed by the word *or*, and then a phrase meaning the same as self-esteem is offset by commas. So, self-esteem means sense of personal worth.

> Before you can apply any study strategy to become the best learner you can be, and before you can achieve any of the goals you have set, you must first be motivated to succeed. Your **motivation**, also known as drive, pushes you to succeed in a task and is especially important in college learning.

Notice in this example how the term *motivation* is followed by the words *also known as* then the synonym *drive*.

TABLE 1.3 TRANSITION WORDS OR PUNCTUATION THAT INDICATE SYNONYM CLUES

TYPE OF CONTEXT CLUE	TRANSITION WORDS OR PUNCTUATION	EXAMPLE (WITH SYNONYM OF BOLDED WORD UNDERLINED)
SYNONYM CLUE	**TRANSITION WORDS OR PHRASES**	

A word or phrase that means the same thing as the one you don't know	• *Or* followed by a synonym of the unknown word
	
	• *Also known as . . .*
	
	• A word later in the sentence (or surrounding sentences) that means the same. This synonym clue may be indicated by the word *this* or *these* following the unknown word.
		Retrieval <u>or recall</u> is a vital part of the memory and learning system.
		
		    Retrieval = recall
		
		Repressing memories can lead to inaccurate recall. This <u>blocking of</u> your recollections may mean that you may not remember the event.
		
		    Repressing means blocking or holding back.

	PUNCTUATION/PLACEMENT	
	• A word that has the same meaning within commas	**Encoding,** or <u>processing</u>, information is a vital part of the memory system since the brain requires repetition to learn.

© Cengage Learning 2013

Purveyors of exotic goods are found in most large American cities. <u>These suppliers</u> have a greater market for their wares when the population is **diverse** <u>or different</u>.

In this example, there are two bold words. The first, *purveyors*, has a synonym in the second sentence. The clue here is the word *these*. With the use of this pronoun, the author must be referring to another word previously used. In this case, the word that means the same as purveyors is *suppliers*. So, a purveyor is a supplier. *Diverse* is followed by the word *or*. So, diverse must mean "different" in this context.

On Your Own RECOGNIZING SYNONYM CONTEXT CLUES

For the following boldfaced words, underline the synonym provided in the surrounding sentence or sentences. Circle the transition word or phrase or punctuation, if there is any, that helped you find the synonym of the unknown word.

(Continued)

FOCUS ON VOCABULARY: Definition and Synonym Context Clues

1. **Encoding** or organizing information is essential for studying.

2. **Prior knowledge,** also known as background knowledge, is essential for activating your brain to learn new information most efficiently.

3. **Procrastination** is the downfall of many a student. This habit of putting off tasks needs to be addressed with good time-management skills.

4. Short-term goals need to be **articulated** or defined before they can work in your favor.

5. Carlos told many short stories about his struggles as a first-year student. His **anecdotes** provided lots of useful tips for surviving the first year.

6. In class discussion, Miranda was **loquacious.** Her talkativeness helped her clarify the important points.

7. In contrast, Bryonie was **taciturn** in class. She was quiet except when called upon directly.

8. Cassandra created a **cacophony** when she dropped her books on the floor. The loud sound was equaled only by the roar of laughter from the rest of the class.

9. The study load was **daunting.** Maurice was unsure if he could overcome how discouraging his workload had become. He decided to employ more effective study strategies in the future.

10. The old shop was **redolent** of garlic. This smell was so over powering that Nancy left the shop and took refuge outside in the fresh air.

Practice Exercise 1: RECOGNIZING DEFINITION AND SYNONYM CONTEXT CLUES

For the following passages, underline the meaning of the boldfaced word or key term. Circle the transition word or phrase or punctuation, if there is any, that helps you find the meaning of the unknown word. Identify which clue—definition or synonym—helped you figure out the meaning of the unknown word.

1. **Life chances** refer to the likelihood of possessing the good things in life: health, happiness, education, wealth, legal protection, and even life itself.

—From SHEPARD. Cengage Advantage Books: *Sociology* 10E.
© 2010 Wadsworth, a part of Cengage Learning, Inc. By permission.

_____

2. **Social mobility** refers to the movement of individuals or groups within a stratification structure.

—From SHEPARD. Cengage Advantage Books: *Sociology* 10E.
© 2010 Wadsworth, a part of Cengage Learning, Inc. By permission.

_____

3. **Procrastination**, or putting off tasks, is the downfall of many students.

_____

4. **Plagiarism** is forbidden in the academic environment. Representing the work of others as your own is an ethical problem that all students must take seriously.

_____

5. A change from one occupation to another at the same general status level is called **horizontal mobility.**

—From SHEPARD. Cengage Advantage Books: *Sociology* 10E.
© 2010 Wadsworth, a part of Cengage Learning, Inc. By permission.

_____

6. But additional more **subtle** life chances exist, and these, too, vary with social class. These less obvious life chances are in good part the product of inequality in the distribution of education, power, prestige, and economic rewards.

—From SHEPARD. Cengage Advantage Books: *Sociology* 10E.
© 2010 Wadsworth, a part of Cengage Learning, Inc. By permission.

_____

7. **Inconsistent discipline**—punishing a child one day for a mistake but not another day—is associated with personality issues later in life.

_____

8. Information in the working memory is **ephemeral,** or fleeting. Spaced practice is necessary to retrieve information when you need it for a test.

_____

9. Mark **vanquished** his opponents at chess. He defeated all but the most able player within 1 hour.

_____

10. Sasha learned that cramming for a test was a **liability.** This disadvantage was made clear to her when she received her test scores back.

_____

APPLICATIONS

These applications will develop your skills of previewing as well as using definition and synonym context clues for vocabulary comprehension. You will practice the reading process. Each application gives more responsibility to the reader as these techniques become more automatic.

APPLICATION

Before you read the whole passage through, preview the reading. Underline or highlight the parts of the reading you'll preview, following these instructions.

1. Read the title. Activate your background knowledge—what do you know about procrastination?
2. Read the first paragraph.
3. Read the headings, if there are any.
4. Read the first sentence of each body paragraph.
5. Read the concluding paragraph.

While you read the passage, answer the questions in the margins about making predictions and understanding vocabulary from context clues. After you are done reading the passage, complete the Comprehension Check questions that follow the reading.

Procrastination: Ten Things to Know
By Hara Estroff Marano

Based on this paragraph, how would you define procrastinators?

1   There are many ways to avoid success in life, but the most sure-fire just might be procrastination. Procrastinators sabotage themselves. They put obstacles in their own path. They actually choose paths that hurt their performance.

2   Why would people do that? I talked to two of the world's leading experts on procrastination: Joseph Ferrari, Ph.D., associate professor of psychology at De Paul University in Chicago, and Timothy Pychyl, Ph.D., associate professor of psychology at Carleton University in Ottawa, Canada. Neither one is a procrastinator, and both answered my many questions immediately.

Why does the author list these ten points? What will they outline?

3   1. Twenty percent of people identify themselves as chronic procrastinators. For them procrastination is a lifestyle, albeit a maladaptive one. And it cuts across all domains of their life. They don't pay bills on time. They miss

opportunities for buying tickets to concerts. They don't cash gift certificates or checks. They file income tax returns late. They leave their Christmas shopping until Christmas Eve.

4   2. It's not trivial, although as a culture we don't take it seriously as a problem. It represents a profound problem of self-regulation. And there may be more of it in the U.S. than in other countries because we are so nice; we don't call people on their excuses ("my grandmother died last week") even when we don't believe them.

5   3. Procrastination is not a problem of time management or of planning. Procrastinators are not different in their ability to estimate time, although they are more optimistic than others. "Telling someone who procrastinates to buy a weekly planner is like telling someone with chronic depression to just cheer up," insists Dr. Ferrari.

6   4. Procrastinators are made, not born. Procrastination is learned in the family milieu, but not directly. It is one response to an authoritarian parenting style. Having a harsh, controlling father keeps children from developing the ability to regulate themselves, from internalizing their own intentions and then learning to act on them. Procrastination can even be a form of rebellion, one of the few forms available under such circumstances. What's more, under those household conditions, procrastinators turn more to friends than to parents for support, and their friends may reinforce procrastination because they tend to be tolerant of their excuses.

7   5. Procrastination predicts higher levels of consumption of alcohol among those people who drink. Procrastinators drink more than they intend to—a manifestation of generalized problems in self-regulation. That is over and above the effect of avoidant coping styles that underlie procrastination and lead to disengagement via substance abuse.

8   6. Procrastinators tell lies to themselves, such as, "I'll feel more like doing this tomorrow," or "I work best under pressure." But in fact they do not get the urge the next day or work best under pressure. In addition, they protect their sense of self by saying "this isn't important." Another big lie procrastinators indulge is that time pressure makes them more creative. Unfortunately they do not turn out to be

(Continued)

more creative; they only feel that way. They squander their resources.

9   7. Procrastinators actively look for distractions, particularly ones that don't take a lot of commitment on their part. Checking e-mail is almost perfect for this purpose. They distract themselves as a way of regulating their emotions such as fear of failure.

10   8. There's more than one flavor of procrastination. People procrastinate for different reasons. Dr. Ferrari identifies three basic types of procrastinators:

What do you think are the definitions of arousal types, avoiders, and decisional procrastinators?

- arousal types, or thrill-seekers, who wait to the last minute for the euphoric rush.
- avoiders, who may be avoiding fear of failure or even fear of success, but in either case are very concerned with what others think of them; they would rather have others think they lack effort than ability.
- decisional procrastinators, who cannot make a decision. Not making a decision absolves procrastinators of responsibility for the outcome of events.

11   9. There are big costs to procrastination. Health is one. Just over the course of a single academic term, procrastinating college students had such evidence of compromised immune systems as more colds and flu, more gastrointestinal problems. And they had insomnia. In addition, procrastination has a high cost to others as well as oneself; it shifts the burden of responsibilities onto others, who become resentful. Procrastination destroys teamwork in the workplace and private relationships.

12   10. Procrastinators can change their behavior—but doing so consumes a lot of psychic energy. And it doesn't necessarily mean one feels transformed internally. It can be done with highly structured cognitive behavioral therapy.

Marano, Hara Estroff. "Procrastination: Ten Things To Know." *Psychology Today Psyched for Success,* 23 August 2003; Article ID: 2711; http://www.psychologytoday.com/articles/index.php?term=pto-20030823-000001&print=1

COMPREHENSION CHECK

TRUE/FALSE QUESTIONS

For the following statements, write a *T* if the statement is true or an *F* if the statement is false based on the reading.

___ 1. Fifty percent of people identify themselves as chronic procrastinators.

___ 2. Procrastinators are made, not born.

___ 3. Procrastination is a symptom of poor planning or time management.

___ 4. Procrastination destroys teamwork in the workplace and in private relationships.

___ 5. Procrastinators can change their behavior.

LITERAL COMPREHENSION—MULTIPLE CHOICE

Circle the best answer for the following questions.

Understanding Main Ideas

6. Based on the list of 10 things you should know about procrastinating, which of the following options does not characterize a procrastinator?

   a. A procrastinator tells lies.

   b. A procrastinator looks for distractions.

   c. A procrastinator is more likely to drink alcohol.

   d. A procrastinator is likely to change behavior as they grow up.

7. What are the three types of procrastinators? (paragraph 10)

   a. Arousal, avoiders, decisional procrastinators

   b. Mature, immature, and unlikely procrastinators

   c. Avoiders, drinkers, and players

   d. Internally motivated, externally motivated, and conscientious procrastinators

Understanding Secondary Information and Locating Information

8. What percentage of people identifies themselves as chronic procrastinators? (paragraph 3)

   a. 20 percent

   b. 50 percent

   c. 65 percent

   d. 70 percent

(Continued)

9. Why doesn't our culture take procrastination seriously? (paragraph 4)

    a. We do not care about procrastinators.

    b. Procrastination is commonplace.

    c. We are too nice and don't confront people.

    d. We are all procrastinators in one way or another.

10. How do you think the family affects the development of procrastinators? (paragraph 6)

    a. Authoritarian parenting may promote procrastination.

    b. Parents who are strict may raise children who do not learn to regulate behavior.

    c. Children of strict parents may see procrastination as a form of rebellion.

    d. All of the given answers.

11. What is the connection between procrastination and alcohol use? (paragraph 7)

    a. Procrastinators are likely to have avoidant coping styles.

    b. Procrastinators are likely to have problems with self-regulation.

    c. Procrastinators are likely to have both avoidant coping styles and problems with self-regulation.

    d. Procrastinators are not likely to drink alcohol.

12. What lies do procrastinators tell themselves? (paragraph 8)

    a. They lie to themselves that they work well and are more creative under pressure.

    b. They lie to themselves that they are procrastinating.

    c. They lie on job applications.

    d. They lie in interviews.

13. Which of the following are the costs of procrastination? (paragraph 11)

    a. Health is affected.

    b. Interpersonal relationships are affected.

    c. Finances are affected.

    d. Both health and interpersonal relationships are affected.

14. Procrastinating college students showed evidence of all of the following physical issues except

    a. More colds and flu

    b. More gastrointestinal problems

    c. More obsessive-compulsive behavior

    d. Insomnia

15. How can procrastination not be a problem of time management? What is procrastination a problem of, then? (paragraph 5) Evidence suggests

    a. Procrastination has more to do with the ability to self-regulate.

    b. Procrastinators are born that way.

    c. Procrastinators are looking for attention.

    d. Procrastinators will grow out of it.

INFERENTIAL COMPREHENSION—MULTIPLE CHOICE

Circle the best answer for the following questions.

Making Inferences

16. Why do procrastinators look for distractions that don't involve much commitment? (paragraph 9) Evidence suggests

    a. They like attention.

    b. They like to have more free time.

    c. They don't have goals.

    d. They look for distractions to deal with their emotions.

Applying Information

17. How can procrastinators change their behavior? (paragraph 12)

    a. Shape up or ship out.

    b. Seek cognitive behavior therapy.

    c. Confront strict parents.

    d. Grow up.

Understanding Sentence Relationships

18. In paragraph 3, why does the author provide a list of examples? How does this list help you understand procrastination?

    a. The author provides the list of examples to illustrate how procrastination spans all aspects of life.

    b. The author wants to challenge the reader.

    c. The author contrasts a procrastinator with an enlightened goal setter.

    d. The author self-identifies as a procrastinator.

(Continued)

19. In paragraph 6, why does the author discuss parenting and childhood?
    a. The author defines procrastination.
    b. The author provides the possible causes for procrastination.
    c. The author lists characteristics of procrastination.
    d. The author shows how procrastinators can solve their problems.

20. Why does the author break down procrastinators into types in paragraph 10? How does this help you understand procrastination?
    a. The author classifies types of procrastinators to clarify and define.
    b. The author shows the effects of procrastination.
    c. The author discusses the symptoms of procrastination.
    d. The author discusses the solutions to procrastination.

INCREASE YOUR COLLEGE-LEVEL VOCABULARY

Based on information in the reading, choose the best answer from the following key terms or concepts (ideas) for each sentence.

procrastination	arousal types	decisional procrastinators
procrastinator	avoiders	

21. Jose was an individual who suffered from _____. He sabotaged himself by delaying doing essential tasks.

22. A person who sabotages himself by failing to complete tasks in a timely manner is called a _____.

23. One form of procrastinator is characterized as an _____ because he or she is a thrill seeker who waits to complete tasks at the last minute for the euphoric rush of the pressure.

24. Another form of procrastinator is an _____. This is an individual who is afraid of failure or even of success. This type of person would rather have others think they lack effort than ability.

25. A third type of procrastinator is a _____. This type of person simply cannot make a decision.

SHORT-ANSWER QUESTIONS

As your instructor assigns, respond to the following questions.

26. What causes procrastination or creates procrastinators? What sentences from the reading support your answer?

27. Can procrastinators change? What would you suggest it takes to change a procrastinator? Use both sentences from the reading and your own ideas to answer these questions.

28. In your opinion, is procrastination a behavior that is learned or a lifestyle choice that is made?

29. Why do you think 1 out of 5 (20%) people considers themselves procrastinators? (paragraph 3)

APPLICATION ②

This reading is from the college success textbook *BAMS: The Essential Guide to Becoming a Master Student*. Before you read the whole passage through, preview the reading. Underline or highlight the parts of the reading you'll preview, following these instructions.

1. Read the title. Activate your background knowledge—what do you know about planning?
2. Read the first paragraph.
3. Read the headings, if there are any.
4. Read the first sentence of each of body paragraph.
5. Read the concluding paragraph.

While you read the passage, answer the questions in the margins about making predictions and understanding key terms from context clues. After you are done reading the passage, complete the Comprehension Check questions that follow the reading.

Planning Sets You Free

What do you think the main point is?

1   An effective plan is flexible, not carved in stone. You can change your plans frequently and still preserve the advantages of planning—choosing your overall direction and taking charge of your life. And even when other people set the goal, you can choose how to achieve it.

2   Planning is a self-creative venture that lasts for a lifetime. Following are eight ways to get the most from this process. The first four are suggestions about goal setting. The rest are about the details of scheduling activities based on your goals.

What do you think the author will discuss next?

3   **1. Back up to a bigger picture.** When choosing activities for the day or week, take some time to lift your eyes to the horizon. Step back for a few minutes and consider your longer-range goals—what you want to accomplish in the next six months, the next year, the next five years, and beyond.

4   Ask whether the activities you're about to schedule actually contribute to those goals. If they do, great. If not, ask whether you can delete some items from your calendar or to-do list to make room for goal-related activities. See if you can free up at least one hour each day for doing something you love instead of putting it off to a more "reasonable" or "convenient" time.

5   **2. Look boldly for things to change.** It's fascinating to note the areas that are off-limits when people set goals.

Money, sex, career, marriage, and other topics can easily fall into the category "I'll just have to live with this."

6   When creating your future, open up your thinking about what aspects of your life can be changed and what cannot. Be willing to put every facet of your life on the table. Staying open-minded can lead to a future you never dreamed was possible.

What do you think the author will discuss next?

Facet is a synonym of what word in the previous sentence?

7   **3. Look for what's missing—and what to maintain.** Goals often arise from a sense of what's missing in our lives. Goal setting is fueled by unresolved problems, incomplete projects, relationships we want to develop, and careers we still want to pursue.

8   However, not all planning has to spring from a sense of need. You can set goals to maintain things that you already have, or to keep doing the effective things that you already do. If you exercise vigorously three times each week, you can set a goal to keep exercising. If you already have a loving relationship with your spouse, you can set a goal to nurture that relationship for the rest of your life.

9   **4. Think even further into the future.** To have fun and unleash your creativity, set goals as far in the future as you can. The specific length of time doesn't matter. For some people, long-range planning might mean 10, 20, or even 50 years from now. For others, planning 3 years ahead feels right. Do whatever works for you.

What do you think the author will discuss next?

10   Once you've stated your longest-range goals, work backward until you can define a next step to take. Suppose your 30-year goal is to retire and maintain your present standard of living. Ask yourself: "In order to do that, what financial goals do I need to achieve in 20 years? In 10 years? In one year? In one month? In one week?" Put the answers to these questions in writing.

11   **5. Schedule fixed blocks of time first.** When planning your week, start with class time and work time. These time periods are usually determined in advance. Other activities must be scheduled around them. Then schedule essential daily activities such as sleeping and eating. In addition, schedule some time each week for actions that lead directly to one of your written goals.

What do you think the author will discuss next?

(Continued)

What do you think the author will discuss next?

12   **6. Set clear starting and stopping times.** Tasks often expand to fill the time we allot for them.

13   Try scheduling a certain amount of time for a reading assignment—set a timer, and stick to it. Students often find that they can decrease study time by forcing themselves to read faster. This can usually be done without sacrificing comprehension.

14   The same principle can apply to other tasks. Some people find they can get up 15 minutes earlier in the morning and still feel alert throughout the day. Plan 45 minutes for a trip to the grocery store instead of one hour. Over the course of a year, those extra minutes can add up to hours.

What do you think the author will discuss next?
What is a synonym for *flex time*?

15   **7. Schedule for flexibility and fun.** Recognize that unexpected things will happen and allow for them. Leave some holes in your schedule. Build in blocks of unplanned time. Consider setting aside time each week marked "flex time" or "open time." Use these hours for emergencies, spontaneous activities, catching up, or seizing new opportunities.

16   Include time for errands. The time we spend buying toothpaste, paying bills, and doing laundry is easy to overlook. These little errands can destroy a tight schedule and make us feel rushed and harried all week. Remember to allow for travel time between locations. Also make room for fun. Take time to browse aimlessly through the library, stroll with no destination, ride a bike, or do other things you enjoy.

What is a synonym for *harried*?

What is a synonym for *aimlessly*?

17   **8. Involve others when appropriate.** Sometimes the activities we schedule depend on gaining information, assistance, or direct participation from other people. If we neglect to inform them of our plans or forget to ask for their cooperation at the outset—surprise! Our schedules can crash.

From MASTER STUDENT. Book Block for Ellis' *BAMS: The Essential Guide to Becoming a Master Student*, 1E. © 2010 Wadsworth, a part of Cengage Learning, Inc. By permission.

COMPREHENSION CHECK

TRUE/FALSE QUESTIONS

For the following statements, write a *T* if the statement is true or an *F* if the statement is false based on the reading.

___   1. Effective planning is flexible.

___   2. Planning is a self-creative venture that lasts for a specific period of time.

___   3. When you are planning your daily schedule, you should ask yourself if these plans will contribute to your long-term goals.

___   4. You should schedule work time and school time around other activities.

___   5. You should not build blocks of unstructured time into your schedule.

LITERAL COMPREHENSION—MULTIPLE CHOICE

Circle the best answer for the following questions.

Understanding Main Ideas

6. According to the author, how does planning "set you free"?

   a. Planning is choosing your overall direction and taking charge of your life.

   b. You are in control of how you attain your goals.

   c. You choose your direction and take charge of your life, and you are in control of how you attain your goals.

   d. Once you have planned, you are free to fill your time with leisure activities.

7. Which of the following is not one of the four suggestions about goal setting?

   a. Back up to the bigger picture.

   b. Look boldly for things to change.

   c. Look for what's missing—and what to maintain.

   d. Do not think too much about the future.

8. Which of the following is not one of the four guidelines for scheduling activities based on your goals?

   a. Schedule unstructured blocks of time first.

   b. Set clear starting and stopping times.

   c. Schedule for flexibility and fun.

   d. Involve others when appropriate.

(Continued)

Understanding Secondary Information and Locating Information

9. According to paragraph 5, what areas are off limits when people set goals?

    a. Money, sex, career, marriage

    b. Money, time, and space

    c. School, recreation, and fun

    d. Nothing is off limits when setting goals.

10. According to paragraph 7, what fuels goal setting?

    a. Unresolved problems and incomplete projects

    b. Relationships we want to develop

    c. Careers we still want to pursue

    d. All of the given answers.

11. According to paragraph 9, how variable are long-term goals?

    a. Goals ought to be set in stone and should not be variable.

    b. Goals need to be set after leisure time is enjoyed.

    c. Different people view long-term goals from different perspectives—some may not be comfortable thinking in years but instead think in months.

    d. Goals should not interfere with your daily life.

INFERENTIAL COMPREHENSION—MULTIPLE CHOICE

Circle the best answer for the following questions.

Making Inferences

12. Using the title of this reading, one could pose the question "How does planning set you free?" How does the author answer this question?

    a. The author suggests that you can control how or when to attain your goals.

    b. The author suggests that one ought to free oneself from planning.

    c. The author says that plans are made to be changed.

    d. The author tells the reader to work school and career goals around daily tasks.

13. What does the author mean by this statement in paragraph 2: "Planning is a self-creative venture that lasts for a lifetime"?

    a. Planning is lifelong.

    b. We should work toward goals throughout our lives.

    c. Planning and goals setting are lifelong activities.

    d. Plans should be made for a short period of time.

Applying Information

14. In paragraph 3, the author says, "Step back for a few minutes and consider your longer-range goals—what you want to accomplish in the next six months, the next year, the next five years, and beyond." Why do you think the author recommends this?

    a. To have a bigger picture of where you are going

    b. To focus on the task at hand

    c. To motivate yourself to accomplish your tasks

    d. To have a bigger picture of where you are going in order to motivate yourself to accomplish your tasks

Understanding Sentence Relationships

15. Consider this statement in paragraph 2: "The first four are suggestions about goal setting. The rest are about the details of scheduling activities based on your goals." Are these 10 suggestions in a random or a specific order?

    a. The order is random.

    b. The order is specific.

    c. The order is both random and specific.

    d. The order is neither random nor specific.

INCREASE YOUR COLLEGE-LEVEL VOCABULARY

Based on information in the reading, write your own sentence for each of the following words using a definition or synonym context clue.

16. Planning (paragraph 1): _____

    _____

17. Facet (paragraph 6): _____

    _____

18. Flex time (paragraph 15): _____

    _____

19. Aimlessly (paragraph 16): _____

    _____

20. Harried (paragraph 16): _____

    _____

(Continued)

SHORT-ANSWER QUESTIONS

As your instructor assigns, respond to the following questions.

21. Why do you think the author entitles this reading "Planning Sets You Free"?

22. Which of the suggestions that the author presents do you feel is the most important to leading an organized, planned life?

23. Which of the author's suggestions do you feel is the least important to helping with time management?

24. Is there a point that is not included in this reading that you feel is important and should be a part of any well-organized life plan?

WRAPPING IT UP

STUDY OUTLINE

This is a list of key terms from this chapter for you to define in an organized format. In the following study outline, fill in the definitions and a brief explanation of the key terms in the Your Notes column. Use the strategy of spaced practice to review these key terms on a regular basis. Use this study guide to review this chapter's key topics.

KEY TERM	YOUR NOTES
Reading process	
Before, during, and after reading strategies	
Background knowledge	
Purpose for reading	
Preview	
Predicting	
Metacognition	
Rehearsal	
Spaced practice	

(Continued)

WRAPPING IT UP

KEY TERM	YOUR NOTES
Active reading strategy	
Active learning	
Active reading	
Sensory memory	
Working memory	
Encoding	
Long-term memory	
Schema	
Cramming	
Context clue	
Transition words	

KEY TERM	YOUR NOTES
Definition clue	
Synonym	
Synonym clue	

WHAT DID YOU LEARN?

Now, go back to the KWL chart at the beginning of this chapter and fill in the L column, noting what you have learned from this chapter.

GROUP ACTIVITY: PANEL DISCUSSION

As a group, find further information on one of the following topics, and present what you find out in a panel discussion where teams become experts on their research question.

- Memory and/or learning
- The causes and effects of procrastination
- How to study effectively
- Achievement
- Characteristics of successful people
- Characteristics of unsuccessful people
- Definitions of success
- Will power and impulse

WRAPPING IT UP

QUESTIONS FOR WRITING, DISCUSSION, OR REFLECTION

1. What do you feel is the most significant piece of information regarding motivation and learning covered in this chapter? What are some ways you could use this information to improve your learning?

2. Several readings in this chapter concern motivation, procrastination, and the relationship to student success. Based on these readings, what do you think you ought to work on next to improve your success in college?

3. What are the qualities needed for an individual to be successful in college? Choose three qualities (behaviors, techniques, or attitudes) that characterize a successful student. Support your answer with specific examples.

4. Choose a textbook you use in another class. Find an example or examples of the following:

   a. A definition context clue

   b. A synonym context clue

5. Choose a reading assigned for another course. Preview the reading and answer the following questions based on your previewing:

   a. What is the main point of the reading?

   b. Into how many sections is the reading divided?

   c. What are the key points in the reading?

6. Read the following quote by a German philosopher, Arthur Schopenhauer, who lived from 1788 to 1860. "Reading is thinking with someone else's head instead of one's own." What do you think he meant by this quote? How does this quote apply to the topic of predicting while you read?

POST-ASSESSMENT

This assessment will help you understand your strengths and weaknesses in learning, understanding, and applying the skills and strategies discussed in this chapter. Preview the following reading. Then read it all the way through and answer the Comprehension Check questions that follow.

Organizing Your Time
By Dianne Hales

1   We live in what some sociologists call <u>hyperculture</u>, a society that moves at warp speed. Information bombards us constantly. The rate of change seems to accelerate every year. Our "time-saving" devices—pagers, cell phones, modems, faxes, palm-sized organizers, laptop computers—have simply extended the boundaries of where and how we work.

2   As a result, more and more people are suffering from "<u>timesickness</u>," a nerve-racking feeling that life has become little more than an endless to-do list. The best antidote is time management, and hundreds of books, seminars, and experts offer training in making the most of the hours in the day. Yet these well-intentioned methods often fail, and sooner or later most of us find ourselves caught in a time trap.

Are You Running Out of Time?

3   Every day you make dozens of decisions, and the choices you make about how to use your time directly affect your stress level. If you have a big test on Monday and a term paper due Tuesday, you may plan to study all weekend. Then, when you're invited to a party Saturday night, you go. Although you set the alarm for 7:00 a.m. on Sunday, you don't pull yourself out of bed until noon. By the time you start studying, it's 4:00 p.m., and anxiety is building inside you.

4   How can you tell if you've lost control of your time? The following are telltale symptoms of poor time management:

- Rushing.
- Chronic inability to make choices or decisions.
- Fatigue or listlessness.
- Constantly missed deadlines.
- Not enough time for rest or personal relationships.
- A sense of being overwhelmed by demands and details and having to do what you don't want to do most of the time.

5   One of the hard lessons of being on your own is that your choices and your actions have consequences. Stress is just one of them. But by thinking ahead, being realistic about your workload, and sticking to your plans, you can gain better control over your time and your stress levels.

From HALES. *An Invitation to Health, Brief Edition (with Personal Health Self Assessments)*, 6E. © 2010 Brooks/Cole, a part of Cengage Learning, Inc. By permission

(Continued)

COMPREHENSION CHECK

Circle the best answer to the questions based on information in the reading.

1 **According to paragraph 1, *hyperculture* is**

A. A society that moves at warp speed.

B. An anxious society.

C. The concept of hyperactivity within individuals.

2 **What type of context clue did you use to answer question 1?**

A. A definition clue

B. A synonym clue

C. A transition word

3 **According to paragraph 2, *timesickness* is defined as**

A. Good and effective actions.

B. A society that moves at warp speed.

C. A nerve-racking feeling that life has become little more than an endless to-do list.

4 **What type of context clue did you use to answer question 3?**

A. A definition clue

B. A synonym clue

C. A transition word

5 **Why do more people suffer from timesickness?**

A. Because they are unmotivated and lazy

B. Because they are part of the hyperculture

C. Because time-saving devices have expanded work hours

6 **According to the reading, how can you cure timesickness?**

A. By becoming part of the hyperculture

B. By using meditation techniques

C. By managing your time

7 **In paragraph 3, the author says, "By the time you start studying, it's 4:00 p.m., and anxiety is building inside you." Why is anxiety building?**

A. Because you are running out of time to get things done because the weekend is almost over

B. Because you feel listless and tired

C. Because the weekend is almost over and you are unable to make choices or decisions

8 If you have these symptoms—rushing, chronic inability to make choices or decisions, and fatigue or listlessness—what is your problem?

A. Poor energy levels
B. Poor time management
C. Poor health

9 According to paragraph 5, what is one consequence of your choices and actions?

A. Stress
B. Hyperactivity
C. Lack of sleep

10 How can you gain control over your time and stress levels?

A. Through internal motivation
B. By thinking ahead, being realistic about your workload, and sticking to your plans
C. Through listlessness and constantly missed deadlines

TOPIC AND POSING QUESTIONS

THEME *Success in College—Your Health*

"First, have a definite, clear practical ideal; a goal, an objective. Second, have the necessary means to achieve your ends; wisdom, money, materials, and methods. Third, adjust all your means to that end."

— ARISTOTLE (GREEK PHILOSOPHER)

OBJECTIVES

In this chapter, you will focus on:

COMPREHENSION SKILLS

Learn how to concentrate on a reading by

- Determining topic
- Posing guide questions

LEARNING HOW TO CONCENTRATE

READING STUDY SKILLS

Learn how to concentrate through

- Motivation
- Time management

VOCABULARY SKILLS

Learn how to concentrate on context clues to determine the meaning of unknown words using

- Antonym clues
- Inference clues

© Cengage Learning 2013

WHY DO YOU NEED TO KNOW THIS?

Problem: Mario, 27, has returned to school after being laid off from his job. He receives financial aid to requalify for a new job through taking classes at his local community college, but he needs to progress in his course-work to move back into the job market as soon as possible. He is unsure of himself since he was never an outstanding student, dropping out of high school at 17 and later attaining a GED. He lives with his wife and two young children and has trouble concentrating on his studies with so many distractions and demands on his time. He has learned about the reading process, but he doesn't know how to a find the most important points in a reading. He doesn't understand how to use the clues the author provides to uncover the topic. Mario is eager to learn and needs a system that will jump-start his college reading load to his best advantage.

© Gary Conner/Index Stock Imagery/Photolibrary

WHAT ADVICE WOULD YOU OFFER TO MARIO?

_____

_____

_____

_____

Solution: To understand what you read, first you need to pinpoint the topic of a reading and use your knowledge about this topic to anticipate the author's most important points. An active reader also poses guide questions while reading to aid concentration. By posing guide questions, you can focus on finding the answers, which enables you to uncover the key points. Mario needs to reconsider how to be an effective learner. To manage a college workload, he needs to assess his motivation and manage his time—both key elements in providing the focus needed for college success. This chapter will provide Mario, and you, with fundamental strategies for college success.

WHAT DO YOU ALREADY KNOW?

What problems do you have with concentrating on difficult readings? In the following chart, respond to each statement twice—once at the beginning of the chapter and again when you have finished reading the chapter. Read each statement and put an *X* in the Agree or Disagree column, depending on your opinion.

| BEFORE | | | AFTER | |
AGREE	DISAGREE		AGREE	DISAGREE
		1. **Effective readers read a passage through and ask guide questions to focus afterward.**		
		2. **Effective readers read the passage through and then determine the topic of the reading.**		
		3. **Effective readers determine the topic of a reading before reading the passage through.**		
		4. **Effective readers pose guide questions before they read to focus their reading.**		

© Cengage Learning 2013

Roman Shcherbakov/Shutterstock

PRE-ASSESSMENT

This pre-assessment will help you measure what you already know and what you need to learn about the reading skills and strategies explored in this chapter. Your results will help you understand your strengths and weaknesses. Read the article, and then answer the Comprehension Check questions that follow.

Students Under Stress
By Dianne Hales

1   More than a quarter of freshmen feel overwhelmed by all they have to do at the beginning of the academic year; by the year's end, 44 percent feel overwhelmed. In research at three universities, underclassmen were most vulnerable to negative life events, perhaps because they lacked experience in coping with stressful situations. Freshmen had the highest levels

of depression; sophomores had the most anger and hostility. Seniors may handle life's challenges better because they have developed better coping mechanisms. In the study, more seniors reported that they faced problems squarely and took action to resolve them, while younger students were more likely to respond passively, for instance, by trying not to let things bother them.

2   First-generation college students—those whose parents never experienced at least one full year of college—encounter more difficulties with social adjustment than freshmen whose parents attended college. Second-generation students may have several advantages: more knowledge of college life, greater social support, more preparation for college in high school, a greater focus on college activities, and more financial resources.

3   The percentage of students seeking psychological help because of stress or anxiety has risen dramatically in the last 15 years. Students say they react to stress in various ways: physiologically (by sweating, stuttering, trembling, or developing physical symptoms); emotionally (by becoming anxious, fearful, angry, guilty, or depressed); behaviorally (by crying, eating, smoking, being irritable or abusive); or cognitively (by thinking about and analyzing stressful situations and strategies that might be useful in dealing with them).

4   A supportive network of friends and family makes a difference. Undergraduates with higher levels of social support and self-efficacy reported feeling less stressed and more satisfied with life than others.

COMPREHENSION CHECK

Circle the best answer to the questions based on information from the reading.

1 **What is the topic of this reading?**

A. Stress
B. Students under stress
C. Stressful situations

2 **What is a good guide question to ask about the title of this reading?**

A. Who are the students under stress?
B. Where is stress on campus?
C. Why is there stress?

3 **Who are the students under stress?**

A. Mainly seniors
B. Mainly sophomores
C. Mainly freshmen and first-generation college students

(Continued)

4 **According to paragraph 2, what are first-generation college students?**

    A. Students whose parents never experienced at least one full year of college

    B. Students who faced problems squarely and took action to resolve them

    C. Students who find school stressful

5 **What type of vocabulary context clue did you use to figure out the term *first-generation college students*?**

    A. Definition clue

    B. Synonym clue

    C. Inference clue

6 **According to paragraph 1, _____ percent of freshmen are stressed at the beginning of the year, whereas ___ percent are stressed by the end of the year.**

    A. 25 percent and 44 percent

    B. 44 percent and 50 percent

    C. Freshmen tend to be more angry than stressed.

7 **According to the reading, the percentage of students seeking psychological help because of stress or anxiety has _____**

    A. Risen in the past 15 years.

    B. Decreased in the past 15 years.

    C. Remained at a steady rate.

8 **Sweating, stuttering, and trembling are examples of what type of stress symptom?**

    A. Physiological

    B. Emotional

    C. Behavioral

9 **What does the word *cognitively* mean in paragraph 3?**

    A. Relating to behavior

    B. Relating to emotions

    C. Relating to thought

10 **What helps lessen stress for students under stress?**

    A. Understanding instructors

    B. Alcohol use

    C. Supportive family and friends

FOCUS ON COMPREHENSION
Determining the Topic and Posing Guide Questions

In Chapter 1, you learned that there is a process to reading in an effective and efficient manner. Before you read, you can take certain steps in order to work with your brain to maximize your comprehension of a reading.

TOPIC

To understand what you are reading, you need to recognize *who* or *what* the passage is about, or the **topic.** Another word for topic is the **subject** of the reading. A topic is not a sentence. A topic is a word or phrase, and it should be specific. The more specific the topic, the easier it will be to determine the author's most important point about the topic, or the author's main idea.

A topic is not a complete sentence. Consider these statements. Which is a word, which is a phrase, and which is a sentence?

   a. Stress management is essential to good health.

   b. Stress management

   c. Stress

Answer *a* is a sentence, so it is not a topic. A sentence must have both a subject and a verb; and in answer *a*, the subject of the sentence is *stress management* and the verb is *is*. Answer *b* is a phrase—a couple of words; this option may be the topic. Answer *c* is a word and may also be a topic.

FOCUS ON COMPREHENSION: Determining the Topic and Posing Guide Questions

On Your Own UNDERSTANDING TOPIC

Put an *X* next to statements that could be topics. Be prepared to explain your answers.

_____ 1. Memory and the brain

_____ 2. The brain's complex memory system is the subject of much research.

_____ 3. Procrastination

_____ 4. Procrastination is the enemy of efficiency.

_____ 5. Motivation and time management

_____ 6. Motivation can come from both internal and external sources.

_____ 7. Intermediate goals are important for long-term success.

_____ 8. Goal setting and active learning

_____ 9. Short-term versus long-term goals

_____ 10. Goals

General Versus Specific _____

When a topic is too **general,** it means that the topic is too broad. For example, health could be a topic. But health is broad or general—many subjects could be discussed about health, like health and stress, or health and student success. When a topic is too **specific,** it means that the topic is too narrow. If not everything in the reading relates to that topic, then the topic is too narrow.

Thinking It Through GENERAL VERSUS SPECIFIC

Read the following passages and then determine which choice is the best topic for the passage by putting an *X* next to it. Put a *G* next to the statement that is too general and an *S* next to the statement that is too specific.

How Are Stress and Coping Related to Physical Health?

A great deal of research has been conducted over the years examining links between stress and physical health. Being under chronic stress suppresses the immune system, resulting in increased susceptibility to viral infections, increased risk of atherosclerosis (buildup of plaque along the walls of arteries so that the arteries become stiffer and restrict blood flow) and hypertension (high blood pressure), and impaired memory and cognition. However, these effects depend on the kind of event. Experiencing negative events tends to lower immune function, whereas experiencing positive events tends to improve immune functioning.

—From KAIL/CAVANAUGH. *Human Development,* 5E. © 2010 Wadsworth, a part of Cengage Learning, Inc. By permission.

___ **Stress**

___ **Hypertension and impaired memory**

___ **Stress, coping, and physical health**

The first option, "stress," is too general. The passage is about stress, but, as the title implies, it is also about more than that. The second option is mentioned in the passage, but it is not what all the sentences in the passage are about. "Hypertension and impaired memory" are just effects of stress on physical health. This option is too specific. The last option—"stress, coping, and physical health"—is the best topic choice because the title suggests that this is what the reading is about. Also, all the sentences in the passage function to provide more information about the relationship among stress, coping, and physical health.

Read this passage and then look at the topics provided.

Tips for Staying Healthy

1. Get enough sleep (at least 8–9 hours a night)
2. Eat a healthy diet that includes at least 5–7 servings of fruits and vegetables daily
3. Take a multivitamin with folic acid and get at least 1300 mg of calcium daily
4. Exercise for at least 30 minutes most days of the week
5. Avoid smoking
6. Learn to manage stress

(Continued)

FOCUS ON COMPREHENSION: Determining the Topic and Posing Guide Questions

7. Take time every day to do something you enjoy! (Read, paint/draw, dance, cook, talk to a friend, etc.)

—"Tips for Staying Healthy" from Center for Young Women's Health Staff.
©2011 Center for Young Women's Health, Children's Hospital Boston. By permission.

Which topic is too general? Which topic is too specific? Which topic best fits the passage?

__Health

__Tips for staying healthy

__Avoid smoking

"Health" is too general to be an effective topic; the passage could be about health and aging, health and stress, health and college students, or various other health issues. Health does not accurately portray what the whole passage is about. "Avoid smoking" is too specific to be the topic because it is only a small part of what the passage is about; it doesn't include the other parts of the passage, such as sleep, diet, and managing stress. "Tips for staying healthy" is the best topic because all the bullets of the passage fall under that general statement. Notice this answer is also the title of the passage. A title often indicates the topic.

On Your Own GENERAL VERSUS SPECIFIC

Read the following passages and then determine which choice is the best topic for the passage by putting an *X* next to it. Put a *G* next to the statement that is too general and an *S* next to the statement that is too specific.

1. **Coping** is any attempt to deal with stress. People cope in several different ways. Sometimes people cope by trying to solve the problem at hand; for example, you may cope with a messy roommate by moving out. At other times, people focus on how they feel about the situation and deal with things on an emotional level; feeling sad after breaking up with your partner would be one way of coping with the stress of being alone. Sometimes people cope by simply redefining the event as not stressful—an example of this approach would be saying that it was no big deal you failed to get the job you wanted. Still others focus on religious or spiritual approaches, perhaps asking God for help.

—From KAIL/CAVANAUGH. *Human Development,* 5E. © 2010 Wadsworth, a part of Cengage Learning, Inc.
By permission.

_ Coping with stress

_ Coping with a focus on religious or spiritual approaches

_ Coping

2. In general, psychological forces are all the internal cognitive, emotional, personality, perceptual, and related factors that influence behavior. Psychological forces have received the most attention of the three main developmental forces. Much of what we discuss throughout this text reflects psychological forces. For example, we will see how the development of intelligence enables individuals to experience and think about their world in different ways. We'll also see how the emergence of self-esteem is related to the beliefs people have about their abilities, which in turn influence what they do.

—From KAIL/CAVANAUGH. *Human Development,* 5E. © 2010 Wadsworth, a part of Cengage Learning, Inc. By permission.

_ Psychology
_ Three main developmental forces
_ Psychological forces

Psychological Forces

3. Psychological forces probably seem familiar because they are the ones used most often to describe the characteristics of a person. For example, think about how you describe yourself to others. Most of us say that we have a nice personality and are intelligent, honest, self-confident, or something similar. Concepts like these reflect psychological forces.

—From KAIL/CAVANAUGH. *Human Development,* 5E. © 2010 Wadsworth, a part of Cengage Learning, Inc. By permission.

_ Psychological forces
_ Describing yourself to others
_ Forces

4. One useful way to organize the biological, psychological, and sociocultural forces on human development is with the **biopsychosocial framework.** The biopsychosocial framework emphasizes that each of the forces interacts with the others to make up development. Let's look at the different elements of the biopsychosocial model in more detail.

—From KAIL/CAVANAUGH. *Human Development,* 5E. © 2010 Wadsworth, a part of Cengage Learning, Inc. By permission.

_ Biological, psychological, and sociocultural forces
_ Human development
_ Biopsychosocial framework

FOCUS ON COMPREHENSION: Determining the Topic and Posing Guide Questions

Finding the Topic

There are three clues for determining a topic of a passage. Some passages have more than one clue to work with. To identify the topic, follow these steps:

1. **Look for a title, subtitle, headings, or subheadings that provide clues.** Often an author will provide information about who or what a passage is about by providing a title, heading, or subheading.

Dangerous Stress

Stress becomes dangerous when it interferes with your ability to live a normal life for an extended period of time. You may feel "out of control" and have no idea of what to do, even if the cause is relatively minor. This, in turn, may cause you to feel continually fatigued, unable to concentrate, or irritable in otherwise relaxed situations. Prolonged stress may also compound any emotional problems stemming from sudden events, such as traumatic experiences in your past, and increase thoughts of suicide.

—Source: The American Psychological Association, http://www.apa.org/helpcenter/ stress.aspx. The American Psychological Practice Directorate gratefully acknowledges the assistance of Sara Weiss, Ph.D., and Nancy Molitor, Ph.D., in developing this fact sheet. © 2010 American Psychological Association

Notice that the topic of this passage is stated in the title: dangerous stress.

2. **Look for bold, colored, or italicized words.** When a passage does not have a title, you need to look at visual clues to help you figure out the topic. These visual clues often indicate a definition or another important point. When an author makes a word stand out with special print, chances are that this is what the paragraph is about. Remember definition clues that you learned about in Chapter 1? Often, a key term is a word or phrase in special print. Consider this example:

A **self-fulfilling prophecy** is anticipating or predicting your reaction to a person, event, or thing. This prediction or anticipation directly or indirectly causes itself to become a reality. An example of a self-fulfilling prophecy is when you convince yourself you will do poorly in a job interview or on a test, and it comes to pass.

—Gamble and Gamble, *Interpersonal Communication in Theory, Practice, and Context*

Since this passage doesn't have a title, you have to rely on other text clues. What stands out in the passage? "Self-fulfilling prophecy." These are boldfaced words, which signal to a reader that the author is emphasizing the term, so it must be important. Because boldfaced words in readings are typically terms that are defined, it is reasonable to assume that the passage will define and explain the term. A definition context clue can not only help you to understand the vocabulary term but also help you determine the topic of a passage.

3. **Look for a word (or words) in the reading that occurs over and over again.** If an author uses a word, words, or a phrase repeatedly or refers to repeated words later in the passage with a pronoun (*he, she, it, they*), then chances are that is what the passage is about—the topic. Not all passages will repeat *exactly* the same words or phrases. Instead, authors often use synonyms to stand in for certain terms. Remember that a synonym is a word or a phrase that means the same as another word or phrase. The word *stress* may be suggested by a synonym like *trauma* or *pressure*. While subtly different, these words mean basically the same thing in certain contexts. Look at the following passage and decide which of the following statements best sums up the topic of the passage.

> Stress may be the most significant inherited risk factor in people who develop heart disease at a young age. According to behavioral researchers, family transmission of emotional and psychosocial stress, specifically anger in males, greatly increases the likelihood of early heart disease. Young adults whose blood pressure spikes in response to stress may be at risk of hypertension as they get older.

—From HALES. *An Invitation to Health, Brief Edition (with Personal Health Self Assessments),* 6E. © 2010 Brooks/Cole, a part of Cengage Learning, Inc. By permission.

What is the best statement of topic?

___Young adults and blood pressure

___Stress

___Stress and heart disease

Without a title or bolded words to use as clues to determine the topic, search out repeated words in the passage. Look at the first sentence: "stress" and "heart disease" are mentioned. In the second sentence, both "stress" and "heart disease" are mentioned again. In the last sentence, "stress" is mentioned as is its toll on the body as a risk for hypertension. With these thoughts in mind, you can eliminate "young adults and blood pressure" because that topic does not include stress. "Stress" is too general a topic because it does not mention heart disease. The best topic is "stress and heart disease" because it is specific enough to cover the contents of the passage but not too general as to be vague and incomplete. Consider this example:

> Time management is a way to find the time for all the things you want and need to do. It helps you decide which things are urgent

FOCUS ON COMPREHENSION: Determining the Topic and Posing Guide Questions

and which can wait. Learning how to manage your time, activities, and commitments can be hard. But doing so can make your life easier, less stressful, and more meaningful.

1. When you manage your time, you decide which tasks and activities are most important to you. Knowing what's important helps you decide how best to spend your time.

2. There are three parts to time management: prioritize tasks and activities, control procrastination, and manage commitments.

—Jeannette Curtis, Stress Management: Managing Your Time, accessed from http://www.webmd.com/balance/stress-management/stress-management-managing-your-time. Used with permission.

The topic of this passage is time management. The phrase *time management*, or related words, like *manage your time*, appears throughout the passage.

QUICK TIPS IDENTIFYING TOPIC

☑ The topic is who or what a passage is about.

☑ The topic can be found in the title; italicized, colored, or boldfaced words; or repeated words in a passage.

☑ Try to narrow the topic into a few words that sum up the whole reading.

☑ Make sure the topic isn't too general or too specific.

☑ A topic is a word or a phrase, not a sentence!

On Your Own DETERMINING THE TOPIC OF A PASSAGE

Write the statement of topic for each of the following passages. Circle any text clues that help you identify the topic.

Biological Forces

1. Prenatal development, brain maturation, puberty, menopause, facial wrinkling, and change in cardiovascular functioning may occur to you as examples of biological forces. Indeed, major aspects of each are determined by our genetic code. For example, many

children resemble their parents, which shows biological influences on development. But biological forces also include the effects of lifestyle factors, such as diet and exercise. Collectively, biological forces can be viewed as providing the raw material necessary and as setting the boundary conditions (in the case of genetics) for development.

—From KAIL/CAVANAUGH. *Human Development*, 5E. © 2010 Wadsworth, a part of Cengage Learning, Inc. By permission.

Topic: _____

2. Why is this trait so prevalent? Is it because you inherited the trait from your parents? Or is it because of where and how you and your parents were brought up? Answers to these questions illustrate different positions on the nature–nurture issue, which involves the degree to which genetic or hereditary influences (nature) and experiential or environmental influences (nurture) determine the kind of person you are. Scientists once hoped to answer these questions by identifying either heredity or environment as the cause of a particular aspect of development. The goal was to be able to say, for example, that intelligence was due to heredity or that personality was due to experience. Today, however, we know that virtually no feature of life-span development is due exclusively to either heredity or environment. Instead, development is always shaped by both: Nature and nurture are mutually interactive influences.

—From KAIL/CAVANAUGH. *Human Development*, 5E. © 2010 Wadsworth, a part of Cengage Learning, Inc. By permission.

Topic: _____

3. More so than ever, many people find that they are working more and enjoying it less. Many people, including working parents, spend 55 to 60 hours a week on the job. More people are caught up in an exhausting cycle of overwork, which causes stress, which makes work harder, which leads to more stress. Even the workplace itself can contribute to stress. A noisy, open-office environment can increase levels of stress without workers realizing it.

—From HALES. *An Invitation to Health, Brief Edition (with Personal Health Self Assessments)*, 6E. © 2010 Brooks/Cole, a part of Cengage Learning, Inc. By permission.

Topic: _____

4. Age is the one variable most consistently associated with burnout: Younger employees between ages 30 and 40 report the highest rates. Both men and women are susceptible to burnout. Unmarried individuals, particularly men, seem more prone to burnout than married workers. Single employees who've never been married have higher burnout rates than those who are divorced.

—From HALES. *An Invitation to Health, Brief Edition (with Personal Health Self Assessments)*, 6E. © 2010 Brooks/Cole, a part of Cengage Learning, Inc. By permission.

Topic: _____

FOCUS ON COMPREHENSION: Determining the Topic and Posing Guide Questions

Finding the Topic in a Longer Passage

Finding topics in a longer passage is not any more difficult than finding a topic in a paragraph. You can look at the topic in a variety of ways. First, there is a topic of a whole reading. You have practiced this from your previewing activities in Chapter 1. Second, there is a topic for a subsection in a reading. A **subsection** is a section of a reading that is indicated by a heading. The heading often provides a clue as to whom or what the section is about, much like a title does for a whole reading. Last, you can determine the topic of each individual paragraph. Basically, you break the whole reading down into smaller parts and find the topic of each part.

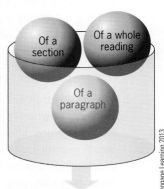

Ways of determining topic

The question to ask yourself remains the same, regardless of the length of the reading passage: who or what is the passage about?

Thinking It Through FINDING THE TOPIC IN A LONGER PASSAGE

Preview the first half of this reading on the stages of stress; then read it all the way through, taking note of the questions in the margin. As you recall from Chapter 1, previewing involves these steps:

1. **Read the title.**
2. **Read the first paragraph.**
3. **Read the headings, if there are any.**
4. **Read the first sentence of each body paragraph.**
5. **Read the concluding paragraph.**

Afterward, write your answers to the questions in the margin. Then read the explanation that follows the reading.

What Causes Stress?

Who or what is the reading about?

1   Of the many biological theories of stress, the best known may be the **general adaptation syndrome (GAS)**, developed by Hans Selye. He postulated that our bodies

constantly strive to maintain a stable and consistent physiological state, called **homeostasis.** Stressors, whether in the form of physical illness or a demanding job, disturb this state and trigger a nonspecific physiological response. The body attempts to restore homeostasis by means of an **adaptive response**.

Who or what is this section about (paragraphs 1 and 2)?

2   Selye's general adaptation syndrome, which describes the body's response to a stressor—whether threatening or exhilarating—consists of three distinct stages:

3   **1. Alarm.** When a stressor first occurs, the body responds with changes that temporarily lower resistance. Levels of certain hormones may rise; blood pressure may increase. The body quickly makes internal adjustments to cope with the stressor and return to normal activity.

Who or what is paragraph 3 about?

4   **2. Resistance.** If the stressor continues, the body mobilizes its internal resources to try to sustain homeostasis. For example, if a loved one is seriously hurt in an accident, we initially respond intensely and feel great anxiety. During the subsequent stressful period of recuperation, we struggle to carry on as normally as possible, but this requires considerable effort.

Who or what is paragraph 4 about?

5   **3. Exhaustion.** If the stress continues long enough, we cannot keep up our normal functioning. Even a small amount of additional stress at this point can cause a breakdown.

Who or what is paragraph 5 about?

—From HALES. *An Invitation to Health, Brief Edition (with Personal Health Self Assessments),* 6E. © 2010 Brooks/Cole, a part of Cengage Learning, Inc. By permission.

Who or what is the reading about? The title of the reading provides a clue to the topic. The reading is about the causes of stress.

What is this section about (paragraphs 1 and 2)? The boldfaced words provide a clue to the topic. This section is about the general adaptation syndrome, homeostasis, and the adaptive response.

What is paragraph 3 about? This paragraph is about the alarm stage. The clue is the boldfaced word.

What is paragraph 4 about? This paragraph is about the resistance stage. The clue is the boldfaced word.

What is paragraph 5 about? This paragraph is about the exhaustion stage. The clue is the boldfaced word.

FOCUS ON COMPREHENSION: Determining the Topic and Posing Guide Questions

On Your Own   FINDING THE TOPIC IN A LONGER PASSAGE

Read the rest of the reading on what causes stress. While you read, answer the questions in the margin. Circle clues that help you identify topic.

6   Among the nonbiological theories is the cognitive transactional model of stress, developed by Richard Lazarus, which looks at the relation between stress and health. As he sees it, stress can have a powerful impact on health. Conversely, health can affect a person's resistance or coping ability. Stress, according to Lazarus, is "neither an environmental stimulus, a characteristic of the person, nor a response, but a relationship between demands and the power to deal with them without unreasonable or destructive costs." Thus, an event may be stressful for one person but not for another, or it may seem stressful on one occasion but not on another. For instance, one student may think of speaking in front of the class as extremely stressful, while another relishes the chance to do so—except on days when he's not well prepared.

Who or what is paragraph 6 about?

7   At any age, some of us are more vulnerable to life changes and crises than are others. The stress of growing up in families troubled by alcoholism, drug dependence, or physical, sexual, or psychological abuse may have a lifelong impact—particularly if these problems are not recognized and dealt with. Other early experiences, positive and negative, also can affect our attitude toward stress–and our resilience to it. Our general outlook on life, whether we're optimistic or pessimistic, can determine whether we expect the worst and feel stressed or anticipate a challenge and feel confident. The when, where, what, how, and why of stressors also affect our reactions. The number and frequency of changes in our lives, along with the time and setting in which they occur, have a great impact on how we'll respond.

Who or what is paragraph 7 about?

8   "Perceived" stress—an individual's view of how challenging life is—undermines a sense of well-being in people of all ages and circumstances. However, good self esteem, social support, and internal resources buffer the impact of perceived stress.

Who or what is paragraph 8 about?

9   Our level of ongoing stress affects our ability to respond to a new day's stressors. Each of us has a breaking point for dealing with stress. A series of too-intense pressures or too-rapid changes can push us closer and closer to that point. That's why it's important to anticipate potential stressors and plan how to deal with them.

Who or what is paragraph 9 about?

—From HALES. *An Invitation to Health, Brief Edition (with Personal Health Self Assessments)*, 6E. © 2010 Brooks/Cole, a part of Cengage Learning, Inc. By permission.

POSING GUIDE QUESTIONS

A **guide question** is a question you create in order to focus your reading. This technique allows you to sift through material as you read to find the key points. When you have a question to answer about a passage, you are actively looking for the answer, which helps you comprehend the material better and improves your concentration. Also, guide questions and the resulting answers form a solid basis for notes that you can review to learn the information.

Use the six journalist prompts to design your questions: who, what, where, when, why, or how. Decide which of the six questions best elicits the key points of the section. Look at the heading in this section: "Posing Guide Questions." What would be reasonable questions to ask yourself while you read this subsection? You could ask the following:

- Who should pose guide questions?
- What are guide questions?
- Where are guide questions posed?
- When are guide questions posed?
- Why pose guide questions?
- How do you pose guide questions?

FOCUS ON COMPREHENSION: Determining the Topic and Posing Guide Questions

Which question would yield the best results? In this case, "Why pose guide questions?" would be the best to pull out the important points. If you asked yourself this question, you would find the key points are (1) posing questions focuses your attention and guides your reading, (2) posing questions improves concentration and comprehension, and (3) the answers to self-generated questions form a basis for notes that you can review to learn new information.

"Who should pose guide questions?" would be a less effective question to ask because the passage doesn't address the answer specifically, although you could make an educated guess that every active reader should use this strategy. The other questions would be OK, but not as focused as asking *why*. How do you know which of the six prompts to use with any given heading? The answer is simple: practice. If you preview a reading, you will develop the skill of predicting what the author's train of thought will be. Don't worry if your questions seem awkward at first; they will improve as you practice.

There are two methods for creating good guide questions: from headings and from the topic.

- **Creating guide questions from headings.** A **heading** is a major section in larger or bold print. A subheading is a smaller section within a major section. A subheading can be recognized by distinct print or size, too, but is smaller in size or fainter in color than a major heading. Turn the headings and subheadings into questions using the journalist questions.

- **Creating guide questions from topic.** If a reading does not have headings or subheadings, you can ask yourself, "Who or what is the passage about?" The answer to this question is the topic of the passage. Once you have determined the topic, use your answer to formulate your own guide question, using one of the journalist question prompts: who, what, where, when, why, or how. This technique is like using headings, but instead of having the author's words to form a guide question, you create your own word or phrase to form your guide question. A specific topic will make your guide question more effective and finding the key points easier. For example, look at this passage:

> For many students, midterms and final <u>exams</u> are the most <u>stressful</u> times of the year. Studies at various colleges and universities found that the incidence of colds and flu soared during <u>finals</u>. Some students feel the impact of <u>test stress</u> in other ways— headaches, upset stomachs, skin flare-ups, or insomnia.
>
> Because of <u>stress's</u> impact on memory, students with advanced skills may perform worse under <u>exam</u> pressure than their less skilled peers. Sometimes students become so preoccupied with the possibility of failing that they can't concentrate on studying. Others,

including many of the best and brightest students, freeze up during <u>tests</u> and can't comprehend multiple-choice questions or write essay answers, even if they know the material.

—From HALES. *An Invitation to Health, Brief Edition (with Personal Health Self Assessments),* 6E. © 2010 Brooks/Cole, a part of Cengage Learning, Inc. By permission.

The topic of this passage is stress and exams. You know that because of the repeated words. What would be a good guide question to ask about this topic? How do exams affect stress? What is the result of exam stress? Asking this guide question allows you to pull out key points. Exam stress results in:

- Increased colds and flu
- Headaches, upset stomachs, skin flare-ups, and insomnia
- Reduced memory capacity
- Poor concentration
- Poor comprehension

Thinking It Through POSING GOOD GUIDE QUESTIONS

Consider the reading "What Causes Stress?" that you worked with in the section on "Thinking It Through" and "On Your Own" on pages 74–77. Create a guide question for each of the sections of this reading. Then read the explanation that follows. Remember, use the journalist's questions—who, what, where, when, why, or how—to begin your guide questions.

1. **Title:** What Causes Stress?

   Guide Question:_____

Subsections:

2. **Paragraphs 1 and 2:** The general adaptation syndrome, homeostasis, and the adaptive response

   Guide Question:_____

3. **Paragraph 3:** The Alarm Stage

   Guide Question:_____

4. **Paragraph 4:** The Resistance Stage

   Guide Question:_____

(Continued)

FOCUS ON COMPREHENSION: Determining the Topic and Posing Guide Questions

5. **Paragraph 5:** The Exhaustion Stage

    Guide Question: _____

6. **Paragraph 6:** Stress and health

    Guide Question: _____

7. **Paragraph 7:** Stress and life

    Guide Question: _____

8. **Paragraph 8:** Perceived stress

    Guide Question: _____

9. **Paragraph 9:** Ongoing stress

    Guide Question:_____

Now, check your guide questions against these sample guide questions. You'll also see the answers to the guide questions, the reason for posing the questions.

1. **Title:** What Causes Stress?

    Guide Question: What causes stress?

    Answer: Stress is caused by a physiological response in three stages

    Subsections:

2. **Paragraphs 1 and 2:** The general adaptation syndrome, homeostasis, and the adaptive response

    Guide Question: What is the general adaptation syndrome, homeostasis, and the adaptive response?

    Answer: General adaptive syndrome is triggered as our bodies constantly strive to maintain a stable and consistent physiological state. Homeostasis is our bodies' effort to maintain a stable and consistent physiological state. The adaptive response is how we try to achieve a stable homeostatic state.

3. **Paragraph 3:** The Alarm Stage

    Guide Question: What is the Alarm Stage?

    Answer: The body's response to stressors with changes that temporarily lower resistance.

4. **Paragraph 4:** The Resistance Stage

    Guide Question: What is the Resistance Stage?

    Answer: The stage when the body mobilizes its internal resources to try to sustain homeostasis.

5. **Paragraph 5:** The Exhaustion Stage

   Guide Question:__What is the Exhaustion Stage?

   Answer: The stage where we cannot keep up our normal functioning.

6. **Paragraph 6:** Stress and health

   Guide Question: What is the connection between stress and health?

   Answer: Stress affects health and health can undermine a person's resistance to stress.

7. **Paragraph 7:** Stress and life

   Guide Question: How does life impact stress?

   Answer: Life experiences affect our resistance to stress.

8. **Paragraph 8:** Perceived stress

   Guide Question: What is perceived stress?

   Answer: Perceived stress is an individual's view of how challenging life is.

9. **Paragraph 9:** Ongoing stress

   Guide Question: What is the effect of ongoing stress?

   Answer: Our level of ongoing stress affects our ability to respond to a new day's stressors.

On Your Own IDENTIFYING TOPIC AND POSING GOOD GUIDE QUESTIONS

This reading is from the American Psychological Association. Preview this reading using the following steps:

1. **Read the title.**
2. **Read the first paragraph.**
3. **Read the headings, if there are any.**
4. **Read the first sentence of each body paragraph.**
5. **Read the concluding paragraph.**

   Next, read the passage all the way through. Write a word or a phrase that is the topic of each section in the reading. Then pose an appropriate guide question about that section.

(Continued)

FOCUS ON COMPREHENSION: Determining the Topic and Posing Guide Questions

Mind/Body Health: Stress: What You Can Do

1   Learning to deal with stress effectively is a worthwhile effort, even if you already consider yourself capable of handling anything life sends your way.

2   Many of the most common long-term stressors—family illness, recovery after injury, career pressures—often arise without warning and simultaneously. Stress management is particularly valuable if your family has a history of hypertension and other forms of heart disease.

3   **Identify the cause.** You may find that your stress arises from something that's easy to correct. A psychologist can help you define and analyze these stressors, and develop action plans for dealing with them.

4   **Monitor your moods.** If you feel stressed during the day, write down what caused it along with your thoughts and moods. Again, you may find the cause to be less serious than you first thought.

5   **Make time for yourself at least two or three times a week.** Even ten minutes a day of "personal time" can help refresh your mental outlook and slow down your body's stress response systems. Turn off the phone, spend time alone in your room, exercise, or meditate to your favorite music.

6   **Walk away when you're angry.** Before you react, take time to mentally regroup by counting to 10. Then look at the situation again. Walking or other physical activities will also help you work off steam.

7   **Analyze your schedule.** Assess your priorities and delegate whatever tasks you can (e.g., order out dinner after a busy day, share household responsibilities). Eliminate tasks that are "shoulds" but not "musts."

8   **Set reasonable standards for yourself and others.** Don't expect perfection.

Who or what is the reading about?

Guide Question: What is the reading about?

Pose a guide question about this reading.

Who or what is this section about?

Pose a guide question about this section.

Who or what is the section about?

What is a good guide question to ask?

Who or what is this section about?

Pose a guide question about this section.

Who or what is this section about?

Pose a guide question about this section.

Who or what is this section about?

Pose a guide question about this section.

Who or what is this section about?

Pose a guide question about this section.

Source: The American Psychological Association, http://www.apa.org/helpcenter/stress.aspx. The American Psychological Practice Directorate gratefully acknowledges the assistance of Sara Weiss, Ph.D., and Nancy Molitor, Ph.D., in developing this fact sheet. © 2010 American Psychological Association.

Practice Exercise 1: IDENTIFYING THE TOPIC OF A PASSAGE AND POSING GUIDE QUESTIONS

For the following passages, identify the topic. Then pose a guide question based on that topic.

1. Stress is difficult for scientists to define because it is a subjective sensation associated with varied symptoms that differ for each of us. In addition, stress is not always a synonym for distress. Situations like a steep roller coaster ride that cause fear and anxiety for some can prove highly pleasurable for others. Winning a race or election may be more stressful than losing but this is good stress.

—From The American Institute of Stress. Used with permission.

Topic: _____

Guide Question: _____

2. We all have stress sometimes. For some people, it happens before having to speak in public. For other people, it might be before a first date. What causes stress for you may not be stressful for someone else. Sometimes stress is helpful—it can encourage you to meet a deadline or get things done. But long-term stress can increase the risk of diseases like depression, heart disease and a variety of other problems. A stress-related illness called post-traumatic stress disorder (PTSD) develops after an event like war, physical or sexual assault, or a natural disaster.

—National Institutes of Health, http://www.nlm.nih.gov/medlineplus/stress.html

Topic: _____

Guide Question: _____

3. Can you do anything to reduce test stress and feel more in control? Absolutely. Another way is through relaxation. Students taught relaxation techniques—such as controlled breathing, meditation, progressive relaxation, and guided imagery (visualization)—a month before finals tend to have higher levels of immune cells during the exam period and feel in better control during their tests.

—From HALES. *An Invitation to Health, Brief Edition (with Personal Health Self Assessments)*, 6E.
© 2010 Brooks/Cole, a part of Cengage Learning, Inc. By permission.

Topic: _____

Guide Question: _____

4. On average, students tended to drink more on days when they were feeling good—possibly because of what the researchers called the "celebratory and social" nature of college drinking. Drinking—and positive emotions—also peaked on weekends.

—From HALES. *An Invitation to Health, Brief Edition (with Personal Health Self Assessments)*, 6E.
© 2010 Brooks/Cole, a part of Cengage Learning, Inc. By permission.

(Continued)

FOCUS ON COMPREHENSION: Determining the Topic and Posing Guide Questions

Topic: _____

Guide Question: _____

5. Many students bring complex psychological problems with them to campus, including learning disabilities and mood disorders like depression and anxiety. "Students arrive with the underpinnings of problems that are brought out by the stress of campus life," says one counselor. Some have grown up in broken homes and bear the scars of family troubles. Others fall into the same patterns of alcohol abuse that they observed for years in their families or suffer lingering emotional scars from childhood physical or sexual abuse.

—From HALES. *An Invitation to Health, Brief Edition (with Personal Health Self Assessments)*, 6E.

© 2010 Brooks/Cole, a part of Cengage Learning, Inc. By permission.

Topic: _____

Guide Question: _____

6. Job Stress

More so than ever, many people find that they are working more and enjoying it less. Many people, including working parents, spend 55 to 60 hours a week on the job. More people are caught up in an exhausting cycle of overwork, which causes stress, which makes work harder, which leads to more stress. Even the workplace itself can contribute to stress. A noisy, open-office environment can increase levels of stress without workers realizing it.

—From HALES. *An Invitation to Health, Brief Edition (with Personal Health Self Assessments)*, 6E.

© 2010 Brooks/Cole, a part of Cengage Learning, Inc. By permission.

Topic: _____

Guide Question: _____

7. Burnout

Burnout is a state of physical, emotional, and mental exhaustion brought on by constant or repeated emotional pressure. No one—regardless of age, gender, or job—is immune. Mothers and managers, fire fighters and flight attendants, teachers and telemarketers feel the flames of too much stress and not enough satisfaction. Many people, especially those caring for others at work or at home, get to a point where there's an imbalance between their own feelings and dealing with difficult, distressful issues on a day-to-day basis. If they don't recognize what's going on and make some changes, their health and the quality of their work suffer.

—From HALES. *An Invitation to Health, Brief Edition (with Personal Health Self Assessments)*, 6E.

© 2010 Brooks/Cole, a part of Cengage Learning, Inc. By permission.

Topic: _____

Guide Question: _____

8. For years therapists encouraged people to "vent" their anger. However, research now shows that letting anger out only makes it worse. "Catharsis is worse than useless," says psychology professor Brad Bushman of Iowa State University, whose research has shown that letting anger out makes people more aggressive, not less. "Many people think of anger as the psychological equivalent of the steam in a pressure cooker that has to be released or it will explode. That's not true. People who react by hitting, kicking, screaming, and swearing aren't dealing with the underlying cause of their anger. They just feel more angry."

—From HALES. *An Invitation to Health, Brief Edition (with Personal Health Self Assessments)*, 6E.
© 2010 Brooks/Cole, a part of Cengage Learning, Inc. By permission.

Topic: _____

Guide Question: _____

9. **Conflict Resolution**

Disagreements are inevitable; disagreeable ways of dealing with them are not. One of the most important skills in any setting—from family room to staff meeting to corporate boardroom—is resolving conflicts. Although many assume that you can't reason with someone who's furious, psychologists have shown that angry people are capable of processing and analyzing information, depending on how it is presented to them.

—From HALES. *An Invitation to Health, Brief Edition (with Personal Health Self Assessments)*, 6E.
© 2010 Brooks/Cole, a part of Cengage Learning, Inc. By permission.

Topic: _____

Guide Question: _____

10. **The Anger Epidemic**

In recent years, violent aggressive driving—which some dub *road rage*—has exploded. Sideline rage at amateur and professional sporting events has become so widespread that a Pennsylvania midget football game ended in a brawl involving more than 100 coaches, players, parents, and fans.

—From HALES. *An Invitation to Health, Brief Edition (with Personal Health Self Assessments)*, 6E.
© 2010 Brooks/Cole, a part of Cengage Learning, Inc. By permission.

Topic: _____

Guide Question: _____

FOCUS ON VOCABULARY
Antonym and Inference Context Clues

You learned in Chapter 1 that context clues should be your first strategy when unlocking the meaning of an unknown word or phrase. A lot of the reading you will encounter in college will have definition clues to help you understand key terms. Continuing to work on recognizing synonym clues will also help you avoid rushing to the dictionary to look up every unknown word. To add to your toolbox of strategies for understanding words in complex college reading, you need to recognize antonym clues and inference clues.

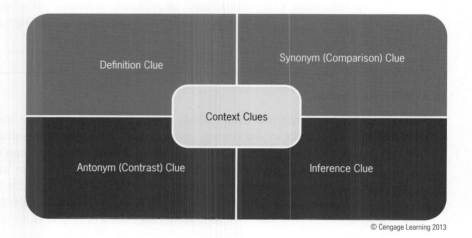

Definition Clue

Synonym (Comparison) Clue

Context Clues

Antonym (Contrast) Clue

Inference Clue

© Cengage Learning 2013

ANTONYM CLUE

Whereas a synonym clue involves a word or phrase that means the *same* as an unknown word, an **antonym clue** is a clue within a reading that means the *opposite* of an unknown word. Like synonym clues, antonym clues, sometimes called contrast clues, may be in the same sentence as the unknown word or in surrounding sentences. Like definition and synonym clues, antonym clues are often recognizable from transition words. As you learned in Chapter 1, transition words are words authors use to help their ideas flow together more seamlessly. Many of the antonym transition words are familiar to you: *on the other hand, conversely, in contrast, but, however, rather than*, and *so on*. Study Table 2.1, paying close attention to the transition words that indicate an antonym clue.

TABLE 2.1 TRANSITION WORDS THAT INDICATE ANTONYM CLUES

TYPE OF CONTEXT CLUE	TRANSITION WORDS	EXAMPLE (WITH ANTONYM OF BOLDED TERM UNDERLINED)
Antonym Clue A word or phrase that means the opposite of the unknown word	• *unlike* • *instead* • *but* • *however* • *on the other hand* • *rather, rather than* • *conversely* • *in contrast* • *whereas*	An instructor may give **tacit** praise for study skills <u>instead of telling you directly</u> how impressed he is with your organization. *Tacit* means "unspoken." <u>Rather than tell the truth</u> about not completing the assignment, the student was **mendacious** and created an excuse. *Mendacious* means "untruthful."

© Cengage Learning 2013

Consider the following examples. The unknown word is circled, and its antonym is underlined. If there is a transition word that helps clarify the antonym, it is highlighted.

> John's interest in psychology was (latent). Unlike John, Steve's passion for psychology was <u>overt</u> and clearly recognizable.

To understand the word *latent*, look to the second sentence that contains the contrast transition *unlike* that reveals that the author flips his thought process to talk about an opposite. The opposite concept here is that John's interest in psychology is latent and Steve's is overt. So, *overt* means the opposite of *latent*. What does *latent* mean? *Latent* means "hidden or not revealed" in this context.

> John's interest in science is (manifest) whereas Steve's interest in science is <u>latent</u>.

In this example, the word *manifest* is unknown but is followed by the contrast transition word *whereas*. This word indicates that the author will talk about something in contrast to something said before. *Manifest*, therefore, is the opposite of *latent*. *Manifest* means "observable."

> John's interest in science is due to his fascination with (empirical) evidence. Conversely, he does not like disciplines where the evidence is <u>not directly observable</u>.

FOCUS ON VOCABULARY: Antonym and Inference Context Clues

In this example, the word *conversely* indicates a contrast to something said previously in the passage. *Empirical* is the opposite of "not directly observable." So, *empirical* means "directly observable."

Not all antonym clues contain an antonym transition word. Even if there are no transition words, the contrast pattern is still there; it is just a bit harder to recognize.

> Remember that once you start medication, it is important not to stop taking it (abruptly.) Certain drugs must be <u>tapered off</u> under the supervision of a doctor or bad reactions can occur.

In this example, there are no contrast or antonym clue words to help you figure out the meaning of *abruptly*. Instead, you have to follow the author's train of thought. Even though the author doesn't use a transition word, the word *abruptly* is the opposite of the phrase *tapered off. Abruptly*, then, means to "stop right away."

> Jeanette's approach to exercise was (lackadaisical.) Trevor approached physical tasks with <u>vigor and energy</u>. Which approach to exercise yields the best results? Trevor's approach to exercise allowed him to lose more weight and gain more muscle.

Lackadaisical is the opposite of "vigor and energy," so it means "listless or without interest."

On Your Own RECOGNIZING ANTONYM CONTEXT CLUES

For the following passages, identify the meaning of the bolded word and write down the definition on the line provided. Also underline the antonym word or phrase, and circle clues that help you figure out the definition, if there are any.

1. The amygdala is known as the **reptilian** part of the brain. Conversely, the frontal cortex is regarded as a more evolved part of the brain.

    _____

2. Tyrone was a **polyglot**. He was fluent in French, Spanish, as well as English. Unlike her brother, Kyla was only fluent in one language.

    _____

3. After the argument, Jill was **seething**. Rochelle, on the other hand, was not mad at all.

    _____

4. Jean-Paul was known throughout North America for his **vivacious** designs. Simone was jealous. Her designs were regarded as ordinary and without life or color.

_____

5. Kana was anxious to travel abroad to become more **sophisticated.** She was tired of being a person without experience and without worldly knowledge.

_____

6. Larissa was known as a **pompous** individual, always talking about her accomplishments and ability. Unlike her, Sienna was modest and unpretentious.

_____

7. I did not find that lecture to be **lucid** at all. It was the most unclear presentation so far this semester. Mr. Griggs should say what he means clearly.

_____

8. In contrast to the dull first speaker at the rally, the politician gave a speech that was timely and **provocative.**

_____

9. Rather than being **fastidious** about his studies, Mark preferred to do his work piecemeal and sloppily.

_____

10. **Sequestered** from the rest of the crew, Jason was not a part of the group.

_____

INFERENCE CLUE

An **inference** is an educated guess. So, an **inference clue** is a clue where you use the information in the surrounding words to make an educated guess about the word that you don't know. You come to a conclusion based on what the author has suggested but has not directly stated. An inference clue does not contain a direct definition of a word as in a definition clue, or a synonym as in a synonym clue, or an antonym

FOCUS ON VOCABULARY: Antonym and Inference Context Clues

TABLE 2.2 CLUES THAT INDICATE INFERENCE CLUES

TYPE OF CONTEXT CLUE	CLUES	EXAMPLE (WITH INFERENCE OF BOLDED TERM UNDERLINED)
Inference Clue An educated guess based on information and reasonable deduction from the sentence or surrounding sentences	A list of examples or a specific example that clarifies the word	The child was **precocious.** She learned to operate the television remote control by 2 years old, read at 3, and could roller skate by 4. In this sentence, three examples are provided to illustrate the child's precocious behavior, all which show how she is advanced for her age. A reasonable inference is that the word *precocious* means advanced for one's age.
	Descriptive details that clarify the word	Short-term memory capacity is so **precarious** that I forced myself to stare at the page and block out everything else. In this example, the descriptive details clarify and give examples of what *precarious* means—one has to focus and concentrate by staring at the page and blocking everything out. A reasonable inference is that precarious means concentration is likely to fail. *Precarious* means "risky, uncertain."

© Cengage Learning 2013

as in an antonym clue. Instead, you use common sense to make a good guess about the unknown word's meaning. Inference clues can be a list of examples or descriptive details that allow you to make an educated guess about the meaning of an unknown word. Study Table 2.2, paying close attention to the part of the sentence that indicates an inference clue.

Inference clues are not necessarily any more difficult than the other types of vocabulary context clues. Although direct clues are not available, other details or examples usually appear in the sentence or surrounding sentences. Read the following sentences, paying attention to the circled word or words and the information provided in the surrounding words.

Inadequate sleep (less than 7 or 8 hours a night) has been tied to many different health problems, including obesity, diabetes, and cancer.

Inadequate means

  a. Too much.

  b. Not enough.

  c. The right amount.

How do you know the meaning of *inadequate*? The word is followed by the phrase in parentheses, "less than 7 or 8 hours," and is then followed by "negative health problems." If inadequate sleep is less than the recommended daily amount of sleep, then *inadequate* must mean not enough. *Obesity* means

  a. Diabetes.

  b. Disease.

  c. Overweight.

How do you know the meaning of *obesity*? There is no direct clue, so in this case, you have to make an educated guess. The best choice is overweight.

> Since caffeine, certain illicit drugs, and even some over-the-counter
> cold medications can aggravate the symptoms of anxiety disorders,
> they should be avoided.

In this example, the word *illicit* is set apart from the over-the-counter drugs as something different. *Illicit*, then, means that the drugs are not available to purchase in a store. These drugs are illegal. *Illicit* means "illegal." Similarly, no direct clues are provided for the word *aggravate*. The sentence does suggest that these drugs, both illicit and over-the-counter, should be avoided because they can aggravate symptoms of anxiety disorders. *Aggravate*, then, must mean "make worse."

> The family is very important in the recovery of a person with an
> anxiety disorder. Ideally, the family should be supportive but not
> help perpetuate their loved one's symptoms.

In this example, for people with anxiety disorders, family should be supportive. The word *but* indicates that the author provides a contrast for something. The contrast here is not a direct antonym clue, however. The family should not perpetuate the symptoms yet should be supportive. *Perpetuate* means "continue or encourage."

> Family members should not trivialize the anxiety disorder or
> demand improvement without treatment. If your family is doing

FOCUS ON VOCABULARY: Antonym and Inference Context Clues

either of these things, you may want to show them this booklet so they can become educated allies and help you succeed in therapy.

In this example, you need to make an educated guess about the meaning of *trivialize.* Family members should not do that or demand improvement. *Trivialize* must have something to do with not taking the condition seriously.

On Your Own   RECOGNIZING INFERENCE CLUES

In the following passages, find the best definition for each boldfaced word and circle the best answer. Then explain how you inferred the meaning of the unknown word.

The **degenerative** brain disease attacks almost everyone who lives long enough, though mind games and puzzles are known to **ward off** the effects.

1.   *Degenerative* means
   a. Destructive.
   b. Strengthening.
   c. Confusing.

How do you know the meaning of the word? _____

_____

_____

2.   *Ward off* means
   a. Increase.
   b. Stop.
   c. Defend against.

How do you know the meaning of the word? _____

_____

But if you're looking to do yourself in, overdo the two-drink-per-day limit and **imbibe** heartily.

3.   *Imbibe* means
   a. To drink.
   b. To stop drinking.
   c. Self destruction.

How do you know the meaning of the word? _____

_____

For the following passages, write down the definition of the boldfaced word. Also, underline any clues that help you figure out the definition.

4. Jolene was concerned that men dated her for **pecuniary** reasons. She is a doctor, drives a sports car, and lives in a nice part of town.

_____

5. The atmosphere in the classroom was **fetid**—all the windows were closed, it was hot, and I felt I could hardly breathe.

_____

6. His manners were **gauche.** He never said thank you, he wiped his nose on his sleeve, and he chewed with his mouth open.

_____

7. The evidence in the trial was **spurious.** As an attorney, Elizabeth knew that she could dispute each and every claim the prosecution made.

_____

8. With their **devious** looks and shifty gazes, the dogs were clearly guilty of stealing the turkey from the table.

_____

9. With her **pensive** looks and soft bearing, Sylvia was thought to embody the saying "still waters run deep."

_____

10. The advertisements for the politician were **ubiquitous.** Everywhere I looked there were billboards, flyers, and television commercials advertising his platform and urging voters to cast their ballots.

_____

Practice Exercise 2: ANTONYM AND INFERENCE CONTEXT CLUES

For the following passages, define the meaning of the boldfaced word on the line provided using antonym or inference context clues. Indicate the type of clue you used to decode the unknown word.

(Continued)

FOCUS ON VOCABULARY: Antonym and Inference Context Clues

1. The opposing view is that differences among people are not simply variations on a theme. **Advocates** of this view argue that human development is inextricably intertwined with the context within which it occurs.

    —From KAIL/CAVANAUGH. Human Development, 5E. © 2010 Wadsworth, a part of Cengage Learning, Inc.
    By permission.

    _____

2. People develop in part because of culture and social influences, not in a **vacuum.**

    _____

3. Unlike middle-class families that emphasize cooperation and discussion, working-class parents emphasize **conformity,** which involves following the rules and refraining from discussion about these rules.

    _____

4. Ongoing stress in your life leads to **chronic** health problems, such as low resistance to infection, tiredness, and low energy.

    _____

5. We can only **surmise** if the modern world is responsible for such ongoing, chronic stress. Research suggests that stress may well be a risk factor for a number of health-related issues.

    _____

6. Jeff was **reticent.** In contrast, Sandy was more outgoing.

    _____

7. **Erudition** is the hallmark of any educated person with a good, expansive vocabulary.

    _____

8. After a hard day at school, Chelsea sought **refuge** in her room. She turned off her phone, dimmed the lights, and lay on her bed, exhausted.

    _____

9. Edward was **lethargic.** In contrast, his sister, Sandra, was energetic and upbeat.

    _____

10. The teacher tended to use **obscure** words. Most of the time I had no clue what she was talking about.

    _____

FOCUS ON READING STUDY SKILLS
Motivation and Time Management

Now that you have an introduction to some strategies to jump-start active learning and reading, consider your ultimate goals of being a college student. Why did you enroll in college? What do you expect to get out of your education? We can all agree that one goal is to succeed and graduate. To be a successful college student, you need to be motivated to succeed.

Motivation is what guides your behavior and gives you direction. Motivation, wanting something badly enough to work for it, pushes you to succeed at a task. In college, it is difficult to manage coursework, complete assignments well and on time, and work toward academic and career goals that you have set for yourself. Motivation is the key to reading, too. You must be motivated to do well in college, and a large part of doing well relies on reading successfully. The more you are aware of what you want to achieve, why you want to achieve it, and how to get there, the more likely you will be successful.

INTERNAL AND EXTERNAL MOTIVATION

Motivation stems from two sources: forces outside yourself and forces within yourself (see Figure 2.1). **External motivation** is when something outside yourself makes you want to succeed, such as family pressure, more money, or a need to keep a job. **Internal motivation** is when something within yourself makes you want to succeed, like wanting to show yourself that you can graduate, the pride that comes from receiving a good grade (rather than the attention of others), or simply because you enjoy learning. Most college students find they are motivated by both internal and external motivation. As you gain some success and self-confidence, you begin to shift more toward being internally motivated and doing well because it makes you feel satisfied. Overall, motivation gives you the will to try harder and stay focused on your goals.

FOCUS ON READING STUDY SKILLS: Motivation and Time Management

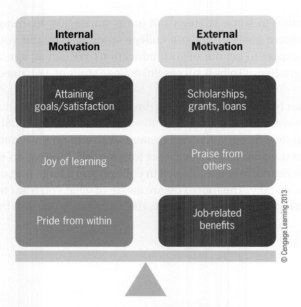

FIGURE 2.1 Types of Motivation

© Cengage Learning 2013

On Your Own ARE YOU MOTIVATED?

Take this quiz to gauge your background knowledge about motivation. Circle the answer that best describes your response. There are no right or wrong answers, but the results of this quiz can help you understand your reasons for being in college. Discuss what you can do to improve your experience with your instructor, a classmate, or adviser.

1. It is the week before midterms. You have a paper due that is worth 25 percent of your final grade. You also have a creative assignment due that looks fun but is not worth more than 5 percent of your grade. What do you do?
    a. Pull an all-nighter to get both done well.
    b. Start with the fun activity and hope you will have the urge to do the essay, even if it's not done well.

c. Do the work for both assignments poorly just to have something to turn in.

d. E-mail your instructor to say you'll be sick tomorrow and need an extension.

2. In one of your courses, the instructor assigns a reading that is optional but looks interesting. You already have a lot to do. What do you do?

a. Read the optional reading and take notes.

b. Scan it for important points.

c. Consider looking at the reading if you have time.

d. There is no way you would read something that is optional.

3. What is the *best* reason to keep your grade point average (GPA) up?

a. Good grades make you feel proud and mean you will have more opportunity to learn.

b. Good grades make life easier all around.

c. You will not get financial aid if your grades drop, and your family will be disappointed.

d. This is just not a priority in your life.

4. You feel frustrated by a difficult assignment you have been asked to complete for a class. How do you respond?

a. Take a break to clear your head and devise an action plan over a few days to accomplish the task.

b. Keep your frustration to yourself and do what you can to get it done.

c. Hand something in, even though you know it's incorrect.

d. Complain to anyone who will listen and give up on the task.

5. You worked hard on an assignment for class, and the results exceeded your expectations. How do you respond?

a. Build on your success by refining your goals and pushing yourself further.

b. Plan to do the next assignment, but not try your best because you already earned one good grade, so you can afford to get a bad grade.

c. Do an incomplete job on the next assignment.

d. Skip the next assignment since you've already proven you can do well.

6. You have been working on a project for school due at the end of the week, but you have encountered some difficulty in judging how well you are doing and what you can do to improve. What do you do?

a. Carry out a self-evaluation, discuss it with your instructor or at a college learning resource center, and modify your project accordingly.

b. Do the part of the assignment that you know is good, and do what you can on the other part.

c. Submit the partial assignment, notifying the instructor that you have hit a roadblock.

d. Tell the instructor that you didn't know the assignment was due until next week.

(Continued)

FOCUS ON READING STUDY SKILLS: Motivation and Time Management

For each *a* answer, give yourself 3 points; for each *b* answer, 2 points; for each *c* answer, 1 point; and for each *d* answer, 0 points.

Total Points: _____

If you scored **15–18:** You are internally motivated and take pride in doing well and learning. You are in college to learn and become educated and love the challenge. You enjoy the assignments because you engage in learning for its own sake. The rewards that come from learning are enough of a reason for you to do anything in college.

If you scored **12–14:** You are sometimes internally motivated *if* you are really interested in the assignment and have time to complete it. However, often you complete things because you *have to* do it for a grade or because you just do not want the hassle of having to stress over grades.

If you scored **6–11:** You are externally motivated. Outside forces make you do work for fear of the consequences if you do not do it. You want to pass your classes, but you would prefer to do the minimum. College is just something you need to do to slide over the finish line and make everyone happy. You focus on the outcome rather than the process of learning.

If you scored **below 6:** You are not motivated, or you give up easily on your assignments. You may consider speaking with an adviser or taking a college success course to see if poor study skills may be affecting your motivation. College success is a big commitment; think long and hard about why you are here and what you want.

1. Does your motivation description accurately describe you? If so, how is it accurate? If not, why is it not accurate?

    _____

    _____

    _____

2. If you got different results than you would have liked, what might you do differently to become more motivated?

    _____

    _____

    _____

MANAGING YOUR TIME

To be a successful college student, you *must* have efficient time-management strategies. **Time management** means using time wisely and efficiently to be productive. Reading is a time-intensive task, especially given the large amount of reading that will be required of you in college, so you must give yourself enough time to read. If you are taking several courses and are employed, or if you have family and other obligations, time management can make the difference between success in college and underachievement. You need to use every spare moment to learn new information and study. The brain absorbs information through repetition, and studying requires repetition, which takes time.

Here are some basic steps for effective time management:

1. Purchase a planner with daily to-do pages, weekly schedules, as well as monthly planning pages.

2. Insert all assignments and tests into your monthly plan.

3. Insert all work and social obligations into your monthly plan.

4. Each day, set short-term goals in your to-do pages, with things you need to achieve that day. If you don't get to something that day, be sure to transfer it to your next day's to-do list.

5. Make note of the chunks of time in your schedule and use them to your advantage.

6. Take advantage of the breaks in between classes or appointments, and bring along notes or vocabulary flash cards to study.

7. Use 10 minutes before or in between classes to scan your notes to refresh your memory and prepare your brain for new learning.

8. Keep up with day-to-day assignments and reading so you have a grasp of the material prior to the class in which it will be discussed.

9. Plan ahead for tests, essays, and projects. Start the assignment early by breaking it into smaller chunks so you'll have time to complete it and make necessary revisions. Overestimate the time you'll need for completing assignments and reviewing information so you're not caught at the last moment.

10. Make sure to build some relaxation time into your schedule *after* study periods with brief rewards between study periods, like getting a snack or watching an episode of your favorite television show.

FOCUS ON READING STUDY SKILLS: Motivation and Time Management

Sample Daily Schedule (Each Block Represents One Half Hour)

Home/Chores, Travel, School, Sports/Activities, Homework, Free time

Time 6:00	Time 6:30	Time 7:00	Time 7:30	Time 8:00	Time 8:30	Time 9:00	Time 9:30
Wake up, Shower, Dress	Breakfast	Bus to School	School →				
Time 10:00	Time 10:30	Time 11:00	Time 11:30	Time 12:00	Time 12:30	Time 1:00	Time 1:30
					School Play Auditions	School →	
Time 2:00	Time 2:30	Time 3:00	Time 3:30	Time 4:00	Time 4:30	Time 5:00	Time 5:30
	Bus from School	Homework →				Soccer Game	→
Time 6:00	Time 6:30	Time 7:00	Time 7:30	Time 8:00	Time 8:30	Time 9:00	Time 9:30
		Set Table, Dinner	Dinner, Take out Garbage	Free Time →			Read Before Bed

© Cengage Learning 2013

FIGURE 2.2 Daily Calendar

There are several methods of keeping track of your time: a daily calendar, a weekly calendar, and a monthly calendar (Figures 2.2, 2.3, and 2.4). Decide which method, or a combination of methods, works best for you. In Figure 2.2, the daily calendar, all time is accounted for and plotted into the appropriate time slot. Inserting all your daily activities into a weekly planner is one way to effectively manage your time (Figure 2.3). An advantage of using a weekly calendar is that you can easily see your commitments for the week and plan ahead for assignments, work, and other obligations.

The benefit of seeing your month laid out, as in Figure 2.4, is you can clearly recognize when you have busy periods ahead. You can then plan to complete tasks during times when you have less pressing assignments. Complete assignments early so you avoid the panic of last-minute cramming.

Your college bookstore will sell a variety of planners, from booklets to smartphones to PDAs (personal digital assistants)—experiment with the different types and see what works best for you. First, write in all the nonchangeable items in your day, such as class times, work hours, and other commitments. Next, assess your unscheduled time, allowing reasonable time for study and preparation of your class assignments. The rule of thumb is to allow 2 hours outside class for homework and study for each hour you spend in the classroom each week. Don't forget to make use of small blocks of time, such as travel time via public transportation or time in between classes. These times can be used to review notes, study vocabulary, or complete short reading tasks.

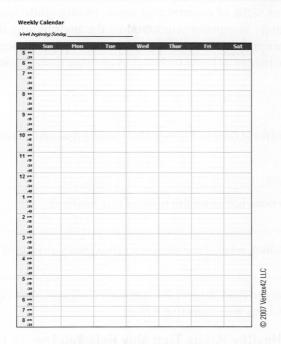

Weekly Calendar

Week beginning Sunday _____

	Sun	Mon	Tue	Wed	Thur	Fri	Sat
5 am							
6 am							
7 am							
8 am							
9 am							
10 am							
11 am							
12 pm							
1 pm							
2 pm							
3 pm							
4 pm							
5 pm							
6 pm							
7 pm							
8 pm							

© 2007 Vertex42 LLC

FIGURE 2.3 Weekly Calendar

January 2012						
SUNDAY	MONDAY	TUESDAY	WEDNESDAY	THURSDAY	FRIDAY	SATURDAY
1	2	3	4	5	6	7
8	9	10	11	12	13	14
15	16	17	18	19	20	21
22	23	24	25	26	27	28
29	30	31				

© Cengage Learning 2013

FIGURE 2.4 Monthly Calendar

APPLICATIONS

These applications will develop your skills of determining topic, posing guide questions, and using context clues for vocabulary comprehension. Follow the instructions for each application, and then answer the Comprehension Check questions. Each application serves to release more responsibility to the reader as these techniques become more automatic.

APPLICATION ①

This reading comes from *U.S. News & World Report*. Preview this reading first and answer these questions:

● Who or what is this reading about? _____

● What is a good guide question to pose based on the topic of this reading? _____

_____

● Based on your preview of this reading, what is the answer to your guide question? _____

_____

Now read the article in its entirety. As you read, answer the questions in the margin. After you read, complete the Comprehension Check questions that follow.

10 Healthy Habits That May Help You Live to 100
By Deborah Kotz

1   The biggest factor that determines how well you age is not your genes but how well you live. Not convinced? A new study of 20,000 British citizens published in the *British Medical Journal* shows that you can cut your risk of having a stroke in half by doing the following four things: being active for 30 minutes a day, eating five daily servings of fruit and vegetables, and avoiding cigarettes and excess alcohol.

Can you infer what centenarians means?

2   While those are some of the obvious steps you can take to age well, researchers have discovered that **centenarians** tend to share certain traits in how they eat, move about, and deal with stress—the sorts of things we can emulate to improve our own aging process. Of course, getting to age 100 is enormously more likely if your parents did. Still, Thomas Perls, M.D., M.P.H., who studies the century-plus set at Boston University School of Medicine, believes that assuming you've side-stepped genes for truly fatal diseases like Huntington's, "there's nothing stopping you from living independently well into your 90s." Heck,

if your parents and grandparents were heavy smokers, they might have died prematurely without ever reaching their true potential lifespan, so go ahead and shoot for those triple digits. Follow these 10 habits, and check out Perls' lifetime risk calculator to see how long you can expect to live.

Don't Retire

3   "Evidence shows that in societies where people stop working abruptly, the incidence of obesity and <u>chronic</u> disease skyrockets after retirement," says Luigi Ferrucci, M.D., Ph.D., director of the Baltimore Longitudinal Study of Aging. The Chianti region of Italy, which has a high percentage of centenarians, has a different take on leisure time. "After people retire from their jobs, they spend most of the day working on their little farm, **cultivating** grapes or vegetables," he says. "They're never really inactive." Farming isn't for you? Volunteer as a docent at your local art museum or join the Experience Corps, a program offered in 19 cities that places senior volunteers in urban public elementary schools for about 15 hours a week.

What is the topic of this section?

Pose a guide question about this section.

Can you infer what cultivating means?

Floss Every Day

4   That may help keep your arteries healthy. A 2008 New York University study showed that daily flossing reduced the amount of gum-disease-causing bacteria in the mouth. This bacteria is thought to enter the bloodstream and trigger inflammation in the arteries, a major risk factor for heart disease. Other research has shown that those who have high amounts of bacteria in their mouth are more likely to have thickening in their arteries, another sign of heart disease. "I really do think people should floss twice a day to get the biggest life expectancy benefits," stresses Perls.

What is the topic of this section?

Pose a guide question about this section.

Move Around

5   "Exercise is the only real fountain of youth that exists," says S. Jay Olshansky, Ph.D., a professor of medicine and aging researcher at the University of Illinois in Chicago. "It's like the oil-and-lube job for your car. You don't have to do it, but your car will definitely run better." Study after study has documented the benefits of exercise to improve mood, mental <u>acuity</u>, balance, muscle mass, and bone health. "And the benefits kick in immediately after your first workout," Olshansky adds. Don't worry if you're not a gym rat. Those who see the biggest payoffs are the ones who go from doing nothing to simply walking around the neighborhood or local mall for about 30 minutes a day. Building muscle with resistance training is also ideal, but yoga classes can

What is the topic of this section?

Pose a guide question about this section.

(Continued)

give you similar strength-training effects if you're not into weight lifting.

Eat a Fiber-Rich Cereal for Breakfast

What is the topic of this section?

Pose a guide question about this section.

Can you infer what *accelerator* means?

6   Getting a serving of whole grains, especially in the morning, appears to help older folks maintain stable blood sugar levels throughout the day, according to a recent study conducted by Ferrucci and his colleagues. "Those who do this have a lower incidence of diabetes, a known **accelerator** of aging," he says.

Get at Least Six Hours of Shut-eye

What is the topic of this section?

Pose a guide question about this section.

7   Instead of skimping on sleep to add more hours to your day, get more to add years to your life. "Sleep is one of the most important functions that our body uses to regulate and heal cells," says Ferrucci. "We've calculated that the minimum amount of sleep that older people need to get those healing REM phases is about six hours." Those who reach the century mark make sleep a top priority.

Consume Whole Foods, Not Supplements

What is the topic of this section?

Pose a guide question about this section.

8   Strong evidence suggests that people who have high blood levels of certain nutrients—selenium, beta-carotene, and vitamins C and E—age much better and have a slower rate of <u>cognitive</u> decline. Unfortunately, there's no evidence that taking pills with these nutrients provides those anti-aging benefits. "There are more than 200 different carotenoids and 200 different flavonoids in a single tomato," points out Ferrucci, "and these chemicals can all have complex interactions that <u>foster</u> health beyond the single nutrients we know about, like lycopene or vitamin C." Avoid nutrient-lacking white foods (breads, flour, sugar) and go for all those colorful fruits and vegetables and dark whole-grain breads and cereals with their host of hidden nutrients.

Be Less Neurotic

What is the topic of this section?

Pose a guide question about this section.

What does *internalize* mean?

9   It may work for Woody Allen, who <u>infuses</u> his worries with a healthy dose of humor, but the rest of us <u>neurotics</u> may want to find a new way to deal with stress. "We have a new study coming out that shows that centenarians tend not to **internalize** things or dwell on their troubles," says Perls. "They are great at rolling with the punches." If this inborn trait is hard to overcome, find better ways to manage when you're stressed. These are all good: yoga, exercise, meditation, tai chi, or just deep

breathing for a few moments. <u>Ruminating</u>, eating chips in front of the TV, binge drinking? Bad, very bad.

Live Like a Seventh Day Adventist

10   Americans who define themselves as Seventh Day Adventists have an average life expectancy of 89, about a decade longer than the average American. One of the basic tenets of the religion is that it's important to cherish the body that's on loan from God, which means no smoking, alcohol abuse, or overindulging in sweets. Followers typically stick to a vegetarian diet based on fruits, vegetables, beans, and nuts, and also get plenty of exercise. They're also very focused on family and community.

Be a Creature of Habit

11   Centenarians tend to live by strict routines, says Olshansky, eating the same kind of diet and doing the same kinds of activities their whole lives. Going to bed and waking up at the same time each day is another good habit to keep your body in the steady <u>equilibrium</u> that can be easily disrupted as you get on in years. "Your physiology becomes frailer when you get older," explains Ferrucci, "and it's harder for your body to bounce back if you, say, miss a few hours of sleep one night or drink too much alcohol." This can weaken immune defenses, leaving you more susceptible to circulating flu viruses or bacterial infections.

Stay connected

12   Having regular social contacts with friends and loved ones is key to avoiding depression, which can lead to **premature** death, something that's particularly **prevalent** in elderly widows and widowers. Some psychologists even think that one of the biggest benefits elderly folks get from exercise is due to strong social interactions that come from walking with a buddy or taking a group exercise class. Having a daily connection with a close friend or family member gives older folks the added benefit of having someone watch their back. "They'll tell you if they think your memory is going or if you seem more withdrawn," says Perls, "and they might push you to see a doctor before you recognize that you need to see one yourself."

What is the topic of this section?

Pose a guide question about this section.

What is the topic of this section?

Pose a guide question about this section.

What is the topic of this section?

Pose a guide question about this section.

Can you infer what premature and prevalent mean?

From "10 Healthy Habits That May Help You Live to 100", by Deborah Kotz, *U.S. News and World Report*, February 20, 2009. Copyright 2009 by *U.S. News & World Report*. Reproduced with permission.

(Continued)

COMPREHENSION CHECK

TRUE OR FALSE QUESTIONS

For the following statements, write a *T* if the statement is true or an *F* if the statement is false based on the reading.

_____ 1. The biggest factor that determines how well you age is your genes.

_____ 2. Centenarians tend to share certain traits that may explain their long lives.

_____ 3. People who live long lives tend to be inactive.

_____ 4. People who live long lives tend to have a good sense of humor.

_____ 5. Centenarians tend to stick to daily routines.

LITERAL COMPREHENSION—MULTIPLE CHOICE

Circle the best answer for the following questions.

Understanding Main Ideas

6. According to the reading, what is the biggest factor that determines how long you will live?

   a. Your genes

   b. How well you live

   c. Moderation with smoking

   d. Moderation with alcohol

7. On what evidence does the author base her statement about how long you will live?

   a. Study of 20,000 British citizens published in the *British Medical Journal*

   b. Study of 20,000 Americans

   c. Cross-cultural studies

   d. Interviews with older people

8. Which of the following is not one of the traits centenarians share?

   a. How they eat

   b. What they find amusing

   c. How they move about

   d. How they deal with stress

Understanding Secondary Information and Locating Information

9. According to paragraph 3, why shouldn't you retire?

   a. In societies where people stop working abruptly, the incidence of obesity and chronic disease skyrockets after retirement.

   b. In societies where people do not work, obesity is the number one killer.

   c. In societies where people do not retire from their job, there is a longer life span.

   d. You should not retire so you can continue to make money to pay for medical expenses.

10. According to paragraph 4, why should you floss each day?

   a. Routine is good for you.

   b. Flossing indicates other health habits are also observed.

   c. It may help keep your arteries healthy.

   d. It will allow you to better relate to other people who also practice good hygiene.

11. According to paragraph 5, which of the following is not a benefit of exercise?

   a. Improved social contacts

   b. Improved mood and mental acuity

   c. Improved balance

   d. Improved muscle mass and bone health

12. According to paragraph 6, why should you eat a fiber-rich cereal for breakfast?

   a. To maintain stable blood sugar levels throughout the day

   b. To maintain regular digestive health

   c. To maintain a regular eating routine

   d. Fiber-rich foods ought to be avoided.

13. According to paragraph 7, why is getting 6 hours of sleep a night so important?

   a. To refresh the mind

   b. To stick to a routine

   c. To stretch muscles and improve circulation

   d. To regulate and heal cells

14. Why should you consume whole foods and not supplements?

   a. To avoid high blood sugar

   b. To have a slower rate of cognitive decline

   c. There's no evidence that whole foods are preferable to supplements.

   d. Supplements alone will not provide sufficient nutrition.

(Continued)

15. Why should you be less neurotic?

   a.   People who live a long life tend not to dwell on or worry about things.

   b.   People who are neurotic annoy other people.

   c.   Neurotic people do not have a healthy sense of humor.

   d.   Neurotic people tend not to worry about important things.

INFERENTIAL COMPREHENSION

Circle the best answer for the following questions.

Making Inferences

16. In paragraph 10, the author cautions readers to live like a Seventh Day Adventist. What is the reputation of this group?

   a.   Seventh Day Adventists are a religious order that lives a healthy lifestyle without knowingly harming their bodies.

   b.   Seventh Day Adventists are often controversial in the medical community.

   c.   Seventh Day Adventists are more likely to take supplements that the body needs to maintain health.

   d.   Seventh Day Adventists are less likely to experience cognitive decline as they age.

17. Why be a creature of habit, as suggested in paragraph 11?

   a.   Centenarians tend to live by strict routines.

   b.   Centenarians eat the same kind of diet and do the same kinds of activities their whole lives.

   c.   The author implies that if we do the same, we can also live a long and healthy life.

   d.   All of the given answers

18. Why is it important to stay connected (paragraph 12)?

   a.   Having regular social contacts with friends and loved ones is key to avoiding depression, which can lead to premature death.

   b.   Having regular social contact implies a higher incidence of exercise.

   c.   Having regular social contact means you are sharper mentally.

   d.   Having regular social contact means you have not retired.

Applying Information

19. The evidence for this article was gathered from a British study. Would the same recommendations apply to American people?

    a. Yes

    b. No

    c. Only the suggestions regarding diet

    d. The suggestion about humor would not apply since the two cultures have different senses of humor.

Understanding Sentence Relationships

20. Are these 10 traits for living a long life arranged in a specific or random order?

    a. Specific order

    b. Random order

    c. Some tips are specific, while other tips are random.

    d. You can't tell from the reading.

INCREASE YOUR COLLEGE-LEVEL VOCABULARY

The following list includes vocabulary words from the reading that you should be able to define from context clues in the reading. The vocabulary word is followed by the paragraph reference. Provide your own definition or synonym of the word, and then use the word in a sentence you have created.

21. chronic (paragraph 3) _____

    _____

22. acuity (paragraph 5) _____

    _____

23. cognitive (paragraph 8) _____

    _____

24. foster (paragraph 8) _____

    _____

25. infuses (paragraph 9) _____

    _____

26. neurotics (paragraph 9) _____

    _____

(Continued)

27. ruminating (paragraph 9) _____

_____

28. equilibrium (paragraph 11) _____

_____

SHORT-ANSWER QUESTIONS

29. Which of the characteristics that the author describes do you feel is the most important for a long, healthy life? Explain your answer.

30. Which characteristics that the author describes do you feel is the least important for a long, healthy life? Explain your answer.

31. Is there another important lifestyle factor that you feel should be included in this list that is not listed? Explain why you would include this factor.

32. The author uses Seventh Day Adventists as models for healthy living. Do you think this example is a realistic one in today's world? Why or why not?

APPLICATION (2)

Here is a reading from the college success textbook called *BAMS: The Essential Guide to Becoming a Master Student.* Preview this reading first and then answer this question:

● What is the topic of this reading? _____

Read the passage all the way through, and write a word or a phrase that sums up the topic of each section in the reading. Afterward, pose a guide question for each section based on the topic. Then answer the Comprehension Check questions that follow the reading.

Five Ways to Resolve Conflict

1   When conflict occurs, we often make statements about another person. We say such things as:

"You are rude."

"You make me mad."

"You must be crazy."

"You don't love me anymore."

What is the topic of paragraph 1?

Pose a guide question based on this topic.

2   These are "You" messages. Usually they result in **defensiveness**. The responses might be:

"I am not rude."

"I don't care."

"No, *you* are crazy."

"No, *you* don't love *me*!"

Can you infer what defensiveness means?

What is the topic of paragraph 2?

Pose a guide question based on this topic.

3   "You" messages are hard to listen to. They label, judge, blame, and assume things that might or might not be true. They demand **rebuttal**.

Can you infer what rebuttal means?

4   The next time you're in conflict with someone, consider replacing "You" messages with "I" messages:

"You are rude" might become "I feel upset."

"You make me mad" could be "I feel angry."

"You must be crazy" can be "I don't understand."

"You don't love me anymore" could become "I'm afraid we're drifting apart."

5   "I" messages don't judge, blame, criticize, or insult. They don't invite the other person to **counterattack**.

"I" messages are also more accurate. They stick to the facts and report our own thoughts and feelings.

Can you infer what counterattack means?

6   Suppose a friend asks you to pick her up at the airport. You drive 20 miles and wait for the plane. No friend. You decide your friend missed her plane, so you wait three hours for the next flight. No friend. **Perplexed** and worried, you drive home.

Can you infer what perplexed means?

(Continued)

The next day, you see your friend downtown.

"What happened?" you ask.

"Oh, I caught an earlier flight."

"You are a rude person," you reply.

7   When you saw your friend, you might have chosen an "I" message instead: "I waited and waited at the airport. I was worried about you. I didn't get a call. I feel angry and hurt. I don't want to waste my time. Next time, you can call me when your flight arrives, and I'll be happy to pick you up."

Can you infer what indisputable means?

8   An "I" message can include any or all of the following five elements.

Pose a guide question for this section.

1. **Observations.** Describe the facts—the **indisputable**, observable realities. Talk about what you—or anyone else—can see, hear, smell, taste, or touch. Avoid judgments, interpretations, or opinions. Instead of saying, "You're a slob," say, "Last night's lasagna pan was still on the stove this morning."

What is the topic of this section?

2. **Feelings.** Describe your own feelings. It is easier to listen to "I feel frustrated" than to "You never help me." Stating how you feel about another's actions can be valuable feedback for that person.

What is the topic of this section?

3. **Wants.** You are far more likely to get what you want if you *say* what you want. If someone doesn't know what you want, she doesn't have a chance to help you get it. Ask clearly. Avoid demanding or using the word *need*. Most people like to feel helpful, not **obligated**. Instead of saying, "Do the dishes when it's your turn, or else!" say, "I want to divide the housework fairly."

Can you infer what obligated means?

What is the topic of this section?

4. **Thoughts.** Communicate your thoughts, and use caution. Beginning your statement with the word "I" doesn't make it an "I" message. "I think you are a slob" is a "You" judgment in disguise. Instead, say, "I'd have more time to study if I didn't have to clean up so often."

· Pose a guide question for this section.

What is the topic of this section?

5. **Intentions.** The last part of an "I" message is a statement about what you intend to do. Have a plan that doesn't depend on the other person. For example, instead of "From now on we're going to split the dishwashing evenly," you could say, "I intend to do my share of the housework and leave the rest."

Pose a guide question for this section.

COMPREHENSION CHECK

TRUE/FALSE QUESTIONS

For the following statements, write a *T* if the statement is true or an *F* if the statement is false based on the reading.

____ 1. "I" statements are more effective for interpersonal communication than "You" statements.

____ 2. "You" statements are more effective for interpersonal communication than "I" statements.

____ 3. "I" statements demand rebuttal.

____ 4. "You" statements should describe your own feelings.

____ 5. "I" statements should describe your feelings.

LITERAL COMPREHENSION—MULTIPLE CHOICE

Circle the best answer for the following questions.

Understanding Main Ideas

6. What type of statements do we often make to others during conflicts?
   a. We make "You" statements.
   b. We make "I" statements.
   c. We should not talk during conflicts.
   d. We use neither "You" nor "I" statements.

7. When we make "You" statements, how do others typically react?
   a. Others understand our feelings.
   b. Others typically get defensive.
   c. Others reply with "You" statements.
   d. Others reply with "I" statements.

8. How should you phrase statements next time you're in conflict with someone?
   a. Consider mixing "You" and "I" statements for the best effect.
   b. Consider walking away from the conflict.
   c. Consider replacing "You" messages with "I" messages.
   d. Consider replacing "I" messages with "You" messages.

(Continued)

9. What are the benefits of "I" statements during conflict?

    a. "I" messages show vulnerability.

    b. "I" messages resolve the conflict.

    c. "I" messages are clear.

    d. "I" messages don't judge, blame, criticize, or insult.

10. How many elements could "I" statements contain (paragraph 8)?

    a. An "I" message can include any or all of the five elements.

    b. An "I" message contains four of the five elements.

    c. An "I" message contains only one of the five elements.

    d. An "I" message cannot contain any of the elements.

11. Which of the following is not one of the five elements in an "I" statement?

    a. Observations

    b. Feelings

    c. Wanting to be right

    d. Thoughts and/or intentions

Understanding Secondary Information and Locating Information

12. How do you include observations in "I" messages?

    a. Describe facts and/or sensations and avoid judgments.

    b. List them before the "I" statement.

    c. Use judgments as observations.

    d. Observe the other person's response.

13. How do you include feelings in "I" statements?

    a. State what the other person did rather than how you feel.

    b. State how the other person feels rather than what you did.

    c. State what the other person feels and what he or she did.

    d. State how you feel rather than what the other person did.

14. How do you use wants in "I" statements?

    a. Tell the other person what you want.

    b. Tell the other person what you need.

    c. Tell the other person what he or she wants.

    d. Tell the other person what he or she needs.

15. How do you communicate thoughts?
    a. Relate the thought to the other person.
    b. Relate the thought to yourself rather than direct it at the other person.
    c. Think about your needs in the situation and express them.
    d. Think about the other person's needs in the situation and be sympathetic.

16. How do you communicate intentions in "I" statements?
    a. The first part of your "I" statement should communicate what you intend to do.
    b. The last part of your "I" statement should communicate what you intend to do.
    c. The first part of your "I" statement should communicate what you intend to ask the other person to do.
    d. The last part of your "I" statement should communicate what you intend the other person to do.

INFERENTIAL COMPREHENSION

Circle the best answer for the following questions.

Making Inferences

17. What is the difference between using an "I" statement and a "You" statement based on the anecdote of waiting for a friend at the airport who didn't arrive?
    a. The reading suggests that "I" statements are less provocative and less threatening so the other person doesn't get defensive.
    b. The reading suggests that "You" statements are less provocative and less threatening so the other person doesn't get defensive.
    c. The reading suggests that "I" statements are better if there is no conflict.
    d. The reading suggests that "You" statements are better if there is no conflict.

Applying Information

18. You are at a friend's house waiting for him to arrive. He said he would be there at 5 P.M. It is now 6 P.M. What should you do, according to the reading?
    a. Use "You" statements when he gets there.
    b. Use "I" statements to express your feelings.
    c. Use "I" statements to express your feelings plus an intention that states what you are going to do.
    d. Use "I" statements to express what he will say once he gets there.

(Continued)

Understanding Sentence Relationships

19. The author begins the reading with a long discussion of "You" and "I" statements, complete with anecdotes and examples. Why does the author do this and not just get to the point?

    a. One possibility is that the author is trying to grab the reader's attention with the anecdotes to make the information relate to the reader's life.

    b. One possibility is that the author is trying to endorse the use of "You" statements.

    c. One possibility is that the author is trying to endorse the use of "I" statements.

    d. The author is distracting the reader so that the main idea will be a surprise.

20. Which of the following tactics does the author use to teach you about "You" and "I" statements?

    a. Comparison and contrast

    b. A list of examples

    c. Classifying the statements into categories

    d. A time line of events

INCREASE YOUR COLLEGE-LEVEL VOCABULARY

For the following words from the reading, write a synonym word or phrase. Then, write an antonym, or phrase that means the opposite, of the original word.

WORD FROM THE READING	SYNONYM	ANTONYM
21. Defensiveness		
22. Counterattack		
23. Perplexed		
24. Indisputable		
25. Obligated		

© Cengage Learning 2013

SHORT-ANSWER QUESTIONS

26. Can you recall a time during a conflict when you used "You" statements? How did the other person respond to you?

27. Can you recall a time during conflict when you used an "I" statement? How did the other person respond to you?

28. The author provides several suggestions for avoiding conflict in communication. Which suggestion do you feel is most effective?

29. Which suggestion do you feel is least effective for avoiding conflict in communication?

30. Brainstorm some additional suggestions to avoid conflict.

WRAPPING IT UP

STUDY OUTLINE

In the following study outline, fill in the definitions and a brief explanation of the key terms in the Your Notes column. Use the strategy of spaced practice to review these key terms on a regular basis. Use this study guide to review this chapter's key topics.

KEY TERM	YOUR NOTES	
Topic		
Subject		
General		
Specific		
Subsection		
Guide question		

KEY TERM	YOUR NOTES
Heading	
Antonym clue	
Inference	
Inference clue	
Motivation	
External motivation	
Internal motivation	
Time management	

WRAPPING IT UP

WHAT DID YOU LEARN?

Now, go back to the questionnaire at the beginning of this chapter on page 62 and fill in the After Reading column, noting if you agree or disagree with the statements after reading this chapter. Have your views changed?

GROUP ACTIVITY: PRESENTATIONS

As a group, find further information on one of the following topics, and present your findings to the class in a short oral report so others can learn from what you know and apply it to their lives.

- Time management
- Habits of healthy people
- Healthy living
- Sharp thinking/brain power
- Longevity (long life)
- Memory and aging
- Conflict resolution

A good oral report includes these features:

- Plan what you want to say, making notes.
- Use clear language to communicate ideas.
- Be brief and to the point, but include major ideas.
- Make sure to reference your sources (where you got the information from).
- Use visuals if an idea is complicated (maps, charts, etc.).
- Look at your audience rather than look down at your notes when possible.
- Ask the audience if they have questions, and do your best to answer them completely.

QUESTIONS FOR WRITING, DISCUSSION, OR REFLECTION

1. What do you feel is the most significant piece of information regarding motivation covered in this chapter? What are some ways you could use this information to improve your success in college?

2. Based on what you have read about healthy living and dealing with conflict and stress, in what ways can you make changes to your life today that will have long-term benefits for you.

3. What are the qualities needed for an individual to manage his or her time given the demands of work, family, and school? Choose three qualities (behaviors, techniques, or attitudes) that characterize well-managed time. Support your answer with specific examples.

4. Choose a textbook you use in another class. Find examples of the following:
   a. An antonym context clue
   b. An inference context clue
   c. Topic determined by a heading
   d. Topic determined by a boldfaced or italicized word
   e. Topic determined by repeated words

5. For another class, try the technique of posing guide questions to focus your reading. Write a paragraph about how the technique worked.

POST-ASSESSMENT

This assessment will help you understand your strengths and weaknesses in learning, understanding, and applying the skills and strategies discussed in this chapter. Preview the following article. Then read it all the way through and answer the Comprehension Check questions that follow.

Stress on Campus
by Dianne Hales

1   Being a student—full-time or part-time, in your late teens, early twenties, or later in life—can be extremely stressful. You may feel pressure to perform well to qualify for a good job or graduate school.

2   To meet steep tuition payments, you may have to juggle part-time work and coursework. You may feel stressed about choosing a major, getting along with a difficult roommate, passing a particularly hard course, or living up to your parents' and teachers' expectations. If you're an older student, you may have children, housework, and homework to balance. Your days may seem so busy and your life so full that you worry about coming apart at the seams. One thing is for certain: You're not alone.

3   According to surveys of students at colleges and universities around the country and the world, stressors are remarkably similar. Among the most common are:

- **Test pressures.**
- **Financial problems.**
- **Frustrations,** such as delays in reaching goals.
- **Problems in friendships** and dating relationships.
- **Daily hassles.**
- **Academic failure.**
- **Pressures** as a result of competition, deadlines, and the like.
- **Changes,** which may be unpleasant, disruptive, or too frequent.
- **Losses,** whether caused by the breakup of a relationship or the death of a loved one.

4   Many students bring complex psychological problems with them to campus, including learning disabilities and <u>mood disorders</u> like depression and anxiety. "Students arrive with the underpinnings of problems that are brought out by the stress of campus life," says one counselor. Some have grown up in broken homes and bear the scars of family troubles. Others fall into the same patterns of alcohol abuse that they observed for years in their families or suffer lingering emotional scars from childhood physical or sexual abuse.

5   Students aren't the only ones complaining about stress on campus. Professors working toward tenure also report high stress levels—particularly women. The reason for this gender difference may be that women take on more responsibility for <u>mentoring</u> female students and for teaching independent study courses with individual students.

COMPREHENSION CHECK

Circle the best answer to the questions based on information from the reading.

1   What is the topic of this reading?

A. Stress

B. Stress on campus

C. Stressful situations

2   What is a good guide question to ask about the title of this reading?

A. Who is stressed on campus?

B. Where is stress on campus?

C. Why is there stress on campus?

3   Why are students under stress?

A. Pressure to perform, financial pressure, and pressure from family

B. Pressure from outside jobs and family demands

C. Pressure to perform, financial pressure, and pressure from job and family

4   Which of the following is not a common pressure, according to research about students and stress?

A. Academic failure

B. Deciding on a major

C. Friendships

5   In paragraph 5, a counselor is quoted as saying, "Students arrive with the underpinnings of problems that are brought out by the stress of campus life."
What does this mean?

A. Many students suffer from prior mental health issues before starting college.

B. Students blame school life for a variety of emotional issues.

C. Healthy people do not demonstrate stressful behaviors.

(Continued)

6 **What are some preexisting mental health issues that students bring to campus?**

A. Learning disabilities, mood disorders, alcohol problems, and family troubles

B. Motivation issues and time-management problems

C. Drug problems

7 **What are examples of mood disorders?**

A. Problems with alcohol and drugs

B. Depression and anxiety

C. Bad moods due to stress

8 **What type of vocabulary context clue did you use to figure out the term *mood disorders*?**

A. Definition clue

B. Synonym clue

C. Inference clue

9 **What does the word *mentoring* mean in paragraph 5?**

A. Advising

B. Teaching

C. Examining

10 **What is the author's main point?**

A. Stress for students is widespread.

B. Stress for students comes with them to college.

C. Alcohol is commonly used to deal with college stress.

MAIN IDEAS

MAIN IDEAS

UNIT 2

© PinkTag/iStockphoto.com

EXPLICIT MAIN IDEAS

THEME *Money and Happiness*

"A good idea plus capable men cannot fail;
it is better than money in the bank." — JOHN BERRY

OBJECTIVES

In this chapter, you will focus on:

COMPREHENSION SKILLS

Learn how to focus on main points in a reading by identifying

- Author's purpose
- Explicit main idea

LEARNING HOW TO FOCUS ON MAIN POINTS

READING STUDY SKILLS

Learn how to focus on main points by

- Zeroing in on goals
- Optimizing your study environment

VOCABULARY SKILLS

Learn how to focus on main meanings of words by understanding

- Prefixes
- Suffixes

© Cengage Learning 2013

WHY DO YOU NEED TO KNOW THIS?

Problem:

Sonia is a young mother of two. She has a high school diploma but has not been in school for over five years. She works full-time and is very busy with her family as well as her job. She has a goal of attaining an associate's degree that will enable her to get a good job working with children as a teacher's aide. Sonia has a good vocabulary and loves to read, but reading for college is another matter. She's never sure what the main idea in a reading is. She's confused by technical, college-level vocabulary. She wants to be able to break a word down into parts to understand all the words she encounters in reading that she doesn't know.

© Sean Justice/Getty Images

WHAT ADVICE WOULD YOU OFFER TO SONIA?

_____

_____

_____

Solution:

Sonia needs to focus on the most important part of a reading to understand it—the main idea. Knowing how to determine the topic of a reading and how to turn a topic into a guide question is a start in determining the main idea. Different disciplines use vocabulary that you don't see in magazines or books for pleasure. Using context clues helps you figure out unknown words, but what if this strategy is not enough? You can look at prefixes and suffixes of a word to help you figure out its meaning. Combine this strategy with finding main ideas, and you're on the right track to understanding college reading material. If Sonia applies these skills, she will find that college reading is more easily understandable and her comprehension improves.

WHAT DO YOU ALREADY KNOW?

Write down five things you know about main ideas and five things you would like to learn. Do not edit your list; just brainstorm. When you have completed this chapter, you will have a chance to see if you have a better understanding of main ideas.

Five Things I Know About Main Ideas	Five Things I Do Not Know About Main Ideas (and would like to find out)
1 _____	1 _____
2 _____	2 _____
3 _____	3 _____
4 _____	4 _____
5 _____	5 _____

PRE-ASSESSMENT

This pre-assessment will help you measure what you already know and what you need to learn about the reading skills and strategies explored in this chapter. Your results will help you understand your strengths and weaknesses. Read the article, and then answer the Comprehension Check questions that follow.

Money = Happiness
By John M. Grohol

1   It turns out that whoever said money can't buy you happiness was wrong.

2   Money can buy you happiness, as long as you give some of the money away.

3   Dunn and colleagues (2008) conducted three studies that examined the relationship between Americans' spending habits and their self-reported happiness. The first study was a national survey conducted on 632 Americans that asked to detail their income and spending habits. The participants were also asked to rate their general happiness level.

4   The researchers found that two things were correlated with greater general happiness levels—higher income (naturally) and spending on gifts for other people or money given to charity.

5   One could argue, well, hey, of course having more income can make you happy. . . . But maybe it's related to either the dollar amount given, or the fact that people who are more likely to give money to charity and others are just inherently happier people by character. So the researchers set out to examine those <u>hypotheses</u> in two separate follow-up experiments.

6   In a small, second study, 16 employees were asked about their general happiness levels before and after receiving their <u>annual</u> bonus. No matter what the size of the actual bonus, employees who spent more of their bonus money on others or charity reported greater general happiness levels than those who spent more of it on themselves.

7   Finally, in a third study of 46 people, researchers discovered that participants who were directed to spend a small amount of money on others (either $5 or $20) reported greater feelings of happiness than those who were directed to spend the same amounts on themselves. Again, the dollar amount didn't matter.

8   The third study suggests that even when the choice isn't ours, we still feel the happiness effects of giving away money to others. And even when the actual value is small ($5).

9   So indeed, money can buy you happiness. As long as you give some of it away.

"Money = Happiness" by John M. Grohol, PSYD. http://psychcentral.com/blog/archives/2008/09/05/money-happiness/. Used with permission.

COMPREHENSION CHECK

Circle the best answer to the questions based on information from the reading.

1 What is the topic of this reading?
   A. Money
   B. Happiness
   C. Money and happiness

2 What is a good guide question to pose about the title of this reading?
   A. Where can money equal happiness?
   B. Why can money buy happiness?
   C. How can money equal happiness?

3 What is the answer to the guide question posed about the title, according to the reading?
   A. Money can buy happiness if you give it away.
   B. Yes, money can buy happiness.
   C. No, money cannot buy happiness.

(Continued)

4 **What is the main idea of this reading?**

A. Money can buy you happiness, as long as you give some of the money away.

B. It turns out that whoever said money can't buy you happiness was wrong.

C. Buying life experiences rather than material possessions leads to greater happiness for both the consumer and those around him or her.

5 **What is the author's primary purpose in writing this article?**

A. To inform us of the research on money and happiness.

B. To persuade us that money doesn't bring happiness.

C. To instruct us on how to use money to attain happiness.

6 **What two things were linked with happiness, according to the three studies that examined the relationship between Americans' spending habits and their self-reported happiness?**

A. Buying life experiences and sharing them with others.

B. Having more money and giving more away.

C. A feeling of being alive and having money.

7 **How many studies proved the point that spending money on others brings happiness?**

A. 2

B. 3

C. 4

8 **Did the experimenters prove that those who tend to give money away are just happier people by nature?**

A. No, in studies people were happier after giving money away regardless of their happiness prior to the gift.

B. Yes, people who give money away are happier by nature prior to the gift.

C. Maybe people who give money away are happier by nature.

9 **In paragraph 5, what does the word *hypotheses* mean?**

A. Experiments

B. Theories

C. Results

10 **In paragraph 6, what part of speech does the ending *-al* mean in the word *annual*?**

A. Noun

B. Verb

C. Adjective

FOCUS ON COMPREHENSION
Author's Purpose and Explicit Main Ideas

In Unit 1, you learned how to zero in on the topic of a passage; now, you are ready to look at the "heart" of a reading. In this chapter and the next, you will develop skills to determine the author's most important point in a reading. First, you should consider why an author has written a text to begin with. Along with all the skills and strategies you have learned so far, such as determining topic and posing guide questions, the purpose an author has for writing is important to consider and will help you determine the main idea.

AUTHOR'S PURPOSE

When an author writes, he or she has a purpose in mind. By thinking about *why* an author has written something, you can understand what the author's motivation behind the task of writing was to begin with. **Author's purpose** refers to the reason the author has for writing. There are four main purposes an author may have in writing:

- To inform
- To instruct
- To persuade
- To entertain

Of course, all authors try to be informative and entertaining to some extent. For our purposes, however, there is a distinct difference between these four reasons for writing. These purposes for writing can often be recognized by specific language. Sometimes an author can have more than one purpose. For example, an author can aim to inform *and* persuade. However, one purpose is predominant, and this purpose is reflected in the author's most important point.

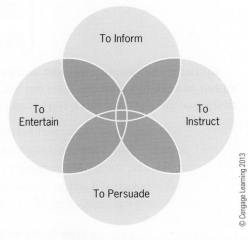

© Cengage Learning 2013

FIGURE 3.1 Author's Purpose An author has a main purpose for writing, but sometimes purposes may intertwine.

FOCUS ON COMPREHENSION: Author's Purpose and Explicit Main Ideas

To Inform

An author may write to inform or explain. The author provides factual information only. An author presents information in an objective manner without imposing his or her personal opinion about the facts on the reader. In this case, an author does not want to convince the reader of his or her point of view or take a side about the facts. The sole purpose of the writing is to convey information in an unbiased, open-minded manner.

Newspaper articles are examples of writing where an author's purpose is to inform. Recall how you used journalists' prompts to develop questions when you read. These same questions—who, what, where, when, why, or how—are used to write news stories. The author does not say what he or she thinks or what you, the reader, should think. You are left to form your own conclusion based on the facts. The author may quote someone else's opinion but will not state his or her own.

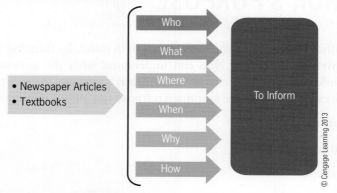

Similarly, the purpose of most authors of academic textbooks is to inform. The author of a biology textbook does not tell you what to think about DNA synthesis, he or she just gives you the facts. Here is an example that has a purpose to inform.

> The statistical disconnect between money and happiness raises a
> question: Why doesn't money make us happy? One answer comes
> from a new study by psychologists at the University of Liege, published
> in Psychological Science. The scientists explore the "experience-
> stretching hypothesis," an idea first proposed by Daniel Gilbert.
>
> —From Wired.com, Jonah Lehrer, "Why Money Makes You Unhappy".
> Copyright © 2010 Condé Nast Publications. By permission.

The author does not take a position on the issue here. Rather, he reports what psychologists have discovered. Although the author quotes what a psychologist says, the author himself reports the comments to inform the reader—notice the straightforward language.

To Instruct

Another purpose an author may have for writing is to instruct the reader about how to do something or how something works. In instructional writing, like informative writing, the author does not provide an opinion about the process or set of instructions. Instead, he or she presents the information in a factual, step-by-step manner and with a neutral tone or attitude. How to assemble something is a classic example of an instructional purpose.

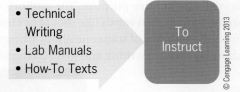

- Technical Writing
- Lab Manuals
- How-To Texts

To Instruct

Instructional writing can be found in many different types of reading, from how-to texts and lab manuals to technical writing texts that show how to complete a process. Office systems texts or readings in other technical courses may use instructional writing. Here is an example that has a purpose to instruct.

Calculate Your Balance

1. Write down your checkbook's current balance at the top of a piece of paper or on the back of your statement (some banks provide a worksheet on the back of each statement for calculating your balance).

2. Subtract amounts for uncleared deposits and bank fees, such as monthly fees or those for (gasp!) bounced checks, and subtract from your calculated total.

3. Add any uncleared checks and the interest you have earned to this figure.

4. Compare the final figure to your bank statement.

—"How to Regularly Balance Your Checkbook" from
http://www.ehow.com/how_2597_regularly-balance-checkbook.html

In this example, the author instructs you about how to keep track of your finances and balance your checkbook. The instruction is a step-by-step process. Also, notice the numbers that illustrate the steps to take to keep track of these expenses.

FOCUS ON COMPREHENSION: Author's Purpose and Explicit Main Ideas

To Persuade

Sometimes an author wants to persuade the reader to adopt a position on an issue. The author has something about which he or she wants to convince the reader. Even if the author's argument is one with which you agree, if that author tries to get the reader to choose a side—usually the author's side—then his or her main purpose is to persuade. In persuasive writing, an author uses **biased words**, also called *loaded* or *slanted language*, that reveal the author's position on an issue. Words or phrases such as *should, ought to,* or *must* also always reveal a persuasive purpose. The author's intent is to change the reader's mind. (Be careful, though, that words like *should* or *ought to* are in the author's voice and do not express the opinion of someone about whom the author is writing.) You will learn more about persuasive writing and loaded language in Chapter 7.

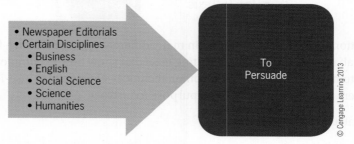

- Newspaper Editorials
- Certain Disciplines
  - Business
  - English
  - Social Science
  - Science
  - Humanities

To Persuade

A newspaper editorial is a good illustration of a persuasive piece of writing. Editorials, usually in the middle of the first section of a newspaper, contain essays that express the opinions of the writers about some topic currently in the news. The authors of these essays take a stand on an issue and try to persuade the reader to agree with them. Humanities, social science, physical sciences, business, and English texts may also have essays or passages in which an author takes a point of view on an issue. Here is an example that has a purpose to persuade.

> Perhaps we should be asking whether financial education is *worthwhile*—and the answer is even more emphatically, yes. While education alone won't guarantee financial well-being, it must be part of the equation—along with adequate information, consumer protection, access to fair and convenient services and a better understanding of social and emotional influences.

—"Does Financial-Literacy Education Work?" Laura Levine from Billitteri, T. J. (2009, September 4). Financial literacy. *CQ Researcher, 19,* 717–740. Copyright © 2009 CQ Press, a division of SAGE Publications, Inc.

The author of this passage takes a position that financial literacy education is worth-while. Notice the wording (*the answer is . . . yes, must*)that shows persuasive intent.

To Entertain _____

Usually in academic writing, an author's primary purpose will be to inform, instruct, or persuade. Magazines, novels, and stories that are read for recreation usually have the purpose of entertaining a reader. In addition to providing entertainment, these types of readings may also inform, instruct, or persuade—the typical purposes of academic reading. A story or poem can be informative or persuasive as well as enter-taining. While an author may intend for his or her audience to enjoy reading a selection, he or she may also want to provoke the reader to think about an issue and see it from the author's point of view. Humor, satire, and sarcasm can also be meant to entertain and persuade. Originally the definition of entertain meant to engage a reader—to grab the reader's attention. So, if you are interested in a topic about which you are reading, you are entertained. Here is an example that has a purpose to entertain.

> Every year, after the lottery, Mr. Summers began talking again about a new box, but every year the subject was allowed to fade off without anything's being done. The black box grew shabbier each year: by now it was no longer completely black but splintered badly along one side to show the original wood color, and in some places faded or stained.

> —From Shirley Jackson, "The Lottery"

In this passage, the author describes a box. She uses a variety of descriptive details to create a mental image in the readers' minds about this object. While writers of litera-ture may often have other purposes for writing, such as to persuade a reader about some larger issue or concern, their main purpose is to entertain by engaging the reader in a story. A reader can also gain insight into an author's issue or larger concern by considering the author's background, which may suggest a certain point of view about a topic embedded in a story or descriptive passage.

- Magazines
- Literature
- Leisure Reading

→

To Entertain

© Cengage Learning 2013

FOCUS ON COMPREHENSION: Author's Purpose and Explicit Main Ideas

TABLE 3.1 AUTHOR'S PURPOSES

AUTHOR'S PURPOSE	TYPICAL READING MATERIAL	VOCABULARY
To Inform	Textbooks Newspapers Nonfiction books	Straightforward language
To Instruct	Manuals, diagrams "How-to" passages Steps in a process Instructions for assembly or task How something works	Detailed language explaining a process or how to do or assemble something Look for numbers or these words: *first, second, next, finally*
To Persuade	Persuasive essays Editorials Written debates	Wording that expresses emotion or point of view, such as adjectives like *terrible, wonderful, suspicious* Look for these words: *ought to, should,* and *must*
To Entertain	Literature (poetry, fiction, drama) Magazines	Symbolism, figurative language, description, humor

Thinking It Through   DETERMINING AN AUTHOR'S PURPOSE

In the following passages, identify whether the author's primary purpose is to inform, instruct, persuade, or entertain. Then read the explanation that follows.

1.   More than 20% of the 292 self-made American billionaires on the most recent list of the World's Billionaires have either never started or never completed college. This is especially true of those destined for careers as technology entrepreneurs: Bill Gates, Steve Jobs, Michael Dell, Larry Ellison, and Theodore Waitt.

> —From Duncan Greenberg, "Billionaire Clusters", *Forbes* Magazine, April 2, 2009.
> Reprinted by permission of Forbes Media LLC © 2011.

Here, the author's purpose is to inform the reader about the number of billionaires who have not completed or even started college. Notice the straightforward language in the passage, suggesting an informative purpose.

2. As the director of a coalition representing hundreds of organizations that conduct and support standards-based financial education, and as the mother of a young son, I believe that financial education is crucial to providing future generations with the knowledge and skills they'll need not only to make smart financial decisions for themselves, but to know when and how to seek help.

    —"Does Financial-Literacy Education Work?" Laura Levine from Billitteri, T. J. (2009, September 4). Financial literacy. *CQ Researcher, 19,* 717–740. Copyright © 2009 CQ Press, a division of SAGE Publications, Inc.

In this passage, the author argues that financial literacy education is effective. The purpose is to persuade because the author expresses her opinion about whether or not we should promote financial literacy to benefit future generations—she believes we should. Notice the wording: *I believe* suggests that the author wants to convince us to adopt her point of view.

3. You can save money each month by reconsidering ways to cut expenses that may have little impact on your enjoyment of life. Here are some steps to take to reduce monthly expenses.

    1. Do you really need those premium cable channels? If not, the first step is to cut out unnecessary expenses for leisure: cable, eating out, buying that morning coffee, and making impulse purchases.
    2. Second, rethink your insurance premiums: Do you really need comprehensive auto insurance instead of just liability insurance? Can you increase your auto and health insurance deductibles? There's a good chance you're overpaying for your insurance.
    3. Last, cut your unlimited phone plan. Cell phone plans can eat up huge chunks of money each month. Track your minutes for 2 months; then reconsider your unlimited plan. You will save a lot in one year.

The author's purpose here is to instruct. The author provides step-by-step instructions on how to achieve your savings goals using clear language and explicit details.

4. Melting pot Harlem—Harlem of honey and chocolate and caramel and rum and vinegar and lemon and lime and gall . . . where the subway from the Bronx keeps right on downtown.

    —Reprinted by permission of Harold Ober Associates Incorporated. Extract by Langston Hughes from *Freedomways* magazine, Summer 1963, Vol. 3, #3. Copyright © 1963.

    Copyright renewed 1991 by Arnold Rampersad and Ramona Bass.

The writing in this passage is descriptive and, as a result, aimed to entertain. Notice the poet's description of Harlem; this description creates a mental picture in the reader's mind.

FOCUS ON COMPREHENSION: Author's Purpose and Explicit Main Ideas

On Your Own   DETERMINING AN AUTHOR'S PURPOSE

In the following passages, identify the author's primary purpose. Take into account the type of language used by the author that indicates his or her purpose for writing.

If the purpose is to inform, write an *I* next to the passage.
If the purpose is to instruct, write an *IN* next to the passage.
If the purpose is to persuade, write a *P* next to the passage.
If the purpose is to entertain, write an *E* by the passage.

_____ 1.   Sales used to be relatively predictable. A popular 1975 book could say with assurance that luggage went on sale in March and the best month to buy a baby carriage was January or August. But these days, with stores pumping out weekly sales circulars and manufacturers introducing new models as fast as they can get them off the assembly line and onto a containership, all bets would seem to be off.

—*Consumer Reports*, "Mark Your Calendars: What's on Sale When."
Copyright 2011 by Consumers Union of U.S., Inc. Yonkers, NY 10703-1057,
a nonprofit organization. By permission.

_____ 2.   What might be helpful is not teaching financial literacy but basic consumer education. Consumers need to know how little they know, how quickly things change and where to get unbiased, accurate information.

But knowledge alone will not be enough.

—"Does Financial-Literacy Education Work?" Lauren E. Willis from Billitteri, T. J. (2009, September 4).
Financial literacy. *CQ Researcher, 19,* 717–740. Copyright © 2009 CQ Press,
a division of SAGE Publications, Inc.

_____ 3.   We found that it's still possible to use the calendar to save money on major purchases. Our researchers combed industry surveys and publications, and consulted our in-house experts to compile the calendar. Consider it a general guide, and keep your eye on those sales circulars anyway because there will always be exceptions. Bear in mind, too, that the best time to save money isn't always the best for selection. In some cases, your bargain might be a discontinued model without all the latest features.

—*Consumer Reports*, "Mark Your Calendars: What's on Sale When."
Copyright 2011 by Consumers Union of U.S., Inc. Yonkers, NY 10703-1057,
a nonprofit organization. By permission.

_____ 4.   Airline tickets tend to be least expensive to buy on Tuesday afternoon through Thursday. Worst days to fare shop are Saturday and Sunday. CDs and DVDs generally come out on Tuesdays and might be on sale for the first one to three weeks. Jewelry sales are common, except around Valentine's Day and the December holidays. So plan to buy early or hope that your beloved will settle for an IOU.

—*Consumer Reports*, "Mark Your Calendars: What's on Sale When."
Copyright 2011 by Consumers Union of U.S., Inc. Yonkers, NY 10703-1057,
a nonprofit organization. By permission.

_____ 5. I would rather be ashes than dust! I would rather that my spark burn out in a brilliant blaze than it be stifled by dry-rot. I would rather be a superb meteor, every atom of me in magnificent glow, than a sleepy and permanent planet.

—Jack London (1916)

_____ 6. 1. Start by writing in the date using any format, as long as it's legible. Use either the current date or a future date for a post-dated check.

2. Write the name of the person or company receiving your check on the line that starts with "Pay to the Order of" or "Payable to."

3. Write the numerical dollar amount of the check in the small space that starts with a dollar sign ($) so that it reads like this: $25.63.

4. Write the same amount using words for whole dollar amounts, a fractional figure for amounts less than a dollar, and a straight line to fill up the remaining space on the line ending with the word "Dollars," like this: Twenty-five and 63/100 _____ Dollars.

5. Sign the signature line at the lower right.

6. Note the check number, date, payee and amount on the check stub or in the check ledger at the front of your checkbook.

7. Subtract the amount of the check so that you will know how much you have left in your account.

—"How to Write a Check" from http://www.ehow.com/how_567_write-check.html

_____ 7. Quantifying happiness isn't an easy task. Researchers at the Gallup World Poll went about it by surveying thousands of respondents in 155 countries, between 2005 and 2009, in order to measure two types of well-being.

—Francesca Levy, "The World's Happiest Countries," Forbes.com © 2010 Forbes.com.

_____ 8. Knowing how difficult the financial marketplace is to navigate could even be paralyzing. We need to redesign the marketplace to comport with realistic expectations about consumers.

—"Does Financial-Literacy Education Work?" Lauren E. Willis from Billitteri, T. J. (2009, September 4). Financial literacy. *CQ Researcher, 19,* 717–740. Copyright © 2009 CQ Press, a division of SAGE Publications, Inc.

_____ 9. A tearing wind last night. A flurry of red clouds, hard, a water colour mass of purple and black, soft as a water ice, then hard slices of intense green stone, blue stone and a ripple of crimson light.

—Virginia Woolf, in her diary, August 17, 1938

(Continued)

FOCUS ON COMPREHENSION: Author's Purpose and Explicit Main Ideas

_____ 10.   Are you aware of how much you spend each month? Financial security requires that you keep track of your expenses. Here is how to do that. First, keep a notebook with you to write down all purchases each day for one month. Next, use a ledger (available with check purchases at your local bank), and make a habit to always balance your checkbook. Insert daily expenses into your account every week. Finally, once you know how much you really spend per month, you can decide to cut back on certain expenses that are not necessary.

MAIN IDEA

Now you will apply the skills of finding the topic of a reading to finding the author's most important point in a passage, or the main idea. The **main idea** is the single most important point the author makes about the topic. This point reflects the author's purpose for writing, and it is general enough that all the supporting points back it up. The main idea can be determined by answering the question "What is the author's most important point about the topic?" The main idea is always expressed as a complete sentence. Remember that a topic is a word or phrase, never a complete sentence. A main idea is never a question, but it can be the answer to a guide question posed about the reading.

On Your Own TOPIC OR MAIN IDEA?

Put an *MI* beside the statements that are a main idea. Put a *T* by the statements that are topics.

___ 1.   How to prepare for an exam

___ 2.   Exam preparation follows several general steps.

___ 3.   Important steps

___ 4.   To prepare for an exam involves important steps, such as taking good notes and using spaced practice to learn.

___ 5.   How you prepare for an exam

When the main idea is expressed in one sentence in a reading passage, it is called an **explicit main idea.** When the main idea is not directly stated in one sentence in a reading, it is called an **implied main idea.** In this chapter, you will focus on explicit main ideas.

There are different words for *main idea,* depending on what type of main idea is at issue. The main idea of a paragraph, if explicit (directly stated in one sentence), is called the **topic sentence.** A topic sentence states the author's most important point about the topic. A main idea of an essay or long passage is called the **thesis.** A thesis can be explicit or directly stated in a sentence, or it can be implied. Regardless of how long a passage or section is, the main idea is always the most important point the author makes.

TABLE 3.2 TYPES OF MAIN IDEA

TERM	DEFINITION
Main idea	The most important point
Explicit (directly stated) main idea	The most important point expressed in one sentence in the reading
Topic sentence	The most important point of a paragraph *when directly stated*
Thesis	The most important point of an essay or longer reading

© Cengage Learning 2013

An author always chooses a topic and purpose about which he or she writes. Based on the purpose, the author selects words or a writing style to express his or her intent. The author also wants to communicate his or her main idea about the topic to the reader. If an author's purpose is to instruct, for example, the topic of the reading will be "how to understand or do something." The main idea will be a general statement about the topic, such as "Follow these three steps to fix a fax machine."

The author also arranges the information, or **supporting details**, in a deliberate pattern of organization. Supporting details are additional information the author provides to back up the main idea. In the previous example, the supporting details would be the steps to follow in order to fix a fax machine.

FOCUS ON COMPREHENSION: Author's Purpose and Explicit Main Ideas

Topic
- The author writes about the topic.

Purpose for Writing
- The author has a purpose for writing about the topic.

Main Idea
- The author's main point is about the topic.
- Reflects the author's purpose.

Supporting Details
- The information that supports the main idea

© Cengage Learning 2013

FIGURE 3.2 The Relationship Between Topic, Purpose, Main Idea, and Supporting Details

QUICK TIPS THINGS TO REMEMBER ABOUT MAIN IDEA

☑ The main idea is *always* expressed as a sentence.

☑ An explicit main idea means the author has written a sentence that expresses the main thought—the author has directly stated the main idea.

☑ The main idea is *never* in a question form, but it is often the *answer* to a question.

☑ Every paragraph has a main idea.

☑ Every longer reading has a main idea.

Finding the Main Idea

Determining the main idea involves thinking through information that the author has provided. The first step is to determine the topic: What or who is the reading about?

Next, consider why the author wrote the passage: What is the author's purpose for writing? Last, answer the question "What is the author's most important point about the topic?" The response is the main idea.

QUICK TIPS STEPS TO FINDING THE MAIN IDEA

1. What is the topic?
2. What is the author's purpose?
3. What is the author's most important point about the topic?
4. The answer to #3 is the main idea.
5. Find that same answer to #3 in a sentence in the reading; this is the explicit main idea.

Once you have determined the main idea, ask yourself several questions to verify your answer. For example, the main idea must be a sentence rather than a phrase or a single word. This sentence must make complete sense by itself and contain the topic and reflect the author's purpose for writing. The main idea must also be general enough to cover all the supporting details, as these details support the main idea.

QUICK TIPS STEPS TO CHECKING THE MAIN IDEA

To make sure you understand the main idea, ask yourself the following questions:

1. Is your main idea a complete sentence (not a phrase)?
2. Does your main idea sentence contain the topic?
3. Does your main idea sentence make sense by itself? (Would someone who hadn't read the passage understand the main point without major clarification?)
4. Does your sentence reflect the author's purpose? (If the author's purpose is to inform, your sentence should not include words like *should*, *must*, and *ought to*, because they indicate a purpose to persuade.)
5. Do the major supporting points backup or support the more general sentence you say is the main point?

FOCUS ON COMPREHENSION: Author's Purpose and Explicit Main Ideas

Location of Main Idea _____

The author's main idea can apply to a paragraph, a section of a reading, or a whole reading and be found anywhere in the reading—the beginning, the middle, or the end. The reasons an author states a main idea at the beginning, middle, or the end of a passage has to do with the reasoning an author uses to put forward his or her point. Sometimes an author states the main point at the beginning and then supports the point with details (see Table 3.3, diagram 1). Other times an author may state the main point at the end of a passage to present support to lead the reader to the main point (see Table 3.3, diagram 3). Authors also use the technique of "hooking" the readers' attention with information at the beginning of a passage, stating the main point in the middle, then follow that point with support (see Table 3.3, diagram 2).

In some cases, clues can point you to the main idea. They are often referred to as *"summative" words* because they summarize the author's main idea about the passage. Summative words usually indicate a main idea at the end of the paragraph or longer reading, but not always.

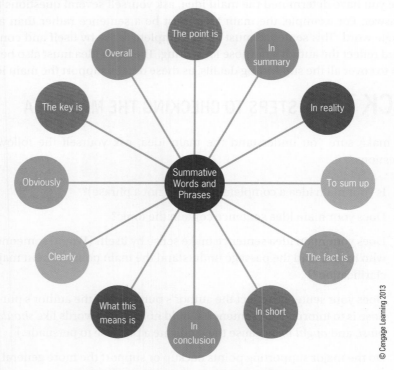

© Cengage Learning 2013

FIGURE 3.3 Summative Words: Words and Phrases Indicating Main Idea Sentence

TABLE 3.3 WHERE ARE TOPIC SENTENCES LOCATED?

At the beginning	MAIN IDEA	<u>More money can lead to more stress.</u> The big salary you pull in from your high-paying job may not buy you much in the way of happiness. But it can buy you a spacious house in the suburbs. Trouble is, that also means a long trip to and from work, and study after study confirms what you sense daily: Even if you love your job, the little slice of everyday hell you call the commute can wear you down. You can adjust to most anything, but a stop-and-go drive or an overstuffed bus will make you unhappy whether it's your first day on the job or your last.
	Details	
In the middle	Details	In attempting to answer these seemingly depressing questions, the new scholars of happiness have arrived at some insights that are, well, downright cheery. <u>Money can help you find more happiness, so long as you know just what you can and can't expect from it.</u> And no, you don't have to buy a Lexus to be happy. Much of the research suggests that seeking the good life at a store is an expensive exercise in futility. Before you can pursue happiness the right way, you need to recognize what you've been doing wrong.
	MAIN IDEA	
	Details	
At the end	Details	Not long ago, most researchers thought you had a happiness "set point" that you were largely stuck with for life. One famous paper said that "trying to be happier" may be "as futile as trying to be taller." The author of those words has since recanted, and experts are increasingly coming to view happiness as a talent, not an inborn trait. <u>Exceptionally happy people seem to have a set of skills—ones that you can learn too.</u>
	MAIN IDEA	

© Cengage Learning 2013

EXPLICIT MAIN IDEA IN A PARAGRAPH

Finding the main idea in a paragraph is an important skill because a main point in a paragraph becomes a major supporting detail of a whole reading. An explicit main idea in a paragraph is called a **topic sentence.** Most often a topic sentence is the first or last sentence in a paragraph. Sometimes, however, the topic sentence can be in the middle of a paragraph.

Look for transition words that indicate a supporting detail to narrow your scope. If there is a transition word or phrase, such as *in addition, furthermore, second,*

FOCUS ON COMPREHENSION: Author's Purpose and Explicit Main Ideas

in contrast, or *on the other hand,* to name a few, this point would be a supporting detail rather than a main idea. Look for a summative word that may indicate the main idea. Look for the sentence that is the general point under which all the examples in the paragraph might fall.

Thinking It Through   DETERMINING TOPIC SENTENCES WITHIN PARAGRAPHS

Consider the following examples of finding the topic sentence of a paragraph. Determine the topic of each paragraph. Clues to the topic are circled. Next, think in your own words what the author's most important point is about the topic. Then look at the paragraph and find a sentence that echoes your main idea. This is the topic sentence—it is underlined.

1. <u>Doing things can bring us more joy than having things.</u> Our preoccupation with stuff obscures an important truth: The things that don't last create the most lasting happiness. That's what Gilovich and Leaf Van Boven of the University of Colorado found when they asked students to compare the pleasure they got from the most recent things they bought vs. the experiences (a night out, a vacation) they spent money on.

   —"Can Money Buy Happiness?" by David Futrelle. From *Money,*
   August 1, 2006. © 2006 *Money.* By permission.

   What is the topic? <u>Things and happiness</u>
   What is the most important point in your own words? <u>Things don't bring happiness.</u>
   Underline the topic sentence.

2. What does experience-stretching have to do with money and happiness? <u>The Liege psychologists propose that, because money allows us to enjoy the best things in life— we can stay at expensive hotels and eat exquisite sushi and buy the nicest gadgets—we actually decrease our ability to enjoy the mundane joys of everyday life.</u> (Their list of such pleasures includes "sunny days, cold beers, and chocolate bars".) And since most of our joys are mundane—we can't sleep at the Ritz every night—our ability to splurge actually backfires. We try to treat ourselves, but we end up spoiling ourselves.

   —From Wired.com, Jonah Lehrer, "Why Money Makes You Unhappy."
   Copyright © 2010 Condé Nast Publications. By permission.

   What is the topic? <u>Money and happiness</u>
   What is the most important point in your own words? <u>Money makes us enjoy life less.</u>
   Underline the topic sentence.

3. You overestimate how much (pleasure) you'll get from having more. Humans are adaptable creatures, which has been a plus during assorted ice ages, plagues and wars. But that's also why you're never all that satisfied for long when good (fortune) comes your way. <u>While earning more makes you (happy) in the short term, you quickly adjust to your new (wealth)— and everything it buys you.</u> Yes, you get a thrill at first from shiny new cars and TV screens the size of Picasso's Guernica. But you soon get used to them, a state of running in place that economists call the "hedonic treadmill."

—"Can Money Buy Happiness?" by David Futrelle. From *Money*,
August 1, 2006. © 2006 *Money*. By permission.

What is the topic? <u>Wealth/money and happiness</u>

What is the most important point in your own words? <u>It seems like money/wealth brings happiness, but not for long.</u>

Underline the topic sentence.

On Your Own DETERMINING TOPIC SENTENCES WITHIN PARAGRAPHS

Read the following paragraphs, and identify the topic, determine the author's most important point about the topic, and then look in the paragraph for a sentence that states this answer—this is the topic sentence. Underline the topic sentence, and compare your answers with a partner.

1. Goldman Sachs has attracted a large share of hungry minds that went on to garner 10-figure fortunes. At least 11 current and recent billionaire financiers worked at Goldman early in their careers, including Edward Lampert, Daniel Och, Tom Steyer and Richard Perry.

—From Duncan Greenberg, "Billionaire Clusters," Forbes Magazine, April 2, 2009.
Reprinted by Permission of Forbes Media LLC © 2011

What is the topic? _____

What is the most important point in your own words? _____
_____

Underline the topic sentence.

2. Applying yourself to something hard makes you happy. We're addicted to challenges, and we're often far happier while working toward a goal than after we reach it. Challenges help you attain what psychologist Mihaly Csikszentmihalyi calls a state of "flow," total absorption in something that stretches you to the limits of your abilities, mental or physical. Buy the $1,000 golf clubs; pay for the $50-an-hour music lessons.

—"Can Money Buy Happiness?" by David Futrelle. From *Money*,
August 1, 2006. © 2006 *Money*. By permission.

(Continued)

FOCUS ON COMPREHENSION: Author's Purpose and Explicit Main Ideas

What is the topic? _____

What is the most important point in your own words? _____

_____

Underline the topic sentence.

3. Friends and family are a mighty elixir. One secret of happiness? People. Innumerable studies suggest that having friends matters a great deal. Large-scale surveys by the University of Chicago's National Opinion Research Center, for example, find that those with five or more close friends are 50% more likely to describe themselves as "very happy" than those with smaller social circles. Compared with the happiness-increasing powers of human connection, the power of money looks feeble indeed. So throw a party, set up regular lunch dates—whatever it takes to invest in your friendships.

> —"Can Money Buy Happiness?" by David Futrelle. From *Money*, August 1, 2006. © 2006 *Money*. By permission.

What is the topic? _____

What is the most important point in your own words? _____

_____

Underline the topic sentence.

4. That's not the only way to get yourself to spend less and appreciate what you have more. Try counting your blessings. Literally. Sit down and make a short list of the things you're grateful for, from your garden to your kids. In a series of studies, psychologists Robert Emmons at the University of California–Davis, and Michael McCullough at the University of Miami found that those who did exercises to cultivate feelings of gratitude, like keeping weekly journals, ended up feeling happier, healthier, more energetic and more optimistic than those who didn't. Gratitude exercises help focus the mind on what really matters in life—which for most people means healthy relationships, not fancy new gadgets.

> —"Can Money Buy Happiness?" by David Futrelle. From *Money*, August 1, 2006. © 2006 *Money*. By permission.

What is the topic? _____

What is the most important point in your own words? _____

_____

Underline the topic sentence.

5. Coping is any attempt to deal with stress. People cope in several different ways. Sometimes people cope by trying to solve the problem at hand; for example, you may cope with a messy roommate by moving out. At other times, people focus on how they feel about the situation and deal with things on an emotional level; feeling sad after breaking up with your partner would be one way of coping with the stress of being alone. Sometimes people cope by simply redefining the

event as not stressful—an example of this approach would be saying that it was no big deal you failed to get the job you wanted. Still others focus on religious or spiritual approaches, perhaps asking God for help.

—From KAIL/CAVANAUGH. *Human Development,* 5E. © 2010 Wadsworth, a part of Cengage Learning, Inc. By permission.

What is the topic? _____

What is the most important point in your own words? _____

_____

Underline the topic sentence.

EXPLICIT MAIN IDEA IN A LONGER PASSAGE

The main idea for a whole reading can be located anywhere in the passage. Most often, the main idea appears in the introduction. The second-most likely place for an explicit main idea is in the conclusion. Remember from Chapter 1 that previewing is an essential reading strategy to get an overview of a reading. The reason that previewing involves reading the entire introductory paragraph as well as the entire concluding paragraph is because the author's main idea of the reading is most likely to be in one of these two spots. However, the main idea can also be in the middle of the reading.

If the reading includes a section indicated by a heading, this section can also have an overall main idea. Think of a section in a reading as a complete, shorter reading within a longer reading. Look at a heading, for example, in a textbook and consider what the author's most important point is about that section. You know how to turn headings into questions—to find the main idea of a section, find the answer to the question you pose about the heading.

To determine the main idea of a longer passage, you follow the same steps you used to determine the main idea of a paragraph. Ask yourself:

1. What is the topic?
2. What is the author's purpose?
3. What is the author's most important point about the topic?
4. The answer to #3 is the main idea.
5. Find that same answer to #3 in a sentence in the reading; this is the explicit main idea.

FOCUS ON COMPREHENSION: Author's Purpose and Explicit Main Ideas

Thinking It Through   FINDING THE MAIN IDEA OF A LONGER PASSAGE

Here you will apply the steps of finding the main idea of a longer passage from a textbook as well as finding the main idea, or topic sentence, of each paragraph. Begin by previewing the passage to figure out the topic, the author's purpose, and the author's main idea. Jot down your responses below or discuss your ideas with a partner. Then look at the explanation following the reading.

1. **What is the topic of the passage?**_____

2. **How many sections are in the reading?**_____

3. **What is the author's purpose?**_____

4. **What is the author's main idea about the topic (in your own words)?** _____

   _____

5. **Underline the main idea of the passage—the sentence that has the same ideas as you**

   wrote in question 4._____

After you've previewed the reading to answer these questions, read the passage completely to check your answers. Make adjustments to your answers if your reading reveals something new. Turn each heading into a question unless it's already in question form. Read to find the answer to the question.

   This passage is from the textbook *Sociology*, 10th edition, by Jon M. Shepard. Note that *stratification* in sociology refers to the levels of income, power, wealth, and prestige (or status) in a society.

Pose this title as a question and read to find the answer.
What are the consequences of stratification?

Consequences of Stratification
by Jon M. Shepard

1   The unequal distribution of income, wealth, power, and prestige has additional consequences for people. Two broad categories of class-related social consequences are *life chances* and *lifestyle*.

Pose this heading as a question and read to find the answer.
What are life chances? The answer is found in the first sentence.

Life Chances

2   *Life chances* refers to the likelihood of possessing the good things in life: health, happiness, education, wealth, legal protection, and even life itself. The

probability of acquiring and maintaining the material and nonmaterial rewards of life is significantly affected by social class level. Power, prestige, and economic rewards increase with social class level. The same is true for education, the single most important gateway to these rewards. But additional more subtle life chances exist, and these, too, vary with social class. These less obvious life chances are in good part the product of inequality in the distribution of education, power, prestige, and economic rewards.

How does social class affect more subtle life chances?

3   The probability of possessing life itself—the most fundamental, precious life chance—declines with social class level. Whether measured by the death rate or by life expectancy, the likelihood of a longer life is enhanced as people move up a stratification structure. This disparity is generated by differences in such things as neighborhood safety, possession of health insurance, quality of medical care, value placed on medical attention, and concern with proper nutrition.

4   <u>In light of differences in life expectancy, it is not surprising that physical health is affected by social class level.</u> Those lower in a stratification structure are more likely to be sick or disabled and to receive poorer medical treatment once they are ill. It is no different for mental health. Persons at lower class levels have a greater probability of becoming mentally disturbed and are less likely to receive therapeutic help, adequate or otherwise.

5   <u>Innumerable other life chance inequalities exist.</u> For example, the poor often pay more for the same goods and services. They are more likely to get caught for committing a crime, and when they are apprehended, they stand a greater chance of being convicted and serving prison time. Critics offer a dramatic example of class-related inferior public service when they contend

What is the answer to this question? The answer has three parts. Part 1 is found in the first sentence of paragraph 3. Part 2 is found in the first sentence of paragraph 4. Part 3 is found in the first sentence of paragraph 5. So the answer to the question is "Social class affects life, health, and other life chance inequalities."

Underline the topic sentence of paragraph 4.

Underline the topic sentence of paragraph 5.

(Continued)

FOCUS ON COMPREHENSION: Author's Purpose and Explicit Main Ideas

the federal government neglected the poor in New Orleans (mostly African Americans) in the evacuation process prior to Hurricane Katrina and in subsequent efforts to deal with the devastating consequences.

Lifestyle

How does social class affect lifestyle?

What is the answer to this question? The answer is in the second sentence of paragraph 6. This is the main idea of the section because paragraphs 6 and 7 discuss aspects of this statement.

6   The rich and the poor are separated by more than money. Social class differences in lifestyle can be observed in many areas of American life, including education, marital and family relations, child rearing, political attitudes and behavior, and religious affiliation.

7   People in higher social classes tend to marry later, experience lower divorce rates, and have better marital adjustment. While working-class and middle-class parents are more alike in childrearing practices than in the past, some differences remain. Compared with the middle class, lower-class parents tend to be less attentive to their children's social and emotional needs; in disciplining, they are more inclined to use physical punishment rather than reasoning. Middle-class parents are more interested in helping their children develop such traits as concern for others, self-control, and curiosity. Finally, working-class parents emphasize conformity, orderliness, and neatness, whereas middle-class parents stress self-direction, freedom, initiative, and creativity.

From SHEPARD. Cengage Advantage Books: *Sociology,* 10E. © 2010 Wadsworth, a part of Cengage Learning, Inc. By permission.

1. **What is the topic of the article?** The consequences of stratification, as indicated in the title.

2. **How many major sections are in the reading?** There are two: life chances and lifestyle. Since these two sections have the same type of heading print and size, they are equal in importance. This means that the main idea must mention both life chances and lifestyle.

3. **What is the author's purpose?** The author's purpose is to inform the reader about the consequences of stratification.

4. **What is the author's main idea about the topic (in your own words)?** The consequences of stratification are affected by two factors: life chances and lifestyle. This main idea statement answers a question you could pose from the title: "What are the consequences of stratification?"

5. **Underline the main idea of the article—the sentence that has the same ideas as you wrote in question 4.** The main idea is the second sentence of the passage: "Two broad categories of class-related social consequences are life chances and lifestyle."

On Your Own FINDING THE MAIN IDEA OF A LONGER PASSAGE

Apply the steps of finding the main idea of a longer passage from a textbook as well as finding the main idea, or topic sentence, of each paragraph. Begin by previewing the article to figure out the topic, the author's purpose, and the author's main idea. Jot down your responses here, or discuss your answers with a partner.

1. What is the topic of the passage? _____

2. How many major sections are in the reading? _____

3. What is the author's purpose? _____

4. What is the author's main idea about the topic (in your own words)? _____

_____

After you've previewed the reading to answer these questions, read the article completely. Make adjustments to your answers if your reading has revealed something new. Turn each heading into a question unless it's already in question form. Read to find the answer to the question. Answer the questions about main idea in the margins. This passage is from the textbook *Sociology*, 10th edition, by Jon M. Shepard.

(Continued)

FOCUS ON COMPREHENSION: Author's Purpose and Explicit Main Ideas

Turn the title into a question.

Underline the answer to the question.

Social Mobility
by Jon M. Shepard

1 **Social mobility** refers to the movement of individuals or groups within a stratification structure. In the United States, the term *mobility* implies an elevation in social class level. Beyond this, it is possible either to move down in social class or to move with little or no change in social class.

Turn this heading into a question.

Underline the answer to the question.

Types of Social Mobility

2 Social mobility can be horizontal or vertical. Both types of mobility can be measured either within the career of an individual—intragenerational mobility— or from one generation to the next—intergenerational mobility.

Answer this question by underlining the topic sentences in paragraphs 3 and 4.

How does horizontal mobility differ from vertical mobility?

3 A change from one occupation to another at the same general status level is called **horizontal mobility**. Examples of intragenerational horizontal mobility are familiar: an army captain becomes a public school teacher, a minister becomes a psychologist, a restaurant server becomes a taxi driver. The daughter of an attorney who becomes an engineer illustrates intergenerational horizontal mobility. Because horizontal mobility involves no real change in occupational status or social class, sociologists are not generally interested in investigating it.

4 Vertical mobility, however, is investigated extensively. In vertical mobility, occupational status or social class moves upward or downward. Vertical mobility can also be intragenerational or intergenerational. The simplest way to measure intragenerational mobility is to compare an individual's present occupation with his or her first one. Someone who began as a dockworker and later became an insurance sales person has

experienced upward intragenerational mobility. Intergenerational mobility involves the comparison of a parent's (or grandparent's) occupation with the child's occupation. If a plumber's daughter becomes a physician, upward intergenerational mobility has occurred. If a lawyer's son becomes a carpenter, downward intergenerational mobility has occurred.

From SHEPARD. Cengage Advantage Books: *Sociology*, 10E. © 2010 Wadsworth, a part of Cengage Learning, Inc. By permission.

Based on your answers to the marginal prompts, what is the main idea of this passage in your own words? Be careful to include the major details.

_____

_____

Practice Exercise 1: AUTHOR'S PURPOSE

Circle the author's purpose in writing the following passages. Look for key words that may indicate purpose.

1. **Advertise other people's products.** If you already have a Web site or a blog, look for vendors that offer related but non-competing products and see if they have an affiliate program. Stick to familiar products and brands—they're easier to sell. To promote those products:

    ● Place simple text or graphical ads in appropriate places on your site

    ● Include links to purchase products you review or recommend in a blog, discussion forum or mailing list you control

    ● Create a dedicated sales page or Web site to promote a particular product

    —Allen, "Make Money Online (Without Spending a Dime)" found online at
    http://entrepreneurs.about.com/od/homebasedbusiness/a/makemoneyonline.htm

    a. To inform

    b. To instruct

    c. To persuade

    d. To entertain

(Continued)

FOCUS ON COMPREHENSION: Author's Purpose and Explicit Main Ideas

2. The mind I love must have wild places, a tangled orchard where dark damsons drop in the heavy grass, an overgrown little wood, the chance of a snake or two, a pool that nobody's fathomed the depth of, and paths threaded with flowers planted by the mind.

—Katherine Mansfield

   a. To inform
   b. To instruct
   c. To persuade
   d. To entertain

3. Friendships are more common between children from the same race or ethnic group than between children from different groups, reflecting racial segregation in American society. Friendships among children of different groups are more common when a child's school and neighborhood are ethnically diverse.

—From KAIL/CAVANAUGH. *Human Development*, 5E. © 2010 Wadsworth,
a part of Cengage Learning, Inc. By permission.

   a. To inform
   b. To instruct
   c. To persuade
   d. To entertain

4. If money is your hope for independence you will never have it. The only real security that a man will have in this world is a reserve of knowledge, experience, and ability.

—Henry Ford

   a. To inform
   b. To instruct
   c. To persuade
   d. To entertain

5. As children develop, their friendships become more complex. For older elementary school children (ages 8 to 11), mutual liking and shared activities are joined by features that are more psychological in nature: trust and assistance. At this age, children expect that they can depend on their friends—their friends will be nice to them, will keep their promises, and won't say mean things about them

to others. Children also expect friends to step forward in times of need: A friend should willingly help with homework or willingly share a snack.

—From KAIL/CAVANAUGH. *Human Development*, 5E. © 2010 Wadsworth,
a part of Cengage Learning, Inc. By permission.

a. To inform

b. To instruct

c. To persuade

d. To entertain

Practice Exercise 2: FINDING EXPLICIT MAIN IDEAS

These passages are from both popular sources and textbooks. For each paragraph, determine the topic. Then formulate a main idea based on the topic in your mind. Last, underline the topic sentence.

1. More than 20% of the 292 self-made American billionaires on the most recent list of the World's Billionaires have either never started or never completed college. This is especially true of those destined for careers as technology entrepreneurs: Bill Gates, Steve Jobs, Michael Dell, Larry Ellison, and Theodore Waitt.

—From Duncan Greenberg, "Billionaire Clusters," Forbes Magazine, April 2, 2009.
Reprinted by Permission of Forbes Media LLC © 2011

2. Adolescence adds another layer of complexity to friendships. Mutual liking, common interests, and trust remain. In fact, trust becomes even more important in adolescent friendships. New to adolescence is intimacy—friends now confide in one another, sharing personal thoughts and feelings. Teenagers will reveal their excitement over a new romance or disappointment at not being cast in a school musical. Intimacy is more common in friendships among girls, who are more likely than boys to have one exclusive "best friend." Because intimacy is at the core of their friendships, girls are also more likely to be concerned about the faithfulness of their friends and worry about being rejected.

—From KAIL/CAVANAUGH. *Human Development*, 5E. © 2010 Wadsworth,
a part of Cengage Learning, Inc. By permission.

3. Understanding the impact of culture is particularly important in the United States, the most diverse country in the world. Hundreds of different languages are spoken, and in many states no racial or ethnic group constitutes a majority. The many customs that people bring offer insights into the broad spectrum of human experience and attest to the diversity of the U. S. population.

—From KAIL/CAVANAUGH. *Human Development*, 5E. © 2010 Wadsworth,
a part of Cengage Learning, Inc. By permission.

(Continued)

FOCUS ON COMPREHENSION: Author's Purpose and Explicit Main Ideas

4. Interestingly, culture plays an important role in how people perceive stress. These differences are grounded in the values people hold. For example, what constitutes stressors varies a great deal between Eastern societies such as India and Western societies such as England. Indians tend to believe that much of life is determined, whereas the British tend to emphasize personal choice and free will. Consequently, frustrations that Britons may feel when free will is thwarted may not be perceived as stressful by Indians. These differences point out the importance of understanding a culture when studying a concept such as stress.

> —From KAIL/CAVANAUGH. *Human Development*, 5E. © 2010 Wadsworth,
> a part of Cengage Learning, Inc. By permission.

5. People develop in the world, not in a vacuum. To understand human development, we need to know how people and their environments interact and relate to each other. That is, we need to view an individual's development as part of a much larger system in which no individual part can act without influencing all other aspects of the system. This larger system includes one's parents, children, and siblings as well as important individuals outside the family, such as friends, teachers, and co-workers. The system also includes institutions that influence development, such as schools, television, and the workplace. At a broader level, the society in which a person grows up plays a key role.

> —From KAIL/CAVANAUGH. *Human Development*, 5E. © 2010 Wadsworth,
> a part of Cengage Learning, Inc. By permission.

6. Your penchant for comparing yourself with the guy next door, like your tendency to grow bored with the things that you acquire, seems to be a deeply rooted human trait. An inability to stay satisfied is arguably one of the key reasons ancient man moved out of his drafty cave and began building the civilization you now inhabit. But you're not living in a cave, and you likely don't have to worry about mere survival. You can afford to step off the hedonic treadmill. The question is: How do you do it?

> —"Can Money Buy Happiness?" by David Futrelle. From *Money*,
> August 1, 2006. © 2006 *Money*. By permission.

7. From a certain perspective, the Amish live without a lot of the stuff most of us consider essential. They don't use cars, reject the Internet, avoid the mall, and prefer a quiet permanence to hefty bank accounts. The end result, however, is a happiness boom. When asked to rate their life satisfaction on a scale of 1 to 10, the Amish are as satisfied with their lives as members of the Forbes 400. There are, of course, many ways to explain the contentment of the Amish. (The community has strong ties, plenty of religious faith and stable families, all of which reliably correlate with high levels of well-being.) But I can't help wonder if part of their happiness is related to experience-stretching. They don't fret about getting the latest iPhone, or eating at the posh new restaurant, or buying the au courant handbag. The end result, perhaps, is that the Amish are better able to enjoy what really matters, which is all the stuff money can't buy.

> —From Wired.com, Jonah Lehrer, "Why Money Makes You Unhappy."
> Copyright © 2010 Condé Nast Publications. By permission.

8. While a healthy marriage is a clear happiness-booster, the kids that tend to follow are more of a mixed blessing. Studies of kids and happiness have come up with little more than a mess of conflicting data. "When you take moment-by-moment readouts of how people feel when they're taking care of the kids, they actually aren't very happy," notes Cornell psychologist Tom Gilovich. "But if you ask them they say that having kids is one of the most enjoyable things they do with their lives."

—"Can Money Buy Happiness?" by David Futrelle. From *Money,* Vol. 35, No. 8, August 1, 2006. © 2006 *Money*. By permission.

9. Women now constitute at least 40% of the industrialized world's paid workforce (World Bank, 1996), and about 60% of the workforce in the United States (U. S. Bureau of the Census, 1998). Immigration continues to affect the ethnic makeup of the North American workforce. For example, in previous years, Mexican, Puerto Rican, and Native American women traditionally showed lower rates of labor force participation, whereas African-American, Chinese, Japanese, and Filipino women showed rates higher than those of white women. However, all over North America, such ethnic differences are rapidly declining. Work, workers, and working are all changing.

—From GALLIANO. *Gender: Crossing Boundaries,* 1E. © 2003 Wadsworth, a part of Cengage Learning, Inc. By permission.

10. Even though stuff seldom brings you the satisfaction you expect, you keep returning to the mall and the car dealership in search of more. "When you imagine how much you're going to enjoy a Porsche, what you're imagining is the day you get it," says Gilbert. When your new car loses its ability to make your heart go pitter-patter, he says, you tend to draw the wrong conclusions. Instead of questioning the notion that you can buy happiness on the car lot, you begin to question your choice of car. So you pin your hopes on a new BMW, only to be disappointed again.

—"Can Money Buy Happiness?" by David Futrelle. From *Money,* Vol. 35, No. 8, August 1, 2006. © 2006 *Money*. By permission.

FOCUS ON VOCABULARY
Recognizing Prefixes and Suffixes

You have learned so far that looking at parts of a reading helps you understand the overall point of the reading most effectively. Similarly, you can improve your comprehension of vocabulary by looking at parts of a word. While your first strategy for decoding an unknown word is looking for context clues, your second strategy is looking at word parts. You do not necessarily have to memorize lists of word parts to use this strategy. In fact, your very best chance at expanding your reading, speaking, and writing vocabulary is to read! Most people who read for about a half hour each day for a year increase their vocabulary by over one thousand words!*

Word parts are called **affixes**. There are three parts of words:

- **Prefixes**—found at the beginning of words

- **Suffixes**—found at the end of words

- **Roots**—found in the middle of words

Not all words have all three of these parts. You'll learn more about root words in Chapter 4. In this chapter, you will learn to recognize prefixes and suffixes.

PREFIXES

Prefixes are the parts of words that come at the beginning of a word. When context clues don't help you figure out the meaning of a word, look at the beginning of the word. Brainstorm other words that have the same beginning or prefix.

For example, let's say you do not know the word *prefix* and it was in this sentence:

> The prefix is found at the beginning of a word.

There is an inference clue here that *prefix* is somehow associated with *beginning*. Think about other words you know that begin with *pre-*: *predict, presume, premeditate, prevent*, and *prescribe*. What do all these words have in common? They all have to do with something coming before, such as *predict*, which means to state or make known in advance. *Presume* means to assume or take for granted.

> I presume you want me to meet you at the usual time.

---

*Anderson, R. C., & Nagy, W. E. (1991). Word meanings. In R. Barr, M. L. Kamil, P. B. Mosenthal, & P. D. Pearson (Eds.), *Handbook of reading research* (Vol. 2, pp. 690–724). Hillsdale, NJ: Erlbaum.

Premeditate means to plan before doing something.

> Since he planned the crime in advance, he was charged with premeditated murder.

Prevent means to keep something from happening.

> I wish I could prevent anything bad from happening to my friend in Iraq.

Prescribe means to set down a rule, or to order a medicine or other treatment.

> The doctor said, "I'll prescribe a medicine that will help clear up your cough."

So, *prefix* means a part of a word that is at the beginning or comes before other parts of a word.

Table 3.4 lists 20 of the most common prefixes used in written English. These prefixes are extremely useful to know because they account for 97 percent of the prefixes you will encounter in your reading. Can you think of other words that contain each prefix? Look up words in the dictionary if none come to mind. Make sure that the word you use has the prefix you need (for more information on using a dictionary, see Chapter 6). Write your additions in the table.

TABLE 3.4 TWENTY COMMON PREFIXES

PREFIX	MEANING	EXAMPLE	OTHER WORDS YOU KNOW THAT USE THIS PREFIX
anti-	against	antidepressant	
de-	opposite, away from	detoxify	
*dis-**	not, opposite of	disease	
en-, em-	cause to	encode, empathy	

(Continued)

© Cengage Learning 2013

FOCUS ON VOCABULARY: Recognizing Prefixes and Suffixes

TABLE 3.4 TWENTY COMMON PREFIXES

PREFIX	MEANING	EXAMPLE	OTHER WORDS YOU KNOW THAT USE THIS PREFIX
fore-	before	foreshadow	
in-, im-	in	intoxicate, imbibe	
*in-, im-, il-, ir-**	not	interminable, improbable, illegal, irrational	
inter-	between	intervention	
mid-	middle	midbrain	
mis-	wrongly	mistake	
non-	not	nonsense	
over-	over	overdose	
pre-	before	prescribe	
*re-**	again	repetition	
semi-	half	semicircle	
sub-	under	submerge	
super-	above	superimpose	
trans-	across	transcript	
*un-**	not	unprepared	
under-	under	underscore	

*Most frequent prefixes that account for 97 percent of prefixed words in printed school English.

On Your Own   USING PREFIXES TO CHANGE THE MEANING OF A WORD

Using one of the following prefixes that negates a word (means "not"), convert these words to their opposite. Use a dictionary to define the word. The first two exercises are completed for you.

dis-   in-   im-   il-   ir-   non-   un-

Original Word	Prefix Added	New Meaning with Prefix
1. Honest	*Dis-* dishonest	Not honest
2. Clean	*Un-* unclean	Not clean
3. Legal		
4. Approve		
5. Reliable		
6. Conformist		
7. Probable		
8. Credible		
9. Regular		
10. Associate		

FOCUS ON VOCABULARY: Recognizing Prefixes and Suffixes

Other common prefixes have to do with numbers. Prefixes that indicate number can be very helpful to recognize as you read. They help you make an educated guess about the meaning of an unknown word. Look at the first column in Table 3.5. These prefixes look familiar to you, no doubt. Can you think of other words that contain each prefix? Write your additions in the table.

TABLE 3.5 NUMBER PREFIXES

PREFIX	MEANING	EXAMPLE	OTHER WORDS YOU KNOW THAT USE THIS PREFIX
uno-, uni-, mono-	one	*Uniform*—one type *Monocle*—one lens The monocle seems to be a uniform characteristic of the archetypal old-fashioned general.	
bi-, di-, duo-	two	*Bisect*—divided into two parts *Dual*—two The astute biologist was attempting to bisect the organism into dual entities.	
tri-	three	*Tricycle*—three wheels The bicycle soon replaces the tricycle for eager drivers.	
quad-	four	*Quadrangle*—four-sided shape At our campus, the quadrangle is the "village square" where student activities are held in nice weather.	

TABLE 3.5 NUMBER PREFIXES

PREFIX	MEANING	EXAMPLE	OTHER WORDS YOU KNOW THAT USE THIS PREFIX
quint-	five	*Quintuplets*—five babies at birth Quintuplets, while exceedingly rare, can occur without the use of fertility drugs.	
dec-, deca-	ten	*Decade*—10 years In the past decade, the adolescent use of "hard" drugs has diminished.	
cent-	hundred	*Centipede*—one hundred legged The centipede is aptly named since "*cent*" means "one hundred" and "*ped*" means "foot."	
milli-	thousand	*Millennium*—one thousand years The dawn of the new millennium in the year 2000 brought both excitement and fear.	
poly-, multi-	many	*Polygamy*—many spouses Polygamy is legal in many other countries, primarily those that have the official religion of Islam. *Multi*—many Multitalented people tend to be successful.	

FOCUS ON VOCABULARY: Recognizing Prefixes and Suffixes

On Your Own   USING NUMBER PREFIXES

Write the meaning of the number prefix beside the following words. Use a dictionary to define the word. The first two exercises are completed for you.

Word	Number Prefix Used	Meaning of Prefix	Meaning of Word
1. Century	*Cent-*	Hundred	100 years
2. Polyglot	*Poly-*	Many	Speaker of many languages
3. Millipede			
4. Monotone			
5. Bifocal			
6. Tripod			
7. Quadruped			
8. Polygamy			
9. Bigamy			
10. Monogamy			

SUFFIXES

Suffixes are the parts of words that come at the end of a word. Suffixes are useful to notice because they can indicate the part of speech of a word, such as whether it is an adjective, noun, adverb, or verb. Look at these examples.

- Beauti<u>ful</u> ⟶ The suffix -*ful* indicates an adjective.
- Beautiful<u>ly</u> ⟶ The suffix -*ly* indicates that the word describes how an action was done, so *beautifully* is an adverb.

Notice how you can convert the following words to another part of speech using a different suffix.

- *Biology* (noun) can be converted to an adjective, a word that modifies a noun, using the suffix -*al* ⟶ *biological*.
- *Happy* (adjective) can be converted to a noun by adding the suffix -*ness* ⟶ *happiness*. By adding -*ly*, *happy* can be converted to an adverb ⟶ *happily*.
- *Intention* (noun) can be converted to an adverb by adding the suffix -*ally* ⟶ *intentionally*.

Not all words can be converted to all four parts of speech, but some can. For example:

> *to comprehend* (infinitive verb)
> *comprehension* (-*ion* indicates noun)
> *comprehensible, comprehensive* (adjective)
> *comprehensively* (adverb)

Table 3.6 lists 20 of the most common suffixes used in written English. Can you think of other words that contain each suffix? Look up words in the dictionary if none come to mind. Write your additions in the table.

FOCUS ON VOCABULARY: Recognizing Prefixes and Suffixes

TABLE 3.6 TWENTY MOST COMMON SUFFIXES

SUFFIX	MEANING	EXAMPLE	OTHER WORDS YOU KNOW THAT USE THIS SUFFIX
-able, -ible	can be done	consumable, digestible,	
-al, -ial	having characteristics of	personal, partial	
-ed*	past tense of verbs	transformed	
-en	made of	sodden	
-er	comparative	stronger	
-er	one who	learner	
-est	comparative	toughest	
-ful	full of	plentiful	
-ic	having characteristics of	enthusiastic	
-ing*	verb form, present participle	transforming	
-ion, -tion, -ation, -ition	act, process	opinion, attraction, duration, partition	
-ity, -ty	state of	mobility	
-ive, -ative, -itive	adjective form of a noun	passive, talkative, sensitive	
-less	without	careless	
-ly*	characteristic of	lively	
-ment	action or process	achievement	

TABLE 3.6 TWENTY MOST COMMON SUFFIXES

SUFFIX	MEANING	EXAMPLE	OTHER WORDS YOU KNOW THAT USE THIS SUFFIX
-ness	state of, condition of	readiness	
-ous, -eous, -ious	possessing the qualities of	porous, igneous, ambitious,	
-s, -es*	more than one	books, boxes	
-y	characterized by	sensory	

© Cengage Learning 2013

*Most frequent suffixes that account for 97 percent of suffixed words in printed school English.

On Your Own   USING SUFFIXES TO CHANGE THE PART OF SPEECH OF A WORD

Convert the following words to other parts of speech using suffixes. Convert each word to an adjective, a noun, and an adverb. Hint: Not all noun forms require a suffix. The first two are completed as an example.

	Adjective	Noun	Adverb
1. attract	attractive	attraction	attractively
2. abuse	abusive	abuse	abusively
3. suggest			
4. create			
5. predict			

© Cengage Learning 2013

(Continued)

FOCUS ON VOCABULARY: Recognizing Prefixes and Suffixes

	Adjective	Noun	Adverb
6. appreciate			
7. talk			
8. invite			
9. combat			
10. force			

Practice Exercise 3: IDENTIFYING PREFIXES AND SUFFIXES

In the following sentences, identify the underlined word parts. Then, write the meaning of the word or its part of speech in the space provided. Don't forget to refer to the tables in the vocabulary section of this chapter to help you determine the best answers.

1. Dwonna was <u>anti</u>-establish<u>ment</u>. She was always fighting against government control in political rallies.

   Prefix means: _____

   Word means: _____

   Part of speech of word based on suffix: _____

2. David was accused of being <u>in</u>sensit<u>ive</u> because of his rude remarks.

   Prefix means: _____

   Word means: _____

   Part of speech of word based on suffix: _____

3. The diplomat was aiming for a <u>bi</u>later<u>al</u> agreement. He wanted both sides to sign the treaty.

   Prefix means: _____

   Word means: _____

   Part of speech of word based on suffix: _____

4. The students were <u>mis</u>inform<u>ed</u>—spring break was after week 8 of the semester, not week 9.

Prefix means: _____

Word means: _____

Part of speech of word based on suffix: _____

5. Jane considered herself <u>fore</u>warn<u>ed</u>. Julio told her that the class was very hard.

Prefix means: _____

Word means: _____

Part of speech of word based on suffix: _____

6. Frank was convicted of the crime since the evidence suggested <u>pre</u>meditat<u>ion</u>.

Prefix means: _____

Word means: _____

Part of speech of word based on suffix: _____

7. The summer is always the season I look forward to, despite the fact the weather has been <u>un</u>predict<u>able</u>.

Prefix means: _____

Word means: _____

Part of speech of word based on suffix: _____

8. Joe reviewed the wrong chapter for class. He was <u>un</u>questioning<u>ly</u> furious.

Prefix means: _____

Word means: _____

Part of speech of word based on suffix: _____

9. According to my instructor, my essay was affected by <u>under</u>develop<u>ment</u>. I got a C, whereas I usually get A's.

Prefix means: _____

Word means: _____

Part of speech of word based on suffix: _____

(Continued)

FOCUS ON VOCABULARY: Recognizing Prefixes and Suffixes

10. Michelle was <u>trans</u>formed by the new attitude and her recent success.

Prefix means: _____

Word means: _____

Part of speech of word based on suffix: _____

FOCUS ON READING STUDY SKILLS
Goal Setting and Study Environments

Setting goals and being motivated are qualities that can make the difference between success and failure in any sphere of life, but these attributes are particularly important in college. You know that motivation and time management are vital to coping with college stress. Setting goals and setting up a workable study environment allow you to stay motivated and remain committed to managing your time. Just as in reading you want to focus on the main points to understand an author's train of thought, in using effective reading study skills, you want to focus on the main point of your efforts and understand your own train of thought. Why are you making the sacrifices day-to-day to remain motivated and successful in college? For most of you, these sacrifices and this motivation have to do with your goals. Setting useable and realistic goals is vital to keep you on track.

SETTING ACHIEVABLE GOALS

Having both internal and external motivation for gaining a college education is the first step to success. Next, you need to consider and act on setting reasonable and achievable goals. Setting goals is important because doing so keeps you motivated and provides both a big picture for you to work toward as well as a step-by-step path for you to travel on along the way.

For some people, setting goals is something automatic and natural. For others, writing down goals seems forced and awkward. But actually *writing down* long-term, intermediate, and short-term goals is effective. If you do not know specifically what you want to accomplish, then how can you accomplish anything? Referring to written goals when things get rough can boost your motivation and put you back on the path to success.

Maybe you find it easy to set a mental plan of something you mean to do, such as doing quality work or getting good grades. But just having intentions may not be enough; convert those intentions into goals. What's the difference? An intention is a very general statement, whereas a goal provides strategies to make something happen. See the difference in the statements here:

FOCUS ON READING STUDY SKILLS: Goal Setting and Study Environments

INTENTIONS	GOALS
I intend to get a B in Reading Improvement this semester.	I will get a B in Reading Improvement this semester by completing all the readings *prior* to the class for which they are assigned.
I plan to pass my classes.	I will use spaced practice for test review by starting to study *at least 5* days before each test.
I will write good papers for college classes.	If I get a disappointing grade on a paper, I will make use of the writing and learning facilities at my college immediately.

© Cengage Learning 2013

Intentions are vague, while goals are concrete and specific. The key is to maintain your dedication to your goals. Too often, you start out motivated and eagerly set goals only to forget about them soon after. Setting and attaining goals requires self-discipline. Self-discipline helps you manage your time and sustain your motivation. Productive goal setting means that you attain the goals you set for the short term and actively work toward the goals you set for the intermediate and long term.

Just as your brain absorbs new information more easily when it's organized, as a student, when you are organized, aware of where you are going, and exactly what you need to accomplish to get there, you can more easily achieve your goals. It's easy for time to slip away, and without a concrete and realistic plan, you'll end up with little to show for that time. Better to have some concrete and realistic ideas of where you want to be by the end of the day, week, month, and year and have a step-by-step plan of how to get where you want to be. To do that, you need to set three types of goals.

- **Long-term goals** are life goals that help you see where you are now in relation to where you want to end up in the future. Long-term goals are important because they help you deal with the pressures, burdens, and sacrifices you make today. Think of long-term goals as the "light at the end of the tunnel" when you are staying up late to complete an assignment due the next day, but they must be something that is reasonably attainable, not just wishful thinking.

  Examples of attainable long-term goals

  — To use your sociology degree to obtain a position in a social service agency working with disadvantaged children

  — To make enough money at that job to afford to live in a decent apartment in the city of your choice

SETTING ACHIEVABLE GOALS   175

Examples of wishful thinking long-term goals

— To become a millionaire by the age of 30

— To be in a position to retire by the age of 35

● **Intermediate goals** are goals that span 2 to 5 years and lead you one step closer to achieving your long-term goal.

Examples of intermediate goals

— To create an action plan to attain an associate of arts degree within 2.5 years

— To transfer to a 4-year college to earn a bachelor's degree in sociology

— To plan out your course of study with an advisor at your college so you know exactly what courses you will need to complete during which semester

— To make sure that the courses for the associate's degree transfer smoothly to the program of study at the 4-year college or university to which you intend to transfer

● **Short-term goals** (which are sometimes called *objectives*) are the goals you set for yourself to accomplish more immediately that lead you to your intermediate and long-term goals. These are usually more weekly or monthly goals.

Examples of short-term goals

— To outline your psychology textbook chapter by Thursday, so you are prepared when the information is presented by your instructor in class on Friday morning

— To earn at least a C in each of your classes this semester, as that would put you in good standing academically

Table 3.7 shows examples of long-term, intermediate, and short-term goals. Notice how the short-term goals are more specific and concrete than the long-term and intermediate goals. Also, notice the words associated with each type of goal.

FOCUS ON READING STUDY SKILLS: Goal Setting and Study Environments

TABLE 3.7 EXAMPLES OF TYPES OF GOALS

LONG-TERM GOAL	INTERMEDIATE GOAL	SHORT-TERM GOALS
<u>I want</u> to be an educational assistant and earn a good living.	<u>I want</u> to achieve an associate's degree in education with a certificate in early childhood education assisting.	<u>I will</u> attend each class. <u>I will</u> review my notes before each class. <u>I will</u> complete all reading prior to the class for which it is assigned. <u>I will</u> sit near the front of the class to focus my attention. <u>I will</u> ask questions to clarify any misunderstandings during the class period.

QUICK TIPS TEN TIPS FOR SETTING GOALS

1. Make your goals specific. The more specific a goal is, the more focused you will be.

2. Make your goals realistic. Don't get sidetracked by wishful thinking.

3. Write your goals down where you can see them. Using a list where you can check off that your goal is attained will help you focus.

4. Make your goal measurable. Be able to cross the goal off your list once it's achieved. To do this, your goal needs to be specific, such as getting a certain grade in a class or attaining a certificate.

5. Make your goals with a specific time period in mind. Add target dates for completion of your goals.

6. Get others to support your goals.

7. Do not get sidetracked by setbacks.

8. Do not get sidetracked by negative people.

9. Review your goals regularly. Read them over to keep them fresh in your mind.

10. Revise your goals regularly. As your plans unfold, your goals should change. Make sure your goals are current. For example, a setback may require that you take longer to attain your degree. Your long-term goal may still be active, but the short-term and intermediate goals may need some adjustments.

On Your Own SETTING LONG-TERM, INTERMEDIATE, AND SHORT-TERM GOALS

Identify several goals for yourself. Be sure to make your short-term goals specific and concrete. It is helpful to begin each objective with the words *I will*.

Long-Term Goals	Intermediate Goals	Short-Term Goals

© Cengage Learning 2013

CREATING A MOTIVATING STUDY ENVIRONMENT

Having an organized study environment that is not distracting will allow you to do your best work and sets you up to learn most efficiently. A **study environment** is a physical and mental space that you create in order to enable you to focus and produce

FOCUS ON READING STUDY SKILLS: Goal Setting and Study Environments

results. To ensure a productive mental "space" for doing your best work requires that you eliminate distractions, which may mean clearing your physical and mental environment. You don't want to be thinking about other concerns as you work on your assignments. Also, you don't want to be distracted and uncomfortable in the environment in which you do your studies. As a result, you want to choose an environment that is conducive to and allows maximum concentration.

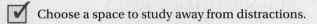

QUICK TIPS CHOOSE YOUR STUDY ENVIRONMENT

- ☑ Choose a space to study away from distractions.

- ☑ Try to study at the same time and in the same space each day. This way, you will learn to associate the space with learning and concentrate more easily.

- ☑ Avoid distractions, such as sounds from television, music, or phones.

- ☑ Eat before you do your work, or study when you're not hungry, so that you aren't distracted.

- ☑ Write down everything you need to do that you think you'll forget *before* you sit down to study so it won't distract your thought process.

- ☑ Make sure you have everything you need *before* you start.

- ☑ Break your assignments into manageable chunks, and set your study time to about 50 minutes to an hour before a 10- to 15-minute break.

- ☑ Do not study on your bed because it may make you feel like sleeping!

- ☑ Study at a time when you feel alert. If you are a night person, study in the evening. If you are a morning person, set your alarm so you can complete some work before you start your day. (To see if you are a morning or night person, refer to the self-assessment in Chapter 5.)

APPLICATIONS

These applications will develop your skills of determining author's purpose, topic, and explicit main ideas, as well as using word parts and context clues for vocabulary comprehension. Follow the instructions for each application, and then answer the Comprehension Check questions. Each application serves to release more responsibility to the reader as these techniques become more automatic.

APPLICATION

This reading, from *Newsweek,* is difficult in terms of vocabulary. But you can read and understand it with concentration, using all the vocabulary skills you have learned. However, some words have been defined in the margin to help you understand the author's train of thought.

Preview this reading first, and then read the article in its entirety. As you read, answer the questions in the margin about finding main ideas. After you read, complete the Comprehension Check that follows the reading.

Why Money Doesn't Buy Happiness
By Sharon Begley

Read to answer the question: Why doesn't money buy happiness?

1   All in all, it was probably a mistake to look for the answer to the eternal question—"Does money buy happiness?"—from people who practice what's called the **dismal** science. For when economists tackled the question, they started from the observation that when people put something up for sale they try to get as much for it as they can, and when people buy something they try to pay as little for it as they can. Both sides in the <u>transaction</u>, the economists noticed, are therefore behaving as if they would be more satisfied (happier, dare we say) if they wound up receiving more money (the seller) or holding on to more money (the buyer). Hence, more money must be better than less, and the only way more of something can be better than less of it is if it brings you greater contentment. The economists' conclusion: the more money you have, the happier you must be.

Underline the main idea of paragraph 1.

Dismal means "depressing."

2   Depressed **debutantes**, suicidal CEOs, miserable **magnates** and other unhappy rich folks aren't the only ones giving the lie to this. "Psychologists have spent decades studying the relation between wealth and happiness," writes Harvard University psychologist Daniel Gilbert in his best-selling "Stumbling

Debutantes means "high-society women."
Magnates means "people of power."

Underline the main idea of paragraph 2 and 3.

(Continued)

Abject means "hopeless."

on Happiness," "and they have generally concluded that wealth increases human happiness when it lifts people out of **abject** poverty and into the middle class but that it does little to increase happiness thereafter."

3   That flies in the face of intuition, not to mention economic theory. According to standard economics, the most important commodity you can buy with additional wealth is choice. If you have $20 in your pocket, you can decide between steak and peanut butter for dinner, but if you have only $1 you'd better hope you already have a jar of jelly at home. Additional wealth also lets you satisfy additional needs and wants, and the more of those you satisfy the happier you are supposed to be.

Underline the main idea of paragraph 4.

Chronically means "constantly."

4   The trouble is, choice is not all it's cracked up to be. Studies show that people like selecting from among maybe half a dozen kinds of pasta at the grocery store but find 27 choices overwhelming, leaving them **chronically** on edge that they could have chosen a better one than they did. And wants, which are nice to be able to afford, have a bad habit of becoming needs (iPod, anyone?), of which an advertising- and media-saturated culture create endless numbers. Satisfying needs brings less emotional well-being than satisfying wants.

Nonlinear means "not straight forward."

Penury means "severe poverty."

Underline the main idea of paragraph 5.

5   The **nonlinear** nature of how much happiness money can buy—lots more happiness when it moves you out of **penury** and into middle-class comfort, hardly any more when it lifts you from millionaire to decamillionaire—comes through clearly in global surveys that ask people how content they feel with their lives. In a typical survey people are asked to rank their sense of well-being or happiness on a scale of 1 to 7, where 1 means "not at all satisfied with my life" and 7 means "completely satisfied." Of the American multimillionaires who responded, the average happiness score was 5.8. Homeless people in Calcutta came in at 2.9. But before you assume that money does buy happiness after all, consider who else rated themselves around 5.8: the Inuit of northern Greenland, who do not exactly lead a life of luxury, and the cattle-herding Masai of Kenya, whose dung huts have no electricity or running water. And proving Gilbert's point about money buying happiness only when it lifts you out of abject poverty, slum dwellers in Calcutta—one economic rung above the homeless—rate themselves at 4.6.

6   Studies tracking changes in a population's reported level of happiness over time have also dealt a death blow to the money-buys-happiness claim. Since World War II the gross domestic product **per capita** has tripled in the United States. But people's sense of well-being, as measured by surveys asking some variation of "Overall, how satisfied are you with your life?" has barely budged. Japan has had an even more **meteoric** rise in GDP per capita since its postwar misery, but measures of national happiness have been flat, as they have also been in Western Europe during its long postwar boom, according to social psychologist Ruut Veenhoven of Erasmus University in Rotterdam. A 2004 analysis of more than 150 studies on wealth and happiness concluded that "economic indicators have glaring shortcomings" as approximations of well-being across nations, wrote Ed Diener of the University of Illinois, Urbana-Champaign, and Martin E. P. Seligman of the University of Pennsylvania. "Although economic output has risen steeply over the past decades, there has been no rise in life satisfaction . . . and there has been a substantial increase in depression and distrust."

Underline the main idea of paragraph 6.

Per capita means "for each person."

Meteoric means "very fast."

7   That's partly because in an expanding economy, in which former luxuries such as washing machines become necessities, the newly **affluent** don't feel the same joy in having a machine do the laundry that their grandparents, suddenly freed from washboards, did. They just take the Maytag for granted. "Americans who earn $50,000 per year are much happier than those who earn $10,000 per year," writes Gilbert, "but Americans who earn $5 million per year are not much happier than those who earn $100,000 per year." Another reason is that an expanding paycheck, especially in an expanding economy, produces expanding **aspirations** and a sense that there is always one more cool thing out there that you absolutely have to have. "Economic success falls short as a measure of well-being, in part because materialism can negatively influence well-being," Diener and Seligman conclude.

Underline the main idea of paragraph 7.

Affluent means *"rich."*

Aspirations means "goals."

8   If money doesn't buy happiness, what does? Grandma was right when she told you to value health and friends, not money and stuff. Or as Diener and Seligman put it, once your basic needs are met "differences in well-being are less frequently due to income, and are more frequently due to factors such as social relationships and enjoyment at work." Other

Underline the main idea of paragraph 8.

(Continued)

researchers add fulfillment, a sense that life has meaning, belonging to civic and other groups, and living in a democracy that respects individual rights and the rule of law. If a nation wants to increase its population's sense of well-being, says Veenhoven, it should make "less investment in economic growth and more in policies that promote good governance, liberties, democracy, trust and public safety."

Underline the main idea of paragraph 9.

9   (Curiously, although money doesn't buy happiness, happiness can buy money. Young people who describe themselves as happy typically earn higher incomes, years later, than those who said they were unhappy. It seems that a sense of well-being can make you more productive and more likely **to show initiative** and other traits that lead to a higher income. Contented people are also more likely to marry and stay married, as well as to be healthy, both of which increase happiness.)

To show initiative means "to be proactive."

Underline the main idea of paragraph 10.

10   If more money doesn't buy more happiness, then the behavior of most Americans looks downright <u>insane</u>, as we work harder and longer, decade after decade, to fatten our W-2s. But what is insane for an individual is crucial for a national economy—that is, ever more growth and consumption. Gilbert again: "Economies can blossom and grow only if people are **deluded** into believing that the production of wealth will make them happy . . . Economies thrive when individuals strive, but because individuals will strive only for their own happiness, it is essential that they mistakenly believe that producing and consuming are routes to personal well-being." In other words, if you want to do your part for your country's economy, forget all of the above about money not buying happiness.

Deluded means "tricked."

"Why Money Doesn't Buy Happiness," by Sharon Begley. From *Newsweek*, Oct 15, 2007, © 2007 The Newsweek/Daily Beast Company LLC. By permission.

COMPREHENSION CHECK

TRUE/FALSE QUESTIONS

For the following statements, write a *T* if the statement is true or an *F* if the statement is false based on the reading.

___   1. Economists believe the more money you have, the happier you must be.

___   2. Psychologists believe that money brings happiness only when it lifts you out of extreme poverty. After that, more money does not really bring happiness.

___   3. A lot of choice in, for example, types of food to buy makes people happier.

___   4. According to studies, people are not that much happier when they have basic needs met and a lot of money.

___   5. According to studies, money does buy happiness for the very rich.

LITERAL COMPREHENSION—MULTIPLE CHOICE

Circle the best answer for the following questions.

Understanding Main Ideas

6. According to the reading, does money buy happiness?
   a. While there is a relationship between money and happiness at the lower-income levels, once you hit a certain income, money does not buy happiness.
   b. Studies show that money does buy happiness.
   c. Money makes people happy when they have a lot of choices to make.
   d. Money does not make very poor people happy.

Understanding Secondary Information and Locating Information

7. What is the "economic theory" in paragraph 3?
   a. The theory that money does not buy choice.
   b. The theory that poor people need more choices.
   c. The theory that money does not buy choice for the rich.
   d. The theory that money ought to buy choice.

8. What is the problem with choice as discussed in paragraph 4?
   a. A bit of choice is bad because it is confusing.
   b. A bit of choice is good; too much choice is confusing.
   c. A lot of choice is better than a little.
   d. A little choice makes people less happy.

9. In paragraph 6, what evidence does the author provide to backup the idea that money does not buy happiness?
   a. Studies have shown that in Japan, the United States, and Western Europe, despite economic growth, happiness ratings have not increased.
   b. Studies have shown that in Japan, the United States, and Western Europe, happiness ratings have increased.
   c. Studies show that happiness increases when we have more choices.
   d. Studies show that there is no relationship between money and happiness in very poor countries.

(Continued)

10. What is the reasoning in paragraph 7 that we are no more satisfied today as we were in past generations?

    a. What was a necessity then is now a luxury.

    b. What was a luxury then is now a necessity.

    c. The more you make, the more you think you need.

    d. We seem to need more now than we did and, as a result, we need more money to attain those needs.

INFERENTIAL COMPREHENSION—MULTIPLE CHOICE

Circle the best answer for the following questions.

Making Inferences

11. The author puts all of paragraph 9 in parentheses. Why do you think she does this?

    a. Because paragraph 9 is not important

    b. Because the point in paragraph 9—that happiness seems to lead to making money—is not directly on topic

    c. Because paragraph 9 is not relevant to the discussion

    d. Because the point in paragraph 9 is the most important point

12. In paragraph 10, the author says that economies thrive when people feel that making money will make them happy. Explain this reasoning.

    a. If Americans realized that money doesn't bring happiness, they wouldn't work as hard and the economy would suffer.

    b. If Americans realize that money brings happiness, they will work less.

    c. If people in other countries realize that money will bring happiness, they will work harder than Americans.

    d. If people in other countries want money, they will move to America.

Applying Information

13. In paragraph 2, the author writes, "Depressed debutantes, suicidal CEOs, miserable magnates and other unhappy rich folks aren't the only ones giving the lie to this." What is the lie?

    a. The lie is that money buys happiness.

    b. The lie is that money does not buy happiness.

    c. These people are lying that they are unhappy.

    d. These people are lying to each other.

14. If psychologists are right that money does not buy happiness, what would this mean to the American economy?

   a. People will work harder.

   b. People will move to countries where money does buy happiness.

   c. People will move here from countries where money does not buy happiness.

   d. People will not work as hard.

Understanding Sentence Relationships

15. Paragraph 3 begins, "That flies in the face of intuition." What does the author mean?

   a. That we find it hard to believe that money does not buy happiness

   b. That economists would agree with this statement

   c. That people in other countries would agree with this statement

   d. That Americans would agree with this statement

INCREASE YOUR COLLEGE-LEVEL VOCABULARY

16. In paragraph 1, what does the prefix and suffix indicate in the word *transaction*? _____

   _____

   List other words that include the prefix *trans-*. _____

17 In paragraph 5, what does the prefix *non-* mean in *nonlinear*? _____

   What part of speech is the word? _____

   List other words that include the prefix *non-*. _____

18. In paragraph 5, what does the word *decamillionaire* mean, based on its prefix? _____

   _____

   What part of speech is the word? _____

   List other words that include the prefix *deca-*. _____

19. In paragraph 5, what does *multi-* mean in *multimillionaires*? _____

   What part of speech is the word? _____

   List other words that include the prefix *multi-*. _____

20. In paragraph 10, what does the prefix *in-* mean in the word *insane*? _____

   What part of speech is the word? _____

   Change this word into its noun form by changing the suffix. _____

   List other words that include the prefix *in-*. _____

(Continued)

SHORT-ANSWER QUESTIONS

21. Do you think money buys happiness?

22. In paragraph 7, the author quotes an expert who says, "But Americans who earn $5 million per year are not much happier than those who earn $100,000 per year." Do you agree with this economic cutoff? At what income level, in your opinion, does money no longer buy happiness?

23. If money does not buy happiness, would you live your life differently?

APPLICATION ②

This reading is from the college sociology textbook *Sociology* by Jon M. Shepard. Preview this reading as you learned in Chapter 1. Then, read it all the way through, responding to the prompts in the margin. Last, answer the Comprehension Check questions that follow the reading.

Do you recall what *stratification* means from earlier in the chapter? *Stratification* refers to the levels of income, wealth, prestige, and power in a society. *Gross domestic product* (or GDP) is a term that refers to the measurement of a country's total money (goods and services) produced. This application concerns a global look at money, wealth, and global economies.

Global Stratification
by Jon M. Shepard

Identification of Economies

1   Thus far, the focus has been on stratification within societies. But scarce desirables—income, wealth, prestige, and power— are also differentially distributed among nations. The gross domestic product (GDP) of a country—the total value of the

Pose a guide question, based on this heading.

Underline the answer to this question.

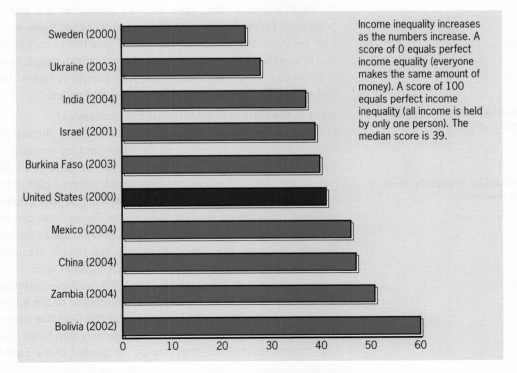

Income inequality increases as the numbers increase. A score of 0 equals perfect income equality (everyone makes the same amount of money). A score of 100 equals perfect income inequality (all income is held by only one person). The median score is 39.

FIGURE 3.4 Levels of Income Inequality Vary Around the World

Source: World Bank, World Development indicators, online database (http://publications.worldbank.org/WDV, accessed May 25, 2007)/ It also appears on the 2007 World Population Data Sheet. (Washington, DC: Population Reference Bureau), 2007.

(Continued)

goods and services it produces in one year—is a reasonably good indicator for classifying countries into economic categories. GDP is useful both because it is a single, measurable economic indicator and because a nation's economic rank is highly correlated with the extent of its prestige and power.

What does the prefix *in-* mean in *inequality*?
What part of speech is inequality?
Underline the main idea of paragraph 2.

Underline the answer to this heading/question.

2   Predictably, levels of income inequality vary around the world, from low income **inequality** in Sweden and Ukraine to moderate income inequality in the United States to high income inequality in Bolivia. The United States' score of 41 reflects greater income inequality than exists in most developed countries.

Where Are the High-Income Economies, and How Wealthy Are They?

3   The richest countries, nearly all capitalistic, include countries such as England, Germany, France, Norway, Finland, Denmark, Sweden, and Switzerland in western Europe; the United States and Canada in North America; Australia and New Zealand in Oceania; and Japan in Asia. A few oil-rich nations, such as Kuwait and the United Arab Emirates, also have high-income economies. High-income economies, spanning approximately one-quarter of the Earth's land surface, have only 15 percent of the world's population (approximately 800 million people). Yet, these countries are in control of most of the wealth. Due to this concentration of wealth, the standard of living of nearly all the people living in these countries, even most of the poor people, is higher than that for the average person in low-income economies.

Underline the answer to this heading/question.

What Is the Nature of Middle-Income Economies?

4   Middle-income economies include, but are not limited to, nations historically founded on or influenced by socialist or communist economies. This encompasses members of the former Soviet Union, many of them **renamed** and now part of the new Commonwealth of Independent States that was created in 1991. Other countries that fell into the Soviet orbit but are not part of the Commonwealth of Independent States include Poland, Bulgaria, the Czech Republic, the Slovak Republic, Hungary, Romania, Estonia, Latvia, Lithuania, and Cuba.

What does the prefix *re-* mean in *renamed*?

5   From the end of World War II until 1989, all these countries, under the political, economic, and military control of the former Soviet Union, constituted the Eastern bloc in the Cold War against the West. These countries are no more densely populated than high-income economies—they occupy 15 percent of the Earth's

land with only 10 percent of the world's population (about 500 million people). Although more prosperous than low-income countries, citizens of middle-income economies do not enjoy the standard of living characteristic of high-income economies. The extent of industrialization in these countries is variable. Most inhabitants of these countries live in urban areas; in comparison to countries with high-income economies, though, a greater percentage of their people live in rural areas and participate in agricultural economic activities.

6   In 1989, eastern European countries (freed of Soviet domination, its socialist economy, and government-controlled bureaucracy) turned to capitalism and its market mechanism. A major source of current political and economic turmoil in the former Soviet Union revolves around the struggle between the socialist and capitalist roads to economic development.

Underline the main idea of paragraph 6.

7   The middle-income category contains other countries that have never been part of the old Soviet bloc. These countries are spread from Mexico, Latin America, and South America to parts of Africa to Thailand, Malaysia, and New Guinea in the Far East.

Underline the main idea of paragraph 7.

What Is Distinctive About Low-Income Economies?

8   The economic base of low-income economies is primarily agricultural. These countries span the globe from south of the United States border to Africa to China to Indonesia. Population density within these countries as a whole is very high. In fact, just over two-thirds of the world's population (more than 5 billion people) live on 60 percent of the Earth's land (Livernash and Rodenburg 1998).

Underline the answer to this heading/question.

9   No single economic system is typical of these economies. Capitalism, socialism, and various combinations of each are practiced. If these countries share no economic ideology, they do share one important economic characteristic: they are **unimaginably** poor. Problems of the poor in high-income countries are real and significant. But most people in low-income economies live annually on less than 7 percent of the official poverty line in the United States. The plight of the poor in low-income countries is particularly bleak because they are trapped in a double bind. Their populations are exploding (due to declining infant mortality rates while they maintain their traditionally high birth rate).

What does the prefix un- mean in unimaginably?

From SHEPARD. Cengage Advantage Books: *Sociology,* 10E. © 2010 Wadsworth, a part of Cengage Learning, Inc. By permission.

(Continued)

COMPREHENSION CHECK

TRUE/FALSE QUESTIONS

For the following statements, write a *T* if the statement is true or an *F* if the statement is false based on the reading.

___ 1. Different societies have different distributions of wealth, power, prestige, and income.

___ 2. A country's GDP is an inaccurate measure of that country's wealth.

___ 3. Levels of income inequality means the degree to which people in a country have the same amount of money.

___ 4. Levels of income inequality means the degree to which people in a country have different amounts of money.

___ 5. The United States' score of 41 reflects greater income inequality than exists in most developed countries.

LITERAL COMPREHENSION—MULTIPLE CHOICE

Circle the best answer for the following questions.

Understanding Main Ideas

6 What are high-income countries?

    a. Countries that are capitalistic and largely Western

    b. Countries that are socialist and Eastern

    c. Countries with a low GDP

    d. Countries that believe money does not buy happiness

7. What are middle-income countries?

    a. Countries with a low GDP

    b. Nations that are historically socialist or communist economies

    c. Western capitalist countries

    d. Eastern countries

8. What are low-income economies?

    a. The economic base of low-income economies is primarily agricultural.

    b. These countries span the globe from south of the United States border to Africa to China to Indonesia.

    c. Both agricultural economies as well as those economies south of the United States, African, China, and Indonesia

    d. The U.S. economy

Understanding Secondary Information and Locating Information

9. According to paragraph 3, what is the standard of living like for high-income economies?

    a. The standard of living is lower than that for the average person in low-income economies.

    b. The standard of living is lower than that for an average person in high-income economies.

    c. The standard of living is higher than that for an average person in high-income economies.

    d. The standard of living is higher than that for the average person in low-income economies.

10. Although more prosperous than low-income countries, why don't citizens of middle-income economies enjoy the standard of living characteristic of high-income economies (paragraph 5)?

    a. The extent of industrialization in these countries is variable.

    b. Most inhabitants of these countries live in urban areas.

    c. Both the variable industrialization and the population mainly in urban areas

    d. Because they are urban populations that are not industrialized

11. Which of the following does not explain why low-income countries are suffering?

    a. The economic base of low-income economies is primarily agricultural.

    b. Population density within these countries as a whole is very high.

    c. They have a relatively small GDP.

    d. They are not enough people living in cities to make money.

INFERENTIAL COMPREHENSION—MULTIPLE CHOICE

Circle the best answer for the following questions.

Making Inferences

12. How does the GDP help identify economies?

    a. The GDP of a country—the total value of the goods and services it produces in one year—allows economists to assess the level of an economy.

(Continued)

　　b.　The GDP of a country—the total value of the goods and services it produces in one year—is *not* helpful in assessing the level of an economy.

　　c.　The GDP is not related to the economy.

　　d.　The GDP may be an indicator of the economy in some countries but not others.

Applying Information

13.　Which of the following factors does not explain why there is such diversity between high-income and low-income countries?

　　a.　Population

　　b.　Religion

　　c.　Economic system

　　d.　GDP

14.　Look at Figure 3.4 about income inequality. Why is the United States near the middle of the graph?

　　a.　The United States has little income inequality.

　　b.　The United States has the most income inequality.

　　c.　The United States has more income inequality than most of the other nations.

　　d.　The United States has less income inequality than most of the other nations.

Understanding Sentence Relationships

15.　Does the author arrange his discussion of economies in a specific order? If so, in what order are they discussed?

　　a.　The economies are discussed from most prosperous to least.

　　b.　The economies are discussed from least prosperous to most.

　　c.　The economies are not discussed in a particular order.

　　d.　There is little discussion of the economies, so it is hard to tell.

INCREASE YOUR COLLEGE-LEVEL VOCABULARY

Define the following key terms from this reading.

16.　GDP:

_____

_____

17.　High-income economies:

_____

_____

18. Middle-income economies:

_____

_____

19. Low-income economies:

_____

_____

20. Global stratification:

_____

_____

Fill out the chart to analyze the prefixes and suffixes for the following words found in Application 2.

WORD FROM THE READING	PREFIX	PREFIX MEANING	SUFFIX	PART OF SPEECH	NEW WORD USING PREFIX
21. predictably					
22. inequality					
23. unimaginably					
24. declining					

© Cengage Learning 2013

SHORT-ANSWER QUESTIONS

25. Do you have experience with someone from a country with a middle- or low-income economy, or have you visited a country with a middle- or low-income economy? What information have you learned about what life is like in this type of economy?

26. If a high-income inequality means there is a big difference between the rich and the poor, explain what other types of inequality may exist in countries with a high degree of income inequality. Use Figure 3.4 as a reference.

27. Look at Figure 3.4 about income inequality across nations. Were you surprised at any of the information? Were you surprised at how the United States ranks in comparison with other countries? Why or why not?

WRAPPING IT UP

STUDY OUTLINE

This is a list of key terms from this chapter for you to define in an organized format. In the following study outline, fill in the definitions and a brief explanation of the key terms in the Your Notes column. Use the strategy of spaced practice to review these key terms on a regular basis. Use this study guide to review this chapter's key topics.

KEY TERM	YOUR NOTES
Author's purpose	
Biased words	
Main idea	
Explicit main idea	
Topic sentence	
Thesis	
Affixes	
Prefixes	
Suffixes	

KEY TERM	YOUR NOTES
Long-term goals	
Intermediate goals	
Short-term goals	
Study environment	

WHAT DID YOU LEARN?

Now, go back to the chart at the beginning of this chapter, noting what you wanted to learn from the chapter about main ideas. Did you learn what you wanted to learn? If not, take action: Ask questions of your instructor, at your college's learning resource center, or of a classmate. Reread parts of this chapter to clarify what you did not understand.

GROUP ACTIVITY: FINDING MAIN IDEAS IN READINGS ABOUT MONEY AND HAPPINESS

As a group, find a short reading on one of the following topics. Determine the author's purpose, highlight the thesis of the article, and underline the explicit main ideas in the paragraphs that contain topic sentences. Present your answers to your class.

- Happiness
- Wealth
- Billionaires
- How to save money
- Credit cards
- Poverty

WRAPPING IT UP

QUESTIONS FOR WRITING, DISCUSSION, OR REFLECTION

1. Several readings in this chapter concern money and happiness. How will this information affect your short-term, intermediate, and long-term goals?

2. Choose a textbook you use in another class and find an example or examples of the following:

    a. A prefix clue

    b. A suffix clue

    c. An explicit main idea of a paragraph

    d. An explicit main idea of a section

    e. An explicit main idea of the whole reading

3. For another class, try the technique of locating main ideas to focus your reading. Write a paragraph concerning how the technique worked.

4. What is your opinion of the relationship between money and happiness. Do you feel that money creates happiness?

 # POST-ASSESSMENT

This assessment will help you understand your strengths and weaknesses in learning, understanding, and applying the skills and strategies discussed in this chapter. Preview the following article. Then read it all the way through, and answer the Comprehension Check questions that follow.

Billionaire Clusters
by Duncan Greenberg

Want to become a billionaire? Up your chances by dropping out of college, working at Goldman Sachs or joining Skull & Bones.

1   Are billionaires born or made? What are the common attributes among the <u>über-wealthy</u>? Are there any true secrets of the self-made?

2   We get these questions a lot, and decided it was time to go beyond the broad answers of smarts, ambition and luck by sorting through our database of wealthy individuals in search of bona fide trends. We analyzed everything from the billionaires' parents' professions to where they went to school, their track records in the early stages of their careers and other experiences that may have put them on the path to extreme wealth.

3   Our admittedly unscientific study of the 657 self-made billionaires we counted in February for our list of the World's Billionaires yielded some interesting results.

4   First, a significant percentage of billionaires had parents with a high aptitude for math. The ability to crunch numbers is crucial to becoming a billionaire, and mathematical prowess is hereditary. Some of the most common professions among the parents of American billionaires (for whom we could find the information) were engineer, accountant and small-business owner.

5   Consistent with the rest of the population, more American billionaires were born in the fall than in any other season. However, relatively few billionaires were born in December, traditionally the month with the eighth highest birth rate. This anomaly holds true among billionaires in the U.S. and abroad.

6   More than 20% of the 292 self-made American billionaires on the most recent list of the World's Billionaires have either never started or never completed college. This is especially true of those destined for careers as technology entrepreneurs: Bill Gates, Steve Jobs, Michael Dell, Larry Ellison, and Theodore Waitt.

7   Billionaires who derive their fortunes from finance make up one of the most highly educated <u>sub-groups</u>: More than 55% of them have graduate degrees. Nearly 90% of those with M.B.A.s obtained their master's degree from one of three Ivy League schools: Harvard, Columbia or U. Penn's Wharton School of Business.

8   Goldman Sachs has attracted a large share of hungry minds that went on to garner 10-figure fortunes. At least 11 current and recent billionaire financiers worked at Goldman early in their careers, including Edward Lampert, Daniel Och, Tom Steyer and Richard Perry.

9   Several billionaires suffered a bitter professional setback early in their careers that heightened their fear of failure. <u>Pharmaceutical</u> tycoon R.J. Kirk's first venture was a flop—an experience he regrets but appreciates. "Failure early on is a necessary condition for success, though not a sufficient one," he told Forbes in 2007.

10   According to a statement read by Phil Falcone during a congressional hearing in November, his botched buyout of a company in Newark in the early 1990s taught him "several valuable lessons that have had a profound impact upon my success as a hedge fund manager."

11   Several current and former billionaires rounded out their Yale careers as members of Skull and Bones, the secret society portrayed with enigmatic relish by Hollywood in movies like *The Skulls* and *W*. Among those who were inducted: investor Edward Lampert, Blackstone co-founder Steven Schwarzman, and FedEx founder Frederick Smith.

(Continued)

COMPREHENSION CHECK

Circle the best answer to the questions based on information in the reading.

1 **What is the topic of this reading?**

A. Billionaires

B. Common traits and billionaires

C. Money and billionaires

2 **What is a good guide question to pose about the title of this reading?**

A. What are common traits for billionaires?

B. How do billionaires become wealthy?

C. Why do billionaires become wealthy?

3 **What is the answer to the guide question posed about the title, according to the reading?**

A. Billionaires become wealthy from hard work and luck.

B. There are several characteristics that are common to billionaires.

C. Billionaires tend to avoid wasting time in college.

4 **What is the main idea of this reading?**

A. Many billionaires have several characteristics in common.

B. To become a billionaire, increase your odds by working at Goldman Sachs.

C. Several billionaires suffered a bitter professional setback early in their careers that heightened their fear of failure.

5 **What is the author's primary purpose in writing this article?**

A. To inform

B. To persuade

C. To instruct

6 **What does the word *über-* mean in *über-wealthy* from paragraph 1?**

A. not

B. very

C. money

7 **What is the main idea of paragraph 4?**

A. A significant percentage of billionaires had parents with a high aptitude for math.

B. The ability to crunch numbers is crucial to becoming a billionaire, and mathematical prowess is hereditary.

C. Some of the most common professions among the parents of American billionaires (for whom we could find the information) were engineer, accountant, and small-business owner.

8 **What is the main idea of paragraph 9?**

A. Several billionaires suffered a bitter professional setback early in their careers that heightened their fear of failure.

B. Pharmaceutical tycoon R. J. Kirk's first venture was a flop—an experience he regrets but appreciates.

C. "Failure early on is a necessary condition for success, though not a sufficient one," he told Forbes in 2007.

9 **In paragraph 9, what part of speech does suffix *-al* indicate in the word *pharmaceutical*?**

A. Noun

B. Adjective

C. Verb

10 **In paragraph 7, what does the prefix *sub-* mean in the word *sub-groups*?**

A. Beyond

B. Within

C. Below/under

IMPLIED MAIN IDEAS

THEME *Personality: Nature Versus Nurture*

"Heredity deals the cards; environment plays the hand."
—CHARLES L. BREWER

OBJECTIVES

In this chapter, you will focus on:

COMPREHENSION SKILLS

Learn how to make inferences

- Determining implied main ideas

LEARNING HOW TO MAKE INFERENCES

READING STUDY SKILLS

Learn how to make inferences to paraphrase

VOCABULARY SKILLS

Learn how to focus on roots to infer the meaning of an unknown word

© Cengage Learning 2013

WHY DO YOU NEED TO KNOW THIS?

Problem:
Jean is a recent high school graduate. He did fairly well in high school, earning Bs and Cs. He was good at reading for the most part. When reading textbooks, he found that most main ideas were explicitly stated in the first sentence. What troubled Jean is that he never understood how to make an educated guess about the author's most important point when the main idea was not stated directly in the first sentence—then it became complicated. He has trouble putting the author's words into his own words. Now, in college, Jean is determined to improve his skills. After all, his goals are too important to him to stumble over his reading any longer.

Stockbyte/Jupiter Images

WHAT ADVICE WOULD YOU OFFER TO JEAN?

_____

_____

_____

_____

Solution:
You make inferences all the time in everyday life. An inference is an educated guess, suggested by details but not explicitly stated. You guess how someone's feeling from the expression on his face, you get the jokes that you see in cartoons, and you get the point of a story a friend is telling you, even when she doesn't tell you what that is in so many words. Like all students, Jean can apply this knowledge to reading. In college reading, you will be expected to make inferences all the time. You use inference when you determine the meaning of an unknown word from context. You also make an inference when you determine an implied main idea. Reading a passage that doesn't have an explicit main idea can be perplexing, but if you ask yourself, "What is the author's most important point about the topic?" and can answer that question, you have figured out an implied main idea. When you can put the author's most important point into your own words, you have paraphrased that point. It's not simple, but if you are determined like Jean, it will become easier with practice.

WHAT DO YOU ALREADY KNOW?

Find out what you already know about genetics—the theme of the readings in this chapter—by completing this quiz. Choose the best answer to each of these questions.

1. Where is your DNA? ____In your cells ____In your blood ____In your reproductive organs	**2.** Who has the exact same DNA as you do? ____Your children ____Your parents ____Only you	**3.** What is a gene? ____The basic unit of hereditary information ____A cell in the human body that causes disease ____A protein found in the human body
4. What is a genome? ____The part of a cell that makes proteins ____An organism's complete set of hereditary information ____All the cells in an organism	**5.** What is the main goal of the Human Genome Project? ____To eliminate the genes that cause disease in humans ____To determine the complete set of hereditary information present in humans ____To enable us to genetically engineer and clone human beings	**6.** If you have a gene for a disease, will you get that disease? ____Yes ____Only if both your parents have the gene ____It depends.

Adapted from "Our Genes/Our Choices," Fred Friendly Seminars, Inc., © 2010 http://www.pbs.org/inthebalance/archives/ourgenes/what_do_you_know.html

PRE-ASSESSMENT

This pre-assessment will help you measure what you already know and what you need to learn about the reading skills and strategies explored in this chapter. Your results will help you understand your strengths and weaknesses. Read the article, and then answer the Comprehension Check questions that follow.

Do Our Genes Make Us Popular?
By Jordan Lite

1   Always the last one picked for kickball? Never get invites to the hottest parties? Blame Mom and Dad.

2   That's right, a new study says genes may influence whether or not you're popular. But DNA, or genetic material, shapes more than popularity, according to the research published today in the *Proceedings of the National Academy of Sciences*. It may also play a role in the number of friends we have—and whether we're integral or insignificant members of a social group.

3   Researchers from Harvard University and the University of California, San Diego, found that genes may be responsible for 46 percent of the <u>variation</u> (or difference) in how popular we are versus other people. Genetics exerts a similar effect on people's varying degrees of connectivity (for example, one person might know many of their friends' pals, but another person may not know any of their friends' other buddies). And DNA has a significant, but lesser influence, on the difference between where one or another of us is located in a social network.

4   The scientists based their findings on data from the National Longitudinal Study of Adolescent Health, a study by the University of North Carolina at Chapel Hill of the influence of health on the social behavior of some 90,000 teens who researchers have been following since 1994. Using information on 552 pairs of twins in the study, the Harvard and U.C. San Diego researchers compared the lists of friends of identical twins with the social circles of same-sex <u>fraternal</u> twins. The networks described by the identical twins resembled one another more than those of the same-sex fraternal twins, suggesting a genetic influence on how people network socially. Twin study designs presume that if identical twins resemble each other more on some trait than fraternal twins do, then genes help explain that trait.

5   "Your social position in a network is not purely of your own making," study co-author Nicholas Christakis, a professor of sociology at Harvard University, tells *ScientificAmerican.com*. "In a very deep sense, our social life is <u>predestined</u>. It's predestined genetically."

6   "It's not the only explanation," he adds. "But there is a discernible and substantial role of genes in your social network position."

7   The study didn't sort out which genes are enhancing or ruining our social lives. Michigan State University research published last year showed that a mutation in the serotonin receptor gene 5-HT2A was linked to variation in popularity. (Serotonin is a brain chemical that regulates mood, anxiety, depression, sleep and sexuality.) The new study examines the

(Continued)

genetics of popularity with a wider lens, examining how much DNA may shape the way we socialize.

8   There may be evolutionary reasons for the variations in our social connectedness, Christakis says. While it may be advantageous to be in the center of a group when rumors are circulating, he says, you're better off being on its fringes if a disease—not gossip—is spreading. But the study didn't explore who might benefit from being popular—and who may be lucky to be on the outs.

9   "We're a social species. We shouldn't be surprised that some aspects of how we're social depends on genetics," Christakis says. "Just like other aspects of your personality of how assertive you are, how risk-averse you are, so does your predilection for having particular kinds of social network architectures" depend on genetics.

COMPREHENSION CHECK

Circle the best answer to the questions based on information from the reading.

1 **What is the topic of this reading?**

A. Some people are more sociable than other people.
B. Genes and social ability
C. Nature versus nurture

2 **What is the main idea of paragraph 2?**

A. Genes may determine both social popularity and our role in social groups.
B. That's right, a new study says genes may influence whether or not you're popular.
C. It may also play a role in the number of friends we have.

3 **What type of main idea is in paragraph 2?**

A. Directly stated
B. Implied
C. Both directly stated and implied

4 **What is the main idea of paragraph 3?**

A. Genes may be responsible for 46 percent of the variation (or difference) in how popular we are versus other people.
B. Genetics exerts a similar effect on people's varying degrees of connectivity.
C. Genes appear to have influence on our behavior in several social areas.

5 **What does the word *variation* mean in the context of this sentence from paragraph 3?**

Researchers from Harvard University and the University of California, San Diego, found that genes may be responsible for 46 percent of the variation (or difference) in how popular we are versus other people.

A. How popular we are when compared with other people
B. Difference
C. Responsibility

6 **What does the word *fraternal* mean in paragraph 4?**

A. Related to mother
B. Related to father
C. Related to brother or sibling

7 **In paragraph 5, what does the word *predestined* mean?**

A. To follow after
B. Predetermined (determined before)
C. Changeable

8 **What do you think the root word *gen* means in the words *genetic* and *gene*?**

A. From the father
B. Kind or breed
C. Related to the brain

9 **What is the implied main idea of the whole reading?**

A. Genes may have links to social ability.
B. Behavior is determined by both nature and nurture.
C. Social ability is different in identical twins.

10 **Based on this reading, which of the following statements is a reasonable inference?**

A. Scientists will continue to explore the link between genetics and sociability.
B. Environment plays a larger role in social skills than does genetics.
C. You can overcome any social problem with effort.

FOCUS ON READING STUDY SKILLS
Paraphrasing

Being able to explain what you read in your own words is necessary to understand what an author communicates in writing. In *Merriam-Webster's Collegiate dictionary*, **paraphrasing** is defined as a restatement of a text, passage, or work giving the meaning in another form. Being able to express the thoughts of another in your own language is an essential skill when deciding what the author's most important point is in a reading. In fact, understanding an implied main idea requires that you develop your skills in paraphrasing.

THE IMPORTANCE OF PARAPHRASING

Paraphrasing is vital to your success in college reading because it is a skill that proves you understand what you read. Although to paraphrase something is to put an author's ideas into your own words, paraphrasing doesn't mean repeating an author's words exactly; it means putting the author's ideas into your own words yet maintaining the same ideas.
    Paraphrasing is effective for three main reasons.

1. **Paraphrasing proves you understood what you read.** Paraphrasing makes you sure you understand what the author has written. If you cannot put a passage into your own words, reread the passage, paying careful attention to context clues to make sure you can figure out the meanings of unfamiliar words. Paraphrasing uses the same skills as monitoring your comprehension (see Chapter 1) as you read. Monitoring your comprehension uses metacognition—thinking about what you are thinking. When you paraphrase, you restate what has been written, so you are also monitoring your comprehension.

2. **Paraphrasing helps you understand relationships between ideas in sentences.** When you rewrite a passage in your own words, you can see more clearly how the author arranges ideas and how these ideas fit together to express the author's thoughts.

3. **Paraphrasing helps you study.** Because organized material and repetition help the brain encode new information in your long-term memory, paraphrasing material is an effective study strategy. Paraphrasing as a study technique is usually only most effective with shorter passages because when you paraphrase, you restate all the author's ideas, so your paraphrase should be about the same length as the original reading.

By permission from *Merriam-Webster's Collegiate® Dictionary*, 11th Edition © 2011 by Merriam-Webster, Incorporated (www.merriam-webster.com).

HOW TO PARAPHRASE

The process for creating a paraphrase of a passage uses these four steps:

1. Read the original passage, applying active reading strategies to understand the author's key points.

2. Try to put the ideas expressed in the reading in your own words without looking back at the passage. Try doing this by saying the ideas aloud.

3. Write down your paraphrase, making sure to choose different vocabulary from what the author uses to express your understanding of the author's ideas.

4. Reread the original as well as your paraphrase to make sure your ideas accurately represent those of the author.

Imagine you had to paraphrase this passage:

How Do Genes Influence Behavior?
By Joseph McInerney

No single gene determines a particular behavior. Behaviors are complex traits involving multiple genes that are affected by a variety of other factors. This fact often gets overlooked in media reports hyping scientific breakthroughs on gene function, and, unfortunately, this can be very misleading to the public.

Which of the following do you think is the better paraphrase?

No single gene determines a particular behavior. People can get misled when science news on genetics is reported.

According to "How Do Genes Influence Behavior" by Joseph McInerney, behaviors are complex traits that are influenced by many genes in addition to other factors. When the media reports on findings about scientific studies on genes, the public may get misled since the interaction between genes, behavior, and other factors is complicated.

"How Do Genes Influence Behavior?" by Joseph McInerney by the U.S. Department of Energy and the National Institutes of Health

FOCUS ON READING STUDY SKILLS: Paraphrasing

Both examples retell the important ideas in the passage, but the second example is better. What are the differences between the two paraphrases? See how the second paraphrase is the same length as the original, but worded more simply? Notice that the paraphrase still uses key terms, such as *genes, complex traits*, and *behavior*. Also, it references the author and the reading passage, which is important.

In the first paraphrase, the wording is the same as the original—exact phrasing is not acceptable in paraphrasing because the goal is to put someone else's ideas into your own words. This paraphrase does not represent all the ideas in the passage: The idea that behaviors are complex involving multiple genes, all of which are affected by other forces, is omitted from the first paraphrase.

GOOD PARAPHRASE	POOR PARAPHRASE
• Is the same length as the original	• Is much shorter or longer than the original
• Uses key terms	• Does not use key terms
• References the author and title	• Does not reference the author and title
• Cuts out unnecessary information	• Includes unnecessary information
• Puts ideas into new wording that communicates the same point	• Consistently uses the same wording as the original (therefore doesn't paraphrase)
• Includes all the major and minor supporting details	• Excludes some major and minor details

When paraphrasing, you reword the ideas rather than translate the key terms. Also, you focus on all the supporting details in the original passage, expressing them in your own words in writing. Later, as you become better at paraphrasing, you can put the author's ideas into your own words *in your head* instead of writing them down.

If you are using a paraphrase of an author's work in an essay or in any other work in class, make sure to give credit to the author of the original because the ideas are the author's, not your own. Claiming ideas that are not your own is called **plagiarism,** an ethical violation that is treated seriously in college and can result in serious consequences. To use a paraphrase of another's ideas, you should directly state the source of your ideas in your paraphrase. Or, your instructors may outline footnote and endnote formats that you can also use to reference other people's ideas within a paper you write.

Paraphrasing is a skill that you develop through practice. It helps you fully understand the complex reading you encounter in college-level texts. It also helps move the new information into your long-term memory through repetition.

QUICK TIPS HOW TO PARAPHRASE

To paraphrase a reading, follow these steps:

1. Read the original passage.

2. Without looking back at the original, try to reword the ideas.

3. Write down your paraphrase.

4. Go back and reread the original, checking to make sure the basic idea is the same.

On Your Own PARAPHRASING A PARAGRAPH

For the following paragraphs from "What Is Behavioral Genetics?" by Joseph McInerney, write a paraphrase. Refer to the Quick Tips: How to Paraphrase to guide you.

1. Sir Francis Galton (1822–1911) was the first scientist to study heredity and human behavior systematically. The term "genetics" did not even appear until 1909, only 2 years before Galton's death. With or without a formal name, the study of heredity always has been, at its core, the study of biological variation. Human behavioral genetics, a relatively new field, seeks to understand both the genetic and environmental contributions to individual variations in human behavior.

    _____

    _____

    _____

    _____

    _____

2. As with much other research in genetics, studies of genes and behavior require *analysis of families and populations* for comparison of those who have the trait in question with those who do not. The result often is a statement of "heritability," a statistical construct that estimates the amount of variation in a population that is attributable to genetic factors. The explanatory power of heritability figures is limited, however, applying only to the population studied and only to the environment in place at the time the study was conducted. If the population or the environment changes, the

(Continued)

FOCUS ON READING STUDY SKILLS: Paraphrasing

heritability most likely will change as well. Most important, heritability statements provide no basis for predictions about the expression of the trait in question in any given individual.

_____

_____

_____

_____

_____

_____

_____

_____
"What Is Behavioral Genetics?" by Joseph McInerney by the U.S. Department of Energy and the National Institutes of Health

Thinking It Through PARAPHRASING A READING

Now that you have had some practice paraphrasing a paragraph, see how you apply your skills to paraphrasing a short reading, the rest of the article "How Do Genes Influence Behavior?" by Joseph McInerney. Keep in mind that a short reading is just an array of paragraphs, so you just need to paraphrase each paragraph. Quickly preview the article to determine the topic of this reading. Determining topic and pattern can help you paraphrase the important ideas.

Topic: _____

If you said that the topic was how genes influence behavior, you are correct. Now, read the paraphrases of these two paragraphs.

ORIGINAL	PARAPHRASE
1 No single gene determines a particular behavior. Behaviors are complex traits involving multiple genes that are affected by a variety of other factors. This fact often gets overlooked in media reports hyping scientific breakthroughs on gene function, and, unfortunately, this can be very misleading to the public.	*According to "How Do Genes Influence Behavior?" by Joseph McInerney, behaviors are complex traits that are influenced by many genes in addition to other factors. When the media reports on findings about scientific studies on genes, the public may get misled since the interaction between genes, behavior, and other factors is complicated.*

ORIGINAL	PARAPHRASE
2 For example, a study published in 1999 claimed that overexpression of a particular gene in mice led to enhanced learning capacity. The popular press referred to this gene as "the learning gene" or the "smart gene." What the press didn't mention was that the learning enhancements observed in this study were short-term, lasting only a few hours to a few days in some cases.	*One example of misleading the public by simplifying the function of genes on behavior is a study on mice that concerned a gene that led to quicker learning when it was "overexpressed." The media described this gene as the "smart" gene or "learning" gene but failed to mention that the gains in learning only lasted a short time, sometimes just hours or days.*

On Your Own PARAPHRASING A READING

In your own words, paraphrase the last three paragraphs of "How Do Genes Influence Behavior?" Write your paraphrase next to the original paragraph in the column provided. Then discuss your rewording of the paragraphs with a partner. Remember to make your paraphrase as clear as you can without using any of the author's original words, unless necessary.

ORIGINAL	PARAPHRASE
3 Dubbing a gene as a "smart gene" gives the public a false impression of how much scientists really know about the genetics of a complex trait like intelligence. Once news of the "smart gene" reaches the public, suddenly there is talk about designer babies and the potential of genetically engineering embryos to have intelligence and other desirable traits, when in reality the path from genes to proteins to development of a particular trait is still a mystery.	

(Continued)

FOCUS ON READING STUDY SKILLS: Paraphrasing

ORIGINAL	PARAPHRASE
4 With disorders, behaviors, or any physical trait, genes are just a part of the story, because a variety of genetic and environmental factors are involved in the development of any trait. Having a genetic variant doesn't necessarily mean that a particular trait will develop. The presence of certain genetic factors can enhance or repress other genetic factors. Genes are turned on and off, and other factors may be keeping a gene from being turned "on." In addition, the protein encoded by a gene can be modified in ways that can affect its ability to carry out its normal cellular function.	
5 Genetic factors also can influence the role of certain environmental factors in the development of a particular trait. For example, a person may have a genetic variant that is known to increase his or her risk for developing emphysema from smoking, an environmental factor. If that person never smokes, then emphysema will not develop.	

"How Do Genes Influence Behavior?" by Joseph McInerney, http://www.ornl.gov/sci/techresources/Human_Genome/elsi/behaviors.html by the U.S. Department of Energy and the National Institutes of Health

FOCUS ON COMPREHENSION
Inferences and Implied Main Ideas

Active readers use a variety of strategies to understand and interact with what they are reading. They use their background knowledge as well as the information in the reading to understand a reading. It also helps to put the author's thoughts into your own words or paraphrase so that you are sure you understand what you have just read. Another step is to focus on making inferences or read between the lines to fully understand an author's train of thought. An author doesn't always come right out and say what the main idea is, and so you must infer what the author means to say. Developing your skills of making inferences is the foundation of understanding an implied main idea.

WHAT ARE INFERENCES?

Inferences are reasonable conclusions based on information in the text. Making an inference is like reading between the lines: You make a guess based on what you have read. Inferences are not directly stated and are *reasonable* conclusions that can be made about a reading. "Reasonable" means that the evidence for the inference is clearly suggested by the text and that the reader can assume further information based on what is stated in the text.

You make inferences all the time in daily life. You draw conclusions about people's body language, facial expressions, and tone of voice even when those people do not tell you directly how they feel—you can just tell. This is making an inference. Making several inferences adds up to drawing an overall conclusion. Based on information you know about a person, you draw conclusions about *why* the person is in such a mood. Suppose your friend approached you and looked downcast and upset. However, when you asked what was wrong, he said, "Nothing—everything's fine," but his tone of voice did not sound happy or fine. There is a difference between what he said and what you feel about his manner. You can infer that he is upset. He has implied he is upset by his downcast mood, despite what he has said.

You also make inferences when you understand a joke or see what's funny in a cartoon. The speaker of a joke does not tell you directly why the joke is funny. You put together the information and infer what is funny. To get a joke or understand what's funny in a cartoon, you use your background knowledge to figure out there is a discrepancy between what you expect and what you get—which makes the joke or cartoon funny. Similarly, when you read a passage, you use your background knowledge to make inferences and draw conclusions about where the author is going with the

FOCUS ON COMPREHENSION: Inferences and Implied Main Ideas

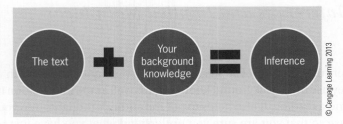

FIGURE 4.1 You make inferences based on your background knowledge plus the information you are reading.

information and what would be a reasonable guess about what an author may mean or suggest (Figure 4.1).

In reading, you need to make inferences to understand the relationships between ideas in a passage. You already use inferences to understand vocabulary in context. Based on surrounding information relative to the word you do not know, you can figure out what the word means. You use inferences to examine word parts to figure out the meaning of the word you don't know. What's important here is that all the evidence suggests a reasonable guess. Inferences are not wild guesses; they are intelligent, informed guesses based on information already available.

Here are a few ways readers make inferences:

- Using context clues

- Using word structure or word part clues

- Making predictions about what will happen next in a reading

- Making predictions about how the information in a reading will be structured

- Determining implied main ideas

- Determining the mood or tone of a reading from the author's choice of words

- Understanding how a character feels

- Understanding events in a reading and why they happened

- Comprehending the author's side on an issue

- Relating to a reading by using background knowledge

Most of the time, an author wants to make a deliberate impression and wants the reader to draw certain inferences. Sometimes, however, readers draw conclusions that the author did not intend. As a reader, you must be careful to draw reasonable inferences. The evidence in the text must provide the support for your inference. You cannot make a reasonable inference based on background knowledge or guessing alone—you must be able to support your conclusion with evidence from the reading.

QUICK TIPS STEPS TO MAKING INFERENCES

1. Consider what each sentence says about the topic.
2. Think about what you know about the information.
3. Ask yourself, What is a reasonable inference to make about this passage based on the information provided in the text?

Thinking It Through MAKING REASONABLE INFERENCES

Read this passage from the PBS program *Nova*, which explores topics related to science.

1990 Human Genome Project

The Human Genome Project is an international research effort to decode the human genome, the complete genetic instructions for a human being. Project leaders originally estimated the work would take 15 years, but with the help of supercomputers and adrenaline, they sequenced the complete human code by 2003. With the final sequence in hand, scientists, doctors, and students have the use of all the DNA information that is key to understanding even the most complex biological systems in our bodies. The possibilities for applications of this information in research are innumerable. At the very least, authorities expect the human code to revolutionize our understanding of human disease.

Put an *X* by the statements that are reasonable inferences based on this passage. Then, read the explanation that follows. Remember, an inference is a *reasonable guess based on information provided in the reading.*

___ 1. Many different countries are involved in the research effort to decode the genome.

This is a reasonable inference based on the information in the first sentence. The author refers to the international effort, so you can infer that many countries are working together to decode the genome.

(Continued)

FOCUS ON COMPREHENSION: Inferences and Implied Main Ideas

___ 2.   The United States leads the effort to decode the human genome.

This statement is not a reasonable inference. Although the United States may be a leader in this field of research, there is no statement in the passage that implies this as a fact. In fact, the United States is not mentioned at all, so you cannot make this assumption.

___ 3.   The effort to decode the human genome took a great deal of dedication and energy on the part of the researchers.

This is a reasonable inference because the second sentence says "with the help of super-computers and adrenaline." Adrenaline is the chemical that gets produced for "fight or flight" in a body when under pressure or threat. The fact that scientists had adrenaline suggests that they worked very hard to finish the sequencing of the genome.

___ 4.   Supercomputers are computers that conduct complex calculations at extraordinary speed.

This is a reasonable inference to make because you can conclude that the prefix *super*-means "above the ordinary." Computers do calculations with accuracy and speed. Super-computers, then, must do these tasks at remarkable levels.

___ 5.   Researchers thought that the task of sequencing the genome would take 15 years, but it took fewer years than originally estimated.

This is not a reasonable inference, not because it is not true—it is true that researchers thought this project would take longer than it did. The reason this is not an inference is because the author explicitly states this information in the second sentence. If a statement is directly mentioned in a passage, it is not an inference since you don't need to make an educated guess—the information is already provided. Notice, though, that the statement above is a paraphrase of the original information in sentence 2 of the passage.

___ 6.   The sequencing of the genome is the most advanced scientific information we have for decoding behavior and disease with profound potential to change our scientific view.

This is a reasonable inference based on the last three sentences of the passage. In these sentences, the author says:

- "DNA information that is key to understanding even the most complex biological systems in our bodies."
- "The possibilities for applications of this information in research are innumerable."
- "At the very least, authorities expect the human code to revolutionize our understanding of human disease."

These points lead to the inference that the sequencing will have an enormous impact on understanding behavior and the functions of the human body—the most significant contribution to the science of humans.

As you can see, making inferences is not necessarily difficult—the key is to consider whether the inferences you make are based on information already provided in the passage.

On Your Own MAKING REASONABLE INFERENCES

Here are some statements from "Genome Facts" from the PBS Website.* With a partner, write one reasonable inference based on each statement. Make sure that your inference statements are based on the statement but are not explicitly stated (in which case, they are not inferences). In addition, write one inference that is *not* a reasonable statement based on the information provided. Be prepared to defend your answers, citing evidence from the statements. Discuss your answers in a small group or in class discussion.

1. Since it began in 1990, the Human Genome Project is estimated to have cost $3 billion.
2. The entire human genome requires three gigabytes of computer data storage space. (One million base pairs of sequence data equals one megabyte of storage space; the human genome has three billion base pairs.)
3. Every second, Human Genome Project computers decode 12,000 letters.
4. For the Human Genome Project, researchers collected blood (female) or sperm (male) samples from a large number of donors. Only a few samples were processed as DNA resources, and the source names remain confidential, so neither donors nor scientists know whose DNA is being sequenced.
5. The human genome sequence generated by the private genomics company Celera was based on DNA samples collected from five donors who identified themselves only by race and sex.
6. The vast majority of DNA in the human genome—about 97 percent—consists of nonge- netic sequences with unknown function, sometimes called "junk DNA."
7. Human DNA is 98 percent identical to chimpanzee DNA.
8. The average amount of genetic difference between any two chimpanzees is four or five times more than the average difference between any two humans, which is 0.2 percent, or one in 500 letters. (This takes into account that human cells, unlike chimpanzee cells, have two copies of the genome.)
9. If two different people started reciting their individual genetic code at a rate of one letter per second, it would take almost eight and a half minutes before they reached a difference.
10. Humans have approximately 30,000 genes.

FOCUS ON COMPREHENSION: Inferences and Implied Main Ideas

IMPLIED MAIN IDEAS

Now that you have some practice with paraphrasing and making reasonable inferences, determining implied main ideas will be clearer. An **implied main idea** is a main idea statement created by the reader when an author does not directly state his or her main point in one sentence within a reading. An implied main idea is an *inference*.

To find implied main ideas, you need to use all the skills outlined in the previous chapters: identifying topic and author's purpose, and using steps to figure out the author's most important point about the topic.

QUICK TIPS STEPS TO FINDING THE IMPLIED MAIN IDEA

The steps for figuring out an implied main idea are very similar to those for finding an explicitly stated main idea, with one additional step.

1. What is the topic?
2. What is the author's purpose?
3. What is the author's most important point about the topic?
4. Write the main idea in your own words.

In Chapter 3, you went back to the reading and found a sentence that stated what you had answered for question 3. In the case of an implied main idea, the sentence that states the main point cannot be found. So, the additional step is #4.

To understand the most important point about anything you read, follow these reasoning steps:

- **Importance of topic in determining an implied main idea.** Determining the topic is necessary to stating a main idea because the topic is always included in a main idea statement. This fact is more significant when determining an implied main idea since you can use the topic to construct it.

- **Importance of the author's purpose in determining an implied main idea.** The author's purpose helps you understand why the author is writing, which is central to understanding the author's train of thought.

Implied main ideas can be made with one of three methods:

- **Method 1:** Topic + existing sentence = implied main idea
- **Method 2:** Sentence + sentence = implied main idea
- **Method 3:** General statement based on supporting details = implied main idea

Method 1: Topic + Existing Sentence = Implied Main Idea

There may be a sentence in the passage that contains the author's most important point about the topic but refers to the topic itself by a pronoun (*he, she, it, they, this,* etc.). To express a complete main idea, you need to add the topic to the sentence that contains the point (see Figure 4.2).

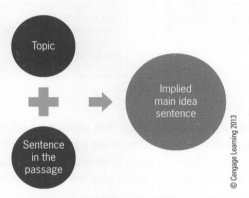

FIGURE 4.2 Method 1: Topic Plus Existing Sentence

© Cengage Learning 2013

Thinking It Through USING METHOD 1

Look at the following three examples of constructing an implied main idea using method 1: adding the topic to an existing sentence. After you read, think about the topic and main idea of the passages. Think of the main idea in your mind, including in your thought the topic of the paragraph. Last, read the explanation that follows.

Example 1

The Human Genome Project is groundbreaking. This scientific breakthrough has revolutionized our understanding of both the potential for disease and human behavior.

(Continued)

FOCUS ON COMPREHENSION: Inferences and Implied Main Ideas

In this example, the topic is the Human Genome Project. The author's purpose is to inform. The second sentence states most of the main point of the passage—that the breakthrough has revolutionized our understanding of both the potential for disease and human behavior. However, the second sentence cannot be an explicit main idea because it does not contain the topic. The main idea always contains the topic. In sentence 2, the pronoun *this* refers to the topic of sequencing of the human genome. So, to construct the implied main idea of this passage, add the topic to sentence 2:

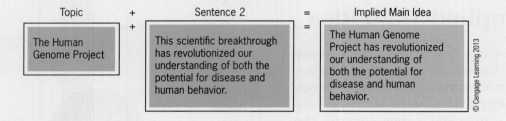

Example 2

As you read this example, think first about who or what the passage is about—this will be the topic. Next, ask yourself, "What is the author's most important point about the topic?" This will lead you to formulate the main idea in your head. Last, look back at the passage and see which sentence almost states the main idea but uses a pronoun to replace the topic.

> Putting all three issues together and using personality to illustrate, we can ask how heredity and environment interact to influence the development of personality, whether the development of personality is continuous or discontinuous, and whether personality develops in much the same way around the world. To answer these kinds of questions, we need to look at the forces that combine to shape human development.
>
> —From KAIL/CAVANAUGH. *Human Development*, 5E. © 2010 Wadsworth,
> a part of Cengage Learning, Inc. By permission.

The topic is questions about the development of personality. The first sentence contains the three issues surrounding the development of personality: hereditary and environment, continuous or discontinuous development, and the development of personality around the world. However, the last sentence states that it is necessary to look at the forces that shape human development—this sentence is important because it sums up the paragraph. In the last sentence, however, the author uses the words *to answer these kinds of questions*. The questions the author refers to are the three issues mentioned earlier. Because the topic is questions about the development of personality, this point needs to be included in the main idea statement. In this case, personality is not mentioned in the last sentence at all. Instead, the author talks about kinds of questions. *Personality* is replaced in this sentence by the word *these*. To correctly state the main idea, then, insert the topic into the existing sentence.

To answer ~~these kinds of~~ questions *about the development of personality*, we need to look at the forces that combine to shape human development.

Example 3

Hand in hand with the emphasis on intimacy is loyalty. Having confided in friends, adolescents expect friends to stick with them through good and bad times. If a friend is disloyal, adolescents are afraid that they may be humiliated because their intimate thoughts and feelings will become known to a much broader circle of people.

—From KAIL/CAVANAUGH. *Human Development*, 5E. © 2010 Wadsworth,
a part of Cengage Learning, Inc. By permission.

In this example, the topic is adolescents and loyalty in friendships. The most important point made in the paragraph is that adolescents expect loyalty from friends. The first sentence almost states this point, but what is missing? The inclusion of adolescents and friendships is missing. Since this is largely who or what the passage is about, these words need to be included in the statement of main idea. The implied main idea is this:

Hand in hand with the emphasis on intimacy is loyalty *in adolescent friendships*.

On Your Own USING METHOD 1

Look at the following paragraphs. Construct an implied main idea using method 1 by adding the topic to an existing sentence from the passage. Write the topic under the paragraph. Next, think of the main idea in your mind, including the topic of the paragraph. Last, find a sentence that almost states the main idea. Add the missing information to this existing sentence, and write it below the paragraph.

(Continued)

FOCUS ON COMPREHENSION: Inferences and Implied Main Ideas

1. More than a century ago, English scientist Sir Francis Galton began to study how genetics influence intelligence. Galton theorized that children inherit their intelligence from their parents. Thus, he believed that genes were responsible for intelligence. In order to test his theory, Galton turned to twin studies.

    —"Nature versus Nurture: Twin and Adoption Studies" http://www.nurture-or-nature.com/
    articles/twin-and-adoption-studies/index.php © 2011 Tree.com, Inc.

    Topic: _____

    Author's purpose: _____

    Implied main idea: _____

    _____

2. While many people have been taught to believe that either genes or the environment and environmental factors determine a person's individual traits and predisposition to diseases and disorders, science is now showing that both of these factors influence an individual's makeup. This is referred to as gene environment interaction.

    —"Gene Environment Interaction" http://www.nurture-or-nature.com/articles/
    gene-enviroment-interaction/index.php © 2011 Tree.com, Inc.

    Topic: _____

    Author's purpose: _____

    Implied main idea: _____

    _____

3. **Social Determinism**

    Social determinism is the opposite of biological or genetic determinism. This concept asserts that social and environmental factors determine a person's characteristics and traits.

    —"Biological Determinism" http://www.nurture-or-nature.com/articles/
    biological-determinism/index.php © 2011 Tree.com, Inc

    Topic: _____

    Author's purpose: _____

    Implied main idea: _____

    _____

4. **DNA Reproduction**

    For a cell to reproduce, each new cell must carry a complete set of DNA, identical to its mother cell. Here is the way this is accomplished:

    1. Cells reproduce by dividing in two.
    2. Before the cell divides the double helix "unzips," dividing into two single strands of DNA.

3. These two strands connect with "free-floating" DNA bases produced by the cell during division.

4. Because the DNA bases only pair up in four different ways, each single strand of DNA pairs up with the correct DNA bases and two copies of the double helix are then available: one for each cell.

—"Testing DNA Knowledge" http://www.healthtree.com/articles/
genetic-testing/what-is-dna/ © 2011 Tree.com, Inc.

Topic: _____

Author's purpose: _____

Implied main idea: _____

_____

5. Not long ago, we were told that learned men and women in lab coats would be able to look into our biological future, using DNA as a crystal ball. But after more research, we're finding that DNA is not absolute. Rather, it works by probabilities and potentialities, and is affected by the environment outside of our cells. The promised crystal ball actually looks more like a murky lake.

—Looking for Trouble, by Greg Fish. From *Business Week*. Copyright © 2008 Bloomberg L.P. By permission.

Topic: _____

Author's purpose: _____

Implied main idea: _____

_____

Method 2: Sentence + Sentence = Implied Main Idea

The second type of implied main idea exists when the author's most important point is divided into two sentences. These sentences must be combined in order to accurately state the main idea in a single sentence (Figure 4.3).

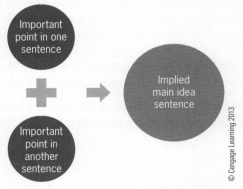

FIGURE 4.3 Method 2: Combine two sentences

FOCUS ON COMPREHENSION: Inferences and Implied Main Ideas

Thinking It Through USING METHOD 2

Look at the following examples using method 2 to construct the implied main idea by combining two sentences into one sentence. After you read, think about the topic and main idea of the passages. Think of the main idea in your mind, including in your thought the topic of the paragraph. Then, read the explanation that follows.

Example 1

What is DNA? Most people understand that DNA carries information we inherit from our parents. The corkscrew shape of DNA is seen in DNA models in science classrooms across the world. But few people really know the reason behind DNA's peculiar structure or how DNA encodes our hereditary traits.

—"Testing DNA Knowledge" http://www.healthtree.com/articles/
genetic-testing/what-is-dna/ © 2011 Tree.com, Inc.

In this informative paragraph, the topic is DNA. The hint to the topic is presented in the opening question. Which two sentences in the paragraph should you combine to answer this question? The second and last sentences both contain essential information to describe what DNA is. The implied main idea is this:

While most people understand that DNA carries information we inherit from our parents, few people know the reason behind DNA's structure or how it encodes hereditary traits.

So, part of the answer to the question is known—DNA is inherited information. But, part of the answer to the question is unknown—why DNA has the particular structure or how it encodes hereditary traits.

Example 2

First-born children are often "guinea pigs" for most parents, who have lots of enthusiasm but little practical experience rearing children. Parents typically have high expectations for their first-borns. With later-born children, parents have more realistic expectations and are more relaxed in their discipline. They are both more affectionate and more punitive toward them, having learned "the tricks of the trade" from earlier children.

—From KAIL/CAVANAUGH. *Human Development*, 5E. © 2010 Wadsworth,
a part of Cengage Learning, Inc. By permission.

In this paragraph, the topic is first-born and later-born children and parenting. The author's purpose is to inform. The first half of the paragraph concerns first-born children and parenting.

The second half of the paragraph concerns how parents are different with later-born children. To state the main idea, both need to be mentioned. To state the main idea, you need to combine two sentences.

> First-born children are often "guinea pigs" for most parents, who have lots of enthusiasm but little practical experience rearing children, but as more children arrive, most parents become more adept at their roles.

Example 3

> That's right, a new study says genes may influence whether or not you're popular. But DNA, or genetic material, shapes more than popularity, according to the research published today in the *Proceedings of the National Academy of Sciences*. It may also play a role in the number of friends we have—and whether we're integral or insignificant members of a social group.
>
> —"Do Our Genes Make Us Popular?" by Jordan Lite http://www.scientificamerican.com/blog/ 60-second-science/post.cfm?id=do-our-genes-make-us-popular--or-no-2009-01-26. Copyright © 2009 Scientific American, Inc. By permission.

In this informative example, the first sentence says that a new study suggests genes influence social success. The passage continues to say that there is more to the possible influence of genes on social ability—genes may also determine how central a player we are to a social group. To correctly state the main idea, you need to take information from the first sentence as well as from the last sentence to compose a complete main point.

> Genes may influence whether or not you're popular (sentence 1) + Genes may also play a role in how many friends we have and also our role in the social group (sentence 3).

So, here is a statement of the implied main idea, using method 2:

> Genes may influence a person's popularity as well as his or her number of friends and role in a social group.

On Your Own USING METHOD 2

Look at the following paragraphs. Construct an implied main idea using method 2 by combining two sentences. Write the topic; then think of the main idea in your mind, including the topic of the paragraph. Last, find two sentences to combine to express the author's complete thought.

(Continued)

FOCUS ON COMPREHENSION: Inferences and Implied Main Ideas

1. **How Is Behavioral Genetics Studied?**
   Traditional research strategies in behavioral genetics include studies of twins and adoptees, techniques designed to sort biological from environmental influences. More recently, investigators have added the search for pieces of DNA associated with particular behaviors, an approach that has been most productive to date in identifying potential locations for genes associated with major mental illnesses such as schizophrenia and bipolar disorder. Yet even here there have been no major breakthroughs, no clearly identified genes that geneticists can tie to disease. The search for genes associated with characteristics such as sexual preference and basic personality traits has been even more frustrating.

   —"How Is Behavioral Genetics Studied?" by Joseph McInerney
   http://www.ornl.gov/sci/techresources/Human_Genome/elsi/behaviors.html
   by the U.S. Department of Energy and the National Institutes of Health

   Topic: _____
   Author's purpose: _____
   Implied main idea: _____
   _____
   _____

2. The opposing view is that differences among people are not simply variations on a theme. Advocates of this view argue that human development is inextricably intertwined with the context within which it occurs. A person's development is a product of complex interaction with the environment, and that interaction is not fundamentally the same in all environments. Each environment has its own set of unique procedures that shape development, just as the "recipes" for different cars yield vehicles as different as a Mini Cooper and a Hummer.

   —From KAIL/CAVANAUGH. *Human Development,* 5E. © 2010 Wadsworth,
   a part of Cengage Learning, Inc. By permission.

   Topic: _____
   Author's purpose: _____
   Implied main idea: _____
   _____
   _____

3. Some of the advantages of genetic fingerprinting include:
   1. ability to forestall or prevent disease through medical intervention and lifestyle changes
   2. encouraging at-risk individuals to begin disease screenings at an earlier age
   3. giving individuals time to prepare emotionally, physically and financially for possible illness.

   Here are some possible drawbacks of genetic fingerprinting:

   - accuracy of tests are dependent on experience and competency of lab personnel
   - emotional turmoil
   - privacy concerns

   —"DNA Fingerprinting and Genetic Disease" http://www.healthtree.com/articles/genetic-testing/

Topic: _____

Author's purpose: _____

Implied main idea: _____

_____

_____

4. The possibility that only children are selfish has been a concern in China, where only children are common because of governmental efforts to limit population growth. However, comparisons in China between only children and children with siblings often find no differences; when differences are found, the advantage usually goes to the only child. Thus, contrary to the popular stereotype, only children are not "spoiled brats" (nor, in China, are they "little emperors" who boss around parents, peers, and teachers). Instead, only children are, for the most part, much like children who grow up with siblings.

—From KAIL/CAVANAUGH. *Human Development,* 5E. © 2010 Wadsworth,
a part of Cengage Learning, Inc. By permission.

Topic: _____

Author's purpose: _____

Implied main idea: _____

_____

_____

5. During genetic tests, technicians look for markers that may indicate a presence of mutated genes associated with an illness. Then they can theorize about the likelihood that the medical problem will develop. For patients with long family histories of particular cancers, insurance company guidelines recommend paying for the tests because their results have proven more certain. Less clear-cut cases, on the other hand, mean too few actionable take aways, too much ambiguity, and too little benefit to the patient to justify covering a test.

—Looking for Trouble, by Greg Fish. From *Business Week.* Copyright
© 2008 Bloomberg L.P. By permission.

Topic: _____

Author's purpose: _____

Implied main idea: _____

_____

_____

FOCUS ON COMPREHENSION: Inferences and Implied Main Ideas

Method 3: General Statement Based on Supporting Details = Implied Main Idea

In some cases, it is up to you to create your own main idea sentence because the author does not provide a sentence that needs the topic added or sentences that combine to create the main idea. This third type of implied main idea occurs when the author presents a series of supporting details only (Figure 4.4). You remember from previous chapters that a *supporting detail* is a point the author includes in a passage to support the main idea. The reader can fairly easily understand what the overall point is, but nothing is stated in the passage as in methods 1 and 2. In method 3, you make an inference to determine the overall point of the passage. As you know, making inferences requires that you make an educated guess based on information provided in the passage. First, determine the topic of the passage, turn the topic into a guide question, and then answer the guide question to determine the implied main idea.

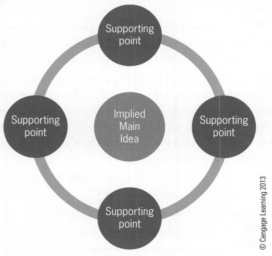

© Cengage Learning 2013

FIGURE 4.4 Method 3: Create a General Statement Based on Supporting Details

Thinking It Through USING METHOD 3

Look at the following three examples of constructing an implied main idea using method 3, creating a general statement based on supporting details. After you read, think about the topic and main idea of the passages. The purpose of each paragraph is to inform. Last, read the explanation that follows.

Example 1

Some researchers think the genes we inherit from our parents play a strong role in guiding our development. Others, however, think our environment has a stronger role in shaping who we will eventually become. Of course, many believe that both environment and genetics play a strong role in our development.

—"Nature versus Nurture: Twin and Adoption Studies" http://www.nurture-or-nature.com/ articles/twin-and-adoption-studies/index.php © 2011 Tree.com, Inc.

In this example, three different views about how genes and environment interact and influence development are provided. The topic then is genes, environment, and development. To accurately state the main idea, you must cover the three supporting points because one major detail is not more important than the other. Use the topic as your guide, and turn it into a question: How are genes, environment, and development viewed? The answer to this question will be the main idea:

There are several opinions about how genes and environment influence development.

Example 2

For instance, a person with two obese parents might, in fact, be quite slender and healthy. This could be due to his access to healthy foods. Also, a person with two parents of less-than-average intelligence could have a higher-than-normal intelligence if he is raised in an environment where education is valued and where learning materials are made accessible.

—"Gene Environment Interaction" http://www.nurture-or-nature.com/articles/ gene-enviroment-interaction/index.php © 2011 Tree.com, Inc.

There are three sentences in this paragraph about obesity, intelligence, and environment. These three sentences present two major details: one concerns obesity, and the other concerns intelligence. What general statement can be made that would cover these two subtopics? One method for expressing the main idea is to take the topic and pose it as a question: What is the relationship between obesity, intelligence, and the environment? The answer to this question will be the main idea.

Both obesity and intelligence can be affected by environment despite the parents' genetic contribution.

(Continued)

FOCUS ON COMPREHENSION: Inferences and Implied Main Ideas

Example 3

When we think of DNA testing services, we often draw upon our memories of it in the latest CSI episode or on paternity tests in talk shows. We hear reports of paternity DNA testing in the news, and find references to ancestry DNA testing on genealogy Web sites. Prenatal DNA testing is now used regularly to screen unborn children for hereditary disorders.

—"DNA Testing" http://www.healthtree.com/articles/genetic-testing/dna-test/ © 2011 Tree.com, Inc.

In this example, the author lists ways that DNA testing is perceived, through television shows, from the news, or Web sites, and its use for testing unborn babies. So, the topic is perceptions of DNA testing. Turning the topic into a question, you can ask, "What are the perceptions of DNA testing?" The answer to this question is the main idea:

There are a variety of sources that influence our perceptions of DNA testing.

or

DNA testing is broadcasted in a variety of ways.

or

DNA testing has become a common topic in our culture.

All of these statements accurately cover the supporting details and convey the topic. Keep in mind that with method 3, everyone will have a slightly different way of expressing the main idea. The important thing to remember is the basic idea will remain the same.

On Your Own USING METHOD 3

Look at the following paragraphs. Construct an implied main idea using method 3 by making a general statement about the supporting details. Write the topic under the paragraph. Next, think of the main idea, including in your thought the topic of the paragraph. Last, write down the statement you have constructed.

1. **What Is DNA Testing?**

    After the DNA is cut, the pieces are placed at one end of a gelatin slab. Drawn through with an electric current, the small pieces of DNA in the gelatin move more quickly than the larger pieces, arranging the cut DNA pieces into ascending order. Once the DNA pieces are organized, the gelatin is replicated for further records.

    —"DNA Testing" http://www.healthtree.com/articles/genetic-testing/dna-test/ © 2011 Tree.com, Inc.

    Topic: _____

    Author's purpose: _____

    Implied main idea: _____

    _____

2. For example, a study published in 1999 claimed that overexpression of a particular gene in mice led to enhanced learning capacity. The popular press referred to this gene as "the learning gene" or the "smart gene." What the press didn't mention was that the learning enhancements observed in this study were short-term, lasting only a few hours to a few days in some cases.

    —"How Do Genes Influence Behavior?" by Joseph McInerney U.S. Department of Energy
    and the National Institutes of Health

    Topic: _____

    Author's purpose: _____

    Implied main idea: _____

    _____

3. **Ancestry and Paternity DNA Testing**

    Ancestry DNA testing can determine if two people come from the same ancestor and even help a person trace their ethnicity to an ancient origin, such as the ongoing National Geographic Genographic project. Similar to ancestry DNA testing is paternity DNA testing, which is often used to identify the father of a child.

    —"Researching Your Ancestry Through DNA Testing" http://www.nurture-or-nature.com/
    articles/researching-ancestry/index.php © 2011 Tree.com, Inc.

    Topic: _____

    Author's purpose: _____

    Implied main idea: _____

    _____

(Continued)

FOCUS ON COMPREHENSION: Inferences and Implied Main Ideas

4. Most DNA tests are done in laboratories by scientists; however, some people use home DNA testing kits to determine relationships which can be found in many pharmacies. Some health clinics also offer free DNA testing, mostly to solve paternity conflicts.

—"Testing DNA: Paternity, Ancestry and Prenatal DNA Testing," http://www.tree.com/health/ genetic-testing-dna-test.aspx ©2011 Tree.com, Inc.

Topic: _____

Author's purpose: _____

Implied main idea: _____
_____

5. **Insurance Coverage of Preventative Genetic Testing**

If insurance covers these preventative efforts, how much money has the insurer spent on fighting the phantoms of patients' concerns? And how much did premiums have to rise to cover all this preventative care based on conjecture? Insurers also worry that companies—wary of the expense ambiguous preventative procedures can entail—may decide not to cover employees based on results of genetic tests. Such genetic discrimination is bound to start court battles, taking a heavy toll on everyone involved.

—Looking for Trouble, by Greg Fish. From *Business Week*.
Copyright © 2008 Bloomberg L.P. By permission.

Topic: _____

Author's purpose: _____

Implied main idea: _____
_____

QUICK TIPS WRITING IMPLIED MAIN IDEA STATEMENTS

When you write your own implied main idea statements, follow these guidelines.

■ **Method 1:** Add the topic to a sentence in the passage that comes close to stating the point you have constructed in your mind.

■ **Method 2:** Combine two sentences to create the main idea.

■ **Method 3:** Check to see if the reading is a series of supporting details that all logically fall under the general statement you have constructed as the main idea, taking into account that all major supporting details are equal in importance.

Keep in mind the following:

☑ Notice if any passage is a list of something and has a general, overriding point that can be summed up in a general statement.

☑ Turn the topic into a question, and then answer the question. That will be the main idea.

☑ Think in terms of summative words or phrases, and imagine explaining the point of a passage to a peer. Start your thinking with "The point is . . ." or "In conclusion . . ." or "To sum up . . . ."

☑ When you see an author compare or contrast two things, consider the possibility of using method 2. In a comparison or contrast passage, an author often states one half of the point in one sentence and the other half of the point in another.

☑ When in doubt, try beginning your implied main idea statement with "There are . . ." or "There is. . . ." This way, you will know you are creating a sentence, not a phrase.

Finding an Implied Main Idea in a Longer Reading

Just as with explicit main ideas, implied main ideas can be for a whole reading, a subsection of a reading, and each paragraph. In almost all passages, there will be a mixture of both implied and explicitly stated main ideas. When you determine an implied main idea of a whole reading, you draw a conclusion based on both stated and unstated main ideas in each of the reading's body paragraphs. An overall main idea is called a **thesis.** A thesis is the main idea of a whole reading—the author's most important point. When you consider a series of main ideas in the body paragraphs of a longer passage, you can infer or deduce what the author's overall point, or thesis, may be. In doing this, you have inferred the implied main idea of a reading. The overall point is not a wild guess, but a reasonable guess based on a series of pieces of information: the topic, how it is organized, the author's purpose, and the major supporting details.

FOCUS ON COMPREHENSION: Inferences and Implied Main Ideas

Thinking It Through   FINDING THE IMPLIED MAIN IDEA OF A LONGER READING

As you approach this longer reading, remember the steps to finding a main idea. Ask yourself the following questions as you read:

1. What is the topic?
2. What is the author's purpose?
3. What is the author's most important point about the topic?
4. Write the main idea in your own words.

Find the topic of each paragraph. Then determine the main idea of each paragraph, whether it is implied or explicit. Last, determine the thesis or main idea of the whole reading.

Genetic Consultation

What is a genetic consultation?

1   A genetic consultation is a health service that provides information and support to people who have, or may be at risk for, genetic disorders. During a consultation, a genetics professional meets with an individual or family to discuss genetic risks or to diagnose, confirm, or rule out a genetic condition.

2   Genetics professionals include medical geneticists (doctors who specialize in genetics) and genetic counselors (certified healthcare workers with experience in medical genetics and counseling). Other healthcare professionals such as nurses, psychologists, and social workers trained in genetics can also provide genetic consultations.

3   Consultations usually take place in a doctor's office, hospital, genetics center, or other type of medical center. These meetings are most often in-person visits with individuals or families, but they are occasionally conducted in a group or over the telephone.

Why might someone have a genetic consultation?

4   Individuals or families who are concerned about an inherited condition may benefit from a genetic consultation. The reasons that a person might be referred to a genetic counselor, medical geneticist, or other genetics professional include:

- A personal or family history of a genetic condition, birth defect, chromosomal disorder, or hereditary cancer.
- Two or more pregnancy losses (miscarriages), a stillbirth, or a baby who died.
- A child with a known inherited disorder, a birth defect, mental retardation, or developmental delay.
- A woman who is pregnant or plans to become pregnant at or after age 35. (Some chromosomal disorders occur more frequently in children born to older women.)

- Abnormal test results that suggest a genetic or chromosomal condition.
- An increased risk of developing or passing on a particular genetic disorder on the basis of a person's ethnic background.
- People related by blood (for example, cousins) who plan to have children together. (A child whose parents are related may be at an increased risk of inheriting certain genetic disorders.)

5   A genetic consultation is also an important part of the decision-making process for genetic testing. A visit with a genetics professional may be helpful even if testing is not available for a specific condition, however.

—From: Genetic Consultation, from US National Library of Medicine.

http://ghr.nlm.nih.gov/handbook/consult?show=all

1. **What is the topic of paragraph 1?** Genetic consultation

2. **What is the main idea of paragraph 1?** The main idea is directly stated in the first sentence. This sentence is the answer to the question—What is a genetic consultation—posed in the heading.

3. **What is the topic of paragraph 2?** Genetics professionals

4. **What is the main idea of paragraph 2?** This paragraph begins by listing two types of genetic professionals. However, further genetic healthcare professionals are listed in the second sentence. Using method 3, the main idea of this paragraph is: There are many genetic professionals who can provide genetic counseling.

5. **What is the topic of paragraph 3?** The location and process of genetic counseling

6. **What is the main idea of paragraph 3?** This paragraph provides information about the location and process of genetic counseling. The first sentence provides information about the location; the second sentence provides information about what to expect the process to be like. Using method 3, the implied main idea is: Genetic counseling takes place in a medical facility and can be conducted in a variety of ways.

7. **What is the topic of paragraph 4?** Why have genetic counseling

8. **What is the main idea of paragraph 4?** The main idea is the answer to the question posed in the heading: Why might someone have a genetic consultation? There are two reasons. First, an individual may seek out counseling. Second, an individual may be referred to a genetics professional. The answer to this question is both in the first sentence—because an individual is concerned about an inherited condition—and in the second sentence— because of several conditions that warrant referral. So, using method 2, the main idea is: Individuals seek a genetic consultation because of a concern about an inherited condition or may be referred to a genetics professional due to several conditions.

9. **What is the topic of paragraph 5?** Genetic counseling

10. **What is the main idea of paragraph 5?** Genetic counseling is important. This main idea is stated in the first sentence.

(Continued)

FOCUS ON COMPREHENSION: Inferences and Implied Main Ideas

11. **What is the main idea of the whole reading?** The title of the reading is genetic consultation. The main idea or thesis of the reading will be the answer to the question: What is the author's most important point about genetic consultation? Can you find a sentence that answers this question directly? The most likely location for a thesis statement is in the introduction. The second most likely place for a thesis statement is the conclusion. A thesis statement can also be within a body paragraph. If it's an implied thesis, it may not even be in the passage—not completely if using methods 1 or 2, and not at all if using method 3. There are two headings in this reading. The first is: What is a genetic consultation? The second is: Why might someone have a genetic consultation? Both sections of this reading are equally important. As a result, the main idea of the whole reading must refer to both of these sections of the reading. The main idea must state what a genetic consultation is and must state why someone may have a genetic consultation. Is there a sentence that combines both ideas? The first sentence of the passage does: *A genetic consultation is a health service that provides information and support to people who have, or may be at risk for, genetic disorders.*

On Your Own FINDING THE IMPLIED MAIN IDEA OF A LONGER READING

As you approach this longer reading, remember the steps to finding a main idea. Ask yourself the following questions as you read:

1. **What is the topic?**
2. **What is the author's purpose?**
3. **What is the author's most important point about the topic?**
4. **Write the main idea in your own words.**

Find the topic of each paragraph. Then determine the main idea of each paragraph, either implied or directly stated. Last, determine the thesis or main idea of the whole reading.

The Genetic Basics: What Are Genes and What Do They Do?

What Are Genes?

What is the topic of paragraph 1?

1   Chromosomes contain the recipe for making a living thing. They are found in almost every cell's nucleus and are made from strands of DNA (deoxyribonucleic

acid). Segments of DNA called "genes" are the ingre-
dients. Each gene adds a specific protein to the recipe.
Proteins build, regulate and maintain your body. For
instance, they build bones, enable muscles to move,
control digestion, and keep your heart beating.

What is the main idea of paragraph 1?

2   Most of our cells contain 46 chromosomes. Sperm
and egg cells contain only 23 chromosomes. When
the sperm and egg cells unite, the resulting fetus
inherits half of its DNA recipe from its mother and
half from its father.

What is the topic of paragraph 2?

What is the main idea of paragraph 2?

3   Two of these 46 chromosomes determine the sex
of a person. A girl inherits two X-chromosomes, one
from her mother and one from her father. A boy inherits one X-chromosome from his mother and a small
Y-chromosome from his father.

What is the topic of paragraph 3?

What is the main idea of paragraph 3?

4   The Austrian monk Gregor Mendel (1822–1884)
was the first person to describe how traits are inherited from generation to generation. He studied how pea
plants inherited traits such as color and smoothness,
and discovered that traits are inherited from parents in
certain patterns. Not until the 20th century did other
scientists take his ideas further. Mendel is considered
to be the father of genetics, although his work was relatively unappreciated until the early 20th century.

What is the topic of paragraph 4?

What is the main idea of paragraph 4?

5   A gene can exist in many different forms, called alleles.
For example, let's say that there is one gene which determines the color of your hair. That one gene may have
many forms, or alleles: black hair, brown hair, auburn
hair, red hair, blond hair, etc. You inherit one allele for
each gene from your mother and one from your father.

What is the topic of paragraph 5?

What is the main idea of paragraph 5?

6   Each of the two alleles you inherit for a gene each
may be strong ("dominant") or weak ("recessive").
When an allele is dominant, it means that the physical
characteristic ("trait") it codes for usually is expressed,
or shown, in the living organism. You need only one
dominant allele to express a dominant trait. You need
two recessive alleles to show a recessive form of a trait.

What is the topic of paragraph 6?

What is the main idea of paragraph 6?

(Continued)

FOCUS ON COMPREHENSION: Inferences and Implied Main Ideas

What is the topic of paragraph 7?

What is the main idea of paragraph 7?

7   For example, mild forms of red/green color blindness are very common, resulting only in the inability to tell apart shades of red and green. The gene for this trait is located on the X-chromosome. A mother who carries this recessive trait has normal red/green vision. Any of her sons who inherit the X-chromosome that carries this trait — the allele for color blindedness — will be mildly red/green color blind. In this chart used to test for color-blindedness, people with normal color vision can see the number seven. People with red/green color blindness cannot see the number seven.

From the National Institutes of Health

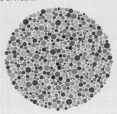

What is the thesis of the reading? _____

_____

_____

_____

Practice Exercise 1:   MAKING INFERENCES

Here are sentences from the PBS Web site about genome facts. Write a reasonable inference for each of the following facts. Remember that reasonable inferences are based on the reading but are not explicitly stated in the reading.

1. The roundworm has 19,098 genes.

   _____

2. The fruit fly has 13,602 genes.

   _____

3. Yeast has 6,034 genes.

   _____

4. The microbe responsible for tuberculosis has approximately 4,000 genes.

   _____

5. There are 100 trillion (100,000,000,000,000) cells in your body.

   _____

6. There are 3 billion (3,000,000,000) base pairs in the DNA code within each cell.

   _____

7. If unwound and tied together, the strands of DNA in one cell would stretch almost 6 feet but would be only 50 trillionths of an inch wide.

   _____

8. If all the DNA in your body was put end to end, it would reach to the sun and back over 600 times (100 trillion times 6 feet divided by 92 million miles).

   _____

9. It would take a person typing 60 words per minute, 8 hours a day, around 50 years to type the human genome.

   _____

10. If all 3 billion letters in the human genome were stacked 1 millimeter apart, they would reach a height 7,000 times that of the Empire State Building.

    _____

"Genome Facts," NOVA/PBS; http://www.pbs.org/wgbh/nova/genome/facts.html © 2010. From FRONTLINE/Tehran Bureau/WGBH Boston. Copyright © updated April 2001, WGBH Educational Foundation.

Practice Exercise 2: FINDING IMPLIED MAIN IDEAS

For the following passages, determine the topic and then determine the implied main idea. Indicate the method you used to determine the implied main idea.

1. ***mtDNA tests:*** This type of DNA test examines the *mitochondrial DNA* a person inherits from his mother. Because mtDNA doesn't change dramatically as it is passed from a mother to her children, a group of related people will have nearly identical mtDNA strands. Consequently, these DNA tests are ideal for determining if two people have a maternal ancestor in common.

   —"Researching Your Ancestry Through DNA Testing" http://www.nurture-or-nature.com/
   articles/researching-ancestry/index.php © 2011 Tree.com, Inc.

Topic: _____

Author's purpose: _____

Implied main idea: _____

_____

Method: _____

(Continued)

FOCUS ON COMPREHENSION: Inferences and Implied Main Ideas

2. Human bodies are made up of trillions of cells. Each of these cells has a nucleus that accommodates chromosomes, which are made up of DNA. Segments of DNA make up genes, and these determine physical traits such as height or eye color.

    —"Inherited Diseases" http://www.healthtree.com/articles/genetic-health/inherited-condition

    Topic: _____

    Author's purpose: _____

    Implied main idea: _____

    _____

    Method: _____

3. For those who don't have contact with their parents or extended families, finding out about their ancestries can help them understand more about who they are. Similarly, knowing about your relatives is an important part of being able to properly take care of yourself, as your genetic makeup can predispose you to certain diseases and/or conditions.

    —"Researching Your Ancestry Through DNA Testing" http://www.nurture-or-nature.com/
    articles/researching-ancestry/index.php © 2011 Tree.com, Inc.

    Topic: _____

    Author's purpose: _____

    Implied main idea: _____

    _____

    Method: _____

4. Once you have obtained both DNA samples, you then send them to the lab (whose address will be specified on the instructions) for testing. Within a month, the lab will mail you back the results of your test. The results typically come as a set of numbers for you and a set for the other person being tested.

    —"Researching Your Ancestry Through DNA Testing" http://www.nurture-or-nature.com/articles/
    researching-ancestry/index.php © 2011 Tree.com, Inc.

    Topic: _____

    Author's purpose: _____

    Implied main idea: _____

    _____

    Method: _____

5. Some of the popular DNA tests are:
    *   AmpFLP
    *   Mitochondrial
    *   PCR
    *   RFLP
    *   STR
    *   Y-Chromosome

RFLP, PCR and STR are commonly used in forensic testing, while Y-Chromosome and Mitochondrial DNA tests are used more frequently in ancestry DNA testing and paternity DNA testing.

—"Testing DNA: Paternity, Ancestry and Prenatal DNA Testing"
http://www.tree.com/health/genetic-testing-dna-test.aspx © 2011 Tree.com, Inc.

Topic: _____
Author's purpose: _____
Implied main idea: _____

_____

Method: _____

6. Serial killers: Is it nature or nurture? This question has been exhaustively examined by researchers for years. If genetics determine our personality and actions, many wonder what leads people to lives of crime and hate.

—"Biological Determinism" http://www.nurture-or-nature.com/articles/
biological-determinism/index.php © 2011 Tree.com, Inc.

Topic: _____
Author's purpose: _____
Implied main idea: _____

_____

Method: _____

7. Are behaviors inbred, written indelibly in our genes as immutable biological imperatives, or is the environment more important in shaping our thoughts and actions? Such questions cycle through society repeatedly, forming the public nexus of the "nature vs. nurture controversy," a strange locution to biologists, who recognize that behaviors exist only in the context of environmental influence. Nonetheless, the debate flares anew every few years, reigniting in response to genetic analyses of traits such as intelligence, criminality, or homosexuality, characteristics freighted with social, political, and legal meaning.

—"What Implications Does Behavioral Genetics Research Have for Society?" by Joseph McInerney
U.S. Department of Energy and the National Institutes of Health

Topic: _____
Author's purpose: _____
Implied main idea: _____

_____

Method: _____

8. What social consequences would genetic diagnoses of such traits as intelligence, criminality, or homosexuality have on society? What effect would the discovery of a behavioral trait associated with increased criminal activity have on our legal system? If we find a "gay gene," will it mean greater or lesser tolerance? Will it lead to proposals that those affected by the "disorder" should

(Continued)

FOCUS ON COMPREHENSION: Inferences and Implied Main Ideas

undergo treatment to be "cured" and that measures should be taken to prevent the birth of other individuals so afflicted?

—"What Implications Does Behavioral Genetics Research Have for Society?" by Joseph McInerney
U.S. Department of Energy and the National Institutes of Health

Topic: _____

Author's purpose: _____

Implied main idea: _____

_____

Method: _____

9. The opposing view is that differences among people are not simply variations on a theme. Advocates of this view argue that human development is inextricably intertwined with the context within which it occurs. A person's development is a product of complex interaction with the environment, and that interaction is not fundamentally the same in all environments. Each environment has its own set of unique procedures that shape development, just as the "recipes" for different cars yield vehicles as different as a Mini Cooper and a Hummer.

—From KAIL/CAVANAUGH. *Human Development*, 5E. © 2010 Wadsworth,
a part of Cengage Learning, Inc. By permission.

Topic: _____

Author's purpose: _____

Implied main idea: _____

_____

_____

Method: _____

10. These labels are not perfect. In some cases, they blur distinctions among ethnic groups. For example, people from both Guatemala and Mexico may be described as Latinos. However, their cultural backgrounds vary on several important dimensions, so we should not view them as being from a homogeneous group. Similarly, the term Asian American blurs variations among people whose heritage is, for example, Japanese, Chinese, or Korean. Whenever researchers have identified the subgroups in their research sample, we will use the more specific terms in describing results. When we use the more general terms, remember that conclusions may not apply to all subgroups within the group described by the more general term.

—From KAIL/CAVANAUGH. *Human Development*, 5E. © 2010 Wadsworth,
a part of Cengage Learning, Inc. By permission.

Topic: _____

Author's purpose: _____

Implied main idea: _____

_____

Method: _____

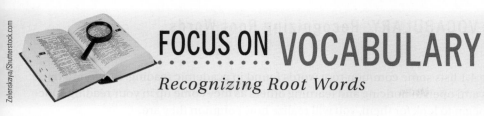

FOCUS ON VOCABULARY
Recognizing Root Words

In Chapter 3, you learned to focus on prefixes and suffixes in a word. Here, you will look at the main part of a word, or its root. Think of looking at a word's root as the same as looking at the main idea of a reading. Many languages have contributed to English and continue to expand and enhance our language. The most common languages that form the basis of English are Latin and ancient Greek, as well as words that come from older versions of English and French. Many of the words we use today originate from these sources.

ROOT WORDS

Root words are the primary units in words. *Primary* refers to the part of a word that cannot be reduced to a smaller unit. Consider the word *prescription*. This word can be divided into three parts:

pre	+	**script**	+	**ion**
prefix	+	root word	+	suffix
before	+	to write	+	means the word is a noun

So, if directly translated, *prescription* means "something that was written before." Consider that doctors write prescriptions to make a patient better. A prescription is written before a person regains his or her health.

In some cases, root words can function as prefixes, or at the beginning rather than the end of the word. The word *autobiographical* is a word that contains two roots. In this case, *auto* functions as a prefix.

auto	+	**bio**	+	**graphic**	+	**al**
prefix	+	root word	+	root word	+	suffix
self	+	life	+	to write	+	indicates an adjective

A direct "translation" of *autobiographical* is "self, life, and writing." Autobiographical writing is writing about one's own life. Notice how a root word is not on its own but rather is accompanied by prefixes and suffixes. You will need to use your knowledge of both prefixes and suffixes when identifying root words.

FOCUS ON VOCABULARY: Recognizing Root Words

Table 4.1 lists some common root words found in academic reading. Be alert to these roots and open to noticing and learning others as they come up in your reading. Once you begin to look for them, you will realize how common they are.

TABLE 4.1 COMMON ROOT WORDS

ROOT WORD	MEANING	EXAMPLE	PREFIX AND/OR SUFFIX USED
anthrop	man/human	*Anthropology*—the study of humans Anthropology is the academic study of humans and culture.	*ology* = study of
astro	star	*Astronaut*—one who travels space Astronauts are specifically trained to cope with the rigors of space travel.	*naut* = sailor (as in *nautical* = water)
bio	life	*Biology*—the study of life Biology is the science of life.	*ology* = study of
demos	people	*Democracy*—government run by the people To live in a democracy provides freedoms and options not found in political systems of dictatorship.	*cracy* = govern, rule
derma	skin	*Epidermis*—outer layer of skin A dermatologist is a medical specialist in the study of the epidermis.	*epi* = over, on
gamy	spouse	*Monogamy*—one spouse Monogamy is the only acceptable legal union in the United States; not so in other countries.	*mono* = one
gen	race, kind, people, breed, grow	*To generate*—to grow Studies have suggested that anti-depressant medication prompts neurons to generate new connections, which takes time.	*erate* = verb form
hydro	water	*Hydrate*—to fill with water To hydrate before long-distance running is as important as it is to all endurance sports.	*ate* = verb form

TABLE 4.1 COMMON ROOT WORDS

ROOT WORD	MEANING	EXAMPLE	PREFIX AND/OR SUFFIX USED
hypno	sleep	*Hypnotism*—the act of putting to sleep/ trance The warmth and gentle hum in the classroom was hypnotic.	*ism* = noun ending *ic* = adjective ending
man(u) *script*	hand write	*Manuscript*—written by hand The manuscript was irreplaceable because no copies had been generated.	
pod/ped	foot *ped* also means "child"	*Pedal*—operated by foot *Pediatrics*—study of child medicine The pediatric nurse was an expert in dealing with the traumatized child.	*al* = adjective ending *iatrics* = from the Greek *iatros*, meaning "healer" or "physician" *ic* = adjective ending
psycho	mind	*Psychology*—the study of the mind To understand the criminal mind, it is necessary to contemplate the psychology of the antisocial act.	*ology* = study of
pop	people	*Populace*—a group of people The populace was excited to welcome the dignitaries to the capital city.	*ace* = noun ending
script	write	*Prescription*—to write before (*pre*) The experts prescribed alternatives to our existing reliance on fossil fuels.	*pre* = before *ion* = noun ending *ed* = verb ending
spec	look	*Spectator*—someone who looks The spectator watched the game with great interest.	*or* = noun ending
terra	earth	*Extraterrestrial*—from outside the earth The terraforming of Mars by making it livable to external life conjures images of extraterrestrial civilizations seen in bad science-fiction movies.	*extra* = beyond *ial* = adjective ending *ing* = verb ending

(Continued)

FOCUS ON VOCABULARY: Recognizing Root Words

TABLE 4.1 COMMON ROOT WORDS

ROOT WORD	MEANING	EXAMPLE	PREFIX AND/OR SUFFIX USED
thermo *meter*	heat measure	*Thermometer*—measure of heat The thermometer indicates that the outside temperature is hovering above freezing.	
ver	truth	*Verify*—to determine truth To verify your risk in assuming a loan of some proportion, banks check three credit reporting agencies.	*ify* = verb ending
zoo	animal	*Zoology*—the study of animals The late Steve Irwin, known as the "Crocodile Hunter," made the study of zoology fascinating and accessible to countless people.	*ology* = the study of
FAMILY RELATIONSHIPS			
mater/matri	mother	*Maternal*—motherly Her maternal instincts compelled her to become a teacher.	*al* = adjective ending
pater/patri	father	*Paternity test*—test of fatherhood Before accepting responsibility for child-support payments, the millionaire insisted on taking a paternity test to assure the child's parentage.	*ity* = noun ending
frater/fratri	brother	*Fraternity*—brotherhood club Fraternity hazing, of long concern, is being banned on an increasing number of college campuses.	*ity* = noun ending
soror	sister	*Sorority*—sisterhood club Sororities have become increasingly popular, although they are not as numerous as fraternities on college campuses.	*ity* = noun ending

On Your Own RECOGNIZING ROOT WORDS

Choose 10 of the root words listed in Table 4.1. Without using the dictionary, write down at least one word that you know containing this root. Next to the word, write a definition using the meaning listed in the chart. Then, write your word in a sentence, providing context clues that clearly reveal the word's meaning. Share your sentences with a partner or in class discussion.

Original Root from Chart	Your New Word and Its Definition	Sentence with Word Using Context Clues
1.		
2.		
3.		
4.		
5.		
6.		
7.		
8.		
9.		
10.		

FOCUS ON VOCABULARY: Recognizing Root Words

Practice Exercise 3:   RECOGNIZING ROOT WORDS

Here are 10 words drawn from the root word list in this chapter. Write a sentence using the word that provides vocabulary clues for its meaning. Alternatively, decode the meaning of these words using your knowledge of prefixes, suffixes, and root words. Refer to Tables 4.1, 3.4, and 3.6.

1. Misanthrope _____

_____

2. Astrology _____

_____

3. Biography _____

_____

4. Democratic _____

_____

5. Bigamy _____

_____

6. Generate _____

_____

7. Hydration _____

_____

8. Psychopath _____

_____

9. Spectator _____

_____

10. Fraternize _____

_____

APPLICATIONS

These applications will develop your skills of understanding inference and implied main ideas as well as strengthen your recognition of word parts. Follow the instructions for each application, and then answer the Comprehension Check questions. Each application serves to release more responsibility to the reader as these techniques become more automatic.

APPLICATION

This reading comes from *Newsweek*. Preview this reading first; then read the article in its entirety. As you read, answer the questions in the margin about finding main ideas. After you read, complete the questions that follow the reading.

What is the topic of this reading? _____

Oh, Brother: How Nature and Nurture Can Conspire to Create Ideologically Opposed Siblings
By Christina Gillham

Ideologically refers to beliefs.

1   Like many brothers, Brad and Dallas Woodhouse share a lot of interests. They both love skiing, *Law & Order*, and following North Carolina State football and basketball. But bring up the subject of politics, and the two veer in sharply different directions.

What is the topic of paragraph 1?

What is the main idea of paragraph 1?

2   "My brother is out to destroy the country," says Dallas, 36, only half jokingly. A Republican, he works for the North Carolina division of Americans for Prosperity, a conservative group that advocates for low taxes and small government. Brad Woodhouse, 41, is the communications director for the **Democratic** National Committee. "My brother is a right-wing nut job," Brad says, also half jokingly.

What method?

What is the topic of paragraph 2?

3   Recently, the brothers have even taken their views public, arguing different sides of the health-care debate—and trading barbs—on media outlets such as CNN.

What is the main idea of paragraph 2?

4   It may seem unusual for two siblings who grew up in the same house, with the same parents, and under more or less the same circumstances to end up on opposite ends of the political spectrum. But it's not that uncommon, researchers say. A quick look around the cultural landscape might prove the point: liberal *New York Times* columnist Maureen Dowd has published lengthy comments by her conservative older brother in her

What method?
What does the root *demo* mean in *democratic*?

(Continued)

What is the topic of paragraph 4?

What is the main idea of paragraph 4?

What method?

What does the root *spec* mean in *spectrum*?

What does the root *psycho* mean in *psychoanalysts*?

What is the topic of paragraph 7?

What is the main idea of paragraph 7?

What method?

What does the root *gen* mean in *genetic*?

5

6

7

8

9

column. And famously liberal actor Alec Baldwin's younger brother Stephen is a born-again Christian conservative.

"Basically, all siblings, animal and human, are hard-wired to compete over parental investment," says Frank Sulloway, a visiting professor at UC Berkeley's Institute of Personality and Social Research and author of *Born to Rebel: Birth Order, Family Dynamics and Creative Lives*. In other words, choosing opposing sides of the political **spectrum** may simply be one manifestation of good, old-fashioned sibling rivalry, born from an unconscious desire to vie for Mom's and Dad's attention and to differentiate oneself from one's sibling.

Sibling rivalry precedes the story of Cain and Abel, of course, and nearly everyone with a brother or sister experiences it in one form or another. **Psychoanalysts** have had a field day with the subject; Sigmund Freud famously described rivalry between brothers as an Oedipal battle for Mom's love. Freud's contemporary, Alfred Adler, believed that siblings differentiate themselves, either consciously or unconsciously, in order to promote the survival of their own genes. "From an evolutionary perspective, it's good for siblings to be different," says Susan McHale, a professor of human development at Pennsylvania State University. "If selection pressures come to prevail, one sibling will survive. If they're all alike, they're all likely to succumb."

But other factors may also contribute to siblings' differing political views. The order in which they were born is one. Sulloway's studies have shown that, in general, older siblings are more likely to be conservative, and second- and later-borns progressively more liberal. The Woodhouse brothers, of course, are a statistical anomaly. Dallas, the conservative one, is the youngest, and Brad, the liberal, is the middle child. Their older sister is apolitical, both brothers say, but leans conservative (Brad says, "I have no doubt she's a Republican. I'm surrounded by 'em").

Of course, when it comes to politics, views are also shaped by life experience. A man who sees his small business heavily taxed may grow into a firm believer in the conservative notion of small government; one who can't afford health insurance might trend more liberal. Dallas says he became a conservative when, as a television reporter, he began to notice what he called "government waste."

But political viewpoints are also something of a **genetic** crapshoot. Recent studies have shown that a person's liberal or conservative viewpoint is partly based on his or her brain activity. Siblings share only about 50 percent of genes, which leaves the remaining 50 percent open to a roll of the dice. So, yes, it's partly your brain that determines whether you vote red or blue (or none of the above).

10   Whether or not all the potential explanations for their beliefs matter to the Woodhouse brothers is doubtful. And, in spite of it all, the brothers maintain that they love each other and are really close. Still, in this contentious political climate, it can be hard to put passions aside. "This stuff heavily divides us," says Dallas. "I think we'll both fight to the bitter end."

"Oh, Brother: How Nature and Nurture Can Conspire to Create Ideologically Opposed Siblings" by Christina Gilham, *Newsweek,* September 24, 2009. © 2009 The Newsweek/Daily Beast Company LLC. By permission.

COMPREHENSION CHECK

TRUE / FALSE QUESTIONS

For the following statements, write a *T* if the statement is true or an *F* if the statement is false based on the reading.

___   1. Like many brothers, Brad and Dallas Woodhouse share a lot of interests.

___   2. The Woodhouse brothers agree on issues of politics.

___   3. Differences between siblings—as in the case of the Woodhouse brothers—are not common.

___   4. Nearly everyone experiences sibling rivalry in one form or another.

___   5. Sibling views and differences are also shaped by life experiences, not just genes.

LITERAL COMPREHENSION—MULTIPLE CHOICE

Circle the best answer for the following questions.

Understanding Main Ideas

6. What is the author's purpose in writing this article?

   a. To inform us about the explanations for such differences between siblings, exploring the nature versus nurture debate.

   b. To persuade us that sibling differences are genetic.

(Continued)

    c. To entertain us about the two fighting brothers.

    d. To instruct us how to get along with our siblings.

7. What reasons are presented that may explain why the Woodhouse brothers may be on different ends of the developmental spectrum?

    a. Parenting differences during childhood

    b. Sibling rivalry, birth order, life experience, and genetics

    c. Different friends and influences in school

    d. Only genetics

8. What is the thesis of the article?

    a. Siblings develop ideological differences because of upbringing.

    b. There are a variety of reasons that siblings may develop ideological differences.

    c. Siblings develop ideological differences due to birth order.

    d. The reasons siblings develop ideological differences is because there are differences in intelligence between siblings.

9. Is the thesis implied or directly stated?

    a. The thesis is implied.

    b. The thesis is directly stated.

    c. The thesis is both directly stated and implied.

    d. There is no thesis in this reading.

10. If the main idea is implied, what method of constructing it did you use?

    a. Method 1

    b. Method 2

    c. Method 3

    d. The thesis is directly stated.

Understanding Secondary Information and Locating Information

11. What are some hypotheses (reasons) that psychoanalysts have come up with that explain sibling rivalry?

    a. Sigmund Freud described rivalry between brothers as an Oedipal battle for Mom's love.

    b. Alfred Adler believed that siblings differentiate themselves, either consciously or unconsciously, in order to promote the survival of their own genes.

    c. Hypotheses include both Oedipal and sibling differentiation theories.

    d. Sibling rivalry is determined by genetics only.

12. According to Sigmund Freud's theory of sibling rivalry,

    a. Brothers compete for the father's attention.

    b. Brothers compete for the mother's attention.

    c. Brothers compete for dominance to promote their own genes.

    d. Brothers compete for attention from friends or peers.

13. How does genetics play a part in determining political orientation (paragraph 9)?

    a. Recent studies have shown that a person's liberal or conservative viewpoint is partly based on his or her brain activity.

    b. Recent studies have shown that political views are completely based on genetics.

    c. Recent studies have suggested that political views are based on environment only.

    d. Studies have disproved that genetics play a part in political orientation.

14. Which of the following examples of rival siblings is not mentioned in this reading?

    a. Alec and Stephen Baldwin

    b. Cain and Abel

    c. The Woodhouse brothers

    d. Michael and Marlon Jackson

15. Siblings share what percentage of their genes?

    a. 25 percent

    b. 50 percent

    c. 75 percent

    d. 100 percent

INFERENTIAL COMPREHENSION—MULTIPLE CHOICE

Circle the best answer for the following questions.

Making Inferences

16. Referring to paragraph 9, make an inference about what the author means in the following quote: "But political viewpoints are also something of a genetic crapshoot."

    a. Crapshoot implies that everyone will manifest the trait.

    b. Crapshoot refers to a game of chance.

    c. Crapshoot implies a random chance of manifesting a trait, like the game of chance from which the term was derived.

    d. Crapshoot implies that the connection between political orientation and genetics has been disproved.

(Continued)

17. Referring to paragraph 9, make an inference about what the author means in the following quote: "So, yes, it's partly your brain that determines whether you vote red or blue (or none of the above)."

    a.   Red refers to conservative politics and blue to liberal politics.

    b.   Blue refers to conservative politics and red refers to liberal politics.

    c.   Red refers to patriotism.

    d.   Blue refers to liberty.

18. In paragraph 2, right wing refers to

    a.   Liberal political beliefs.

    b.   Conservative political beliefs.

    c.   Unfocused thinking.

    d.   Incorrect thinking.

Applying Information

19. Based on this reading, you can assume that

    a.   All siblings demonstrate differences based on genetics.

    b.   All siblings demonstrate differences based on upbringing.

    c.   All siblings demonstrate differences based on environment.

    d.   All of the given answers.

Understanding Sentence Relationships

20. The author explores possible explanations for sibling differences in this reading. Is the focus on the causes of the differences between the two brothers' political views or the effects?

    a.   Causes of differences

    b.   Effects of the differences

INCREASE YOUR COLLEGE-LEVEL VOCABULARY

The following words are used in this reading. Based on your knowledge of root words, use each word in an original sentence. Then create another word using the same root word. Write the new word in a sentence clearly using context clues.

21. Democratic _____

    Sentence: _____

    New word using the same root: _____

    New word used in a sentence: _____

    _____

22. Spectrum _____

   Sentence: _____

   New word using the same root: _____

   New word used in a sentence: _____

   _____

23. Psychoanalyst _____

   Sentence: _____

   New word using the same root: _____

   New word used in a sentence: _____

   _____

24. Genetic _____

   Sentence: _____

   New word using the same root: _____

   New word used in a sentence: _____

   _____

SHORT-ANSWER QUESTIONS

25. Which of the theories of sibling rivalry discussed in the reading is most convincing? Provide specific examples to support your opinion.

26. In your opinion, is sibling rivalry a learned or innate trait?

27. What is your birth order? How do you feel being the only, youngest, middle, or oldest has affected the development of your personality?

APPLICATION ②

Here is a reading from the college human development textbook *Human Development: A Life-Span View*, 5th edition. Preview this reading as you learned in Chapter 1. Then read it all the way through, responding to the prompts in the margin. Last, answer the Comprehension Check questions that follow the reading.

Recurring Issues in Human Development
By Robert V. Kail and John C. Cavanaugh

Nature Versus Nurture

1   Think for a minute about a particular characteristic that you and several people in your family have, such as intelligence, good looks, or a friendly and outgoing personality.

What is the topic of paragraph 2?

What is the main idea of paragraph 2?

2   Why is this trait so prevalent? Is it because you inherited the trait from your parents? Or is it because of where and how you and your parents were brought up? Answers to these questions illustrate different positions on the **nature–nurture issue,** which involves the degree to which genetic or hereditary influences (nature) and experiential or environmental influences (nurture) determine the kind of person you are. Scientists once hoped to answer these questions by identifying either heredity or environment as the cause of a particular aspect of development. The goal was to be able to say, for example, that intelligence was due to heredity or that personality was due to experience. Today, however, we know that virtually no feature of life-span development is due exclusively to either heredity or environment. Instead, development is always shaped by both: Nature and nurture are mutually interactive influences.

Continuity Versus Discontinuity

What is the topic of paragraph 3?

What is the main idea of paragraph 3?

What method?

3   Think of some ways in which you remain similar to how you were as a 5-year-old. Maybe you were outgoing and friendly at that age and remain outgoing and friendly today. Examples like these suggest a great deal of continuity in development. Once a person begins down a particular developmental path—for example, toward friendliness or intelligence—he or she stays on that path throughout life. According to this view,

if Ricardo is a friendly and smart 5-year-old then he should be friendly and smart as a 25- and 75-year-old.

4   The other view—that development is not always continuous—is illustrated in the Hi and Lois cartoon. Sweet and cooperative Trixie has become assertive and demanding. In this view, people can change from one developmental path to another and perhaps several times in their lives. Consequently, Ricardo might be smart and friendly at age 5, smart but obnoxious at 25, and wise but aloof at 75!

What is the topic of paragraph 4?

What is the main idea of paragraph 4?

5   The **continuity–discontinuity issue** concerns whether a particular developmental phenomenon represents a smooth progression throughout the life span (continuity) or a series of abrupt shifts (discontinuity). Of course, on a day-to-day basis, behaviors often look nearly identical, or continuous. But when viewed over the course of many months or years, the same behaviors may have changed dramatically, reflecting discontinuous change.

What is the topic of paragraph 5?

What is the main idea of paragraph 5?

Universal Versus Context-Specific Development

6   In some cities in Brazil, 10- to 12-year-olds sell fruit and candy to **pedestrians** and passengers on buses. Although they have little formal education and often cannot identify the numbers on the money, they handle money proficiently. In contrast, 10- to 12-year-olds in the United States are formally taught at home or school to identify numbers and to perform the kinds of arithmetic needed to handle money. Can one theory explain development in both groups of children? The **universal versus context-specific development issue** concerns whether there is just one path of development or several. Some theorists argue that, despite what look like differences

What is the topic of paragraph 6?

What is the main idea of paragraph 6?

What does the root *ped* mean in *pedestrians*?

(Continued)

in development, there is really only one fundamental developmental process for everyone. According to this view, differences in development are simply variations on a fundamental developmental process in much the same way that cars as different as a Chevrolet, a Honda, and a Porsche are all products of fundamentally the same manufacturing process.

What is the topic of
paragraph 7?

What is the main idea of
paragraph 7?

7   The opposing view is that differences among people are not simply variations on a theme. Advocates of this view argue that human development is inextricably intertwined with the context within which it occurs. A person's development is a product of complex interaction with the environment, and that interaction is not fundamentally the same in all environments. Each environment has its own set of unique procedures that shape development, just as the "recipes" for different cars yield vehicles as different as a Mini Cooper and a Hummer.

What method?

8   As is the case for the other two issues, individual development reflects both universal and context-specific influences. For example, the basic order of development of physical skills in infancy is essentially the same in all cultures. But how those skills are focused or encouraged in daily life may differ across cultures.

What is the topic of
paragraph 9?

What is the main idea of
paragraph 9?

9   Putting all three issues together and using personality to illustrate, we can ask how heredity and environment interact to influence the development of personality, whether the development of personality is continuous or discontinuous, and whether personality develops in much the same way around the world. To answer these kinds of questions, we need to look at the forces that combine to shape human development.

What method?

From KAIL/CAVANAUGH. *Human Development*, 5E. © 2010 Wadsworth, a part of Cengage Learning, Inc. By permission.

COMPREHENSION CHECK

TRUE / FALSE QUESTIONS

For the following statements, write a *T* if the statement is true or an *F* if the statement is false based on the reading.

____ 1. Nature has to do with hereditary influences.

____ 2. Nurture has to do with hereditary influences.

____ 3. The continuity hypothesis states that personality develops more or less smoothly.

____ 4. The discontinuity hypothesis states that personality develops more or less smoothly.

____ 5. Some human characteristics are universal (across cultures).

LITERAL COMPREHENSION—MULTIPLE CHOICE

Circle the best answer for the following questions.

Understanding Main Ideas

6. What is the author's main purpose in writing this article?

   a. To inform

   b. To persuade

   c. To instruct

   d. To entertain

7. What is the thesis of the article?

   a. Nature versus nurture is an ongoing debate.

   b. To understand the development of personality, it is important to consider several issues/factors.

   c. Personality is primarily influenced by nature.

   d. Personality is primarily influenced by nurture.

8. Is the thesis implied or directly stated?

   a. The thesis is implied.

   b. The thesis is directly stated.

   c. The thesis is both implied and directly stated.

   d. There is no thesis.

9. If the thesis is implied, what method to construct it did you use?

   a. Method 1

   b. Method 2

(Continued)

    c.   Method 3

    d.   The thesis is directly stated.

10. Today, researchers would agree with which of the following points of view?

    a.   Identifying either heredity or environment as the cause of a particular aspect of development is the goal of research.

    b.   The goal is to be able to say, for example, that intelligence is due to heredity or that personality is due to experience.

    c.   Heredity is more powerful than environment.

    d.   No feature of life-span development is due exclusively to either heredity or environment. Instead, development is always shaped by both.

Understanding Secondary Information and Locating Information

11. The nature versus nurture debate concerns

    a.   Whether a particular developmental phenomenon represents a smooth progression throughout the life span (continuity) or a series of abrupt shifts (discontinuity).

    b.   Whether there is just one path of development or several.

    c.   The degree to which genetic or hereditary influences (nature) and experiential or environmental influences (nurture) determine the kind of person you are.

    d.   Whether parents are the strongest influence on the development of personality in offspring.

12. The continuity-discontinuity issue concerns

    a.   Whether a particular developmental phenomenon represents a smooth progression throughout the life span (continuity) or a series of abrupt shifts (discontinuity).

    b.   Whether there is just one path of development or several.

    c.   The degree to which genetic or hereditary influences (nature) and experiential or environmental influences (nurture) determine the kind of person you are.

    d.   Whether parents are the strongest influence on the development of personality in offspring.

13. The universal versus context-specific development issue concerns

    a.   Whether a particular developmental phenomenon represents a smooth progression throughout the life span (continuity) or a series of abrupt shifts (discontinuity).

    b.   Whether there is just one path of development or several.

    c.   The degree to which genetic or hereditary influences (nature) and experiential or environmental influences (nurture) determine the kind of person you are.

    d.   Whether parents are the strongest influence on the development of personality in offspring.

14. If your personality is similar now to how you were as a young child, this would support which of the following concepts in human development?

    a. Nature

    b. Nurture

    c. Continuity

    d. Discontinuity

15. The development of physical skills, such as small-motor skills, in young childhood illustrates which of the following development theories?

    a. Universal

    b. Context-specific

    c. Continuity

    d. Discontinuity

INFERENTIAL COMPREHENSION—MULTIPLE CHOICE

Circle the best answer for the following questions.

Making Inferences

16. Explain the following statement from paragraph 7: "The opposing view is that differences among people are not simply variations on a theme."

    a. This means that people in different places are the same.

    b. This means that people in different places are not the same.

    c. This means people cannot be understood.

    d. This means that science cannot answer the question.

17. Explain the following statement from paragraph 7: "Each environment has its own set of unique procedures that shape development, just as the 'recipes' for different cars yield vehicles as different as a Mini Cooper and a Hummer."

    a. This means that similarities occur if the environment is different because of universal development.

    b. This means that development is psychologically determined.

    c. This means that development is genetically determined.

    d. This means that different places influence the development of behavior.

18. Why does the author use cars as a comparison with human development in paragraphs 6 and 7?

    a. The analogy with the cars is included to highlight differences over similarities.

    b. The analogy with the cars is included to highlight similarities over differences.

(Continued)

   c. The analogy with cars is to show similarities between the physical body of a human and that of cars.

   d. The analogy with cars shows that we can "construct" our own behavior just as we can design different types of cars.

Applying Information

19. What is the message of the *Hi and Lois* cartoon?

   a. The change in Trixie's behavior illustrates the continuity hypothesis.

   b. The change in Trixie's behavior illustrates universal traits.

   c. The change in Trixie's behavior illustrates the discontinuity hypothesis.

   d. The change in Trixie's behavior illustrates context-specific traits.

Understanding Sentence Relationships

20. Is the author's primary aim in writing this subsection to provide a discussion of differences within each issue or similarities?

   a. Differences

   b. Similarities

   c. Both differences and similarities

   d. Neither differences nor similarities

INCREASE YOUR COLLEGE-LEVEL VOCABULARY

Define the following key issues.

21. Nature-nurture issue: _____

_____

_____

_____

22. Continuity-discontinuity issue: _____

_____

_____

_____

23. Universal versus context-specific development issue: _____

_____

_____

_____

24. Provide examples of the following concepts:

   • Nature: _____

_____

_____

- Nurture: _____
  _____
  _____

- Continuity: _____
  _____
  _____

- Discontinuity: _____
  _____
  _____

- Universal: _____
  _____
  _____

- Context specific: _____
  _____
  _____

SHORT-ANSWER QUESTIONS

25. Do you think that people from different environments are fundamentally similar, or do different environments yield fundamentally different types of people? Support your answer with specific examples.

26. Regarding the subject of human behavior, are you an advocate of the continuity or discontinuity side of the issue? Do people remain fundamentally the same throughout life, or do they change substantially? Provide specific examples to support your opinion.

27. Which do you think has the most influence on personality development, nature or nurture? Provide specific examples to support your answer.

28. a) Think of a specific example of a character trait you have or someone you know has that you attribute to nature. Describe your reasoning.

    b) Think of a specific example of a character trait you attribute to nurture. Describe your reasoning.

WRAPPING IT UP

STUDY OUTLINE

This is a list of key terms from this chapter for you to define in an organized format. In the following study outline, fill in the definitions and a brief explanation of the key terms in the Your Notes column. Use the strategy of spaced practice to review these key terms on a regular basis. Use this study guide to review this chapter's key topics.

KEY TERM	YOUR NOTES
Paraphrasing	
Plagiarism	
Inferences	
Implied main idea	
Method 1	
Method 2	
Method 3	
Thesis	
Root word	

WHAT DID YOU LEARN?

Now, go back to the "What Do You Know?" quiz about genetics at the beginning of this chapter. Retake the quiz. Has your score improved? Write a brief paragraph outlining what you know now about genetics after reading this chapter that you did not know before.

GROUP ACTIVITY: DEBATE—NATURE OR NURTURE?

Divide into teams, or as your instructor assigns, and take a side on the following case study. Make sure to read all the steps and consider your opinions carefully.

A Pregnant Woman's Real-Life Dilemma*

Let's consider the ethical dilemma in *Making Better Babies* that Kathleen McAuliffe actually faced at the age of thirty-eight in terms of these five steps:

1   A 38-year-old medical writer, Kathleen, and her husband are very excited about having their first child. Because of her age, she is encouraged to consider genetic testing and ultimately consents. When the test results are back, she learns that she has a 10–12 percent probability of producing a child with symptoms that include profound deformities and retardation. Although Ms. McAuliffe is devastated, her husband remains more optimistic.

2   There are three major stakeholders: Ms. McAuliffe, her husband, and the genetic counselor. Ms. McAuliffe is willing to abort in order to avoid bringing a seriously handicapped child into the world and having to devote her life to the intensive care it would require. Her husband is more comfortable with the probability that their child would be healthy, but comes to believe that the decision of whether to proceed with the pregnancy is ultimately his wife's. The genetic counselor has the job of providing information in the most non-directive way possible, dealing with what Ms. McAuliffe refers to as "the really fuzzy odds that [the patient] might not have a clue what to make of." (Here, depending on who the other stakeholders are perceived to be, there may be social concerns about discriminating against the disabled, or religious concerns about violating respect for person.)

3   The major ethical conflict is whether or not to terminate the pregnancy.

*Adapted from "Our Genes/Our Choices," Fred Friendly Seminars, Inc., © 2010 http://www.pbs.org/inthebalance/archives/ourgenes/should_we.html

WRAPPING IT UP

4   Options include aborting the child (which would be legal and medically justifiable) or carrying the pregnancy to term (because the risk factors may be considered low, because of concerns about discriminating against the unwanted, or because of religious prohibitions). A future option may be to genetically engineer the fetus to eliminate the genetic flaw.

5   You're now ready to develop your own ethical position. Do you think that Ms. McAuliffe should abort the baby or carry it to term? What is the reasoning behind your position?

In short, thinking ethically in a situation means organizing the facts, values, conflicts, and options for resolution in order to determine the best course of action. Once you have worked through the steps outlined above, you're ready to take a position that is informed by the situation in all its nuanced complexity.

QUESTIONS FOR WRITING, DISCUSSION, OR REFLECTION

1. What do you feel is the most significant piece of information regarding genetics covered in this chapter? What are some ways you could use this information to improve your motivation in college?

2. What is your opinion on genetic testing? How do these tests help us? What ethical considerations are involved in such testing?

3. What is your opinion on the nature–nurture debate? Provide specific examples and reasons to backup your opinion.

4. Research the Human Genome Project. What was involved in this effort? Who was involved? Paraphrase sections of your reading to simplify the ideas.

5. Choose a textbook you use in another class. Find examples of root words, and decode their meaning.

6. For another class, try the technique of locating implied main ideas of a whole reading, a subsection of a reading, or a paragraph.

7. Find a newspaper or magazine article on the topic of your choice or one related to the theme of this chapter. Find three examples of implied main ideas.

 # POST-ASSESSMENT

This assessment will help you understand your strengths and weaknesses in learning, understanding, and applying the skills and strategies discussed in this chapter. Preview the following article. Then read it all the way through and answer the Comprehension Check questions that follow.

Self-Confidence: Nature or Nurture?
By Ray B. Williams

1   Is self-confidence something that you're born with or is it taught and developed? It's the classic nature vs. nurture question. While current wisdom has been for some time that it's mostly nurture, there's some surprising new research that indicates we may be genetically predisposed to be self-confident.

2   Smart children on balance do well in school. That may seem obvious, but there are a lot of exceptions to that rule. Some kids with high IQs don't ever become academic superstars, while less gifted kids often shine.

3   Why? Psychologists have focused on things like self-esteem and self-confidence—how good children think they are—to explain these outcomes. And the assumption has always been that such psychological traits are shaped mostly by parenting—by parents' beliefs and expectations and modeling. Researchers like Albert Bandura have argued that the initial efficacy experiences are centered in the family. But as the growing child's social world rapidly expands, peers become increasingly important in children's developing self-knowledge of their capabilities. So, until now, an individual's self-confidence was seen to be based on upbringing and other environmental factors.

4   Behavioral geneticist Corina Greven of King's College in London and her colleague, Robert Plomin of the Institute of Psychiatry, argue that self-confidence is more than a state of mind—but rather is a genetic predisposition. Their research, published in the June, 2009 issue of *Psychological Science,* is a rigorous analysis of the heritability of self-confidence and its relationship to IQ and performance.

5   They studied more than 3700 pairs of twins, both identical and <u>fraternal</u> twins, from age seven to age ten. Comparing genetically identical twins to non-identical siblings allows scientists to sort out the relative contributions of genes and the environment. Contrary to accepted wisdom, the researchers found that children's self-confidence is heavily influenced by heredity—at least as much as IQ is. Indeed, as-yet-unidentified self-confidence genes appear to influence school performance independent of IQ genes, with shared environment having only a negligible influence.

6   The fact that self-confidence is heritable does not mean it is unchanging, of course. Siblings share a lot of influences living in basically the same home and community, but there are always worldly influences pulling them apart. A genetic legacy of self-confidence merely opens up many possible futures.

7   Greven and Plomin also found that children with a greater belief in their own abilities often performed better at school, even if they were actually less intelligent. They also concluded that same held true for athletes, with ability playing a lesser role than confidence.

8   So this study, supporting the nature argument for self-confidence should put the cat among the pigeons with coaches, psychologists, trainers and parenting experts, who have argued for some time that nurturing had the most significant influence on developing self-confidence.

(Continued)

COMPREHENSION CHECK

Circle the best answer to the questions based on information in the reading.

1 **What is the topic of this reading?**

A. Self-confidence is something that you're born with.

B. Self-confidence: nature or nurture?

C. Nature versus nurture

2 **What is the main idea of paragraph 1?**

A. Is self-confidence something that you're born with, or is it taught and developed?

B. Whether or not self-confidence is something you're born with or taught is the classic nature-versus-nurture question.

C. Current wisdom has been for some time that it's mostly nurture.

3 **What type of main idea is in paragraph 1?**

A. Explicit

B. Implied—method 1

C. Implied—method 2

4 **What is the main idea of paragraph 2?**

A. Smart children on balance do well in school.

B. That may seem obvious, but there are a lot of exceptions to that rule.

C. There are exceptions to a smart child doing well at school.

5 **What type of main idea is in paragraph 2?**

A. Explicit

B. Implied—method 1

C. Implied—method 2

6 **What is the main idea of paragraph 7?**

A. Greven and Plomin also found that children with a greater belief in their own abilities often performed better at school, even if they were actually less intelligent.

B. They also concluded that same held true for athletes, with ability playing a lesser role than confidence.

C. Self-confidence promotes success.

7 **What type of main idea is in paragraph 7?**

A. Explicit

B. Implied—method 1

C. Implied—method 3

8 **What is a reasonable inference you can make about paragraph 8?**

A. People should reconsider the role of nurture in self-confidence and performance.

B. People should reconsider the role of nature in self-confidence and performance.

C. People should understand that self-confidence can be learned.

9 **In paragraph 5, what does the root word *frater* mean in the word *fraternal*?**

A. Type of kind

B. Brother

C. Identical

10 **What is the main idea of the whole reading?**

A. While current wisdom has been for some time that self-confidence is mostly nurture, there's some surprising new research that indicates we may be genetically predisposed to be self-confident.

B. While current wisdom has been for some time that it's mostly nature, there's some surprising new research that indicates we may be genetically predisposed to be self-confident.

C. Nurture provides the basis for self-confidence.

OBJECTIVES

This application includes a full textbook chapter, "Chapter 2: Learning About Learning," from a popular college success textbook, *Focus on College Success*, by Constance Staley. In this application, you will focus on transferring your reading and study skills to a college-level textbook chapter and be stepped through how to approach a full-length chapter reading. You already have some background knowledge about learning from your reading in Chapters 1–4. Also, you have a spectrum of skills for both studying and comprehending college reading and vocabulary to help you learn and understand the information. Now, you can practice transferring these skills to a real college textbook chapter, something you will have to do in all of your college courses. While reading this chapter may seem difficult, you will find the content of this chapter to be interesting, and the reading skills you've learned already will help make reading the chapter easier. Also, you'll learn a few more ways to approach a reading:

- Surveying a chapter
- Using textbook features
- Applying what you have learned to a full-length chapter
- Understanding test-taking strategies: Taking objective tests

FOCUS ON COMPREHENSION
Using Textbook Features

SURVEYING A CHAPTER

Recall that you learned about previewing a reading in Chapter 1. When you preview a reading, you are skimming a reading more closely to determine important features. However, previewing is a better strategy for reading shorter passages. To look over whole textbook chapters, however, you use a similar strategy called *surveying* designed for entire chapters. **Surveying,** or quickly scanning a reading, helps you consider what you already know about the topic, connect your prior knowledge to the reading, and prime your brain for learning new information.

Although you can preview just a section of a textbook chapter, when you first encounter a full chapter, you will look over the entire chapter and make a mental note of the title, boldfaced words, headings, and graphics. Both previewing and surveying techniques involve very rapid reading (about 1,000 words per minute). "Regular" reading, whether for study or pleasure, varies from between 150 and 300 words per minute, depending on the reading task and the reader's familiarity with the topic. The primary difference between previewing and surveying is the purpose for gaining the overview and the scope or length of the reading passage (see Table 4.2). Note that you

TABLE 4.2 THE DIFFERENCE BETWEEN PREVIEWING AND SURVEYING A READING

	PREVIEWING	SURVEYING
Purpose	Get an overview of <u>an essay, article, or section of a textbook chapter</u> before reading	Get an overview <u>of a textbook chapter or long passage</u> before reading
Goal	Provide <u>more precise information on</u> topic, structure, and main idea of a shorter passage or section of a long passage	Provide a <u>general overview</u> of topic and structure to plan your reading task in a long passage
Steps	1. Read the title. 2. Read the first paragraph. 3. Reading the headings, if there are any. 4. Read the first sentence of each body paragraph. 5. Read the concluding paragraph.	1. Read the title. 2. Activate your prior knowledge. 3. Predict what the chapter will cover. 4. Flip through the pages of the chapter. 5. Turn the title and headings into questions. 6. Scan for words you don't know and circle them. 7. Repeat step 3.

FOCUS ON COMPREHENSION: Using Textbook Features

survey a textbook chapter to gain an overview of the whole chapter, and you preview sections of the chapter to gain more insight into the content.

Surveying a reading involves quickly scanning the reading and considering what you already know about the topic of the reading so your brain will be ready to learn new information. To survey a reading, do the following:

1. **Read the title.** Ask yourself, "What is the chapter about?" This helps you determine the topic of the chapter.

2. **Activate your background knowledge.** Ask yourself, "What do I already about this topic?" Jot down some things you know about the topic based on the title (or discuss it with a partner). This step is important because you are preparing your memory to accept new information on the topic. So, don't skip this part!

3. **Predict what the chapter will cover.** Make a short list of what you think the chapter could cover.

4. **Flip through the pages of the chapter.** Read the headings and boldfaced words, and look at the diagrams or pictures.

5. **Turn the title and headings into questions.** This helps you hone in on content and organization or use the chapter objectives at the beginning and turn them into question form to guide your reading. You learned how to pose questions in Chapter 2—it's the same technique used here.

6. **Scan for words you don't know and circle them.** As you read, figure out the meaning of these words using vocabulary context clues, word part clues, or a dictionary, if necessary.

7. **Repeat step 3.** What do you *now* think the reading will cover?

These steps will provide you with a general overview of the structure of the chapter and helps set up your brain to process the information.

USING TEXTBOOK FEATURES

When you survey a textbook chapter, you will encounter a lot of textbook features that are designed to help you learn the information in the chapter. A **textbook feature** is any feature of a textbook provided to aid a student's learning of the material. There are many types of textbook features, and most textbooks have several in common. Most, however, do not have all of these features.

Features Within a Chapter _____

Chapters of textbooks include learning features to help clarify and organize the material. Here are descriptions of frequently used chapter features:

1. **Introductions** introduce the information in the chapter. These introductions function to prime the brain for accepting the new information by outlining what the chapter will cover and possibly what real-life applications the content may have.

2. **Objectives** are usually presented as an outline of key subjects or topics to be discussed in the chapter. Sometimes objectives are also called *outlines*, *key concepts*, or *goals*. Try the technique of turning these objectives into questions to pinpoint key information in the chapter for study.

3. **Chapter headings and subheadings** provide information on what the text will discuss. As you know from Chapter 2, using headings and subheadings to your advantage is a quality of an active learner and reader. Turn headings into questions to focus your reading.

4. **Key terms** are usually boldfaced within the chapter text and sometimes appear in the margins along with a definition. A list of key terms can also sometimes be found at the beginning and end of a chapter with page references. Key terms are the important terms that the chapter covers and instructors usually expect students to know these terms.

5. **Boxes, charts, tables, graphic aids,** or **other visuals** often summarize key information in a chapter or section of a chapter, or they prompt you to reflect on the chapter contents.

6. **Featured readings, case studies,** or **applications** are not just ordinary readings but specific readings that are related to or in addition to the contents of a textbook chapter. The purpose of these readings is to make the ideas and concepts in a chapter apply to current issues or life in general. For example, an anthropology chapter may discuss key terms and concepts related to kinship and include a modern-day newspaper article that relates the anthropological concepts to modern, American life. This feature usually applies to science and social science textbooks, like psychology or biology, rather than English composition texts. These features allow you to apply what you've learned to actual situations, enhancing your ability to apply and analyze the chapter information.

7. **Chapter summaries** usually appear at the end of chapters and summarize key information of the whole chapter. The summaries always include the main ideas and major supporting details of a chapter, so it is important you pay attention to this feature if a chapter includes them. Most often, the chapter summaries will answer the questions you posed from the chapter objectives.

FOCUS ON COMPREHENSION: Using Textbook Features

8. **Study questions, review exercises, quizzes,** or **other activities** are found at the end of the chapter and sometimes within the chapter. These features allow students to test whether they really know the chapter information or practice using skills that the chapter explains. They also can provide a structured review in preparation for a test or activity related to the chapter and help you make predictions about what test questions might cover.

Keep in mind that textbook chapters have some or many of these features even if they are referred to by a different name, or some features may overlap functions. Be alert to these learning aids that help you get the most out of your reading and studying.

On Your Own   FINDING CHAPTER FEATURES

Survey the chapter in this Textbook Application, "Learning About Learning." Take note of any of the features you learned about. Put an X in the box next to the feature if it is included. Next, choose a chapter from this textbook, *Landscapes: Groundwork for College Reading*, and put an X in the boxes that correspond with a feature.

Feature	Textbook Application: "Learning About Learning"	*Landscapes* Chapter #_____
Introduction		
Headings and subheadings		
Objectives		
Key terms		
Boxes, charts, tables, graphic aids, or other visuals		
Featured readings, case studies, or applications		
Chapter summaries		
Study questions, review exercises, quizzes, or other activities		

Now, list the chapter features that correspond with each of the features the Textbook Application includes.

1. **Introduction**
   • _____

2. **Objectives**
   • _____
   • _____
   • _____

3. **Key terms**
   • _____

4. **Boxes, charts, tables, graphic aids, or other visuals**
   • _____
   • _____
   • _____

5. **Featured readings, case studies, or applications**
   • _____

6. **Chapter summaries**
   • _____

7. **Study questions, review exercises, and other learning devices**
   • _____
   • _____
   • _____
   • _____
   • _____
   • _____
   • _____
   • _____
   • _____

As you can see, this chapter offers a lot of learning support to help readers reflect on and learn the important information. Also note the lively, colorful pictures. Why did the author include the photographs?

FOCUS ON COMPREHENSION: Using Textbook Features

Features Within a Textbook _____

Textbooks include other organizational features to help the reader locate information, identify key terms, and provide supplemental information. These features are included at the beginning of a textbook, like the table of contents, or at the end of a textbook, like a glossary, index, or appendices. Almost all textbooks for college include a table of contents and an index. Many other texts have online resources for further practice and study. Here are the most common features:

1. The **table of contents,** at the front of a textbook, provides you with the location and sequence of chapters, topics, and readings in a text. The given page numbers allow you to flip directly to that chapter or section.

2. A **glossary,** at the back of a textbook, provides the definitions of all the key concepts and vocabulary outlined in all the chapters. This is like a dictionary just for that textbook. Some texts include glossaries if the vocabulary and key terminology is central to the book, such as in an introductory content course.

3. The **index,** at the back of a textbook, allows you to look up a specific concept or topic and find on which pages in a text this concept was discussed.

4. An **appendix** (or **appendices**) can vary from book to book and usually includes other relevant information that expands upon the information discussed in a textbook. Examples of appendices may be maps, charts, further exercises, or readings.

On Your Own FINDING TEXTBOOK FEATURES

Look through *Landscapes* and two other textbooks you are using currently for other courses, and put an *X* in the box if the text contains the features.

	Landscapes	Textbook 1	Textbook 2
Table of contents			
Glossary			
Index			
Appendix (appendices)			

© Cengage Learning 2013

APPLYING WHAT YOU HAVE LEARNED TO A FULL-LENGTH TEXTBOOK CHAPTER

"Chapter 2: Learning About Learning" from *Focus on College Success* by Constance Staley

Apply what you have learned so far in Units 1 and 2 and this Textbook Application about surveying and previewing a chapter, identifying topic and paraphrasing, and recognizing explicit and implied main ideas to the included chapter: "Learning About Learning." Remember, survey the whole chapter, and then preview each section before you read. In addition, use your knowledge of vocabulary context clues, prefixes, suffixes, and root words to increase your comprehension.

EIGHT STEPS TO APPROACHING THIS TEXTBOOK READING

There are eight steps to approaching a textbook chapter. These steps apply to all textbooks, but you will practice them here with the included full-length chapter on page 281.

Step 1: Survey the chapter, paying special attention to the textbook features. To survey the chapter, do the following:

1. Read the title.
2. Activate your background knowledge.
3. Predict what the chapter will cover.
4. Flip through the pages of the chapter.
5. Turn the title, headings, and subheadings into questions in the chart provided here.

CHAPTER TITLE	CHAPTER TITLE AS A QUESTION
"Learning About Learning"	
MAJOR HEADINGS AND SUBHEADINGS	**MAJOR HEADINGS AND SUBHEADINGS AS QUESTIONS**

Learning and the Brain
    Use It or Lose It
    Ask Questions and Hardwire Your Connections	

Take Charge and Create the Best Conditions for Learning	

(Continued)

FOCUS ON COMPREHENSION: Using Textbook Features

Multiple Intelligences: How Are You Smart? Translate Content into Your Own Intelligences Use Intelligence-Oriented Study Techniques Choose a Major and Career That Fit Your Intelligences Develop Your Weaker Intelligences	
How Do You Perceive and Process Information? Using Your VARK Preferences	
What Role Does Your Personality Play? Interpreting Your SuccessTypes Learning Style Type Profile Using Your SuccessTypes Learning Style Type Profile	

© Cengage Learning 2013

6. In the chapter, scan for words you don't know and circle them.

7. Repeat number 3.

Step 2: Read the chapter objectives at the beginning of the chapter carefully—these are the key areas you will learn about.

You're about to discover . . .

✔ How learning changes your brain

✔ How people are intelligent in different ways

✔ How you learn through your senses

✔ How your personality affects your learning style

✔ How to become a more efficient and effective learner

Step 3: In the right hand column of the chart provided, pose each objective as a question.

OBJECTIVE	OBJECTIVE AS A QUESTION
How learning changes your brain	
How people are intelligent in different ways	
How you learn through your senses	

OBJECTIVE	OBJECTIVE AS A QUESTION
How your personality affects your learning style	
How to become a more efficient and effective learner	

Notice, there are *five* major sections to this textbook chapter and there happen to be *five* major objectives (now questions) based on the textbook chapter! If the chapter you are reading for college does not have objectives listed, take each section at a time, turning the headings into questions. In this chapter, the objectives do not directly match the major headings, but they are very close in meaning. Don't let that confuse you—just use the questions you wrote for the major headings guide how you match the objectives to the major sections.

Step 4: Read each section, looking for the answers to the questions you created from the headings, or looking for the answers to the objectives posed as questions.

Step 5: As you read, answer the questions posed by your objective questions or guide questions in your notebook. Remember, you are reading to pull out major ideas, so make sure to focus on answering the question posed rather than writing down interesting information that is not central to the reading.

MAJOR HEADINGS AND SUBHEADINGS	MAJOR HEADINGS AND SUBHEADINGS AS QUESTIONS	LIST OF OBJECTIVES

Learning and the Brain
    Use It or Lose It
    Ask Questions and Hardwire Your Connections
	How does learning change your brain?
	How do you use it or lose it?
	How do you ask questions to hardwire your connection?
		✔ How learning changes your brain

Take Charge and Create the Best Conditions for Learning	How do you take charge and create the best conditions for learning?	✔ How to become a more efficient and effective learner

Multiple Intelligences: How Are You Smart?
    Translate Content into Your Own Intelligences
    Use Intelligence-Oriented Study Techniques
	How are people intelligent in different ways? What are multiple intelligences? How are people smart?
	How do you translate content into your own intelligences?
	What are intelligence-oriented study techniques?
		✔ How people are intelligent in different ways

(Continued)

FOCUS ON COMPREHENSION: Using Textbook Features

MAJOR HEADINGS AND SUBHEADINGS	MAJOR HEADINGS AND SUBHEADINGS AS QUESTIONS	LIST OF OBJECTIVES
Choose a Major and Career That Fit Your Intelligences Develop Your Weaker Intelligences	How do you choose a major and career that fit your intelligences? How do you develop your weaker intelligences?	
How Do You Perceive and Process Information? Using Your VARK Preferences	How do you learn through your senses? How do you use your VARK preferences?	✓ How you learn through your senses
What Role Does Your Personality Play? Interpreting Your SuccessTypes Learning Style Type Profile Using Your SuccessTypes Learning Style Type Profile	How does personality affect your learning style? How do you interpret your SuccessTypes Learning Style Type Profile? How do you use your SuccessTypes Learning Style Type Profile?	✓ How your personality affects your learning style

© Cengage Learning 2013

Step 6: In addition to any unknown words that you circled when you surveyed the chapter, circle any other words that are unfamiliar, and use context clues or word part clues to help you make a guess about the word's meaning.

Step 7: Using the notes you created that answer the guide questions you posed from step 2, identify the following on a separate piece of paper for each subsection:

a. How does learning change your brain?

b. How are people intelligent in different ways?

c. How do you learn through your senses?

d. How does personality affect your learning style?

e. How do you become a more efficient and effective learner?

Step 8: Based on your careful reading and note taking of the chapter, prepare to take an objective test on the information to test your comprehension. After you read the chapter, you will learn more about objective tests and take some practice quizzes.

Note that the first three headings have been turned into questions. The answers to these questions are highlighted in purple as a model. Continue with this strategy throughout the chapter, reading to answer the questions posed from the subheadings. Highlight the answers to these questions as you read.

chapter 2 Learning about Learning

You're about to discover . . .
- ✔ How learning changes your brain
- ✔ How people are intelligent in different ways
- ✔ How you learn through your senses
- ✔ How your personality affects your learning style
- ✔ How to become a more efficient and effective learner

READINESS CHECK | What do you **Know?**

Before beginning this chapter, take a moment to answer these questions. Your answers will help you assess how ready you are to focus.

1 = not very/not much/very little/low   10 = very/a lot/very much/high

How much do you already know?

Based on reading the "You're about to discover. . ." list and skimming this chapter, how much do you think you probably already know about this chapter's subject?

1 2 3 4 5 6 7 8 9 10

See if you can answer these questions about learning to learn before you read.

1. **What does the term "multiple intelligences" mean? Can you name three different types of intelligences?**

2. **What does VARK stand for? Can you identify the letters as they relate to students' preferences for taking in information?**

3. **What does your personality have to do with how you learn? Give several examples.**

How motivated are you to learn more?

In general, how motivated are you to learn more by reading this chapter?

1 2 3 4 5 6 7 8 9 10

How much do you think this information might affect your success in college?

1 2 3 4 5 6 7 8 9 10

How much do you think this information might affect your career success after college?

1 2 3 4 5 6 7 8 9 10

How ready are you to read now?

How ready are you to focus on this chapter—physically, intellectually,

and emotionally? Circle a number for each aspect of your readiness to focus.

1 2 3 4 5 6 7 8 9 10

If any of your answers is below a 10, you might want to pay attention to whatever is distracting you before you start reading. For example, if you're feeling scattered, take a few moments to settle down and focus.

Finally, how long do you think it will take you to complete this chapter from start to finish?

_____ Hour(s) _____ Minutes

© Cengage Learning 2013

Go to the HEAD of the Class: Learning and the Brain

How does learning change the brain?

> **?** challenge **"** reaction ***** insight **!** action

Challenge: What is learning? Can you define the process?

Reaction: _____

EXERCISE 2.1

Assessing Your Views on Learning

The following statements represent common student views on learning. Think about each statement, and mark it true or false based on your honest opinion.

_____ 1. Learning is often hard work and really not all that enjoyable.

_____ 2. Memorization and learning are basically the same thing.

_____ 3. The learning done in school is often gone in a few weeks or months.

_____ 4. In college, most learning takes place in class.

_____ 5. Learning is usually the result of listening to an instructor lecture or reading a textbook.

_____ 6. The best way to learn is by working alone.

_____ 7. Most students know intuitively how they learn best.

_____ 8. Teachers control what students learn.

_____ 9. Learning only deals with subjects taught in school.

_____ 10. The learning pace is controlled by the slowest learner in the class.

You probably noticed that many of these statements attempt to put learning in a negative light. How many did you mark true? This chapter will help you understand more about learning as a process and about yourself as a learner. As you read, your goal should be to use the insights you gain to become a better learner.

L et's start our exploration of the learning process close to home—in our own heads. What's going on up there, anyway? While your hands are busy manipulating test tubes in chemistry lab, or your eyes are watching your psychology professor's PowerPoint presentation, or your ears are taking in a lecture on American politics, what's your brain up to? The answer? Plenty.

This chapter will help you understand how you learn best. In some ways, learning is learning—everyone learns according to the same general principles. For example, new research shows that in many ways, the old one-two-three method still works best: read, close the book, and write down what you remember. Amazingly, it works like a charm. You just have to discipline yourself to do it, and then go back to the book and continue to fill in the gaps.[1]

In other ways, however, you have your own distinct learning preferences. Perhaps you catch on quickly and prefer that teachers clip right along. Or maybe you like chewing over material at a slower pace, especially if it's complex. Maybe you consider yourself to be a hands-on learner. You learn best when someone gives you some guidance, hands over the controls, and lets you have at it. Many students find it easier to learn by doing things themselves, rather than by watching their instructors do things. Math can be a good example. If that's the case for you, you'll have to create hands-on ways to reinforce your learning either in class or outside of class. This chapter will help you find ways to do that.

Use It or Lose It

The human brain consists of a complex web of connections between neurons. This web grows in complexity as it incorporates new knowledge. But if the connections are not reinforced frequently, they degenerate. As you learn new things, you work to hardwire these connections, making them less susceptible to degeneration. When your professors repeat portions of the previous week's lecture or assign follow-up homework to practice material covered in class, they're helping you to form connections between neurons through repeated use—or, in other words, to learn. Repetition is vital to learning. You must use and reuse information in order to hardwire it. Think of it this way: People say that practice makes perfect. But practice also makes learning "permanent, automatic and transferable to new situations."[2]

Giving your brain the exercise it needs—now and in your years after college—will help you form connections between neurons that, if you keep using them, will last a lifetime. From a biological point of view, that's what being a lifelong learner means. The age-old advice "use it or lose it" is true when it comes to learning.

How do you use it or lose it?

How do you ask questions and hardwire your connections?

Ask Questions and Hardwire Your Connections

Your professors have been studying their disciplines for years, perhaps decades. They have developed extensive hardwired connections between their brain neurons. They are *experts*. Woodrow Wilson once said, "I not only use all the brains I have, but all that I can borrow." Think of college as an ideal time to borrow some excellent brains—your professors'!

By contrast, you are a *novice* to whatever discipline you're studying. You've not yet developed the brain circuitry that your professors have developed. This realization points to a potential problem. Sometimes professors are so familiar with what they already know from years of traveling the same neuron paths that what you're learning for the first time seems obvious to them. Without even realizing it, they can expect what is familiar to them to be obvious to you. Sometimes, it isn't obvious at all. One learning expert says this: "The best learners . . . often make the worst teachers. They are, in a very real sense, perceptually challenged. They cannot imagine what it must be like to struggle to learn something that comes so naturally to them."[3] Think of how challenging it is when you try to teach something that you understand thoroughly to another person who doesn't, like teaching someone who has never used a computer before how to upload an assignment.

Since you're a novice, you may not understand everything your professors say. Ask questions, check, clarify, probe, and persist until you do understand. Sometimes your confusion is not due to a lack of knowledge, but a lack of the correct knowledge. You may be getting interference from misinformation or unproductive habits of thinking and learning that have become hardwired in your brain. For example, you may study for a test by doing only one thing—reading and re-reading the textbook when you actually need to do more than that. It's important to be familiar with an array of study tools and choose the ones that work best for you and the subject matter you're trying to learn.

Think of it this way. Learning often involves "messy journeys back, forth and across" new territory.[4] Some of the neural connections you brought with you to college are positive and useful, and some are counterproductive. When you learn, you not only add new connections, but you rewire some old connections. While you're in college, you're under construction![5]

Take Charge and Create the Best Conditions for Learning

Throughout this discussion, we've been talking about internal processes in your brain. *Your* brain, not anyone else's. The bottom line is this: Learning must be *internally initiated*—by you. It can only be *externally encouraged*—by someone else. You're in charge of your own learning. Learning changes your brain.

© Colin Anderson/Blend Images/Corbis

> " When we come to know something, we have performed an act that is as biological as when we digest something."
>
> **Henry Plotkin, *Darwin Machines and the Nature of Knowledge* (1994)**

Let's look at food as an analogy: If learning is a process that is as biological as digestion, then no one can learn for you, in the same way that no one can eat for you. The food in the refrigerator doesn't do you a bit of good unless you walk over, open the door, remove the object of your desire, and devour it. It's there for the taking, but you must make that happen. To carry the analogy further, you eat on a daily basis, right? "No thanks, I ate last week" is a senseless statement. Learning does for your brain what food does for your body. Nourish yourself!

Brain researchers tell us the best state for learning has ten conditions. Read each one, along with some suggestions about how to get there.

1. **You're intrinsically motivated (from within yourself) to learn material that is appropriately challenging.**

   > **Examine where your motivation to learn comes from.** Are you *internally* motivated because you're curious about the subject and want to learn about it or externally motivated to get an A or avoid an F? Can you generate your own internal motivation, rather than relying on external motivators? This book has built-in reminders to boost your intrinsic motivation. Use them to your advantage as a learner.

Don't look now, but you're a very busy person! If you were watching a movie of your life at this moment, what would the scene look like? A cell phone in your hand, a website open on your computer screen, your iPod plugged in, and this book propped in your lap? So much to do, so little time! All we can hope for is that some scientist somewhere will invent a way to get a bigger, better brain! But let's face it: brain enhancement surgery won't be available any time soon.

Even so, scientists have been busy recently learning more about this heady organ of ours. From birth to adolescence, we lay the brain's basic circuitry. Stimulation is critical. When children grow up in isolated, sterile environments, their brains suffer. But when they grow up in fertile, rich environments, their brains thrive. The more our moms and dads read to us and play learning games with us, the better. Scientists used to think that our basic circuitry is hardwired for life by the time we're adults. But new brain research focuses on neuroplasticity. It is possible to build a better brain, especially after traumatic injury, because the brain is more "plastic" than previously thought—not plastic like a Barbie doll, but plastic in that it can "reshape" itself, based on what science has discovered. In a fascinating new book, *The Brain That Changes Itself,* Dr. Norman Doidge recounts miraculous stories of patients whose injured brains have been rewired to work better. If you want some interesting reading, take a look.[6]

Syakobchuk Vasyl, 2009. Used under license from Shutterstock.com

What's the secret to a healthy brain? When we think of fitness, most of us think from the neck down—strong abs, bulging pecs, and tight glutes. But brain health tops them all. New evidence shows that physical exercise helps our brains shrug off damage, reinforce old neural networks, forge new ones, and ultimately result in a better brain!

Current research focuses on a protein called BDNF (for brain-derived neurotrophic factor). BDNF, which helps nerve cells in our brains grow and connect, is important for development in the womb, but it's also important in adult brains. Simply put: it helps us learn. According to researchers, rats that eat a high-calorie, fast-food diet and have a couch-potato lifestyle have less BDNF in their brains. Omega-3 fatty acids found in fish normalize BDNF levels and counteract learning disabilities in rats with brain injuries. Scientists are working to see if the same thing may be true for humans.[7]

"Exercise your brain. Nourish it well. And the earlier you start the better," scientists tell us.[8] New research indicates that education is a great way to nourish our brains. People who are less educated have twice the risk of getting Alzheimer's disease in later life, and less educated people who have ho-hum, non-challenging jobs have three to four times the risk. According to researchers, "College seems to pay off well into retirement."[9] It can help you build a better brain!

> **Adjust the level of challenge yourself.** If you're too challenged in a class, you can become anxious. Make sure you're keeping up with the workload. In many disciplines, you must know the fundamentals before tackling more advanced concepts. Your professor will provide the baseline challenge for everyone in the class. But it's up to you to fine-tune that challenge for yourself. Get extra help if you aren't quite up to the task or bump up the challenge a notch or two so that you're continually motivated to learn.

> Learning is not so much an additive process, with new learning simply piling up on top of existing knowledge, as it is an active, dynamic process in which the connections are constantly changing and the structure reformatted."
>
> **K. Patricia Cross, Professor Emerita of Higher Education, University of California, Berkeley**

2. **You're appropriately stressed, but generally relaxed.**

> **Assess your stress.** No stress at all is what you'd find in a no-brainer course. Some stress is useful; it helps engage you in learning. How stressed are you—and why—when you get to class? Are you overstressed because you haven't done the reading and hope you won't be called on? Prepare for class so that you're ready to jump in. Or are you understressed because you don't value the course material? Consider how the information can be useful to you—perhaps in ways you've never even thought of.

© Larry Harwood Photography. Property of Cengage Learning

> **Attend to your overall physical state.** Are you taking care of your physical needs so that you can stay alert, keep up with the lecture, and participate in the discussion?

3. **You enter into a state researchers call "flow" when you're so totally absorbed in what you're doing that you lose track of everything else.**[10]

> **Identify the kinds of learning situations that help you "flow."** Do you get fully engaged by hands-on activities? Do you find that certain courses naturally capture your attention so that you're surprised when it's time for class to end? Understanding your own preferences as a learner are key here.

> **Think about what you can do as a learner to get yourself there.** Not all classes or subjects will naturally induce a flow state in you, so ask yourself what *you* can do to focus on learning and exclude distractions.

> They know enough who know how to learn."
>
> **Henry Brooks Adams, American journalist and historian, 1838–1918**

4. **You're curious about what you're learning, and you look forward to learning it.**

> ➤ **Get ready to learn by looking back and by looking ahead.** When you're about to cross the street, you must look both ways, right? Keep that image in mind because that's what you should do before each class. What did class consist of last time? Can you predict what it will consist of next time? Considering the big picture can help you fit your learning into a larger whole.

> ➤ **Focus on substance, not style.** Despite society's obsession with attractiveness, grooming, and fashion, a student's job is to ask: What can I learn from this person? Passing judgment on physical appearance just encourages you to play the blame game and derails your learning.

5. **You're slightly confused, but only for a short time.**[11]

> ➤ **Use confusion as a motivator.** You may not be getting the lecture's main points because you don't understand new terms used along the way. Look them up early on in the learning process. Ask yourself what background information would help things click—and find out the answers to those questions. As one learning expert explains, "solving problems brings pleasure," which gives you and your brain a sense of satisfaction.[12]

> ➤ **Ask questions!** To your professor, questions indicate *interest*, not *idiocy*. Don't be afraid to probe more deeply into the material.

6. **You search for personal meaning and patterns.**

> ➤ **Ask yourself: What's in it for me?** Why is knowing this important? How can I use this information in the future? Instead of dismissing material that appears unrelated to your life, try figuring out how it *could* relate. You may be surprised!

> ➤ **Think about how courses relate to one another.** How does this new knowledge align with other things you're learning in other courses? Does sociology have anything to do with history? Psychology with economics?

7. **Your emotions are involved, not just your mind.**

> ➤ **Evaluate your attitudes and feelings.** Do you like the subject matter? Do you admire the teacher? Remember that high school teacher, the one whose class you just couldn't stand? Not every class will be your favorite. That's natural. But if a class turns you off as a learner, instead of allowing your emotions to take over, ask why and whether your feelings are in your best interest.

> **Make a deliberate decision to change negative feelings.** Fortunately, feelings can be changed. Hating a course or disliking a professor can only build resentment and threaten your success. It's possible to do a one-eighty and transform your negative emotions into positive energy.

8. **You realize that as a learner you use what you already know in constructing new knowledge.**[13]

> **Remember that passive learning is an oxymoron.** When it comes to learning, you are the construction foreman, building on what you already know to construct new knowledge. You're not just memorizing facts someone else wants you to learn. You're a full partner in the learning process!

> **Remind yourself that constructing knowledge takes work.** No one ever built a house by simply sitting back or just hanging out. In your college courses, you must identify what you already know and blend new knowledge into the framework you've built in your mind. By constructing new knowledge, you are building yourself into a more sophisticated, more polished, and most certainly, a more educated person.

9. **You understand that learning is both conscious and unconscious.**

> **Watch where your mind goes when it's off duty.** Does learning take place when you're not deliberately trying to learn? Some of what you learn will be immediately obvious to you, and some will dawn on you after class is over. Pay attention to your indirect learning and move it into your line of vision.

> **Remember that both kinds of learning are important.** Both conscious learning and unconscious learning count. There are no rules about when and where learning can occur.

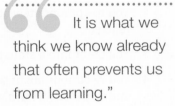

It is what we think we know already that often prevents us from learning."

Claude Bernard, French physiologist (1813–1878)

10. **You're given a degree of choice in terms of what you learn, how you do it, and feedback on how you're doing.**

> **Make the most of the choices you're given.** College isn't a free-for-all in which you can take any classes you like toward earning a

degree. However, which electives you choose will be up to you. Or if your instructor allows you to write a paper or shoot a video, choose the option that will be more motivating for you. When you receive an assignment, select a topic that fires you up. It's easier to generate energy to put toward choices you've made yourself.

> **Use feedback to improve, and if feedback is not given, ask for it.** It's possible to get really good at doing something the wrong way. Take a golf swing or a swimming stroke, for

CONTROL: *YOUR TOP-TEN LIST*

Reflect on yourself as a learner in your toughest class this term. How optimal are the conditions for learning? Put a checkmark in the box if any of the following conditions are present. If not, beside each item, write in a suggestion to help create the condition and improve your own learning.

Ten Conditions for Optimal Learning   **Course Title:** _____

1. You're intrinsically motivated to learn material that is appropriately challenging. ☐ _____

2. You're appropriately stressed, but generally relaxed. ☐ _____

3. You enter into a state researchers call flow. ☐ _____

4. You're curious about what you're learning, and you look forward to learning it. ☐ _____

5. You're slightly confused, but only for a short time. ☐ _____

6. You search for personal meaning and patterns. ☐ _____

7. Your emotions are involved, not just your mind. ☐ _____

8. You realize that as a learner you use what you already know in constructing new knowledge. ☐ _____

9. You understand that learning is both conscious and unconscious. ☐ _____

10. You're given a degree of choice in terms of what you learn, how you do it, and feedback on how you're doing. ☐ _____

example. Without someone intervening to give you feedback, it may be difficult to know how to improve. Your instructors will most likely write comments on your assignments to explain their grades. Assessing your work is their job; it's what they must do to help you improve. Take their suggestions to heart and try them out.

Multiple Intelligences:
How Are You Smart?

? **challenge** >> **reaction**   * **insight** > ! **action**

Challenge: Are people smart in different ways? How so?

Reaction: _____

EXERCISE 2.2

Multiple Intelligences Self-Assessment

On each line, put check-marks next to all the statements that best describe you.

Linguistic Intelligence: **The capacity to use language to express what's on your mind and understand others ("word smart")**

_____ I'm a good storyteller.

_____ I enjoy word games, puns, and tongue twisters.

_____ I'd rather listen to the radio than watch TV.

_____ I've recently written something I'm proud of.

_____ I can hear words in my head before I say or write them.

_____ When riding in the car, I sometimes pay more attention to words on billboards than I do to the scenery.

_____ In high school, I did better in English, history, or social studies than I did in math and science.

_____ I enjoy reading.

Logical-Mathematical Intelligence: **The capacity to understand cause/effect relationships and to manipulate numbers ("number/reasoning smart")**

_____ I can easily do math in my head.

(continued)

_____ I enjoy brainteasers or puzzles.

_____ I like it when things can be counted or analyzed.

_____ I can easily find logical flaws in what others do or say.

_____ I think most things have rational explanations.

_____ Math and science were my favorite subjects in high school.

_____ I like to put things into categories.

_____ I'm interested in new scientific advances.

Spatial Intelligence: **The capacity to represent the world visually or graphically ("picture smart")**

_____ I like to take pictures of what I see around me.

_____ I'm sensitive to colors.

_____ My dreams at night are vivid.

_____ I like to doodle or draw.

_____ I'm good at navigating with a map.

_____ I can picture what something will look like before it's finished.

_____ In school, I preferred geometry to algebra.

_____ I often make my point by drawing a picture or diagram.

Bodily-Kinesthetic Intelligence: **The capacity to use your whole body or parts of it to solve a problem, make something, or put on a production ("body smart")**

_____ I regularly engage in sports or physical activities.

_____ I get fidgety when asked to sit for long periods of time.

_____ I get some of my best ideas while I'm engaged in a physical activity.

_____ I need to practice a skill in order to learn it, rather than just reading or watching a video about it.

_____ I enjoy being a daredevil.

_____ I'm a well-coordinated person.

_____ I like to think through things while I'm doing something else like running or walking.

_____ I like to spend my free time outdoors.

Musical Intelligence: **The capacity to think in music, hear patterns and recognize, remember, and perhaps manipulate them ("music smart")**

_____ I can tell when a musical note is flat or sharp.

_____ I play a musical instrument.

_____ I often hear music playing in my head.

_____ I can listen to a piece of music once or twice, and then sing it back accurately.

_____ I often sing or hum while working.

_____ I like music playing while I'm doing things.

_____ I'm good at keeping time to a piece of music.

_____ I consider music an important part of my life.

Interpersonal Intelligence: **The capacity to understand other people ("people smart")**

_____ I prefer group activities to solo activities.

_____ Others think of me as a leader.

_____ I enjoy the challenge of teaching others something I like to do.

_____ I like to get involved in social activities at school, church, or work.

_____ If I have a problem, I'm more likely to get help than tough it out alone.

_____ I feel comfortable in a crowd of people.

_____ I have several close friends.

_____ I'm the sort of person others come to for advice about their problems.

Intrapersonal Intelligence: **The capacity to understand yourself, who you are, and what you can do ("self-smart")**

_____ I like to spend time alone thinking about important questions in life.

_____ I have invested time in learning more about myself.

_____ I consider myself to be independent minded.

_____ I keep a journal of my inner thoughts.

_____ I'd rather spend a weekend alone than at a place with a lot of other people around.

_____ I've thought seriously about starting a business of my own.

_____ I'm realistic about my own strengths and weaknesses.

_____ I have goals for my life that I'm working on.

Naturalistic Intelligence: **The capacity to discriminate between living things and show sensitivity toward the natural world ("nature smart")**

_____ Environmental problems bother me.

_____ In school, I always enjoyed field trips to places in nature or away from class.

_____ I enjoy studying nature, plants, or animals.

_____ I've always done well on projects involving living systems.

_____ I enjoy pets.

_____ I notice signs of wildlife when I'm on a walk or hike.

_____ I can recognize types of plants, trees, rocks, birds, and so on.

_____ I enjoy learning about environmental issues.

(continued)

Which intelligences have the most check marks? Write in the three intelligences in which you had the most number of check marks.

_____   _____   _____

Although this is an informal instrument, it can help you think about the concept of multiple intelligences, or MI. *How* are you smart?

Based on Armstrong, T. (1994). *Multiple intelligences in the classroom.* Alexandria, VA: Association for Supervision and Curriculum Development, pp. 18–20.

Have you ever noticed that people are smart in different ways? Consider the musical genius of Mozart, who published his first piano pieces at the age of five. Or think about Tiger Woods, who watched his father hit golf balls and mimicked his dad's swing while still in his crib. When he was two, Tiger played golf with comedian and golfer Bob Hope on national television, and he was featured in Golf Digest at the age of five. Not many of us are as musically gifted as Mozart or as physically gifted as Tiger Woods, but we all have strengths. We're all smart in different ways. You may earn top grades in math, and not-so-top grades in English, and your best friend's grades may be just the opposite.

According to Harvard psychologist Howard Gardner, people can be smart in at least eight different ways. Most schools focus on particular types of intelligence, linguistic and logical-mathematical intelligence, reflecting the three R's: reading, writing, and 'rithmetic. But Gardner claims intelligence is actually multifaceted. It can't be measured by traditional one-dimensional standardized IQ tests and represented by a three-digit number: 100 (average), 130+ (gifted), or 150+ (genius). Gardner defines intelligence as "the ability to find and solve problems and create products of value in one or more cultural setting."[14] Although we all have ability in all eight intelligences, most of us, he claims, are strong in two or three.[15]

So instead of asking the traditional question "How smart are you?" a better question is "How are you smart?" The idea is to find out *how*, and then apply this understanding of yourself to your academic work in order to achieve your best results.

Translate Content into Your Own Intelligences

Do you sometimes wonder why you can't remember things for exams? Some learning experts believe that memory is intelligence-specific. You may have a good memory for people's faces but a bad memory for their names. You may be able to remember the words of a country-western hit but not the dance steps that go with it. The Theory of Multiple Intelligences may explain why.[16]

Examine your own behaviors in class. If your instructors use their linguistic intelligence to teach, as many do, and your intelligences lie elsewhere, can you observe telltale signs of your frustration? Instead of zeroing in on the lecture, do you fidget (bodily-kinesthetic), doodle (spatial), or socialize (interpersonal)? You may need to translate the information into your own personal intelligences, just as you would if your professor speaks French and you speak English. If you're having learning problems in one of your classes, it may be partially due to a case of mismatched intelligences between yours and your instructor's.

Let's say one of your courses this term is "Introduction to Economics," and the current course topic is the Law of Supply and Demand. Basically, "the theory of supply and demand describes how prices vary as a result of a balance between product availability at each price (supply) and the desires of those with purchasing power at each price (demand)."[17] To understand this law, you could read the textbook (linguistic); study mathematical formulas (logical-mathematical); examine charts and graphs (spatial); observe the Law of Supply and Demand in the natural world, through the fluctuating price of gasoline, for example (naturalist); look at the way the Law of Supply and Demand is expressed in your own body, using food as a metaphor (bodily-kinesthetic); reflect on how and when you might be able to afford something you desperately want, like a certain model of car (intrapersonal); or write (or find) a song that helps you understand the law (musical). You needn't try all eight ways, but it's intriguing to speculate about various ways to learn that may work for you, rather than assuming you're doomed because your intelligences don't match your instructor's.

Use Intelligence-Oriented Study Techniques

What if your strongest intelligence is different from the one through which course material is presented? What can you do about it? Take a look at the following techniques for studying using different intelligences. Tweaking the way you study may make a world of difference.

Linguistic --→	1. Rewrite your class notes. 2. Record yourself reading through your class notes and play it as you study. 3. Read the textbook chapter aloud.
Logical Mathematical --→	1. Create hypothetical conceptual problems to solve. 2. Organize chapter or lecture notes into logical flow. 3. Analyze how the textbook chapter is organized and why.
Spatial --→	1. Draw a map that demonstrates your thinking on course material. 2. Illustrate your notes by drawing diagrams and charts. 3. Mark up your textbook to show relationships between concepts.
Bodily–Kinesthetic --→	1. Study course material while engaged in physical activity. 2. Practice skills introduced in class or in the text. 3. Act out a scene based on chapter content.
Musical --→	1. Create musical memory devices by putting words into well-known melodies. 2. Listen to music while you're studying. 3. Sing or hum as you work.
Interpersonal --→	1. Discuss course material with your classmates in class. 2. Organize a study group that meets regularly. 3. Meet a classmate before or after class for coffee and course conversation.
Intrapersonal --→	1. Keep a journal to track your personal reactions to course material. 2. Study alone and engage in internal dialogue about course content. 3. Coach yourself on how to best study for a challenging class.
Naturalistic --→	1. Search for applications of course content in the natural world. 2. Study outside (if weather permits and you can resist distractions). 3. Go to a physical location that exemplifies course material (for example, a park for your geology course).

Choose a Major and Career That Fit Your Intelligences

If linguistic intelligence isn't your most developed type, but spatial intelligence is, architecture would probably be a much better major for you than English. If you've had a job you hated in the past, perhaps the Theory of Multiple Intelligences can help you understand why. Take a look at Figure 2.1 for ideas about careers that emphasize particular intelligences and famous achievers in each category.

Intelligence Type	Careers in Intelligences	Well-Known Examples
Linguistic	journalist teacher lawyer talkshow host	Diane Sawyer Your instructor Lin Wood Oprah Winfrey
Logical-Mathematical	accountant engineer computer programmer	Henry W. Bloch (H&R Block) Dean Kamen, inventor Bill Gates, entrepreneur
Spatial	architect artist artistic director	Norma Merrick Sklarek, first African American woman architect, designed the Los Angeles International Airport Terminal Christo, environmental artist Grant Major, Academy Award Winner, *Lord of the Rings: The Return of the King*, 2003
Bodily-Kinesthetic	professional athlete coach actor	Serena Williams, tennis player Bill Parcells, Dallas Cowboys Brad Pitt
Musical	musician composer	Alicia Keys, pop singer John Williams, composer/conductor
Interpersonal	salesperson teacher counselor	Sam Walton, Wal-Mart Founder (1918–1992) Your instructor Carl Rogers (1902–1987)
Intrapersonal	theorist researcher philosopher	Ilya Prigogine (1917–2003), Nobel prize winner, chemistry, 1977 John Wheeler, physicist W. V. Quine, American philosopher (1908–2000)
Naturalistic	landscape architect anthropologist botanist	Frederick Law Olmsted (1822–1903) Jane Goodall Peter Raven

© Cengage Learning 2013

FIGURE 2.1

Choosing an Intelligence-Based Career

Develop Your Weaker Intelligences

It's important to cultivate your weaker intelligences. Why? Because life isn't geared to one kind of intelligence. It's complex. Even in the particular career fields listed for each intelligence in the preceding chart, more than one intelligence may be required. A photo journalist for *National Geographic*, for example, might need linguistic intelligence, spatial intelligence, interpersonal intelligence, and naturalist intelligence. Being well-rounded, as the expression goes, is truly a good thing. Artist Pablo Picasso once said, "I am always doing that which I cannot do, in order that I may learn how to do it." Remember that no one is naturally intelligent in all eight areas. Each individual is a unique blend of intelligences, and most people are strong in only two or three.[17] But the Theory of Multiple Intelligences claims that we all have the capacity to develop all of our eight intelligences further. That's good news! Howard Gardner puts it this way: "We can all get better at each of the intelligences, although some people will improve in an intelligence area more readily than others, either because biology gave them a better brain for that intelligence or because their culture gave them a better teacher."[18]

How Do You Perceive and Process Information?

? challenge	" reaction	* insight	! action

Challenge: You've lived with yourself for many years now, but how well do you know yourself as a learner?

Reaction: List as many descriptive phrases about your learning preferences as you can. For example, you might write, "I learn best when I listen to an instructor lecture" or "I learn best when I make color-coded binders for each class." Use this activity to discover some specifics about your learning style.

_____

_____

_____

Style—we all have it, right? What's yours? Baggy jeans and a T-shirt? Sandals, even in the middle of winter? A stocking cap that translates into I-just-rolled-out-of-bed-before-class? When it comes to appearance, you have your own style.

Think about how your mind works. For example, how do you decide what to wear in the morning? Do you turn on the radio or TV for the weather forecast? Jump on the Internet? Stick your head out the front door? Throw on whatever happens to be clean? We all have different styles, don't we?

So what's a learning style? A learning style is defined as your "characteristic and preferred way of gathering, interpreting, organizing, and thinking about information."19 The way you perceive information and the way you process it—your perceiving/processing preferences—are based in part on your senses. Which sensory modalities do you prefer to use to take in information—your eyes (visual-graphic or visual-words), your ears (aural), or all your senses using your whole body (kinesthetic)? Which type of information sinks in best? Do you prefer teachers who lecture? Teachers who use visuals such as charts, web pages, and diagrams to explain things? Or teachers who plan field trips, use role-plays, and create simulations?

To further understand your preferred sensory channel, let's take this example. You decide to buy a new car and you must first answer many questions: What kind of car do you want to buy—an SUV, a sedan, a sports car, a van, or a truck? What are the differences between various makes and models? How do prices, comfort, gas mileage, and safety compare? Who provides the best warranty? Which car do consumers rate highest? How would you go about learning the answers to all these questions?

Visual: Some of us would look. We'd study charts, graphs, and photographs comparing cars, mileage, fuel tank capacity, maintenance costs, and customer satisfaction. We learn from pre-organized, visual representations.

Aural: Some of us would listen. We'd ask all our friends what kind of cars they drive and what they've heard about cars from other people. We'd pay attention as showroom salespeople describe the features of various cars. We learn through sounds by listening.

Read/Write: Some of us would read or write. We'd buy a copy of *Consumer Reports* annual edition on automobiles, or copies of magazines like *Car and Driver*, and write lists of each car's pros and cons. We learn through words by reading and writing.

Pascal Genest /iStockphoto.com

Kinesthetic: Some of us would want to do it. We'd go to the showroom and test drive a few cars to physically try them out. We learn through experience when all our sensory modalities are activated.

What would you do? Eventually, as you're deciding which vehicle to buy, you might do all these things, and do them more than once. But learning style theory says we all have preferences in terms of how we perceive and process information.

After reading the car-buying description, you probably have a gut feeling about your own style. However, take a few minutes to answer the questions about yourself in Exercise 2.3—for confirmation or revelation—to verify your hunches or to learn something new about yourself.

You can take the VARK online at http://www.vark-learn.com/english/page.asp?p=questionnaire and your results will be tabulated for you.

Using Your VARK Preferences

Knowing your preferences can help you in your academic coursework. It's estimated that 60 percent of the population is multimodal, which gives most of us flexibility in the way we learn.[22] A lower score in a preference simply means that you are more comfortable using other styles. To learn more about your results and suggestions for applying them, see Figure 2.2 for your preferred modality.

Learning style descriptions aren't meant to put you into a cubbyhole or stereotype you. And they certainly aren't meant to give you an excuse when you don't like a particular assignment. You may learn to adapt naturally to a particular instructor or discipline's preferences, using a visual modality in your economics class to interpret graphs and a kinesthetic modality in your chemistry lab to conduct experiments.

Of course, you'll be required to use all four modalities in college. You'll have to read your literature assignments and write your English papers, even if read/write isn't your preferred style. Different disciplines require different kinds of information access. As one skeptic of learning styles writes, "At some point, no amount of dancing will help you learn more algebra." Actually, some teachers do use dance to help students learn math, and there are plenty of other kinesthetic techniques that work well, like solving actual problems, rather than simply re-reading a chapter in your math book.[24]

Regardless, you may also find that you need to deliberately and strategically re-route your learning methods in some of your classes,

	Everyday Study Strategies	Exam Preparation Strategies
VISUAL	• Convert your lecture notes to a visual format. • Study the placement of items, colors, and shapes in your textbook. • Put complex concepts into flowcharts or graphs. • Redraw ideas you create from memory.	• Practice turning your visuals back into words. • Practice writing out exam answers. • Recall the pictures you made of the pages you studied. • Use diagrams to answer exam questions, if your instructor will allow it.
AURAL	• Read your notes aloud. • Explain your notes to another auditory learner. • Ask others to "hear" you understanding of the material. • Record your notes or listen to your instructors' podcasts. • Realize that your lecture notes may be incomplete. You may have become so involved in listening that you stopped writing. Fill your notes in later by talking with other students or getting material from the textbook.	• Practice by speaking your answers aloud. • Listen to your own voice as you answer questions. • Opt for an oral exam if allowed. • Imagine you are talking with the teacher as you answer questions.
READ/WRITE	• Write out your lecture notes again and again. • Read your notes (silently) again and again. • Put ideas and principles into different words. • Translate diagrams, graphs, etc., into text. • Rearrange words and "play"with wording. • Turn diagrams and charts into words.	• Write out potential exam answers. • Practice creating and taking exams. • Type out your answers to potential test questions. • Organize your notes into lists or bullets. • Write practice paragraphs, particularly beginnings and endings.
KINESTHETIC	• Recall experiments, field trips, etc. Remember the real things that happened. • Talk over your notes with another "K" person. • Use photos and pictures that make ideas come to life. • Go back to the lab, your manual, or your notes that include real examples. • Remember that your lecture notes will have gaps if topics weren't concrete or relevant for you. • Use case studies to help you learn abstract principles.	• Role-play the exam situation in your room (or the actual classroom). • Put plenty of examples into your answers. • Write practice answers and sample paragraphs. • Give yourself practice tests.

FIGURE 2.2

Visual, Aural, Read/ Write, and Kinesthetic Learning Strategies

and knowing your VARK preferences can help you do that. Learning to capitalize on your preferences and translate challenging course material into your preferred modality may serve you well. Remember these suggestions about the VARK, and try them out to see if they improve your academic results.

1. VARK preferences are not necessarily strengths. However VARK is an excellent vehicle to help you reflect on how you learn and begin to reinforce the productive strategies you're already using or select ones that might work better.

2. If you have a strong preference for a particular modality, practice multiple suggestions listed in Figure 2.2 for that particular modality. Reinforce your learning through redundancy.

3. Remember that an estimated 60 percent of people are multimodal. In a typical classroom of 30 students (based on VARK data):

   > 17 students would be multimodal,

   > 1 student would be visual,

   > 1 student would be aural,

   > 5 students would be read/write,

   > 6 students would be kinesthetic,

   and the teacher would most likely have a strong read/write preference![25]

4. If you are multimodal, as most of us are, it may be necessary to use all your modalities to boost your confidence in your learning. Practice the suggestions for all of your preferred modalities.

5. While in an ideal world, it would be good to try to strengthen lesser preferences, you may wish to save that goal for later in life. Fleming's students eventually convinced him that college isn't the place to experiment. Academic results are important, and often scholarships and graduate school acceptance hang in the balance. You, too, may decide it's better to try to strengthen existing preferences now and work on expanding your repertoire later. This book will give you an opportunity to practice your VARK learning preferences—whatever they are—in each chapter.

What Role Does Your Personality Play?

? **challenge** > " **reaction** | * **insight** > ! **action**

Challenge: How does your personality affect your learning style?

Reaction: _____

One of the best things about college, no matter which one you've chosen to attend, is meeting so many different kinds of people. At times you may find these differences intriguing. At other times, they may baffle you. Look around and listen to other students, and you'll start to notice. Have you heard students voicing totally opposite opinions about college life by saying things like this?

"There's no way I can study in the dorm. It's way too noisy."	"There's no way I can study in the library. It's way too quiet."
"My roommate is terrific! We're getting along great."	"My roommate is unbearable! I can hardly stand being around him."
"I'm so glad I've already decided on a major. Now I can go full steam ahead."	"I have no idea what to major in. I can think of six different majors I'd like to choose."
"My sociology prof is great. She talks about all kinds of things in class, and her essay tests are actually fun!"	"My sociology prof is so confusing. She talks about so many different things in class. How am I supposed to know what to study for her tests?"[27]

You're likely to run into all kinds of viewpoints and all kinds of people, but as you're bound to discover in college, differences make life much more interesting! Perhaps your friends comment on your personality by saying, "She's really quiet," or "He's the class clown," or "He's incredibly logical," or "She trusts her gut feelings." What you may not know is how big a role your personality traits like these play in how you prefer to learn and your academic success.[28]

The Myers-Briggs Type Indicator® (MBTI) is the most well known personality assessment instrument in the world. Each year, approximately four million people worldwide obtain significant insights about their personalities, their career choices, their interaction with others, and their learning styles by completing it.

This chapter will introduce you to a shorter instrument based on the MBTI, the SuccessTypes Learning Style Type Indicator. Created by Dr. John Pelley at Texas Tech University, this instrument focuses specifically on your personality type and how you prefer to learn. If you are able to complete the full Myers-Briggs Type Indicator in the class for which you're using this textbook, or through your college counseling center or learning center, do so. You'll learn even more about yourself.

© Cengage Learning 2013

Here's an important point: Both the SuccessTypes Learning Style Type Indicator and the Myers-Briggs Type Indicator show you your preferences. These instruments are not about what you *can* do. They're about what you *prefer* to do. That's an important distinction. Here's an illustration. Try writing your name on the line below.

_____

Now put the pen in your other hand, and try writing your name again.

_____

What was different the second time around? For most people, the second try takes longer, is less legible, probably feels odd, and requires more concentration. But could you do it? Yes. It's just that you prefer doing it the first way. The first way is easier and more natural; the second way makes a simple task seem like hard work! It's possible that you might have to try "writing with your other hand" in college—doing things that don't come naturally. Practice, rehearsal, and focus might be extra important, but you can do it!

Throughout this book, you will find "Your Type Is Showing" features. These articles will summarize MBTI research that investigates the chapter's topic. They are intended to pique your interest and invite you to go beyond what you see in the chapter. Chances are you'll be fascinated by what you can learn about yourself through the MBTI. But in the meantime, let's zero in on how your personality affects your learning style, specifically.

EXERCISE 2.4

The SuccessTypes Learning Style Type Indicator

Each of the following statements represents opposites in your thinking when you are learning. Choose the one that describes the way you really are. It is common to want to choose the one that represents what you want to be or what others think you ought to be. Try to imagine that you are learning for yourself and not for a teacher and that there is no grade involved. For example, you are learning about something that interests you like a new hobby or outside interest. Just choose the description that best fits you, and write the letter associated with that sentence in the box to the left, and you will total them when you are done.

1. ☐   E   I study best with other people.
         I   I study best by myself.

2. ☐   E   When I study with other people, I get the most out of expressing my thoughts.
         I   When I study with other people, I get the most out of listening to what others have to say.

3. ☐   E   When I study with other people, I get the most out of quick, trial-and-error thinking.
         I   When I study with other people, I get the most out of thinking things through before I say them.

4. ☐   E   I prefer to start my learning by doing something active and then considering the results later.
         I   I prefer to start my learning by considering something thoroughly and then doing something active with it later.

5. ☐   E   I need frequent breaks when I study and interruptions don't bother me.
         I   I can study for very long stretches and interruptions are *not* welcome.

6. ☐   E   I prefer to demonstrate what I know.
         I   I prefer to describe what I know.

7. ☐   E   I like to know what other people expect of me.
         I   I like to set my own standards for my learning.

8. ☐   S   I am more patient with routine or details in my study.
         N   I am more patient with abstract or complex material.

9. ☐   S   I am very uncomfortable with errors of fact.
         N   I consider errors of fact to be another useful way to learn.

10. ☐   S   I am very uncomfortable when part of my learning is left to my imagination.
          N   I am bored when everything I am supposed to learn is presented explicitly.

11. ☐   S   I prefer to learn fewer skills and get really good at them.
          N   I prefer to keep learning new skills and I'll get good at them when I have to.

(continued)

12. [ ] S I learn much better in a hands-on situation to see what is.

N I learn much better when I'm thinking about the possibilities to imagine what might be.

13. [ ] S I prefer to learn things that are useful and based on established principles.

N I prefer to learn things that are original and stimulate my imagination.

14. [ ] S I always re-examine my answers on test questions just to be sure.

N I usually trust my first hunches about test questions.

15. [ ] S I emphasize observation over imagination.

N I emphasize imagination over observation.

16. [ ] S I'm more comfortable when the professor sticks closely to the handout.

N I'm likely to get bored if the professor sticks closely to the handout.

17. [ ] T I prefer to have a logical reason for what I learn.

F I prefer to see the human consequences of what I learn.

18. [ ] T I prefer a logically organized teacher to a personable teacher.

F I prefer a personable teacher to a logically organized teacher.

19. [ ] T I prefer group study as a way to give and receive critical analysis.

F I prefer group study to be harmonious.

20. [ ] T I prefer to study first what should be learned first.

F I prefer to study first what appeals to me the most.

21. [ ] T The best way to correct a study partner is to be blunt and direct.

F The best way to correct a study partner is to be tactful and understanding.

22. [ ] J I prefer to study in a steady, orderly fashion.

P I prefer to study in a flexible, even impulsive, way.

23. [ ] J I stay on schedule when I study regardless of how interesting the assignment is.

P I tend to postpone uninteresting or unpleasant assignments.

24. ☐ J I tend to be an overachiever in my learning.

 P I tend to be an underachiever in my learning.

25. ☐ J I prefer to structure my study now to avoid emergencies later.

 P I prefer to stay flexible in my study and deal with emergencies when they arise.

26. ☐ J I prefer to give answers based on the information I already have.

 P I prefer to seek more information before deciding on an answer.

27. ☐ J I prefer to finish one assignment before starting another one.

 P I prefer to have several assignments going at once.

28. ☐ J I like well defined learning assignments.

 P I like learning from open-ended problem solving.

Let's boil it down to four letters:

E or I ☐ Record the letter which occurred the most for questions 1–7.

S or N ☐ Record the letter which occurred the most for questions 8–16.

T or F ☐ Record the letter which occurred the most for questions 17–21.

J or P ☐ Record the letter which occurred the most for questions 22–28.

Adapted from Table 5.1 in *SuccessTypes for Medical Students*, J. W. Pelley and B. K. Dalley (Texas Tech Univ. Extended Learning, 1997). Used by permission of John W. Pelley.

You can take the SuccessTypes Learning Style Type Indicator online at http://www.ttuhsc.edu/SOM/success/page_LSTI/LSTI.htm.

Interpreting Your SuccessTypes Learning Style Type Profile

Look at your four-letter profile. Are you an ESFP? An ESTP? An INTJ? What do those four letters say about you? There are many sources of information about the sixteen possible combinations of letters, or type, in books and online resources.[29] However, here are some things you need to know about measuring psychological type.

First, most abbreviated type indicators—even this one—are not scientifically reliable. They are designed to illustrate type, not prove it. As the instrument's creator asserts, "Your type is the starting line, not the finish line. . . . Type is more than the sum of its parts."[30]

Second, the SuccessTypes Learning Style Type Indicator forces you to make a choice between two opposites. That's because, theoretically, you can't simultaneously prefer two opposite things at once. That doesn't mean you'd never under any circumstances choose the other one. It just means that most of the time the one you chose would be your preference.

Third, any Myers-Briggs type instrument answers four questions about you (see Figure 2.3 for further explanations of typical characteristics of the preferences):

1. What energizes you and where do you direct energy? E or I

2. How do you gather information and what kind of information do you trust? S or N

3. How do you make decisions, arrive at conclusions, and make judgments? T or F

4. How do you relate to the outer world? J or P

Using Your SuccessTypes Learning Style Type Profile

What does it all mean? Now that you know some important things about yourself as a learner, there are several other points about learning styles you should know.

First, look at your first and second letters (ES, IS, EN, or IN). Statistically, twice as many instructors as students are Introverted Intuitives (IN). By and large, students are Extraverted Sensors (ES), preferring concrete, practical learning, while instructors often prefer theories and learning for its own sake.[31]

Now look at your second and last letters (SP, SJ, NP, or NJ). Three times as many college students prefer sensing and perceiving (SP) as their professors, who are likely to be intuitive and judging (NJ). Generally, students want a more concrete, flexible approach to learning while instructors like to teach abstract, structured theories.[32]

While simply knowing about these mismatches is good, it's important to go further and act on that knowledge. As a single learner in a larger class, you will need to adjust to the teaching style of your instructor in ways such as the following:

> **Translate for maximum comfort.** The way to maximize your comfort as a learner is to find ways to translate from your instructor's preferences to yours. If you know that you prefer

Extravert (E)

"How do you recharge your batteries"? Students who prefer extraversion pay attention to people and things around them. That's also where they get their energy. As learners, they:

- Learn best when actively involved
- Like to study with others
- Like backgroud noise while studying
- Don't particularly enjoy writing papers
- Want teachers to encourage discussion in class

Introvert (I)

Students who prefer introversion focus on the world inside their heads. They pay attention to their own thoughts, feelings, and ideas, and draw energy from their inner experience. As learners, they:

- Learn best by pausing to think
- Like to study alone
- Say they aren't good public speakers
- Need to study in quiet
- Want teachers to give clear lectures

Sensing (S)

What kind of information do you rely on? Students who are sensors become aware of things that are real through their senses: sound, touch, taste, feel, and smell. They focus on what is happening in the here and now. As learners, they:

- Look for specific information
- Memorize facts
- Follow instructions
- Like hands-on experiences
- Want teachers to give clear assignments

Intuition (N)

Students who trust their intuition, or sixth sense, look for patterns, possibilities, and the big picture. As learners, they:

- Look for quick insights
- Like theories and abstract thinking
- Read between the lines
- Create their own directions
- Want teachers to encourage independent thinking

Thinking (T)

Students who are thinkers like to make decisions objectively using logic, principles, and analysis. They weigh evidence in a detached manner. As learners, they:

- Use logic to guide their learning
- Like to critique ideas
- Learn through challenge and debate
- Can find flaws in an argument
- Want teachers to present logically

Feeling (F)

Students who are feelers value harmony and focus on what is important to them or to others when they make decisions. As learners, they:

- Want information to apply to them personally
- Like to please their teachers
- Find value or good in things
- Learn when they are supported or appreciated
- Want teachers to establish rapport with students

Judging (J)

Students who are judgers like to make quick decisions, settle things, and structure and organize their worlds. As learners, they:

- Like more formal class structures
- Plan their work in advance
- Work steadily toward their goals
- Like to be in charge
- Want teachers to be organized

Perceiving (P)

Students who are perceivers want to adapt to the world around them. They don't like to close off options; instead they'd rather experience whatever comes up. As learners, they:

- Like informal learning situations
- Enjoy spontaneity
- Stay open to new information
- Work in energy bursts
- Want teachers to entertain and inspire

FIGURE 2.3

Learning Style Preferences

Source: Based on J. K. DiTiberio & A. L. Hammer. (1993). *Introduction to Type in College.* Palo Alto, CA: Consulting Psychologists Press.

feeling over thinking, and your instructor's style is based on thinking, make the course material come alive by personalizing it. How does the topic relate to you, your lifestyle, your family, and your future choices?

> **Make strategic choices.** While learning preferences can help explain your academic successes, it's also important not to use them to rationalize your nonsuccesses. An introvert could say, "I could have aced that assignment if the professor had let me work on an individual project instead of a group one! I really hate group projects." Become the best learner you can be at what you're naturally good at. But also realize that you'll need to become more versatile over time. In the workforce, you won't always be able to choose what you do and how you do it. Actively choose your learning strategies, rather than simply hoping for the best. Remember: no one can learn for you, just as no one can eat for you.

> **Take full advantage.** College will present you with an extensive menu of learning opportunities. You will also build on your learning as you move beyond your general, introductory classes into courses in your chosen major—and across and between disciplines. Don't fall victim to the temptation to rationalize and victimize as some students do ("I could have been more successful in college if . . . I hadn't had to work so many hours . . . I hadn't had a family to support . . . my friends had been more studious . . . my roommate had been easier to live with . . . my professors had been more supportive. . . ." If, if, if. College may well be the most concentrated and potentially powerful learning opportunity you'll ever have.

Ultimately, learning at your best is up to you. Early on, this chapter discussed Multiple Intelligences. Like most people, you are probably strongest in two or three. Within your multiple intelligences, you have preferences as a visual, aural, read/write, kinesthetic, or multimodal learner. And surrounding those two aspects of your learning is your personality itself. That affects *how* you prefer to learn in many different ways. You know much more about yourself than you did at the beginning of this chapter, or perhaps you've validated what you've suspected all along. Each chapter of this book will remind you of your VARK preferences with special activities to reinforce your preferred sensory modalities. And you'll have a chance to re-explore your SuccessType Learning Style preferences in short sections called "Your Type Is Showing," in which you'll get a short flash of current research findings on the Myers-Briggs Type Indicator and the chapter's particular focus.

Gaining the insights provided in this chapter and acting on them have the potential to greatly affect your college success. Understand yourself, capitalize on your preferences, build on them, focus, and learn!

VARK It!

Complete the recommended activity for your preferred VARK learning modality. If you are multimodal, select more than one activity. Your instructor may ask you to (a) give an oral report on your results in class, (b) send your results to him or her via e-mail, (c) post them online, or (d) contribute to a class chat.

Marcela Barsse/MarsBars /iStockphoto.com; Johanna Goodyear/Dreamstime.com; Nadezda Firsova /iStockphoto.com; Pascal Genest/iStockphoto.com

Visual: Put together a collage of photos that represents how you learn. Post it on the course blog or website, assemble it on a posterboard, or make a Power-Point slide show.

Aural: Discuss your 1) multiple intelligences, 2) VARK preferences, or 3) personality factors that affect learning with your friends or family. See if they can predict their own scores (generally).

Read/Write: Write a one-page summary of what you have learned about yourself as a result of reading this chapter.

Kinesthetic: Use a variety of kinesthetic learning techniques to prepare for an upcoming quiz or exam in this class or another one. Did the techniques help you master the material? Report your results.

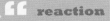

| ? challenge | " reaction | * insight | ! action |

Now What Do You Think?

1. What are your most developed intelligences? Describe a situation in which you excelled as a learner and how the Theory of Multiple Intelligences helps explain your success.

2. What is or are your VARK preferences? Are they what you predicted? How will you capitalize on them to learn at your best?

3. How does your personality affect your learning? Provide an example of how you can make the best use of what you know now about your approach to learning based on your personality type.

4. This chapter asked you to assess your learning in three different ways by thinking about your multiple intelligences, sensory modalities, and personality. How do your three assessments fit together for you? How is the new picture of yourself as a learner similar to or different from what you used to think about yourself? How will it change the way you approach learning in the future?

REALITY CHECK | What did you Learn?

On a scale of 1 to 10, answer the following questions now that you've completed this chapter.

1 = not very/not much/very little/low   10 = very/a lot/very much/high

In hindsight, how much did you already know about this subject before reading the chapter?

1 2 3 4 5 6 7 8 9 10

Can you answer these questions about learning more fully now that you've read the chapter?

1. **What does the term "multiple intelligences" mean? Can you name three different types of intelligences?**

2. **What does VARK stand for? Can you identify the letters as they relate to students' preferences for taking in information?**

3. **What does your personality have to do with how you learn? Give several examples.**

How useful might the information in this chapter be to you? How much do you think this information might affect your success in college?

1 2 3 4 5 6 7 8 9 10

How much do you think this information might affect your career success after college?

1 2 3 4 5 6 7 8 9 10

How long did it actually take you to complete this chapter (both the reading and writing tasks)?

_____ Hour(s) _____ Minutes

Take a minute to compare these answers to your answers from the "Readiness Check" at the beginning of this chapter. What gaps exist between the similar questions? How might these gaps between what you thought before starting the chapter and what you now think after completing the chapter affect how you approach the next chapter in this book?

FOCUS ON TEST-TAKING STRATEGIES
Taking Objective Tests

Objective tests measure your ability to understand facts and ideas. The word *objective* refers to the idea that only one answer is considered the best answer. Subjective tests, covered in Units 3-4 Textbook Application, are like essay tests or short-answer tests, and more complicated because there is not just one correct answer. Both types of tests are common in college. There are three types of objective tests: **multiple choice, true/false, fill-in-the-blank,** and **matching word/concepts with definitions or statements.**

QUICK TIPS GENERAL TIPS FOR TAKING OBJECTIVE TESTS

- ■ Read through the test first.

- ■ Plan your time and aim to move quickly, skipping and marking questions you can't answer easily. You can come back to those after you have finished with all the questions you can answer easily and confidently.

- ■ Sometimes, the answers to questions you do not know are suggested in other questions later in the test, so be on the lookout for any hints to answers in other questions.

MULTIPLE-CHOICE QUESTIONS

Multiple-choice test questions can be intimidating, but remember that you usually have four answers to choose from (a, b, c, or d). Here are some strategies to help you correctly answer multiple choice questions:

- • Eliminate possible answers that you know are incorrect to increase your odds of choosing the right answer.

- • Try rephrasing the questions in your own words, as this may help you eliminate answers that you know are incorrect.

- • Answers that are absolute, such as those that contain the words *always* and *never*, are usually incorrect; few things in life are absolute.

- • Usually, an answer contains qualifiers—words such as *sometimes, often,* or *usually*.

FOCUS ON TEST-TAKING STRATEGIES: Taking Objective Tests

- Longer answers are often correct, as it takes longer to explain a difficult concept completely.

- Answers with *all of the above* or *none of the above* deserve careful consideration because they are often correct. Of course, you must always read through all answers first to make an informed decision.

- Students who change their first answer after second-guessing themselves tend to have been correct the first time! It's a good rule of thumb, then, to change your answer only if you are sure the new one is correct. When in doubt, go with your first instinct.

TRUE/FALSE QUESTIONS

With true/false questions, you have a 50 percent chance of guessing correctly. Here are some strategies for answering true/false questions:

- There are usually more true items than false items. One reason for this is that instructors may make up tests that explain a key term or concept in the material. It is easier use the true statement than to create a clever statement that is false.

- If part of a statement is true and the rest is false, the entire answer must be considered false.

- Qualifiers such as *sometimes, often,* or *usually* are often true.

FILL-IN-THE-BLANK QUESTIONS

Fill-in-the-blank questions are usually testing your knowledge of a key term, topic, or idea, and you have to be able to pick out the answer from a bank of answers or use your own recall to provide the answer. Here are some strategies for answering fill-in-the-blank questions:

- Check to see if there are clues to indicate the number of words in the answer. For example, if there are three spaces, the answer may contain three words.

- Often words, key terms or concepts will not be asked about twice. Remember to cross off the possible answers as you use them.

MATCHING QUESTIONS

Matching involves choosing a key term or concept that aligns with a definition or statement related to the key term. Here are some strategies for answering matching questions:

- Start with the easiest matches and cross them out.

- Look for other questions that contain the key words that are in the matching question you are struggling with, and use your knowledge of context clues to help you decide.

- Sometimes there are more possible answers than terms with which they can be matched.

- Be careful to go with your first instinct. If you can use a term more than once, do not be afraid to do so.

On Your Own PRACTICING OBJECTIVE TEST-TAKING STRATEGIES

Here are test questions based on this Textbook Application for you to practice your objective test-taking skills. Your instructor will let you know if these questions are to be answered with or without your notes and individually or in groups.

MULTIPLE-CHOICE QUESTIONS

For the following questions, choose the best answer based on the reading.

1. According to Gardner, there are four types of learning styles. They are
   a. Visual, Aural, Read/Write, and Kinesthetic.
   b. Visual, Aural, Read, and Write.
   c. Visual, Aural, Intrinsic, and Extrinsic.
   d. Read, Write, Kinesthetic, and VARK.

2. Learning style is defined as
   a. Visual.
   b. Your characteristic and preferred way of gathering, interpreting, organizing, and thinking about information.
   c. Being smart in at least eight different ways.
   d. Understanding that learning is both conscious and unconscious.

(Continued)

FOCUS ON TEST-TAKING STRATEGIES: Taking Objective Tests

3. Which of the following does not correspond with how your brain learns?
    a. Prior knowledge is important for new learning.
    b. As you learn new things, you work to hardwire these connections.
    c. Hardwiring connections makes them less susceptible to degeneration.
    d. Learning is conscious but not unconscious.

4. How do you take charge and create the best conditions for learning?
    a. Be intrinsically motivated.
    b. Search for personal meaning and patterns.
    c. Use what you already know for construction knowledge.
    d. The best conditions for learning are: intrinsic motivation, search for personal meaning and use of background knowledge.

5. How are the SuccessTypes Learning Style Type Indicator and the Myers-Briggs indicator alike?
    a. Both the SuccessTypes Learning Style Type Indicator and the Myers-Briggs Type Indicator show you your learning preferences.
    b. Both the SuccessTypes Learning Style Type Indicator and the Myers-Briggs Type Indicator determine if college is the best fit for you.
    c. Neither the SuccessTypes Learning Style Type Indicator and the Myers-Briggs Type Indicator shows you your preferences.
    d. Both the SuccessTypes Learning Style Type Indicator and the Myers-Briggs Type Indicator tell you what you *cannot* do.

6. The SuccessType Indicator is
    a. Scientifically reliable.
    b. Not scientifically reliable.
    c. Reliable, but the degree to which the indicator is reliable depends on the test taker.
    d. Reliable, but it depends on the instructor who administers it.

7. If any Myers-Briggs type instrument answers four questions about you, which of the following *is not* one of the four questions it answers?
    a. How do you gather information, and what kind of information do you trust?
    b. How do you make decisions, arrive at conclusions, and make judgments?
    c. How do you relate to the outer world?
    d. Are you intrinsically or extrinsically motivated?

8. Which of the following does *not* apply to how you translate your learning preferences to your college career and life?
    a. Use intelligence-oriented study techniques.

b. Choose a major and career that fit your intelligences.

c. Attempt to learn the style that best suits the teaching style of your instructor.

d. Develop your weaker intelligences.

9. A kinesthetic learning style refers to

a. Physical action and hands-on learning.

b. Read/write preferences.

c. Aural or hearing.

d. Visual rather than listening.

10. As a single learner in a larger class, you will need to adjust to the teaching style of your instructor in all of the following ways *except*

a. Translate for maximum comfort.

b. Make strategic choices.

c. Learn along with the primary style of the rest of the class.

d. Take full advantage of learning opportunities.

TRUE/FALSE QUESTIONS

Write a *T* by statements that are true, according to the reading. Write an *F* by statements that are false, according to the reading.

____ 1. As you learn new things, you work to hardwire these connections in your brain, making them less susceptible to degeneration.

____ 2. Learning must be *externally initiated*.

____ 3. Giving your brain the exercise it needs—now and in your years after college—will help you form connections between neurons that, if you keep using them, will last a lifetime.

____ 4. To be a successful student, you don't need to be curious about what you're learning.

____ 5. Learning is both conscious and unconscious.

____ 6. In college, you're given a degree of choice in terms of what you learn, how you do it, and feedback on how you're doing.

____ 7. Sometimes your confusion is not due to a lack of knowledge but a lack of the correct knowledge.

____ 8. According to Harvard psychologist Howard Gardner, people can be smart in at least five different ways.

____ 9. The SuccessTypes Learning Style Type Indicator forces you to make a choice between three opposites.

(Continued)

FOCUS ON TEST-TAKING STRATEGIES: Taking Objective Tests

____ 10. A learning style is defined as your "characteristic and preferred way of gathering, interpreting, organizing, and thinking about information."

FILL-IN-THE-BLANK QUESTIONS

1. The four types of learning styles are

   - _____
   - _____
   - _____
   - _____

2. Choose the best answer from the given words for each of the following statements.

linguistic	logical/mathematical	spatial	bodily/kinesthetic
musical	interpersonal	naturalistic	intrapersonal

   a. Learns best by reading the textbook _____

   b. Learns best by examining charts and graphs _____

   c. Learns best by studying mathematical formulas _____

   d. Turns facts into songs to learn _____

   e. Applies new concepts to situations in the natural world _____

   f. Learns through doing experiments or activities _____

   g. Learns best working with others as in a study group _____

   h. Learns best studying alone _____

MATCHING QUESTIONS

On the left side of the chart are key terms from the Textbook Application. On the right side are definitions. Match the correct definition with its key term by writing the letter of the correct definition beside the key term.

KEY TERM	DEFINITION
____ 1. kinesthetic	a. Learning Style Type Indicator
____ 2. aural	b. Driven from within
____ 3. intrinsically motivated	c. Preferred way of learning
____ 4. learning style	d. Hands-on learning style
____ 5. SuccessTypes	e. Learning style based on hearing

RELATIONSHIPS BETWEEN IDEAS

UNIT

3

Subbotina Anna/Shutterstock.com

PATTERNS OF ORGANIZATION

THEME *Sleep and Dreams*

"I suppose I have a really loose interpretation of 'work,' because I think that just being alive is so much work at something you don't always want to do. The machinery is always going. Even when you sleep." — ANDY WARHOL, AMERICAN ARTIST

OBJECTIVES

In this chapter, you will focus on:

COMPREHENSION SKILLS

Learn how to recognize the structure of a reading passage with

• Patterns of organization

LEARNING TO RECOGNIZE STRUCTURE

READING STUDY SKILLS

Learn how to determine the structure of graphic aids

VOCABULARY SKILLS

Learn how to recognize transition words to determine the author's thought pattern

© 2013 Cengage Learning

WHY DO YOU NEED TO KNOW THIS?

Problem:
Rachel is a full-time student aiming for a degree in nursing. She also has a full-time job and three small children who have just started elementary school. Rachel's plate is full. Since time is the biggest issue in her life, Rachel needs to be able to pull out key points in her reading assignments quickly and accurately. She also needs to find a good way to recall information for tests because the time just isn't there to read and then reread her textbooks more than once. Rachel wants to increase her comprehension of complicated passages and make sure she knows what's important.

Custom Medical Stock Photo/Newscom

WHAT ADVICE WOULD YOU OFFER TO RACHEL?

_____

_____

_____

_____

Solution:
A key strategy that can help Rachel learn what is important in a passage is to determine how the passage is organized. Readings have a primary pattern of organization, and so do paragraphs. In fact, sentences have patterns that link ideas within them and with other sentences. This relationship between ideas lets you know what's important and what is not. For example, if you are reading something that focuses on differences between two or more things, identifying the primary pattern of organization as contrast will help you confirm your understanding of the main idea and the relationships between the major supporting details. You will be able to learn the information and apply it on tests.

WHAT DO YOU ALREADY KNOW?

What do you already know about sleep and how it affects you as a student? To determine whether you might be suffering from sleep deprivation, answer true or false to these questions.

Are You Getting Enough Sleep?

1.	It's a struggle for me to get out of bed in the morning.	True	False
2.	I need an alarm clock to wake up at the appropriate time.	True	False
3.	Weekday mornings I hit the snooze bar several times to get more sleep.	True	False
4.	I often sleep extra hours on weekend mornings.	True	False
5.	I often need a nap to get through the day.	True	False
6.	I have dark circles around my eyes.	True	False
7.	I feel tired, irritable, and stressed out during the week.	True	False
8.	I have trouble concentrating and remembering.	True	False
9.	I feel slow with critical thinking, problem solving, and being creative.	True	False
10.	I often fall asleep in boring meetings or lectures or in warm rooms.	True	False
11.	I often feel drowsy while driving.	True	False
12.	I often fall asleep watching TV.	True	False
13.	I often fall asleep after heavy meals.	True	False
14.	I often fall asleep while relaxing after dinner.	True	False
15.	I often fall asleep within five minutes of getting into bed.	True	False

—From *Power Sleep* by James B. Maas, Ph.D. and M L Wherry. Copyright © 1998 by James B. Maas, Ph.D. By permission.

Scoring instructions: If you answered true to three or more items, you probably are not getting enough sleep. Keep in mind that people differ in their individual sleep needs.

PRE-ASSESSMENT

This pre-assessment will help you measure what you already know and what you need to learn about the reading skills and strategies explored in this chapter. Your results will help you understand your strengths and weaknesses. Read the article, and then answer the Comprehension Check questions that follow.

What Happens When You Sleep?
By the National Sleep Foundation

1   When we sleep well, we wake up feeling refreshed and alert for our daily activities. Sleep affects how we look, feel and perform on a daily basis, and can have a major impact on our overall quality of life.

2   To get the most out of our sleep, both quantity and quality are important. Teens need at least 8½ hours—and on average 9¼ hours—a night of uninterrupted sleep to leave their bodies and minds rejuvenated for the next day. If sleep is cut short, the body doesn't have time to complete all of the phases needed for muscle repair, memory consolidation and release of hormones regulating growth and appetite. Then we wake up less prepared to concentrate, make decisions, or engage fully in school and social activities.

How Does Sleep Contribute to All of These Things?

3   Sleep architecture follows a pattern of alternating REM (rapid eye movement) and NREM (non-rapid eye movement) sleep throughout a typical night in a cycle that repeats itself about every 90 minutes.

What Role Does Each State and Stage of Sleep Play?

4   **NREM** (75% of night): As we begin to fall asleep, we enter NREM sleep, which is composed of stages 1–4.

5   **Stage 1**
   ● Between being awake and falling asleep
   ● Light sleep

6   **Stage 2**
   ● Onset of sleep
   ● Becoming disengaged from surroundings
   ● Breathing and heart rate are regular
   ● Body temperature drops (so sleeping in a cool room is helpful)

7   **Stages 3 and 4**
   ● Deepest and most restorative sleep
   ● Blood pressure drops
   ● Breathing becomes slower
   ● Muscles are relaxed
   ● Blood supply to muscles increases
   ● Tissue growth and repair occurs
   ● Energy is restored
   ● Hormones are released, such as: Growth hormone, essential for growth and development, including muscle development.

8   **REM** (25% of night): First occurs about 90 minutes after falling asleep and recurs about every 90 minutes, getting longer later in the night.
   ● Provides energy to brain and body
   ● Supports daytime performance
   ● Brain is active and dreams occur
   ● Eyes dart back and forth
   ● Body becomes immobile and relaxed, as muscles are turned off

9   In addition, levels of the hormone cortisol dip at bed time and increase over the night to promote alertness in morning.

(Continued)

10   Sleep helps us thrive by contributing to a healthy immune system, and can also balance our appetites by helping to regulate levels of the hormones ghrelin and leptin, which play a role in our feelings of hunger and fullness. So when we're sleep deprived, we may feel the need to eat more, which can lead to weight gain.

11   The one-third of our lives that we spend sleeping, far from being "unproductive," plays a direct role in how full, energetic and successful the other two-thirds of our lives can be.

—"What Happens When You Sleep?" by the National Sleep Foundation.
http://www.sleepfoundation.org/article/how-sleep-works/what-happens-when-you-sleep

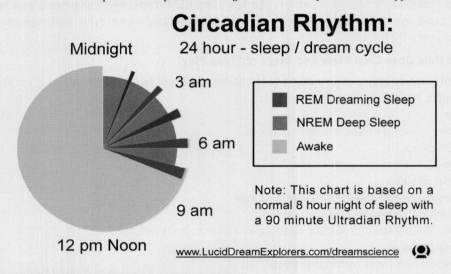

FIGURE 5.1 The 24-Hour Sleep/Wake Cycle
http://www.luciddreamexplorers.com/dreamscience/ Used with kind permission from Richard Hilton.

COMPREHENSION CHECK

Circle the best answer to the questions based on information from the reading.

1   **What happens when you sleep, according to the passage?**

A. You alternate between four stages of sleep.

B. Muscle repair, memory consolidation, and release of hormones regulating growth and appetite occur in your body.

C. While you alternate between the stages of sleep, your body regulates, repairs, and processes its systems.

2   **If a person is sleep deprived, he or she suffers from which of the following symptoms?**

A. Wakes up less prepared to concentrate or engage fully in school and social activities

B. Is less able to make decisions

C. Has problems with both concentration and decision-making processes

3 If one wakes up less prepared to concentrate and make decisions after a lack of sleep, this is what kind of relationship?

A. Cause and effect relationship

B. Comparison and contrast relationship

C. Problem and solution relationship

4 As we begin to fall asleep, we enter NREM sleep, which is composed of stages 1–4. This stage comprises which amount of our night's sleep?

A. 25 percent

B. 75 percent

C. 50 percent

5 According to Figure 5.1, we spend more time in which stage of sleep?

A. REM

B. NREM

C. Stage 1 sleep

6 REM means _____, while NREM means _____.

A. Real; unreal

B. Abnormal; normal

C. Rapid eye movement; nonrapid eye movement

7 How many stages of NREM sleep are there?

A. Three

B. Four

C. Two

8 During which stage(s) are we getting the most restorative sleep?

A. 1 and 2

B. 3 and 4

C. All stages

9 The stages of NREM sleep are organized or listed in which of the following patterns?

A. Sequence order list

B. Cause and effect

C. Comparison and contrast

10 The word *so* in the last sentence of paragraph 10 indicates

A. Sequence order list.

B. Cause and effect.

C. Comparison and contrast.

© Zelenskaya/Shutterstock.com

FOCUS ON VOCABULARY
Recognizing Transition Words

Using your background knowledge, what do you already know about transition words? You are probably familiar with many of the transition words used in college writing. They are not complicated words. You may not have considered before, however, how important they are to notice. For example, you look at transition words to figure out context clues for vocabulary. Many of the words to watch out for when you use context clues are also the clues used in organizational patterns. For example, consider these transition words for antonym context clues: *unlike, instead, but, however, on the other hand, rather*, and *conversely*. Remember how helpful they are to finding out the meaning of a word you don't know? They will prove even more helpful to you in understanding the structure of ideas in a reading.

Transitions Signal Patterns

In Chapters 1 and 2, you learned to recognize four vocabulary context clues: definition, synonym, antonym, and inference clues. Here, you will revisit the textual clues and transition words. Why? These transition words and textual clues can also signal a pattern organizing an author's thoughts. Seeing the relationship between ideas an author presents is a vital skill to understanding how an author organizes information in a reading. See Table 5.1 and consider the connection between the vocabulary

TABLE 5.1 TRANSITION WORDS USED IN VOCABULARY CONTEXT CLUES AND PATTERNS OF ORGANIZATION

TYPE OF CONTEXT CLUE	TRANSITION WORDS OR PUNCTUATION	ASSOCIATED PATTERN OF ORGANIZATION
Definition Clue A definition (phrase) of a term, often in boldface or italics	**Transition Words** • *is* • *is defined as* • *means* **Punctuation/Formatting** • : (colon) followed by definition • — (dash) followed by definition • , (comma) followed by definition • **boldface** • *italics* • definition offset by parentheses (or brackets)	**Definition and Example Pattern** • A definition context clue followed by additional supporting examples that support and illustrate the definition • Additional information is often preceded by phrases such as: *For example, for instance, to illustrate*, or *to explain*.

© Cengage Learning 2013

TABLE 5.1   TRANSITION WORDS USED IN VOCABULARY CONTEXT CLUES AND PATTERNS OF ORGANIZATION

TYPE OF CONTEXT CLUE	TRANSITION WORDS OR PUNCTUATION	ASSOCIATED PATTERN OF ORGANIZATION
Synonym Clue A word or phrase that means the same thing as the one you don't know	**Transition Words** • *Or* followed by a synonym of the unknown word • *Also known as...* • A word later in the sentence (or surrounding sentences) that means the same **Punctuation/Placement** • A word that has the same meaning within commas	**Comparison Pattern** • A comparison of ideas in a passage where similarity is emphasized • *Like, same as, similarly, just as, or*
Antonym/ Contrast Clue A word or phrase that means the opposite of the unknown word	• *unlike* • *instead* • *but* • *however* • *on the other hand* • *rather* • *conversely*	**Contrast Pattern** • A contrast of ideas in a passage where difference is emphasized • This pattern uses the same transition words and phrases as an antonym/contrast vocabulary context clue.

context clues and patterns of organization. In these cases, the same transition words and clues apply and you'll learn a few more.

   Transition words, sometimes also called signal words, are words or phrases authors use to introduce the reader to the pattern of organization, or thought pattern, of their writing and relationships between ideas within the writing. The prefix *trans-* means "across." When you make a *trans*ition from high school to college, you bridge the gap between the two levels. *Trans*ition words, <u>then</u>, link ideas in a logical progression from one idea to the other. These words will look familiar to you <u>because</u> they are used frequently in writing to make the ideas flow together and to indicate important points. Transition words are <u>also</u> called signal words <u>because</u> they signal how the author is arranging ideas. Later, you will find lists of transition words for each type of pattern of organization.

FOCUS ON VOCABULARY: Recognizing Transition Words

TABLE 5.2 SEVEN COMMON PATTERNS OF ORGANIZATION AND THEIR TRANSITIONS

	RANDOM ORDER LIST	SPECIFIC ORDER LIST	DEFINITION AND EXAMPLE	CLASSIFICATION
Description	Information to support the main idea is arranged in a random order.	Information to support the main idea is arranged in a specific order: order of importance, chronological or time order, process or sequence.	The paragraph contains one definition context clue, followed by examples to clarify or support the definition.	Information is categorized according to types or kinds and contains two or more definitions.
Transition words or phrases and other clues	(same as some sequence) *First, second, third, last, finally, next, then,* bullets, numbers, letters, *also, another, furthermore, moreover*	*First, second, third, last, finally, next, then,* bullets, numbers, letters, *also, another, furthermore, moreover,* stages, steps	*Means, is defined as, is,* colon, parentheses, (or brackets), dashes followed by the definition, bold, italics, colored words or terms	More than one boldfaced, italicized, colored word or term; groups, types, categories, classes, factors

First, transition words function to show the relationships within a sentence, a paragraph, subsection, or an entire reading. Transition words can also introduce major supporting details and minor supporting details. In addition, these words help ideas flow more smoothly in writing. Furthermore, transition words improve understanding between connected thoughts and indicate a logical organization between ideas. In short, they function to "lubricate" the parts of a reading to make them work smoothly together. As a result, your understanding of these ideas proceeds smoothly in your mind while you are reading.

In these previous two paragraphs, several main points were made, signaled by transition words. You could ask, "What is the role of transition words?" and these would be your answers:

1. They show the relationships within a sentence, paragraph, or whole reading.

2. They introduce supporting details.

3. They help ideas flow more smoothly in writing.

	COMPARISON–CONTRAST	CAUSE–EFFECT	PROBLEM–SOLUTION
Description	The information in the passage contains two or more items that are compared or contrasted or both.	The information in the passage concerns causes or effects or both.	The information in the passage explores a problem and/or solutions to a problem.
Transition words or phrases and other clues	Compare—*similarly, likewise, like, both, same, also* Contrast—*on the other hand, unlike, in contrast, however, but, while, rather than, whereas, although, nevertheless*	Cause—*because, the reasons, why, is caused by, is due to* Effect—*thus, therefore, consequently, as a result, the effect, leads to*	Problem—*the problem is, of concern* Solution—*the solution is, to solve this problem*

4. They improve understanding between connected thoughts and indicate a logical organization between ideas in a reading.

5. They facilitate the comprehension of ideas to connect more smoothly in your mind.

Points 1 through 5 are supporting details that backup the overall point of the paragraph about the topic—the role of transition words. You will learn more about supporting details in Chapter 6. Did you notice the underlined words in these paragraphs? These are transition words. Go back to these passages and notice how these words help to make the ideas easier to follow. You would still be able to understand the two paragraphs without the transition words, but they make the ideas flow better, don't they?

Table 5.2 shows an overview of the seven major patterns of organization about which you will learn in this chapter. Notice the transition words or phrases or the text clues (punctuation, bold print, etc.) that are common in each type of pattern. You will move through these patterns gradually in the chapter.

FOCUS ON VOCABULARY: Recognizing Transition Words

On Your Own SIGNALING PATTERNS WITH TRANSITIONS

Circle the best answer for the relationship between the ideas in the following passages. Use Table 5.2 to identify the transition words to help you choose the best answer. Underline transition words and circle the best answer.

Example 1: <u>Because</u> the music was too loud, I was not able to get to sleep; <u>consequently</u>, I did not do well on my algebra test.

    a. comparison

    b. contrast

    c. simple listing

    (d.) cause and effect

Example 2: <u>**Sleep deprivation** is</u> a condition where an individual accumulates a sleep debt that leaves him exhausted.

    a. comparison

    (b.) definition

    c. simple listing

    d. classification

1. My first child was very different from my second child in terms of the amount of time she'd sleep.

    a. comparison

    b. contrast

    c. specific order

    d. cause and effect

2. There are several tips that I follow every day to get a good night's sleep: no caffeine close to bedtime, no smoking, and no watching television in bed.

    a. comparison

    b. contrast

    c. simple listing

    d. specific order

3. To get a good night's sleep, first do not eat and drink within 3 hours of bedtime; next, make getting ready for bed a relaxing ritual; last and most important, do not read or watch television in bed, which may reenergize your mind.

   a. classification

   b. definition

   c. specific order

   d. simple listing

4. "*Sleep bruxism,* also known as nocturnal tooth grinding, <u>is</u> the medical term for clenching or grinding teeth during sleep." (National Sleep Foundation)

   a. comparison

   b. definition

   c. simple listing

   d. cause and effect

5. There are several varieties of dreams that I enjoy: flying dreams, successful dreams, and comedies.

   a. comparison

   b. contrast

   c. simple listing

   d. definition

6. "Occasional bruxism may not be harmful. When it occurs regularly, it can result in moderate to severe dental damage, facial pain, and disturbed sleep." (National Sleep Foundation)

   a. comparison

   b. description

   c. contrast

   d. cause and effect

7. If your problem is sleep walking episodes, one solution is to create a safe sleep environment.

   a. simple listing

   b. definition

   c. specific order

   d. problem or solution

(Continued)

FOCUS ON VOCABULARY: Recognizing Transition Words

8. Grinding of teeth or jaw clenching that occurs during sleep is the definition of bruxism, a common condition.

    a. simple listing

    b. definition

    c. cause and effect

    d. classification

9. Using data derived from the answers to poll questions, the National Sleep Foundation found five clusters or "sleep personality" types.

    a. comparison

    b. contrast

    c. cause and effect

    d. classification

10. If you have a problem sleeping on a regular basis, these solutions could help you get the rest you need.

    a. problem or solution

    b. contrast

    c. definition

    d. comparison

FOCUS ON COMPREHENSION
Recognizing Patterns of Organization

In the first two units of this book, you learned strategies to look at the overall organization of a reading by surveying or previewing and by applying active reading strategies to work with your brain to learn. In this chapter, you will build on those skills and focus on the structure of a reading by learning to recognize patterns of organization. Like the topic and main idea, patterns of organization can apply to the whole reading, sections, or paragraphs.

Relationships Between Ideas_____

Relationships between ideas are the "threads" that connect the thoughts in a reading and allow those written thoughts to make sense. An author's goal is to make sure the reader understands how ideas within a sentence connect to one another as well as understand the connection between ideas from one sentence to another sentence, and from one paragraph to another paragraph. An author arranges supporting details in a reading, often indicated by transition words or phrases that clarify, reflect, and support the most important point.

Not having sufficient time to complete my assignment was a problem I solved by using active management techniques.

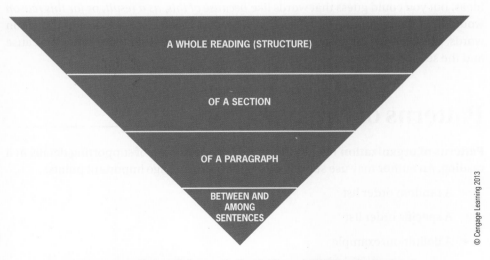

© Cengage Learning 2013

FIGURE 5.2 Determining an Author's Thought Pattern Is Useful for Understanding Not Only a Whole Reading or Parts of a Reading, but Also How Ideas Connect Between Sentences.

FOCUS ON COMPREHENSION: Recognizing Patterns of Organization

In this example, notice the transition words: *problem* and *solved*. Here, these words clarify that my problem led to a solution—the relationship between ideas is one of problem and solution.

Sometimes an author does not use transition words, but there is still a relationship between the ideas. In this case, you need to infer or make an educated guess about the relationships by applying what you already know.

Consider this passage:

> The United States has just experienced the greatest economic crisis since the Great Depression. People are likely to experience high stress levels and high unemployment rates this year.

What is the relationship between ideas in these two sentences?

a. Sentence 1 restates the ideas found in sentence 2.

b. Sentence 2 states the result of sentence 1.

c. Sentence 2 gives an example of the point made in sentence 1.

d. Sentence 2 describes the statement made in sentence 1.

Sentence 1 states that there has been an economic crisis of large proportion. Sentence 2 states that stress levels and unemployment will be high. Notice that there are no transition words to clarify the relationship between the ideas in the two sentences. The answer is b. The relationship between ideas is that sentence 2 *follows from* or is the *result of* sentence 1. In these sentences, there are no transition words to connect the ideas, but you could guess that words like *because of this, as a result,* or *for this reason* would fit at the beginning of the second sentence. Despite the absence of transition words, the ideas are connected by cause and effect. The first sentence states the cause and the second sentence states the effect.

Patterns of Organization_____

Patterns of organization refer to the author's organization of supporting details in a reading. An author may use seven major patterns to arrange important points:

- A random order list

- A specific order list

- A definition/example

- Classification

- Cause and/or effect

- Problem and/or solution

- Comparison and/or contrast

Patterns of organization function to provide a structure to a reading, a section, a paragraph or individual sentences in a paragraph. Patterns of organization reveal how an author arranges the information, which helps you understand the "skeleton" of the piece of writing—the bones that support the "flesh" of the reading. To continue with this metaphor, the "skeleton" is how the author organizes ideas as a whole—a careful arrangement of relationships between ideas. The "flesh" is all the details that the author includes to explain more about his or her topic. You want to see the skeleton of the reading, so you can understand and remember what the author is trying to communicate about the topic. Understanding how the author arranges the information also helps you understand the main idea. Also, if you do not have much background knowledge about the topic of the reading, looking for the pattern of organization will help you—if you can follow the author's train of thought more effectively, you will have less difficulty comprehending the reading and you can focus on the main idea.

This "skeleton" is known by several names: *pattern of organization, organizational pattern, author's writing pattern, rhetorical mode,* and *writing structure,* depending on the class in which the topic is discussed. In reading classes, *pattern of organization* is the most common name; in English classes, *writing pattern* and *rhetorical mode* are the most common names. Whatever the name, the central idea remains the same.

QUICK TIPS   BENEFITS OF RECOGNIZING PATTERNS OF ORGANIZATION

Learning how to recognize patterns of organization in a reading will help you:

- ◼ Comprehend the material.

- ◼ Process the information into your memory.

- ◼ Retrieve the information learned from your long-term memory.

- ◼ Understand how to structure your notes or graphic organizers (outlines, charts, webs, summaries) to study the information.

- ◼ Understand what probable questions you will be asked on a test.

- ◼ Understand how to structure written responses to test questions.

FOCUS ON COMPREHENSION: Recognizing Patterns of Organization

BENEFITS OF PATTERNS	USES OF PATTERNS

• Improved comprehension
   • Understanding the main idea
   • Understanding the arrangement of major supporting details
   • Understanding the relationship between major and minor supporting details
• Prediction of the main points in a passage
• Easier memorization of information
• Improved writing
	• In a whole reading
	• In a section
	• Relationships between ideas
	   • In a paragraph
	   • Within a sentence or between sentences

© Cengage Learning 2013

SUPPORTING DETAILS

Details within a reading are called **supporting details** because they support the author's main idea. Supporting details are additional information in a passage that explain or illustrate a main idea. Supporting details are arranged in a reading according to the pattern of organization. Stop and think about how logical this is: An author writes a passage about the causes of sleep disturbances—this is the topic. What would the author logically discuss? Perhaps a series of causes or reasons that lead to sleep disturbances. The main idea may be that there are several causes for sleep disturbances. These causes or reasons are the major points that support the main idea—the supporting details.

Supporting details can be classified as major details or minor details. **Major details** are primary points that directly support the main idea. **Minor details** are secondary points that support a major detail. You will learn more about major and minor details in Chapter 6.

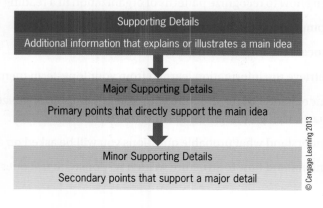

© Cengage Learning 2013

Patterns of organization fall into three main categories:

- Patterns that list
  - Simple list
  - Specific list

- Patterns that define or classify
  - Definition and example
  - Classification

- Two-part patterns
  - Cause and/or effect
  - Problem and/or solution
  - Compare and/or contrast

PATTERNS THAT LIST

Patterns that list include a random order list and a specific order list. A **random order list**, sometimes called a simple list, occurs when an author uses a series of supporting points in a random order. The order of the supporting points could be changed and the passage would still make sense. However, a **specific order list** means that the supporting details must be in a certain order to make sense. The author put the supporting details in an order *for a reason*. Some types of specific order lists are order of importance, chronological or time order, and sequence or process order. Review the transition words that indicate patterns that list in Table 5.3.

TABLE 5.3 TRANSITION WORDS THAT INDICATE PATTERNS THAT LIST

PATTERN OF ORGANIZATION	TRANSITION WORDS AND PUNCTUATION
Random Order	
Random order list	*also, another, in addition, first, second, third, for example;* punctuation (bullets, dashes); numbers (1, 2, 3, etc.); letters (*a, b, c*)
Specific Order	
Order of importance	*most important, finally, primarily*
Chronological or time order	*first, second, third, next, then, after, later, afterward,* dates
Sequence or process order	*first, second, third, next, then, after, later, finally, initially, follows, followed by,* stages, steps

FOCUS ON COMPREHENSION: Recognizing Patterns of Organization

RANDOM ORDER LIST

Random order list means that the items the author lists can be arranged in any order and still make sense. Every piece of writing is a list of something, whether causes, effects, similarities, differences, or steps in a process. So be careful not to oversimplify and see everything as a random order list. Always eliminate other patterns of organization before you choose random order list as the pattern.

> Creating a safe sleep environment is critical to preventing injury during sleepwalking episodes. <u>For example,</u> if your child sleepwalks, don't let him or her sleep in a bunk bed. <u>Also,</u> remove any sharp or breakable objects from the area near the bed, install gates on stairways, and lock the doors and windows in your home.
>
> —"Sleepwalking," National Sleep Foundation
> http://www.sleepfoundation.org/article/sleep-related-problems/sleepwalking

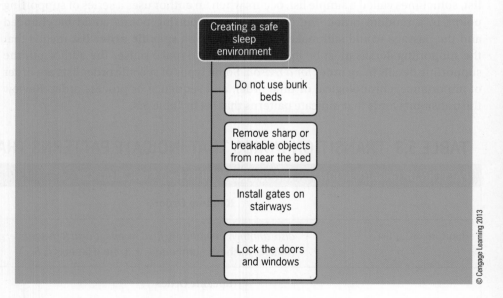

© Cengage Learning 2013

The main idea in this example is directly stated in the first sentence. The list of examples outlining how to keep the sleepwalker safe are listed in a random order following the transition words and phrases *for example* and *also*:

- Don't let him or her sleep in a bunk bed.
- Remove any sharp or breakable objects from the area near the bed.

- Install gates on stairways.
- Lock the doors and windows in your home.

Notice how these points are not in a specific order? The order of the points could be switched around and the passage's meaning would not be affected. The author could have chosen to mention lock the doors and windows before install gates on stairways, and the meaning of the passage would still be the same.

SPECIFIC ORDER LIST

To determine if a list is in a random order or a specific order, ask yourself, "Do these supporting points need to be in this order to make sense?" If your answer is yes, then the supporting details are in a specific order. Here are some examples of specific order listing patterns:

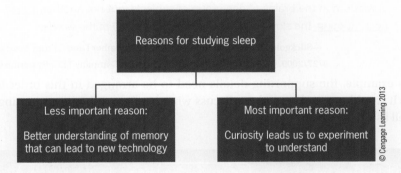

- **Order of importance** means the supporting details in the list need to be in order of significance to convey the author's point. Usually, the last detail is the most important reason for, or an example of, the author's main idea.

> A better understanding of how sleep knits our memories together could lead to new technologies that improve learning, memory and creativity, and even help treat some psychiatric disease. But perhaps <u>the most important reason</u> for studying sleep is simply this: we are a curious species; we spend about a third of our lives asleep; and we realize how little we understand about that third of our lives. So we continue experimenting, hoping to understand sleep better. And perhaps someday we will. After we've slept on it.
>
> —Stickgold and Wehrwein "Sleep Now, Remember Later". From *Newsweek*, 4/27/2009, © 2009 The Newsweek/Daily Beast Company LLC. By permission.

FOCUS ON COMPREHENSION: Recognizing Patterns of Organization

In this example, the transition phrase *the most important reason* indicates that the reasons are arranged in a deliberate order in the passage, with the most important reason last.

- **Chronological order** (or time order) arranges details by how it unfolds over time, such as events in history that occur over time. (The word *chronological* comes from the Greek root word *chronos* that means "time.") Here is an example of information organized according to time. Notice the underlined transition phrases.

> How sleep helps us consolidate memories is still largely a mystery. A recent study from the University of Lubeck, in Germany, offers one clue. Subjects were given a list of 46 word pairs to memorize, <u>just before sleep. Shortly after they fell asleep,</u> as they reached the deepest stages of sleep, electrical currents were sent through electrodes on their heads to induce very slow brain waves. Such slow waves were induced at random in the brains of one group of subjects, but not another. <u>The next morning,</u> the slow-wave group had better recall of the words.
>
> —Stickgold and Wehrwein "Sleep Now, Remember Later." From *Newsweek,* 4/27/2009, © 2009 The Newsweek/Daily Beast Company LLC. By permission.

In this example, the supporting details need to be arranged in this order to make sense. It would not make sense to discuss what happened the next morning before they fell asleep, would it?

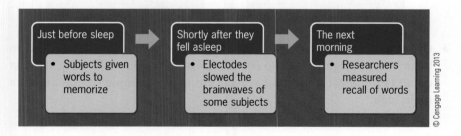

- **Sequence** or **process order,** like chronological order, indicates certain steps need to be followed in order for the result to make sense, such as the steps in a recipe or stages of growth. The difference between chronological order and sequence order is the subject matter. In sequence order, the author uses stages or steps rather than a clear timeline in hours, weeks, or days.

Sleep also seems to be the time when the brain's two memory systems—the hippocampus and the neocortex—"talk" with one another. Experiences that become memories are laid down <u>first</u> in the hippocampus, obliterating whatever is underneath. If a memory is to be retained, <u>it must be shipped from</u> the hippocampus to a place where it will endure—the neocortex, the wrinkled outer layer of the brain where higher thinking takes place.

—Stickgold and Wehrwein "Sleep Now, Remember Later." From *Newsweek,* 4/27/2009, © 2009 The Newsweek/Daily Beast Company LLC. By permission.

In this example, memories must first be laid down in one part of the brain, the hippocampus, before they are sent to the neocortex where they are stored.

QUICK TIPS WHEN IS A LIST A LIST?

This flow chart shows questions to ask yourself to distinguish between a random order list and a specific order list.

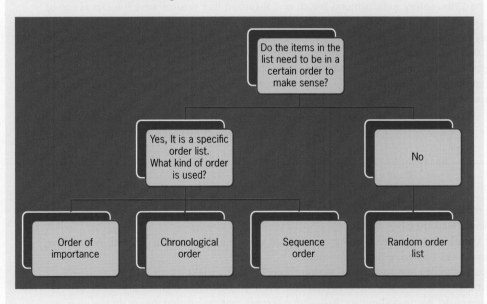

© Cengage Learning 2013

FOCUS ON COMPREHENSION: Recognizing Patterns of Organization

On Your Own   IDENTIFYING PATTERNS THAT LIST

Read the following passages, and identify the pattern of organization in each as either a random order list or a specific order list. If it is a specific order list, indicate if it is order of importance, chronological order, or sequence order.

1. Sleep happens in cycles. When we fall asleep, we initially enter a light stage of sleep and then progress into increasingly deeper stages. Both light and deep sleep stages are called non-REM (rapid eye movement) sleep. After about 90 minutes, we enter the first stage of REM sleep, which is the dreaming portion of sleep, and throughout the night we alternate between stages of REM and non-REM sleep.

   —"Narcolepsy and Sleep", National Sleep Foundation
   http://www.sleepfoundation.org/article/sleep-related-problems/narcolepsy-and-sleep

   _____

2. Thousands of years ago, dreams were seen as messages from the gods, and in many cultures, they are still considered prophetic. In ancient Greece, sick people slept at the temples of Asclepius, the god of medicine, in order to receive dreams that would heal them. Modern dream science really begins at the end of the 19th century with Sigmund Freud, who theorized that dreams were the expression of unconscious desires often stemming from childhood. He believed that exploring these hidden emotions through analysis could help cure mental illness. The Freudian model of psychoanalysis dominated until the 1970s, when new research into the chemistry of the brain showed that emotional problems could have biological or chemical roots, as well as environmental ones. In other words, we weren't sick just because of something our mothers did (or didn't do), but because of some imbalance that might be cured with medication.

   — Kantrowitz, Springen, Wingert, and Ulick, "What Dreams are Made of". From *Newsweek*, 8/9/2004, © 2004 The Newsweek/Daily Beast Company LLC. By permission.

   _____

3. There's a lot of advice out there about getting good sleep; here are tips that work for me:
   1. Exercise most days, even if it's just to take a walk.
   2. No caffeine after 7:00 p.m.
   3. An hour before bedtime, avoid doing any kind of work that takes alert thinking. Addressing envelopes—okay. Analyzing an article—nope.
   4. Adjust your bedroom temperature to be slightly chilly.
   5. Keep your bedroom dark. Studies show that even the tiny light from a digital alarm clock can disrupt a sleep cycle. We have about six devices in our room that glow bright green; it's like sleeping in a mad scientist's lab. The Big Man's new pet, a Roomba (yes, he loves his robot vacuum), gives out so much light that I have to cover it with a pillow before bed.

6. Keep the bedroom as tidy as possible. It's not restful to fight through chaos into bed.

—"Good habits for good sleep," from "Tips...to get a good sleep" by Gretchen Rubin, March 24, 2010
http://shine.yahoo.com/channel/health/tips-to-get-good-sleep-1229593/

---

4. If sleep won't come:

   1. Breathe deeply and slowly until you can't stand it anymore.
   2. If your mind is racing (you're planning a trip, a move, Christmas shopping; you're worried about a medical diagnosis), write down what's on your mind. This technique really works for me.
   3. Slather yourself with body lotion. It feels good and also, if you're having trouble sleeping because you're hot, it cools you down.
   4. If your feet are cold, put on socks.
   5. Stretch your whole body.
   6. Have a warm drink. Some people claim that warm milk contains melatonin and trytophan and so helps induce sleep, but in fact, a glass of milk doesn't contain enough to have any effect. But it's still a soothing drink. My nighttime favorite: 1/3 mug of milk, add boiling water, one packet of Equal, and a dash of vanilla. A real nursery treat.
   7. Yawn.
   8. Stretch your toes up and down several times.
   9. Tell yourself, "I have to get up now." Imagine that you just hit the snooze alarm and in a minute, you're going to be marching through the morning routine. Often this is an exhausting enough prospect to make me fall asleep.

—"Good habits for good sleep," from "Tips...to get a good sleep" by Gretchen Rubin, March 24, 2010
http://shine.yahoo.com/channel/health/tips-to-get-good-sleep-1229593/

---

5. Re-frame your sleeplessness as a welcome opportunity to snatch some extra time out of your day. I get up and tackle mundane chores, like paying bills, organizing books, or tidying up. Then I start the day with a wonderful feeling of having accomplished something even before 6:45 am.

—"Good habits for good sleep," from "Tips...to get a good sleep" by Gretchen Rubin, March 24, 2010 http://shine.yahoo.com/channel/health/tips-to-get-good-sleep-1229593/

---

6. It is important to observe healthy sleep habits. First, make sure that you avoid eating or drinking close to sleep time. Also, refrain from active thinking activities close to bed time that may keep you awake. Most importantly, go to bed at a reasonable time to make sure you have at least seven to eight hours of sleep.

—"Good habits for good sleep," from "Tips...to get a good sleep" by Gretchen Rubin, March 24, 2010 http://shine.yahoo.com/channel/health/tips-to-get-good-sleep-1229593/

FOCUS ON COMPREHENSION: Recognizing Patterns of Organization

PATTERNS THAT DEFINE OR CLASSIFY

Patterns that define or classify are definition/example and classification. These patterns allow an author to make a point and then elaborate on or further explain that point to make sure the reader understands it. These patterns are common in textbook readings because often a concept is introduced, a definition is stated, an idea or series of ideas are put into types or categories, and then examples of the concept are discussed. Review the transition words that indicate patterns that define or classify in Table 5.4.

TABLE 5.4 TRANSITION WORDS THAT INDICATE PATTERNS THAT DEFINE OR CLASSIFY

PATTERN OF ORGANIZATION	TRANSITION WORDS AND PUNCTUATION
Definition/example	Punctuation following a boldfaced term (dash, comma, colon, parentheses), italics of term, *is defined as, is known as, means, is*
Classification	Two (or more) types, groups, *classified as, classes, category, kinds of, types of, characterized by*

© Cengage Learning 2013

DEFINITION/EXAMPLE

Definition/example is commonly used in college textbooks or in writing with many complicated ideas. This pattern is useful for stating a key term or the meaning of an important word and then providing examples to further explain that term. The key term itself is often in special print, such as boldface, italics, or color. A definition pattern always contains a definition vocabulary context clue. In the following passage, look at the transition words and punctuation clues for this pattern. Do they look familiar? They are the same clues that indicate a definition vocabulary context clue that you learned in Chapter 1.

> Sleep talking, formally known as somniloquy, is a sleep disorder defined as talking during sleep without being aware of it. Sleep talking can involve complicated dialogues or monologues, complete gibberish or mumbling. The good news is that for most people it is a rare and short-lived occurrence. Anyone can experience sleep talking, but the condition is more common in males and children.

—"Sleep Talking", National Sleep Foundation
http://www.sleepfoundation.org/article/sleep-related-problems/sleep-talking

In this example, the term *sleep talking* is defined. Notice the clues: *known as, is,* and *defined as.* Then information that pertains to the definition is discussed. In this case, there are no transition phrases such as *for example,* or *to illustrate* to introduce the examples, but the definition is clearly stated.

Sleep talking is a sleep disorder defined as talking during sleep without being aware of it.		
Can involve dialogues or monologues or gibberish or mumbling.	It is rare and short-lived.	Condition is most common in males and children.

© Cengage Learning 2013

CLASSIFICATION

Classification patterns simplify a difficult concept by breaking down a complex idea into manageable parts or categories. This type of pattern is common in college 100-level classes. Because introductory classes function largely to introduce you to the vocabulary of the discipline, patterns that provide terminology and put concepts into categories or types are common.

Classification often contains vocabulary definition clues. However, classification is different from definition because the supporting details are specifically there to show the different categories or to divide a concept into different groups or types.

> There are several different <u>types</u> of memory—including declarative (retrievable, fact-based information), episodic (events from your life) and procedural (how to do something)—and researchers have designed ways to test each of them. In almost every case, whether the test involves remembering pairs of words, tapping numbered keys in a certain order or figuring out the rules in a weather-prediction game, "sleeping on it" after first learning the task improves performance. It's as if our brains squeeze in some extra practice time while we're asleep.

> —Stickgold and Wehrwein, "Sleep Now, Remember Later". From *Newsweek*, 4/27/2009, © 2009 The Newsweek/Daily Beast Company LLC. By permission.

In this example, the author divides memory into three different categories: declarative, episodic, and procedural. Each of these types of memory is defined in parentheses

FOCUS ON COMPREHENSION: Recognizing Patterns of Organization

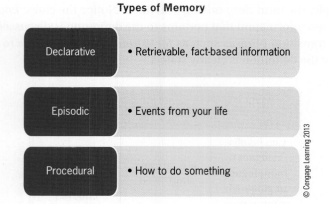

Types of Memory

Declarative	• Retrievable, fact-based information
Episodic	• Events from your life
Procedural	• How to do something

© Cengage Learning 2013

following the key term. But the main pattern is classification because the categories of memory is the main idea of the passage, not the definitions of the kinds of memories. Classification patterns often contain two or more definitions, whereas a definition pattern of organization contains just one definition.

On Your Own IDENTIFYING PATTERNS THAT DEFINE AND CLASSIFY

Read the following passages and identify the pattern of organization in each as either definition/example or classification.

1. What we call "sleep" involves transitions between three different states: wakefulness, rapid eye movement (REM) sleep, which is associated with dreaming, and non rapid eye movement (N-REM) sleep. There are a variety of characteristics that define each state, but to understand REM Behavior Disorder it is important to know that it occurs during REM sleep.

    —"REM Behavior Disorder and Sleep", National Sleep Foundation
    http://www.sleepfoundation.org/article/sleep-related-problems/rem-behavior-disorder-and-sleep

2. Restless Legs Syndrome (RLS) is a neurologic sensorimotor disorder that is characterized by an overwhelming urge to move the legs when they are at rest. The urge to move the legs is usually, but not always, accompanied by unpleasant sensations. It is less common but possible to have RLS symptoms in the arms, face, torso, and genital region. RLS symptoms occur during inactivity and

they are temporarily relieved by movement or pressure. Symptoms of RLS are most severe in the evening and nighttime hours and can profoundly disrupt a patient's sleep and daily life.

—"Restless Legs Syndrome (RLS) and Sleep", National Sleep Foundation
http://www.sleepfoundation.org/article/sleep-related-problems/restless-legs-syndrome-rls-and-sleep

---

3. Many Americans experience sleep disorders that involve dreaming. These include nightmares, sleep terrors, and REM sleep behavior.

Nightmares are dreams with vivid and disturbing content. They are common in children during REM sleep. They usually involve an immediate awakening and good recall of the dream content. Sleep terrors are often described as extreme nightmares. Like nightmares, they most often occur during childhood, however they typically take place during non-REM (NREM) sleep.

Similar to sleep terrors, but more common in adults, is REM sleep behaviors. This involves complex, vigorous, or violent behaviors, sometimes associated with dream-like thoughts and images.

—"Nightmares and Sleep", National Sleep Foundation
http://www.sleepfoundation.org/article/sleep-related-problems/nightmares-and-sleep

---

4. Narcolepsy is a neurological disorder caused by the brain's inability to regulate sleep-wake cycles normally. The main features of narcolepsy are excessive daytime sleepiness and cataplexy. The disease is also often associated with sudden sleep attacks, insomnia, dream-like hallucinations, and a condition called sleep paralysis. Its prevalence in the developed world is approximately the same as that of multiple sclerosis or Parkinson's disease. However, with increased public education about narcolepsy and physician training in the diagnosis and treatment of sleep disorders, these figures are expected to rise.

—"Narcolepsy and Sleep", National Sleep Foundation
http://www.sleepfoundation.org/article/sleep-related-problems/narcolepsy-and-sleep

---

5. Scientists who study our rhythms are known as chronobiologists. To study human circadian rhythms, researchers have isolated people from all cues that might suggest when to sleep. These people begin to operate on a 25-hour day.

—"Sleep: More Than Meets the (Shut-)Eye" Ethel Gofen, *Current Health* 2,
a *Weekly Reader* publication. v17. n5 (Jan 1991): p4(8)

FOCUS ON COMPREHENSION: Recognizing Patterns of Organization

TWO-PART PATTERNS

Two-part patterns of organization are cause and effect, problem and solution, and comparison and contrast. Each of these patterns shows the relationship between two or more distinct features. Sometimes a passage will contain both parts of a two-part pattern of organization. For example, a passage may discuss both causes and effects. Most often, however, a passage will focus on one part of the two-part pattern, like just causes or just effects.

You are familiar with transition words that indicate comparison and contrast already. Comparison transition words and phrases are the same as many of the clue words that signal a synonym vocabulary context clue. Similarly, contrast transition words and phrases are the same as many of the clue words that signal an antonym vocabulary context clue. Review the signal words that indicate two-part patterns in Table 5.5.

TABLE 5.5 TRANSITION WORDS THAT INDICATE TWO-PART PATTERNS

PATTERN OF ORGANIZATION	TRANSITION WORDS
Cause	*is caused by, causes, for the reason, because, due to, being that, in that, inasmuch as, since, that is why*
Effect	*the effect is, consequently, as a result, results in, leads to, thus, as a consequence, hence, so, accordingly, therefore, for this reason*
Problem	*the problem is, the issue is, the question is*
Solution	*can be solved by, the solution is, the cure is*
Comparison	*likewise, like, similar to, similarly, in the same way, equally, by the same token, in a like manner, comparable, in common, neither, both, same*
Contrast	*however, but, in contrast, on the other hand, conversely, although, nevertheless, yet, while, whereas, still, though, otherwise, some people . . . others*

© Cengage Learning 2013

CAUSE AND EFFECT

Cause and effect patterns show causes of a situation or phenomenon, or the effects or results of a situation or phenomenon to show the relationship between ideas. Some passages may show both causes and effects.

A better understanding of how sleep knits our memories together could <u>lead to</u> new technologies that improve learning, memory and creativity, and even help treat some psychiatric disease.

—Stickgold and Wehrwein, "Sleep Now, Remember Later". From *Newsweek,*
4/27/2009, © 2009 The Newsweek/Daily Beast Company LLC. By permission.

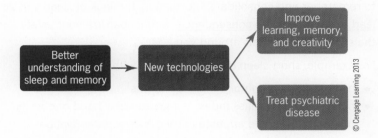

In this example, there is a direct cause and effect relationship between the ideas: a better understanding of sleep and memory leads to new technologies to improve learning, memory, and creativity and treatment of psychiatric disease. The cause is a better understanding of sleep and memory. The effect is new technologies to help us.

Here is an example of a cause structure. Notice how this passage is different from the previous example.

If you have difficulty sleeping, it is essential to determine whether an underlying disease or condition is <u>causing</u> the problem. Sometimes insomnia is <u>caused</u> by pain, digestive problems or a sleep disorder. Insomnia may <u>also signal</u> depression or anxiety.

—"Can't Sleep? What To Know About Insomnia," National Sleep Foundation.
http://www.sleepfoundation.org/article/sleep-related-problems/insomnia-and-sleep

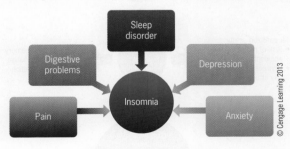

In this passage, five reasons or causes that result in insomnia are discussed. The outcome or effect is insomnia. However, several causes for this outcome are discussed in the passage. Therefore, the passage has a cause pattern of organization. Pain, digestive problems, a sleep disorder, depression, or anxiety all lead to or result in insomnia.

FOCUS ON COMPREHENSION: Recognizing Patterns of Organization

Here is an example of effect structure. Unlike the cause example, this example concerns more than one effect and only one cause.

> Though scientists are still learning about the concept of basal sleep need, one thing sleep research certainly has shown is that sleeping too little can not only inhibit your productivity and ability to remember and consolidate information, but lack of sleep can also <u>lead to</u> serious health <u>consequences</u> and jeopardize your safety and the safety of individuals around you.
>
> For example, short sleep duration is <u>linked</u> with:
> - Increased risk of motor vehicle accidents
> - Increase in body mass index — a greater likelihood of obesity due to an increased appetite caused by sleep deprivation
> - Increased risk of diabetes and heart problems
> - Increased risk for psychiatric conditions including depression and substance abuse
> - Decreased ability to pay attention, react to signals or remember new information

—Excerpted from "How Much Sleep Do We Really Need?", National Sleep Foundation.
http://www.sleepfoundation.org/article/how-sleep-works/how-much-sleep-do-we-really-need

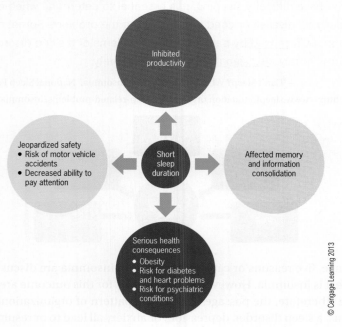

© Cengage Learning 2013

This passage discusses the effects of short sleep duration. Short sleep duration is the cause of all these symptoms. There are many effects from this one cause.

PROBLEM AND SOLUTION

A specific type of cause and effect pattern is **problem and solution.** This pattern focuses on problems that lead to solutions, or a particular problem that has one or more solutions.

> Do not take any naps the day after you've lost sleep. When you feel sleepy, get up and do something. Walk, make the bed, or do your errands.
>
> —"How to Get a Good Night's Sleep", http://www.k-state.org/counseling/topics/life/sleep. html, Originally written in 1989 by David G. Danskin, Ph.D., University Counseling Services; adapted and modified in 1997 by Dorinda Lambert, Ph.D. for use on the Internet.

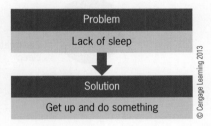

In this example, the problem is lost sleep. The solution is to walk or do something. This next example focuses on the problems of adolescent sleepiness.

> Busy schedules are only part of the problem. During adolescence, the body's internal clock gets pushed back so that a person doesn't feel sleepy until later in the evening.
>
> —Weir, Kirsten. "Who needs sleep? Maybe you do. Here's what you need to know about slumber, from A to Zzzzzzz's. (YOUR BODY)." *Current Health* 2, (Oct 2005): 16(4). Published and copyrighted by Weekly Reader Corporation. By permission.

FOCUS ON COMPREHENSION: Recognizing Patterns of Organization

This next example concerns solutions rather than problems.

> Some people find that a gentle stretching routine for several minutes just before getting into bed helps induce sleep. Others practice relaxation techniques. Libraries or bookstores have books on developing stretching or relaxation routines.

—"How to Get a Good Night's Sleep," http://www.k-state.org/counseling/topics/life/sleep.html, Originally written in 1989 by David G. Danskin, Ph.D., University Counseling Services; adapted and modified in 1997 by Dorinda Lambert, Ph.D. for use on the Internet.

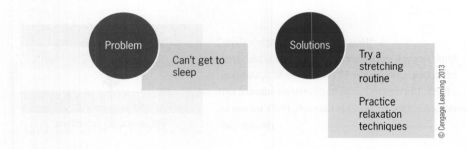

COMPARISON AND CONTRAST

Comparison and contrast show similarities and/or differences between two or more things or ideas. The passage usually emphasizes similarities (comparisons) or differences (contrasts).

> Inge Strauch, a psychology professor at the University of Zurich, has collected 550 dreams from a group of twenty-four 9- to 15-year-olds she studied in her lab over a period of two years. She found that children dreamed about animals more often than adults and were more likely to report being victims than aggressors. They were also more likely to have "fantastic" dreams, <u>while</u> adults' dreams tend to contain more elements of reality. A typical fantastic dream from a 10-year-old Strauch studied included a cat asking for directions to the "cat bathroom." <u>Similarly</u>, an 11-year-old boy dreamed that a snake wanted to go up a ski lift.

—Kantrowitz, Springen, Wingert, and Ulick, "What Dreams Are Made Of."
From *Newsweek*, 8/9/2004, © 2004 The Newsweek/Daily Beast Company LLC. By permission.

Differences between child and adult dreams	• Children dreamed about animals more than adults • Children were the victims in dreams more than adults • Children were more likely than adults to have "fantastic" dreams
Similarities between children's dreams	• 10-year-old's dream about the cat asking directions • 11-year-old's dream about snake on ski lift

© Cengage Learning 2013

In this paragraph, the authors contrast the content of dreams for young people with those of adults. Young people dreamed more about animals and being victims, and had more "fantastic" dreams than adults. This information shows differences or contrast. The authors then discuss similarities between young people's dreams in the study, which shows comparison. Note the comparison transition word *similarly* in the last sentence as well as the contrast transition word *while* in the second last sentence.

> The <u>common denominator</u> of <u>both</u> (non-human) mammals
> and humans is the existence of rapid eye movement (REM) sleep,
> the sleep state that is associated with dreams. <u>Both</u> humans and
> all other mammals display the <u>same</u> level of brain activity and
> increased heart rate variability during REM sleep.
>
> —"Animals' Sleep: Is There a Human Connection?," National Sleep Foundation,
> http://www.sleepfoundation.org/article/how-sleep-works/
> animals-sleep-there-human-connection

In this example, the author uses several transition words that indicate comparison.

> <u>Some</u> people complain because they sleep "only" five or six
> hours each night. <u>Yet</u> many of these people awake rested in the
> morning and function well during the day. Five or six hours of sleep
> is all they need most of the time. They don't have insomnia.
>
> <u>Other people</u> feel tired after eight hours of sleep. They need more
> than the "normal" seven to eight hour average. Just one more hour
> of sleep often gives these people the rest they need.
>
> —"How to Get a Good Night's Sleep," http://www.k-state.org/counseling/topics/life/sleep.
> html, Originally written in 1989 by David G. Danskin, Ph.D., University Counseling Services;
> adapted and modified in 1997 by Dorinda Lambert, Ph.D. for use on the Internet.

In this example, the author contrasts the amount of sleep some need as compared to others. Notice the transitions that indicate contrast.

FOCUS ON COMPREHENSION: Recognizing Patterns of Organization

On Your Own   IDENTIFYING TWO-PART PATTERNS

Read the following passages, and identify the pattern of organization in each as either cause and effect, problem and solution, or comparison and contrast.

1. Adults need about eight hours of sleep each night, but young people need even more. "Kids from about 10 to 18 need a little more than nine hours of sleep a night, on average," says Mary Carskadon, a sleep researcher and member of the NSF task force on sleep and teens. Yet Carskadon has found that most teens sleep an average of seven hours a night.

    —Weir, Kirsten. "Who needs sleep? Maybe you do. Here's what you need to know about slumber, from A to Zzzzzzz's. (YOUR BODY)." *Current Health* 2, (Oct 2005): 16(4). Published and copyrighted by Weekly Reader Corporation. By permission.

2. Difficulty in effectively managing normal, everyday stress in life is a common problem. A frequent reaction to daily stresses is insomnia, either sleep-onset insomnia or sleep-interrupting insomnia. A good stress-management program helps you learn how to manage those frequent stressors and go more easily through each day.

    —"How to Get a Good Night's Sleep," http://www.k-state.org/counseling/topics/life/sleep.html, Originally written in 1989 by David G. Danskin, Ph.D., University Counseling Services; adapted and modified in 1997 by Dorinda Lambert, Ph.D. for use on the Internet.

3. Sleep loss affects personal safety on the road. The National Highway Traffic Safety Administration has estimated that approximately 100,000 motor vehicle crashes each year result from a driver's drowsiness or fatigue while at the wheel. Driving at night or in the early to mid afternoon increases the risk of a crash because those are times that our biological clocks make us sleepy. Drowsy driving impairs a driver's reaction time, vigilance, and ability to make sound judgments. Many adolescents are chronically sleep-deprived and hence at high risk of drowsy-driving crashes. In one large study of fall-asleep crashes, over 50 percent occurred with a driver 25 years old or younger.

    —National Institutes of Health, http://science-education.nih.gov/supplements/nih3/sleep/guide/info-sleep.htm

4. In fact, about two thirds of the characters in men's dreams are men; gender is more evenly divided in women's dreams. These differences appear to be true in many different cultures. Men's dreams also involve more physical aggression than women's dreams; they're more likely to be about chasing, punching, breaking, stealing or killing, Domhoff says. A more typical expression of aggression in women's dreams would be rejection or an insult ("That dress makes you look fat").

    —Rakoczy, "What Dreams Are Made Of." From *Newsweek*, 8/9/2004, © 2004 The Newsweek/Daily Beast Company LLC. By permission.

5. Problems with sleep can be due to lifestyle choices and can result in problem sleepiness—that is, feeling sleepy at inappropriate times. Environmental noise, temperature changes, changes in sleeping surroundings, and other factors may affect our ability to get sufficient restful sleep. Short-term problem sleepiness may be corrected by getting additional sleep to overcome the sleep deficit. In other cases, problem sleepiness may indicate a sleep disorder requiring medical intervention. Alcohol abuse can cause or exacerbate sleep disorders by disrupting the sequence and duration of sleep states. Alcohol does not promote good sleep, and consuming alcohol in the evening can also exacerbate sleep apnea problems.

—National Institutes of Health, http://science-education.nih.gov/supplements/nih3/sleep/guide/info-sleep.htm

QUICK TIPS STEPS TO DETERMINING PATTERN OF ORGANIZATION

To determine the pattern of organization of a reading, follow these steps:

1. Ask yourself, What is the author trying to do: list, define or categorize, explore two or more things: causes and/or effects, problems and/or solutions, or differences (contrast) and/or similarities (comparison)?

2. If your answer to question 1 is list, then decide if the reading lists

- Steps or items in a random order, so that the details would make sense in any order.

- Items arranged according to importance.

- Steps organized by time.

- Steps in a process.

3. If your answer to question 1 is define or categorize,

- Is a definition given along with examples?

- Does it break a big concept into different parts, classifications, or categories?

(Continued)

FOCUS ON COMPREHENSION: Recognizing Patterns of Organization

4. If your answer to question 1 is that the passage is a two-part pattern, does it

- ■ Show causes or effects?
- ■ Outline a problem and its solution?
- ■ Show comparison and/or contrast?

Thinking It Through   PATTERN OF ORGANIZATION OF A LONGER PASSAGE

Now, apply everything you have learned thus far to a longer passage.

- First, consider the topic.
- Next, ask yourself, "What is the author's most important point about the topic?"
- Then, ask, "What is the author's main pattern of organization, based on the main idea?" Finding the pattern of organization of a longer passage uses the same steps you've learned from finding the pattern in paragraphs.

Read this passage, and then answer the questions that follow. Afterward, read the explanation of the answers.

How to Get a Good Night's Sleep

Set a Bedtime Schedule Using These Two Steps

1   First, try to go to bed at about the same time every night. Be regular. Most people get hungry at 7 a.m., noon, and 6 p.m. because they've eaten at those times for years. Going to bed at about the same time every night can make sleep as regular as hunger.

2   Second, go to bed later when you are having trouble sleeping. If you're only getting five hours of sleep a night during your insomnia period, don't go to bed until just five hours before your wake-up time. For instance, if you've been waking up at 7 a.m., don't go to bed until 2 a.m. No naps! Make the time you spend in bed sleep time. Still some insomnia? Go to bed proportionately later.

3   Then, as your time in bed becomes good sleep time, move your going-to-bed time back 15 to 30 minutes a night and do that for a week or so.

4   This is the opposite of what we want to do: we want to go to bed earlier to make up the lost sleep. Learn to do what many sleep laboratories teach—go to bed later the night after losing sleep.

1 Topic:_____

2 Main Idea:_____

3 Pattern of Organization:_____

—"How to Get a Good Night's Sleep", http://www.k-state.org/counseling/topics/life/sleep.html,

Originally written in 1989 by David G. Danskin, Ph.D., University Counseling Services;

adapted and modified in 1997 by Dorinda Lambert, Ph.D. for use on the Internet.

This passage is about the steps to getting a good night's sleep. The word *steps* provides a clue to both the main idea and the pattern of organization. Steps suggest that the ideas are in a specific order list. The main idea is that there are two steps to getting a good night's sleep. The heading of the passage suggests this main idea. You have to complete the steps in this particular order for it to make sense. So, the pattern of organization is sequence order.

On Your Own   FINDING THE PATTERN OF ORGANIZATION IN A LONGER PASSAGE

Determine the pattern of organization of this longer passage. First, consider the topic. Next, ask yourself: "What is the author's most important point about the topic?" Then, ask yourself: "What is the author's main pattern of organization, based on the main idea?"

Solutions for Sleep Deprivation

1   The number one recommendation from doctors and sleep specialists for those concerned about sleep deprivation in college is to exercise. Exercise can help establish healthy sleeping patterns and will make it easier to fall asleep at the end of the day.

2   It is important to note, however, that you should not exercise right before bedtime, as exercise stimulates the body and will make falling asleep more difficult for a while. Experts recommend exercising at least three hours before bedtime.

3   Naps can be helpful, but only if planned properly. Experts suggest napping only once a day in the early afternoon and for no more than 20 or 30 minutes. Taking long naps can affect your ability to fall asleep at bedtime.

4   Additionally, experts recommend setting aside at least a few days per week for a full night's sleep. While it is recommended that people sleep and wake the same time every day

(Continued)

FOCUS ON COMPREHENSION: Recognizing Patterns of Organization

in order to maintain a healthy sleep schedule, some experts recommend trying to get more sleep at least a couple of times a week. Even if you can't get eight hours every night, getting eight hours one or two days each week will help prevent long-term health issues.

1 Topic: _____

2 Main Idea:_____

3 Pattern of Organization: _____

—"Solutions for Sleep Deprivation College Students and Sleep Deprivation", http://www.sleep-deprivation.com
/articles/causes-of-sleep-deprivation/students-and-sleep.php

MIXED PATTERNS

Sometimes an author uses more than one pattern of organization to express his or her points about the topic. An author may also use transition words that indicate more than one type of pattern within a reading. This can be confusing because you, as the reader, may not know which pattern is the main pattern. The rule of thumb is that the main pattern of organization is the one that is reflected in the author's main idea about the topic.

Thinking It Through   RECOGNIZING MIXED PATTERNS

Look at this passage from the National Institute of Health, noting the transition words as you read.

1. Pay attention to the underlined transition words or phrases that indicate a pattern of organization.

2. Write down the patterns (two or more) that are indicated in the passage.

3. Decide which pattern is the main pattern.

Seasonal affective disorder (SAD). A change of seasons in autumn brings on both a loss of daylight savings time (fall back one hour) and a shortening of the daytime. As winter progresses, the day length becomes even shorter. During this season of short days and long nights, some individuals develop symptoms <u>similar</u> to jet lag <u>but</u> more severe. These symptoms include decreased appetite, loss of concentration and focus, lack of energy, feelings of depression and despair, and excessive sleepiness. Too little bright light reaching the biological clock in the SCN* appears to bring on this recognized form of depression in susceptible individuals. <u>Consequently</u>, treatment often involves using light therapy.

—National Institutes of Health, http://science-education.nih.gov/supplements/nih3/sleep/guide/info-sleep.htm

---

*Note that SCN refers to the **suprachiasmatic nucleus,** which is the area of the brain that controls the biological clock—our inner clock that regulates our sleeping and waking cycles.

1. In this passage there are several clues to the pattern:
   - Seasonal affective disorder (SAD) is in italics, indicating a definition.
   - *Similar*—indicating comparison
   - *But*—indicating contrast
   - *Consequently*—indicating cause and effect

2. This passage shows potential to be a definition/example, comparison and contrast, or cause and effect passage. All these patterns are represented in the paragraph. However, if you could pinpoint the main pattern of organization, which would you choose?

3. The main pattern of organization is reflected in the main idea statement—find the main idea. The topic of the passage is seasonal affective disorder. The main idea of the passage is that SAD is a mood disorder that is caused by a lack of light. What pattern of organization is best reflected in the main idea statement? If you chose cause and effect, you are correct.

Now try again with this example:

Unlike some animals, humans are active during daylight hours. This pattern is called diurnal activity. Animals that are awake and active at night (for example, hamsters) have what is known as nocturnal activity. For humans and other diurnally active animals, light signals the time to awake, and sleep occurs during the dark. Modern society, however, requires that services and businesses be available 24 hours a day, so some individuals must work the night shift. These individuals no longer have synchrony between their internal clocks and external daylight and darkness signals, and they may experience mental and physical difficulties similar to jet lag and SAD.

—National Institute of Health, http://science-education.nih.gov/supplements/nih3/sleep/guide/info-sleep.htm

1. There are several transition words that indicate comparison and contrast:
   - *unlike*
   - *however*
   - *similar*

   However, a key term—diurnal activity—is defined in the first sentence. Also, nocturnal activity is defined. So, there are two definitions in this passage.

2. The two possible patterns of organization, then, are definition/example and comparison and contrast. Which is the main pattern?

3. The topic of this paragraph is the internal clock and disruptions. The author's main point is that our internal clock is regulated by light, but we often live in conditions that interrupt our normal sleep/wake cycle. What pattern of organization is signified by this main idea? If you chose comparison and contrast, you are correct.

(Continued)

FOCUS ON COMPREHENSION: Recognizing Patterns of Organization

And here's another example to practice with:

Why You Need More Sleep Tonight

- **It Makes You . . . Healthy**
  Skimping on shut-eye has the potential to be deadly: "Chronic sleep debt raises your risk for high blood pressure, heart disease, diabetes, and obesity," says Dr. Emsellem. Your immune system is compromised too, "so you're more susceptible to catching every virus that comes along."

- **It Makes You . . . Smarter**
  Though your body shuts down, your brain buzzes with activity as you sleep. That's when it sorts, processes, consolidates, and stores the masses of information you absorbed during the day. "Sleep is crucial for learning, cognition, memory, and performance," says Dr. Epstein. In fact, a Harvard study showed that adults who got a good night's sleep performed 44 percent better on a memory test 12 hours later, compared with those who stayed awake.

- **It Makes You . . . Slim**
  Recent research reveals "a very close relationship between insufficient sleep and the inability to lose or stabilize weight," says Dr. Emsellem. A likely reason: Sleep debt interferes with the function of hormones that regulate how efficiently the body burns fat.

- **It Makes You . . . Coordinated**
  Harvard scientists have found that after trying a new motor task—playing a piano minuet, doing an aerobics routine—a good night's rest solidifies what you've learned, making it easier and more automatic the next day. "Studies show that your brain replays the same sequences during the night," explains Dr. Emsellem. "The next day, you just know the moves—it's no longer a conscious act."

—"4 Reasons To Sleep More. Why You Need More Sleep Tonight," http://www.fitnessmagazine.com/
health/spirit/get-to-sleep-guide/5-steps-to-a-good-nights-sleep/?page=7 © Laurel Naversen Geraghty.
Used with kind permission of the author.

1. There are indications of more than one pattern of organization.

   - The title contains the word *why* that indicates cause
   - The supporting points are arranged in bullets that indicate a list
   - Are the bulleted points in a specific order? No, they are in a random order.

2. The two patterns are random order list and cause and effect.

3. The main point of the passage is that there are several *reasons* you ought to get a good night's sleep. Therefore, the main pattern of organization is cause and effect (a list of reasons). Remember that random order list is always your last choice when choosing a pattern of organization. In this case, cause and effect trumps random order list as your first choice.

On Your Own RECOGNIZING MIXED PATTERNS

The following passages have transition words that indicate a mixed pattern of organization. Refer to the table on pages 328 and 329, "Seven Common Patterns of Organization and Their Transitions" to review the clues needed to determine the pattern of organization. Underline these clues as you read.

Sleepwalking, formally known as somnambulism, is a behavior disorder that originates during deep sleep and results in walking or performing other complex behaviors while asleep. It is much more common in children than adults and is more likely to occur if a person is sleep deprived. Because a sleepwalker typically remains in deep sleep throughout the episode, he or she may be difficult to awaken and will probably not remember the sleepwalking incident.

—"Sleepwalking," National Sleep Foundation, http://www.sleepfoundation.org/article/sleep-related-problems/sleepwalking

1. What is the topic based on this passage?
   a. Sleepwalking
   b. Deep sleep
   c. Episodes
2. What is the main idea of this passage?
   a. Because a sleepwalker typically remains in deep sleep throughout the episode, he or she may be difficult to awaken and will probably not remember the sleepwalking incident.
   b. It is much more common in children than adults.
   c. Sleepwalking, formally known as somnambulism, is a behavior disorder that originates during deep sleep and results in walking or performing other complex behaviors while asleep.
3. What mixed patterns are used this passage?
   a. Definition/example and comparison and contrast
   b. Definition/example and cause and effect
   c. Definition/example and classification
4. What is the main pattern of organization? _____

Other drugs that college students may take that can affect sleep include:
- certain anti-depressants
- diet pills
- illegal drugs, including cocaine and methamphetamines
- nicotine
- oral contraceptives containing hormones
- steroids.

—Solutions for Sleep Deprivation, College Students and Sleep Deprivation http://www.sleep-deprivation.com /articles/causes-of-sleep-deprivation/students-and-sleep.php, © 2011 Tree.com, Inc.

(Continued)

FOCUS ON COMPREHENSION: Recognizing Patterns of Organization

5. What is the topic based on this passage?
    a. Drugs
    b. College students and drugs
    c. Drugs that affect sleep
6. What is the main idea based on this passage?
    a. There are several drugs that students may take that affect sleep.
    b. Certain anti-depressants affect sleep.
    c. Here are some tips to get a good night's sleep.
7. What mixed patterns are used this passage?
    a. Cause and effect and list
    b. Sequence order and list
    c. Classification and list
8. What is the main pattern of organization? _____

> Problems related to sleep are among the most common psychological disorders, but often are under diagnosed and under treated. In the United States, 50 to 70 million people suffer from some form of chronic sleep problem. The most common sleep disorder is *insomnia,* the chronic inability to fall or stay asleep. A sleep disorder among children three to eight years old is a *night terror*—a panic attack during stage 4 NREM sleep. Victims sit up in bed, scream, stare into space, and talk without making sense. They seldom wake and have little memory of the event. Night terrors are not *nightmares,* which are common, anxiety-producing dreams that occur during REM sleep among adults and children. An immature nervous system might be the cause of night terrors. This disorder is treated with prescription drugs.
>
> —From Stephen L. Franzoi, *Psychology: A Discovery Experience,* pp. 439–446, © 2010 Cengage South-Western.

9. What is the topic based on this passage?
    a. Nightmares
    b. Night terror
    c. Problems related to sleep
10. What is the main idea based on this passage?
    a. Problems related to sleep are among the most common psychological disorders, but often are under diagnosed and under treated.
    b. A sleep disorder among children three to eight years old is a night terror—a panic attack during stage 4 NREM sleep.
    c. An immature nervous system might be the cause of night terrors.
11. What mixed patterns are used this passage?
    a. Classification and problem and solution
    b. Sequence order and list
    c. Classification and list
12. What is the main pattern of organization? _____

Practice Exercises 1: IDENTIFYING PATTERNS OF ORGANIZATION

Read the following passages and determine the best pattern of organization. Circle transition words that indicate the pattern of organization.

1. **Warm bath, yes; shower, no**

   Take a long, hot bath before going to bed. This helps relax and soothe your muscles. Showers, on the other hand, tend to wake you up. Insomniacs should avoid showers in the evening.

   —"How to Get a Good Night's Sleep," http://www.k-state.org/counseling/topics/life/sleep.html, Originally written in 1989 by David G. Danskin, Ph.D., University Counseling Services; adapted and modified in 1997 by Dorinda Lambert, Ph.D. for use on the Internet.

2. In ancient times, when people wondered what dreams meant, they felt that dreams were messages from the gods. In Egypt, when a person was distressed about something, he would sleep in the temple. Upon awakening, a priest, called the Master of the Secret Things, would interpret his dreams. In the fifth century, the Greek philosopher Heraclitus proposed that dreams were created in the dreamer's mind.

   —From "What Dreams Mean", http://answers.yourdictionary.com/reference/what-do-dreams-mean.html

3. Drinking before bed can increase the number of times you wake up during the night. This prevents your body from getting enough deep sleep, which the body needs in order to function properly. An ongoing lack of deep sleep can lead to daytime fatigue.

   —Solutions for Sleep Deprivation, College Students and Sleep Deprivation http://www.sleep-deprivation.com/articles/causes-of-sleep-deprivation/students-and-sleep.php

4. If you think you might be suffering from sleep apnea, visit your doctor. He or she might have you spend the night in a sleep clinic, where physicians will monitor you while you sleep. If they determine that apnea is affecting you, they may treat it with medications or with a mechanical device that you can wear while you sleep.

   —Weir, Kirsten. "Who needs sleep? Maybe you do. Here's what you need to know about slumber, from A to Zzzzzzz's. (YOUR BODY)." *Current Health* 2, (Oct 2005): 16(4). Published and copyrighted by Weekly Reader Corporation. By permission.

5. The short-term effects of too little sleep are obvious enough. Too little shut-eye can leave you feeling fuzzy-headed and unable to concentrate. "Almost all teenagers, as they reach puberty, become

   (Continued)

FOCUS ON COMPREHENSION: Recognizing Patterns of Organization

walking zombies because they are getting far too little sleep," says Cornell University psychologist James Maas in the American Psychological Association's Monitor on Psychology. Over time, skimping on sleep can cause a sleep debt to accumulate, and that can have serious consequences."

—Weir, Kirsten. "Who needs sleep? Maybe you do. Here's what you need to know about slumber, from A to Zzzzzzz's. (YOUR BODY)." *Current Health* 2, (Oct 2005): 16(4). Published and copyrighted by Weekly Reader Corporation. By permission.

6. You dream when you are sleeping. Sleep is an **altered state of consciousness**, which is an awareness of yourself and your surroundings that is noticeably different from your normal state of consciousness. The most common altered state is *sleep,* a non-waking state of consciousness in which you typically remain motionless and are only slightly responsive to your surroundings.

—From Stephen L. Franzoi, *Psychology: A Discovery Experience*, pp. 439-446, © 2010 Cengage South-Western.

7. New studies are also revealing that sleep debt can mess with metabolism, the chemical processes that occur within an organism to sustain life. "If you aren't getting enough sleep, you're likely to eat more and also process food differently," Carskadon reports. Those metabolic changes can lead to weight gain and related health problems, including diabetes.

—Weir, Kirsten. "Who needs sleep? Maybe you do. Here's what you need to know about slumber, from A to Zzzzzzz's. (YOUR BODY)." *Current Health* 2, (Oct 2005): 16(4). Published and copyrighted by Weekly Reader Corporation. By permission.

8. Some mammals, such as humans, sleep primarily at night, while other mammals, such as rats, sleep primarily during the day. Furthermore, most (but not all) small mammals tend to sleep more than large ones. In some cases, animals have developed ways to sleep and concurrently satisfy critical life functions.

—From the National Institutes of Health, http://science-education.nih.gov/supplements/nih3/sleep/guide/info-sleep.htm

9. Biological rhythms are of two general types. **Exogenous rhythms** are directly produced by an external influence, such as an environmental cue. They are not generated internally by the organism itself, and if the environmental cues are removed, the rhythm ceases. **Endogenous rhythms,** by contrast, are driven by an internal, self-sustaining biological clock rather than by anything external to the organism.

—From the National Institutes of Health, http://science-education.nih.gov/supplements/nih3/sleep/guide/info-sleep.htm

10. The first series of cases of RBD (REM Behavior Disorder) was described in 1985 by Mark Mahowald, MD, and Carlos Schenck, MD, of the University of Minnesota. In *Principles and Practice of Sleep Medicine*, they outlined several case histories of people with RBD:

- A 77-year old minister had been behaving violently in his sleep for 20 years, sometimes even injuring his wife.
- A 60-year old surgeon would jump out of bed during nightmares of being attacked by "criminals, terrorists and monsters."
- A 62-year old industrial plant manager who was a war veteran dreamt of being attacked by enemy soldiers and fought back in his sleep, sometimes injuring himself.
- A 57-year old retired school principal was inadvertently punching and kicking his wife for two years during vivid nightmares of protecting himself and family from aggressive people and snakes.

—"REM Behavior Disorder and Sleep", National Sleep Foundation, http://www.sleepfoundation.org/article
/sleep-related-problems/rem-behavior-disorder-and-sleep

FOCUS ON READING STUDY SKILLS

Reading Graphics

Just as you determine topic and pose questions based on written text, you can apply these same strategies to reading graphics. A **graphic** is a visual representation of information that an author includes to illustrate an important point. The fact that an author chooses to include a graphic tells you that the information is important. Textbooks frequently contain charts, tables, graphs, illustrations, figures, cartoons, photographs, and other graphic material. Even though the information is graphic rather than written, the same process applies to finding the important information.

Types of Graphics

There are many different types of graphics. To "read" graphics, you need to consider the pattern of organization the author uses. An author chooses the type of graphic that best expresses the information. Some types of graphics lend themselves to different patterns of organization. For example, a time line clearly shows a specific order list using chronological order. A bar graph shows comparison and contrast. A cycle graphic accurately shows sequence, and a hierarchy graphic lends itself to cause and effect. See Table 5.6 for the types of graphic aids you may encounter in a college textbook.

A **graph** shows the relationship between two or more variables. Sometimes, as in the case with a line graph or bar graph, two *axes* indicate the components being compared: the x or horizontal axis and the y or vertical axis. The components of a graph are usually labeled across the axes (see Figure 5.3). It is important to look at this information and the title to help determine the topic of the graph. Then, look at the line the graph presents—this is the main idea of the graphic.

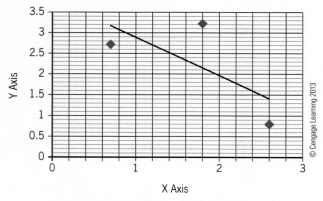

FIGURE 5.3 Parts of a Graph

TABLE 5.6 TYPES OF GRAPHIC AIDS

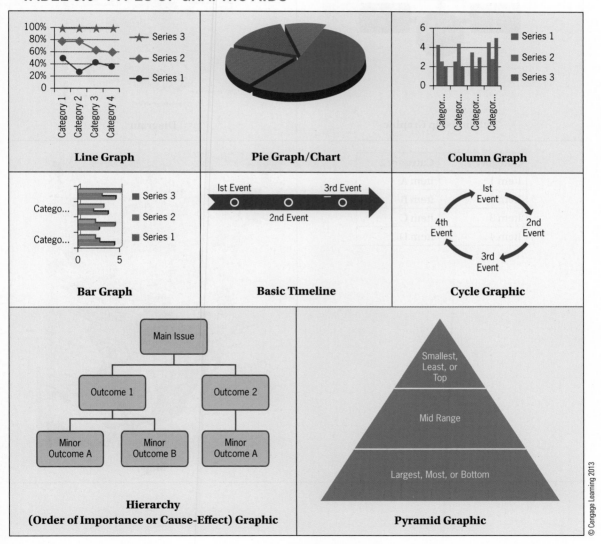

Line Graph

Pie Graph/Chart

Column Graph

Bar Graph

Basic Timeline

Cycle Graphic

**Hierarchy
(Order of Importance or Cause-Effect) Graphic**

Pyramid Graphic

(Continued)

FOCUS ON READING STUDY SKILLS: Reading Graphics

TABLE 5.6 TYPES OF GRAPHIC AIDS

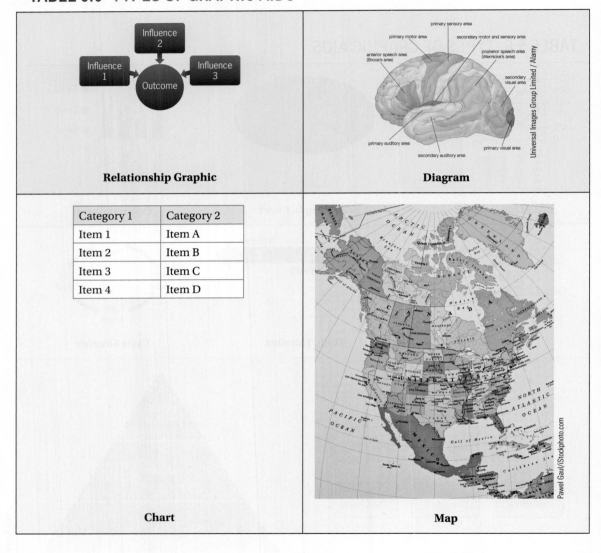

Relationship Graphic		**Diagram**
Chart		**Map**

Universal Images Group Limited / Alamy

Pawel Gaul/iStockphoto.com

Thinking It Through   READING GRAPHICS

Just like reading text, the goal of reading graphics is to determine the author's most important point about the topic. You use the same process to understand a graphic as you do to understand a reading.

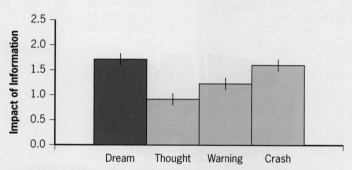

FIGURE 5.4 Impact of Negative Information on People's Plane Travel Plans.

From When Dreaming is Believing: The (Motivated) Interpretation of Dreams. Morewedge, Carey K.; Norton, Michael I. *Journal of Personality and Social Psychology*, 2009, Vol. 96, No. 2, 249–264. © 2009 American Psychological Association. By permission.

1. Determine the topic or subject. Who or what is Figure 5.4 about? *The graphic is about the impact of negative information on people's plane travel plans.*

2. Determine a question to pose about the topic. *What is the impact of negative information on people's plane travel plans?*

3. Look at the structure of Figure 5.4. What are the parts? *This is a bar graph. The parts concern the different negative influences on people's attitude towards plane travel.*

4. Answer your question: What is important about the impact of negative information on people's plane travel plans? *People are most influenced by a dream of a plane crash than conscious thoughts, or warnings of an actual plane crash event.*

5. What is the implied main idea of Figure 5.4? *People are impacted by negative information with regard to travel plans, especially bad dreams.*

FOCUS ON READING STUDY SKILLS: Reading Graphics

On Your Own READING GRAPHICS

Answer the questions that follow these graphics, then discuss them with a partner or in class discussion.

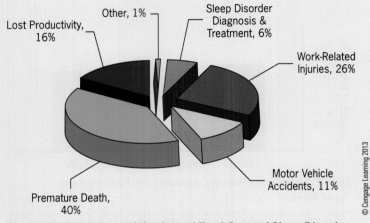

FIGURE 5.5 Percentage of the Annual Total Costs of Sleep Disorders in Western Countries

© Cengage Learning 2013

1. Determine the topic or subject. Who or what is Figure 5.5 about? _____
   _____

2. Pose a question about the topic. _____

3. Look at the structure of Figure 5.5. What are the parts? _____
   _____
   _____

4. Answer the question you posed. _____
   _____

5. What is the implied main idea of Figure 5.5? _____
   _____

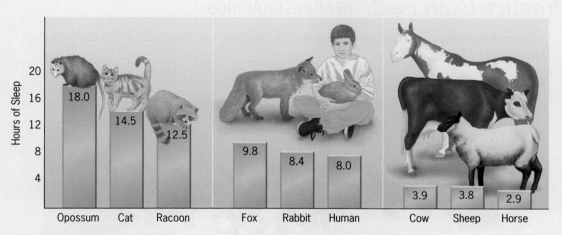

FIGURE 5.6 Sleep Times for Various Species
Large grazing animals, such as cows and horses, eat frequently and are quite vulnerable to surprise attacks from predators. Such animals tend to sleep very little. Small, quick animals, such as cat and rodents, are less vulnerable to attack and sleep a great deal.

From NAIRNE. *Psychology,* 5E. © 2009 Wadsworth, a part of Cengage Learning, Inc. By permission.

1. Determine the topic or subject. Who or what is Figure 5.6 about? _____

_____

2. Pose a question about the topic. _____

3. Look at the structure of Figure 5.6. What are the parts? _____

_____

4. Answer the question you posed. _____

5. What is the implied main idea of Figure 5.6? _____

_____

FOCUS ON READING STUDY SKILLS: Reading Graphics

Practice Exercise 2:   READING GRAPHICS

Answer the questions that follow these graphics; then discuss them with a partner or in class discussion.

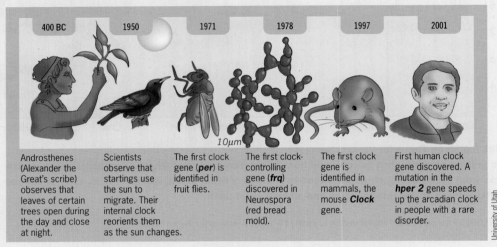

400 BC	1950	1971	1978	1997	2001
Androsthenes (Alexander the Great's scribe) observes that leaves of certain trees open during the day and close at night.	Scientists observe that startings use the sun to migrate. Their internal clock reorients them as the sun changes.	The first clock gene (*per*) is identified in fruit flies.	The first clock-controlling gene (*frq*) discovered in Neurospora (red bread mold).	The first clock gene is identified in mammals, the mouse **Clock** gene.	First human clock gene discovered. A mutation in the **hper 2** gene speeds up the arcadian clock in people with a rare disorder.

10μm

University of Utah

FIGURE 5.7 History of Our Understanding of Biological Clocks

1. Determine the topic or subject. Who or what is Figure 5.7 about? _____

_____

2. Pose a question about the topic. _____

_____

3. Look at the structure of Figure 5.7. What are the parts? _____

_____

4. Answer the question you posed. _____

_____

5. What is the implied main idea of Figure 5.7? _____

_____

TABLE 5.7 DREAM THEORIES

THEORY	EXPLANATION	MEANING OF DREAM	IS MEANING OF DREAM HIDDEN?
Psychoanalytic	Dreams are anxiety-producing wishes originating in the unconscious mind.	Latent content of dream revealed; unconscious wishes.	Yes, by manifest content of dreams
Off-line	Dreaming consolidates and stores information input during the day, allowing you to have a smaller and more efficient brain.	Previous day's experiences are reprocessed in dreams.	Not necessarily
Activation-synthesis	Dreams are the forebrain's attempt to interpret random neural activity.	Dream content is only vaguely related to your daily experiences, but there is little, if any, meaning in the dream.	No real meaning to hide

6. Determine the topic or subject. Who or what is Table 5.7 about? _____

_____

7. Pose a question about the topic. _____

_____

8. Look at the structure of Table 5.7. What are the parts? _____

_____

9. Answer the question you posed. _____

_____

10. What is the implied main idea of Table 5.6? _____

_____

(Continued)

FOCUS ON READING STUDY SKILLS: Reading Graphics

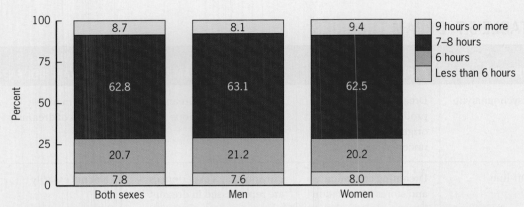

FIGURE 5.8 Age-Adjusted Percentage of Usual Hours of Sleep in a 24-hour Period Among Adults Aged 18 Years and Over, by sex: United States, 2004–2006

Data from CDC, NCHS, National Health Interview Survey, 2004–2006

11. Determine the topic or subject. Who or what is Figure 5.8 about? _____

_____

12. Pose a question about the topic. _____

_____

13. Look at the structure of Figure 5.8. What are the parts? _____

_____

14. Answer the question you posed. _____

_____

15. What is the implied main idea of Figure 5.8? _____

_____

APPLICATIONS

These applications will develop your skills of identifying transitions and patterns of organization. Follow the instructions for each application, and then answer the Comprehension Check questions. Each application serves to release more responsibility to the reader as these techniques become more automatic.

APPLICATION

This passage is from the *Associated Content*—an online news magazine associated with Yahoo—about nightmares. Read the article, answering the questions in the margins. Then, answer the Comprehension Check questions that follow the reading.

Nightmares: What Do They Mean?
Are They Just Scary Inventions of Our Minds?
By Kassidy Emmerson

1   Nightmares are pretty much the same as dreams: they happen when we are asleep, and our subconscious minds conjure them up. Except, what sets nightmares apart from dreams, is the fact that nightmares are never happy experiences. Instead, they are always dark, scary, and maybe even evil in nature. And, nightmares can be so disturbing that they often wake us up suddenly from our sleep. When we do wake up from having a nightmarish dream, we are usually nervous, scared, or shaken up. Our hearts are racing and it's difficult to fall back asleep.

What pattern does the transition word instead *indicate?*

2   Children are thought to experience nightmares more than adults do. Children around the ages of three to five are the most susceptible to these nighttime scares. Stressful events such as being left alone, watching a monster movie on television, being in the dark, et cetera, can easily create fears in a young child. The stress and fears can then manifest into a nightmare.

What does susceptible *mean?*

3   Nightmares can typically be classified into four categories. That is, there are four usual themes to our nightmares. Either we are being chased, we are falling, we are being attacked, or, we are stuck. No matter which theme your nightmare follows, experts say that our nightmares are caused by stress in our lives. Experience a traumatic experience or a stress situation, and you're likely to have a nightmare about it.

What is the pattern of organization of paragraph 3?

(Continued)

What pattern does the transition word *therefore* indicate?

4   The experts also say that nightmares are "<u>red flags</u>" from our subconscious minds. Something is wrong in our lives. Therefore our subconscious minds are trying to alert us to the fact that we have an unresolved problem. A nightmare is the mind's way of bringing the problem to our attention so we can resolve it in real life.

What is the pattern of organization of paragraph 5?

5   So, although these nighttime experiences aren't pleasant, if you analyze your nightmares, you may be able to find out how to stop from having them. For example, if you have a nightmare where you are falling, it can mean that you're worried. The falling in your nightmare may represent your inner need to feel free and unburdened. If you have a scary dream where you are trapped, you may feel "trapped" in real life.

What is the pattern of organization of paragraph 6?

6   Another example is a dream that you can't move your body in, or that you can only move in slow motion. This could represent your feelings that your life is stuck in a rut. If you can't speak in your nightmares, this could mean that you feel you can't express your inner feelings.

7   One of the most popular nightmares that people have is one in which they are naked or not fully dressed in public. Having nothing to do with sexuality or the love of streaking, these nightmares usually mean we feel unprepared or are "not up to par". And, we're afraid that other people will see our inadequacies. Since the others in a dream such as this don't notice our nakedness, this means that we are looking at ourselves in a way that nobody else is.

What does the prefix *in-* mean in *inadequacies*?

What does the prefix *sub-* mean in *subconscious*?

What is the pattern of organization of paragraph 8?

8   So, nightmares are not really terrifying experiences that are conjured up by our subconscious in order to scare us. Instead, they are our mind's way of alerting us to a problem we have. Our subconscious mind is telling us that we have a problem that needs to be resolved. Or, that the steps we are taking to try and end the problem aren't working. Therefore, we need to rethink the problem and come up with a new way to solve it. Once the problem in your daily life is solved, your nightmares should end.

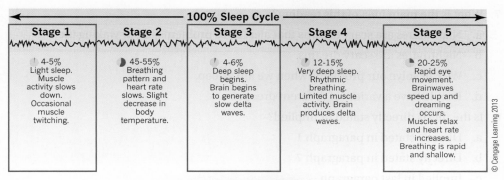

FIGURE 5.9 100% Sleep Cycle

COMPREHENSION CHECK

TRUE/FALSE QUESTIONS

For the following statements, write *T* if the statement is true or *F* if the statement is false based on the reading.

____ 1. Children ages 3 to 5 are the most susceptible to having nightmares.

____ 2. A nightmare where you're falling can mean you strive for freedom in your life.

____ 3. Solve the problem your nightmare represents, and the scary dreams should stop.

____ 4. If you can't speak in your nightmares, this could mean that you feel "trapped" in life.

____ 5. Nightmares are terrifying experiences conjured up by our subconscious to scare us.

LITERAL COMPREHENSION—MULTIPLE CHOICE

Circle the best answer for the following questions.

Understanding Main Ideas

6. What is the topic of this reading?

   a. Dreams

   b. Problems during sleep

   c. Nightmares

   d. Sleep

(Continued)

7. What is the main idea of this reading?

   a. Nightmares are scary dreams that alert us to problems in our waking life.

   b. Nightmares are scary dreams.

   c. We can solve our problems when we are asleep.

   d. People have a variety of different dreams.

8. Is the thesis directly stated or implied?

   a. Directly stated in paragraph 1

   b. Directly stated in paragraph 7

   c. Implied in last paragraph

   d. Implied in paragraph 2

9. What is the main idea of paragraph 3?

   a. Nightmares can typically be classified into four categories.

   b. We are being chased, we are falling, we are being attacked, or we are stuck.

   c. No matter which theme your nightmare follows, experts say that our nightmares are caused by stress in our lives.

   d. A nightmare is the mind's way of bringing the problem to our attention so we can resolve it in real life.

Understanding Secondary Information and Locating Information

10. Into how many categories are nightmares classified (paragraph 3)?

    a. Two

    b. Three

    c. Four

    d. One

11. What causes nightmares, according to paragraph 3?

    a. A guilty conscience

    b. Stress

    c. Physical problems

    d. Experts do not know what causes nightmares.

12. How do experts think you can stop nightmares?

    a. Don't think about them.

    b. See a therapist immediately.

    c. Ask a friend what it means.

    d. Analyze them.

13. What does having a nightmare in which you are falling probably mean?

    a. You're worried.

    b. Your nightmare may represent you inner need to feel free and unburdened.

    c. You are worried and may need to feel free.

    d. You may have a fall in the near future.

14. If someone has nightmares in which he or she is naked or not fully dressed in public, it probably means

    a. He or she feels inadequate.

    b. He or she can foretell the future.

    c. He or she has health problems.

    d. He or she is being ridiculed by other people at work.

15. According to Figure 5.9, in what stage of sleep do we spend most time?

    a. Stage 1

    b. Stage 2

    c. Stage 3

    d. Stage 4

16. According to Figure 5.9, during which stage does dreaming take place?

    a. Stage 1

    b. Stage 2

    c. Stage 4

    d. Stage 5

INFERENTIAL COMPREHENSION—MULTIPLE CHOICE

Circle the best answer for the following questions.

Making Inferences

17. What does the term *red flags* mean in paragraph 4?

    a. Celebration

    b. A warning

    c. Surrender

    d. Solution to a problem

(Continued)

Applying Information

18. If your friend was going to a job interview and had a dream the night before about going to the interview not properly dressed, what might that dream suggest?

    a. He feels ashamed of himself.

    b. He feels inadequate for the job.

    c. He has a fear of falling.

    d. He feels he can't speak at the interview.

Understanding Sentence Relationships

19. What is the main pattern of organization of this reading?

    a. Problem and solution

    b. Definition/example

    c. Random order list

    d. Sequence order

20. Two primary patterns of organization in paragraph 1 are

    a. Cause and effect and comparison and contrast.

    b. Definition/example and classification.

    c. Sequence order and random order listing.

    d. Problem and solution and classification.

INCREASE YOUR COLLEGE-LEVEL VOCABULARY

For the following passages from the reading, underline the transition words, phrases, or clues that help you predict the author's thought pattern. Circle the transitions or clue words, and write the thought pattern next to the statement.

21. Nightmares are pretty much the same as dreams: they happen when we are asleep, and our subconscious minds conjure them up. _____

22. Nightmares can typically be classified into four categories. _____

23. There are four usual themes to our nightmares. _____

24. No matter which theme your nightmare follows, experts say that our nightmares are caused by stress in our lives. _____

25. Although these nighttime experiences aren't pleasant, if you analyze your nightmares, you may be able to find out how to stop from having them. _____

26. Another example is a dream in which you can't move your body or you can only move in slow motion. _____

27. Since the others in a dream such as this don't notice our nakedness, this means that we are looking at ourselves in a way that nobody else is. _____

28. Nightmares are not really terrifying experiences that are conjured up by our subconscious in order to scare us. Instead, they are our mind's way of alerting us to a problem we have. _____

29. Our subconscious mind is telling us that we have a problem that needs to be resolved. _____

30. Therefore, we need to rethink the problem and come up with a new way to solve it. _____ _____

SHORT-ANSWER QUESTIONS

31. Explain the possible causes of nightmares and their effects.

32. Why do you think children are more likely to suffer from frequent nightmares as compared to adults?

33. What is the strangest nightmare you have had? What do you think was the cause of that nightmare?

34. Complete the following chart using information in the reading.

TYPE OF NIGHTMARE	EXPLANATION
falling	
	feel stuck in life
naked or not fully dressed in public	
trapped	

APPLICATION ②

This application is an excerpt from *What Is Psychology? Essentials,* an introductory college psychology textbook. Read the excerpt and answer the questions in the margins. Then, answer the Comprehension Check questions following the reading.

Sleep, Dreaming, and Circadian Rhythm
By Ellen Pastorino and Susann Doyle-Portillo

FUNCTIONS OF SLEEP: WHY DO WE SLEEP, AND WHAT IF WE DON'T?

What is the pattern of organization of this section?

1   What would happen if you tried to stay awake? William C. Dement, a pioneer in sleep research, actually tried this experiment himself. Dement's lack of sleep made him a danger to himself and others, but he was not in danger of dying from lack of sleep. Eventually he fell asleep. In the same way that you cannot hold your breath until you die, you cannot deprive yourself of all sleep. Sleep always wins. We drift into repeated microsleeps. A **microsleep** is a brief (3- to 15-second) episode of sleep that occurs in the midst of a wakeful activity. We are typically unaware of its occurrence unless we are behind the wheel of a car, steering a ship, or flying a plane. In such circumstances, microsleeps could cause a disaster. Yet microsleeps appear to help us survive by preventing total sleep deprivation.

What pattern does the transition word yet indicate?

2   Sleep ensures our continued physical and mental health in several ways.

What pattern does this sentence suggest will follow?

3   • *Sleep restores body tissues and facilitates body growth.* Sleep allows your immune system, nervous system, and organs time to replenish lost reserves and energy and to repair any cellular damage. This prepares the body for action the next day and ensures the continued health of the body. Sleep also activates growth hormone, which facilitates physical growth during infancy, childhood, and the teen years. Lack of adequate sleep can also affect energy levels, often making us feel drowsy and fatigued.

4   • *Sleep increases immunity to disease.* During sleep, the production of immune cells that fight off infection increases. Therefore, your immune system is stronger when you receive the appropriate amount of sleep. When you deprive your body of sleep, your natural immune responses are

What does the transition word therefore indicate?

reduced. This is in part why you are encouraged to sleep and rest when you are ill. This effect on immunity occurs after as few as two days of not sleeping or even several days of partial sleep deprivation. For college students, this may mean you are more susceptible to colds and flu at midterm and final exam time. You are more likely to sleep less at these times, thereby decreasing your immune system's ability to combat illnesses. Fortunately, after a night or several nights of recovery sleep, your natural immune functions return to normal. Sleeping truly is good medicine.

5 • *Sleep keeps your mind alert.* When people do not get enough sleep, they are more likely to be inattentive and easily distracted. Sleep makes your body more sensitive to norepinephrine—the neurotransmitter that keeps you alert during the day.

What is the definition of *norepinephrine*?

6 • *Sleep helps learning and memory.* When you sleep, information that you have reviewed or rehearsed is more likely to be remembered.

7   • In order to get information into your memory, you must *encode* it, or do something to remember the information. This may mean repeating the information over and over again, visualizing the information, or associating it with a personal experience. When information is thoroughly encoded, it can be more easily transferred to long-term memory so that we can retrieve it later.

What does the transition word *so* indicate?

8   • Sleep allows you to better store material that was actually processed (that is, encoded well enough) during studying. Information that you can't readily retrieve in the morning probably wasn't encoded well enough, and you will need to study it again. You can see the advantage of a good night's sleep before an exam.

9   • Sleep's connection to memory processing may also explain why problem solving seems to improve after a night's sleep. You may think about a problem repeatedly during the day, frustrated by your inability to find a solution. The next day you awaken with a solution in mind. This suggests that pertinent details about the problem are processed during sleep. The phrase "sleep on it" really does have merit.

What is the pattern of organization of paragraph 9?

10 • *Sleep enhances your mood.* Sleep activates many chemicals that influence your emotions and mood. Consequently, if

What does the transition word *consequently* indicate?

(Continued)

you are deprived of sleep, you are more likely to be irritable, cranky, and unhappy, in addition to being tired.

Besides cause and effect, what pattern is used in paragraph 11?

11   Research also suggests that sleep may have evolved as a necessary behavior for humans. When humans lived in caves, it was dangerous for them to go out at night to hunt for food because they had very little night vision and were relatively small compared to other species. If they did go outside at night, they were likely to be the food for larger predators. Humans who stayed inside the cave at night were more likely to survive and produce offspring. Over time, these offspring may have adapted to the pattern of nighttime sleeping and daytime hunting and gathering.

12   As you can see, sleep is a necessity, not a luxury. Sleep offers many benefits to our functioning and ensures that we will be healthy, alert, and happy.

HOW MUCH SLEEP DO WE NEED?

What is the pattern of organization of this section?

13   People show differences in the amount of sleep they need. Here are some sleep factors and facts:

What is the pattern of organization of paragraph 14?

14   • *Age.* The older we get, the less sleep we need (Figure 5.10). Babies require a lot of sleep, between 16 and 18 hours a day. Preschoolers require less sleep, about 10 to 12 hours a day, typically including a midday nap. Teenagers and young adults need less sleep than children, but they still require 8 to 10 hours of sleep a night. However, just one in five teenagers gets an optimal 9 hours of sleep on school nights. On average, college students sleep 6.1 hours—2 hours less than they need—each night. One study of 191 undergraduates found that the majority exhibited some form of sleep disturbance. Adults, on average, sleep 6.8 hours a night on weekdays.

What is the pattern of organization of paragraph 15?

15   • *Lifestyle (Environment).* Our habits and our environment also influence the amount of sleep we need or get. If you were raised in a home in which everyone was up early on the weekends to do chores, you adapted to a different sleep schedule than someone who slept until 10 A.M. or noon on weekends. In one study of college students, good sleepers were more likely to have regular bedtime and rise time schedules than poorer sleepers. Keep in mind, too, that stressors and responsibilities change as we get older. Living on one's own, parenting, or job responsibilities also bring about changes in our sleep schedule.

16 • *Genetics.* Genes may also play a role in the amount of sleep that each of us requires. For example, studies that measured the sleep patterns of identical twins compared to fraternal twins found more similar sleep needs among identical twins. Additional research also suggests that genes may influence our propensity to be either "night owls" or "early birds." Some people may be genetically predisposed to get up early in the morning and go to bed earlier, whereas others may prefer getting up later and going to bed later.

What does the root word *frater* mean in *fraternal*?

What does the transition word *whereas* indicate?

From PASTORINO/DOYLE-PORTILLO. *ACP What Is Psychology*, 2E. © 2008 Wadsworth, a part of Cengage Learning, Inc. By permission.

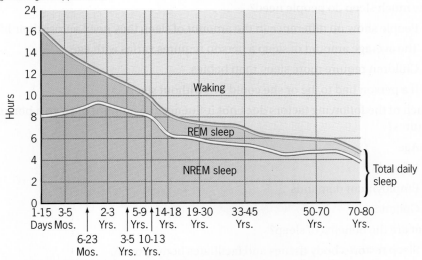

FIGURE 5.10 Sleep Duration over the Lifespan

From Ontogenetic Development of Human Sleep-Dream Cycle, by H. P. Roffwarg, J. N. Muzino and W. C. Dement, Science, 1966, 152:604–609. Copyright 1966 by the AAAS. Reprinted by permission.

COMPREHENSION CHECK

TRUE OR FALSE QUESTIONS

For the following statements, write *T* if the statement is true or *F* if the statement is false based on the reading.

____ 1. Norepinephrine is the neurotransmitter that keeps you alert during the day.

____ 2. During sleep, the production of immune cells that fight off infection increases.

____ 3. College students are *not* more susceptible to colds and flu at midterm and final exam time.

____ 4. The elderly and teenagers require the same average amount of sleep.

____ 5. Based on Figure 5.10, we spend more time in REM than in NREM sleep as adults.

(Continued)

LITERAL COMPREHENSION—MULTIPLE CHOICE

Circle the best answer for the following questions.

Understanding Main Ideas

6. Why do we sleep?
   a. Sleep keeps your mind alert.
   b. Sleep helps learning and memory.
   c. Sleep enhances your mood.
   d. All of the given answers.

7. How much sleep do people need?
   a. People show no difference in the amount of sleep they need across their lifespan.
   b. The average amount of sleep a person requires varies with age.
   c. Children require more sleep than babies.
   d. If a person had to, he or she could live without sleep.

8. Which of the following factors does not influence the amount of sleep a person requires?
   a. Age
   b. Lifestyle
   c. Employment demands
   d. Genetics

9. What are the benefits of sleep?
   a. Sleep restores body tissues and facilitates body growth.
   b. Sleep increases immunity to disease.
   c. Sleep keeps your mind alert.
   d. All of the given answers.

Understanding Secondary Information and Locating Information

10. What would happen if you tried to stay awake?
    a. Eventually, you would die.
    b. Your body would shut down.
    c. You would eventually fall asleep.
    d. Your immunity to disease would be affected.

11. What are microsleeps?
    a. A brief episode of sleep that occurs in the midst of a wakeful activity
    b. 3- to 15-second burst of energy

   c. The body's way of improving memory

   d. Insomnia

12. What is the function of microsleeps?

   a. They appear to help us survive by preventing total sleep deprivation.

   b. They are long periods of consciousness that allow our mood to stabilize.

   c. They are an indication of sleep apnea.

   d. They are an indication of insomnia.

13. In what ways does sleep repair the body?

   a. One study of 191 undergraduates found that the majority exhibited some form of sleep disturbance.

   b. Some people may be genetically predisposed to get up early in the morning and go to bed earlier, whereas others may prefer getting up later and going to bed later.

   c. Sleep allows your immune system, nervous system, and organs time to replenish lost reserves and energy and to repair any cellular damage.

   d. Sleep activates many chemicals that influence your emotions and mood.

14. How soon does a lack of sleep affect your immune system?

   a. You can overcome the adverse effects of sleep deprivation through taking vitamins.

   b. After as few as 2 days of not sleeping or even several days of partial sleep deprivation.

   c. The immune system is affected by sleep deprivation after the first week of wakefulness.

   d. Lack of sleep does not affect the immune system.

15. How does sleep keep your mind alert?

   a. Sleep makes your body more sensitive to norepinephrine.

   b. Sleep affects your body rather than your mind.

   c. Sleep triggers your immune system that in turn triggers your ability to concentrate.

   d. All of the given answers.

INFERENTIAL COMPREHENSION—MULTIPLE CHOICE

Circle the best answer for the following questions.

Making Inferences

16. If a person did not get sufficient sleep for a period of time, what conclusion could you draw about his or her health?

   a. Her body would work adequately but her mind and concentration would be affected.

   b. Her mind and concentration would work adequately, but her body would be affected.

   c. Neither her body nor her mind would be affected.

   d. Both her body and her mind would be affected.

(Continued)

17. If a person is sleep deprived, what would be the probable outcome?

    a. The person would fall asleep and sleep for days.

    b. The person would experience microsleeps about which he or she would be unaware.

    c. The person would not be affected by a lack of sleep.

    d. The person's norepinephrine levels would increase sharply.

Applying Information

18. If you were counseling a college friend about the importance of sleep, what would be your best advice, based on the information in this reading?

    a. Make sure to get the most sleep during stressful times.

    b. Make sure to get less sleep during stressful times.

    c. Make sure to get less sleep during exams.

    d. Stress leads to improved sleep.

Understanding Sentence Relationships

19. What is the main pattern of organization in this section of the reading—Functions of Sleep: Why Do We Sleep, and What If We Don't?

    a. Cause and effect

    b. Comparison and contrast

    c. Definition/example

    d. Random order list

20. What are the main patterns of organization in Figure 5.10?

    a. Definition/example and cause and effect

    b. Sequence order and comparison and contrast

    c. Problem and solution

    d. Random order listing

INCREASE YOUR COLLEGE-LEVEL VOCABULARY

Underline the transition word that indicates the author's pattern of organization in each of the following sentences. Then paraphrase the sentence using *another* transition word for the same pattern of organization.

Example:

One <u>solution</u> for insomnia is to avoid caffeine within a few hours of bedtime.

Pattern: <u>Problem and solution</u>

New sentence: <u>Refraining from consuming caffeine before bed is one way to solve insomnia.</u>

21. In such circumstances, microsleeps could cause a disaster.

    Pattern: _____

    New sentence: _____

22. Lack of adequate sleep can also affect energy levels, often making us feel drowsy and fatigued.

    Pattern: _____

    New sentence: _____

23. Research also suggests that sleep may have evolved as a necessary behavior for humans.

    Pattern: _____

    New sentence: _____

24. People show differences in the amount of sleep they need.

    Pattern: _____

    New sentence: _____

25. Studies that measured the sleep patterns of identical twins compared to fraternal twins found more similar sleep needs among identical twins.

    Pattern: _____

    New sentence: _____

SHORT-ANSWER QUESTIONS

26. Discuss why we sleep and what factors influence the amount of sleep we need.

27. What mind and body processes function better with sufficient sleep? Make sure to explain your answer using specific examples.

28. What mind and body processes are compromised without enough sleep? What happens? Make sure to provide specific examples to support your answer.

WRAPPING IT UP

STUDY OUTLINE

This is a list of key terms from this chapter for you to define. In the following study outline, fill in the definitions and a brief explanation of the key terms in the Your Notes column. Use the strategy of spaced practice to review these key terms on a regular basis. Use this study guide to review this chapter's key topics.

KEY TERM	YOUR NOTES	
Transition words		
Relationships between ideas		
Patterns of organization		
Random order list		
Specific order list		
Definition/example		
Classification		
Cause and effect		
Problem and solution		
Comparison and contrast		
Graphics		
Supporting details		

KEY TERM	YOUR NOTES
Major details	
Minor details	
Order of importance	
Chronological order	
Sequence or process order	
Graph	

WHAT DID YOU LEARN?

At the beginning of this chapter, you assessed your sleep deprivation level. Now, respond to this quiz by answering either "Day" or "Evening" to find out if you are a morning or night person.

Roman Shcherbakov/Shutterstock

1.	I prefer to work during the	Day	Evening
2.	I enjoy leisure-time activities most during the	Day	Evening
3.	I feel most alert during the	Day	Evening
4.	I get my best ideas during the	Day	Evening
5.	I have my highest energy during the	Day	Evening
6.	I prefer to take classes during the	Day	Evening
7.	I prefer to study during the	Day	Evening
8.	I feel most intelligent during the	Day	Evening
9.	I am most productive during the	Day	Evening
10.	When I graduate, I would prefer to find a job with _____ hours.	Day	Evening

—From "Day persons, night persons, and variability in hypnotic susceptibility" by B. Wallace in *Journal of Personality and Social Psychology*, 1993, 64, 827–833 (Appendix, p.833). Copyright © 1993 by the American Psychological Association. Adapted with permission.

Scoring instructions: If you answered "Day" to eight or more items, you are probably a morning person. If you answered "evening" to eight or more items, you are probably a night person.

WRAPPING IT UP

GROUP ACTIVITY: SLEEP STUDY

As a group, find further information on one of the following topics. Present your findings to the class. How can you apply this information to your life as a student?

- Research the connection between sleep deprivation and driving.
- What information can a student use to deal with sleep debt?
- Research the theories of dreams. Poll your class or others to assess which of the theories is the most popular.

QUESTIONS FOR WRITING, DISCUSSION, OR REFLECTION

1. What do you feel is the most significant piece of information regarding sleep covered in this chapter? What are some ways you could use this information to improve your health in college?
2. What is your opinion on the purpose of dreams? Do you believe they are significant or of no real importance?
3. Have you ever gone for a long time without sleep? What did you notice about your mental and physical states?
4. Research sleep disorders. Which two do you think are most serious?
5. Choose a textbook you use in another class. Find examples of transition words that reveal a pattern of organization.
6. For another class, try the technique of locating patterns of organization of a whole reading, a section of a reading, or a paragraph.
7. Find a newspaper or magazine article on the topic of your choice or one related to the theme of this chapter. Find three examples of patterns of organization.
8. Choose a passage on sleep or from a reading in another class. Create a graphic that accurately represents the information. Defend why you chose the format of the graphic—how does it suit the pattern of organization in the reading passage?

POST-ASSESSMENT

This assessment will help you understand your strengths and weaknesses in learning, understanding, and applying the skills and strategies discussed in this chapter. Preview the following article. Then read it all the way through and answer the Comprehension Check questions that follow.

How Bad Dreams Can Lead to High Anxiety
By *Mail On Sunday* Reporter

1   One in 20 people suffers with frequent or chronic nightmares, writes Roger Dobson.

2   In one of the biggest studies in the area, results show that bad dreams are associated with health problems—from insomnia, fatigue and headaches, to depression and anxiety.

3   Mental health problems, such as depression, were five times more common in men and women who had regular nightmares.

4   "The high correlation between nightmare frequency and sleep related daytime consequences underlines the fact that nightmares might have a strong effect on the wellbeing of the patient, and should be treated," says Dr Michael Schredl, of the Sleep Laboratory at the Central Institute of Mental Health in Mannheim, Germany.

5   Nightmares are defined as frightening dreams that awaken people from rapid eye movement or REM sleep, a time when there are high levels of brain activity.

6   In the new Chinese research, psychiatrists investigated nightmares in 9,000 adults, looking at the frequency, as well as who has them and any links with ill health.

7   The results showed that 5.1 percent of people have frequent nightmares, defined as at least one a week. They were more common among women, with 6.2 percent having one at least once a week compared to 3.8 percent of men.

8   Those in the neurotic category were also more likely to have scary dreams, and researchers say there is evidence of a genetic susceptibility, too.

9   Frequency was also linked to income and unemployment. Those on the lowest incomes were 2.3 times more likely to have three or more nightmares a week compared to the more affluent.

10 Higher levels of stress associated with lower incomes and social status may predispose some people to nightmares.

11 In turn, greater frequency was also linked to an increased risk of insomnia and to a higher risk of daytime fatigue, headaches, and difficulty getting up in the morning.

12 Results also show that the risk of having a psychiatric disorder was 5.7 times greater for those with frequent nightmares compared with those without.

(Continued)

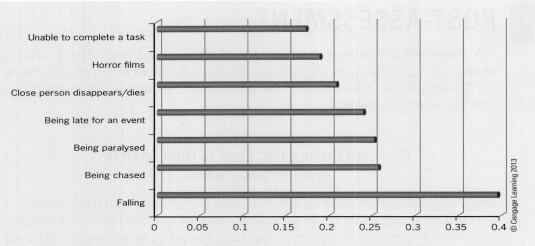

Percentage of Study Participants Reporting Type of Dream

FIGURE 5.11 The Top Nightmares in the Study

COMPREHENSION CHECK

Circle the best answer to the questions based on information in the reading.

1 **Based on the title, what do you expect the pattern of organization to be?**

A. Comparison and contrast

B. Cause and effect

C. Definition/example

2 **What is the relationship between ideas in paragraph 2?**

A. Comparison and contrast

B. Cause and effect

C. Definition/example

3 **What is the relationship between ideas in paragraph 4?**

A. Sequence

B. Classification

C. Cause and effect

4 **What is the relationship between ideas in paragraph 5?**

A. Sequence

B. Classification

C. Definition/example

5   **What is the relationship between ideas in paragraph 7?**

A. Comparison and contrast
B. Classification
C. Problem and/or solution

6   **What is the relationship between income, social status, stress, and nightmares, according to paragraph 10?**

A. The higher your income, the higher the risk of nightmares.
B. The lower your income, the higher the risk of nightmares.
C. There is no relationship between income and the likelihood of having nightmares.

7   **Which of the following consequences can result from a higher incidence of nightmares?**

A. Insomnia, daytime fatigue, and psychiatric disorders.
B. Headaches and difficulty getting up in the morning.
C. All the given answers can be an effect of nightmares.

8   **Which of the following transition words indicates a cause and effect pattern in paragraph 4?**

A. Correlation
B. Frequency
C. Consequences

9   **Which two organizational patterns are indicated in Figure 5.11?**

A. Sequence order and comparison and contrast
B. Problem and solution and random order list
C. Definition/example and comparison and contrast

10   **According to Figure 5.11, about how many people in the study reported having dreams about being chased?**

A. 2.5 percent
B. 50 percent
C. 25 percent

SUPPORTING DETAILS

THEME *The World of Work*

*"To be successful, a woman has to be much better at
her job than a man."*

— GOLDA MEIR, FORMER PRIME MINISTER OF ISRAEL

OBJECTIVES

In this chapter, you will focus on:

COMPREHENSION SKILLS

Identify and organize
supporting details

- Text marking and
  annotating
- Taking notes from
  a reading

USING SUPPORT TO FIND OUT MORE

READING STUDY SKILLS

Assess reading rate and monitor
comprehension to support your
study skills

VOCABULARY SKILLS

Use supporting resources to
understand unknown words

- Using dictionaries
  and glossaries
- Using strategies for
  learning key terms

© Cengage Learning 2013

WHY DO YOU NEED TO KNOW THIS?

Problem:

Raul is improving his ability to find main ideas in his reading for college. In fact, he uses this strategy in all his reading now—for school and for work. Raul works full-time as a supervisor in a warehouse but attends community college to get his associate's degree in business, so he can move up the corporate ladder. The problem is, once Raul is finished with his reading, he has trouble remembering the key points by the time the test is at hand.

Katharine Andriotis / Alamy

WHAT ADVICE WOULD YOU OFFER TO RAUL?

_____

_____

_____

_____

Solution:

Like Raul, all college students need to read efficiently and learn effectively. Increasing comprehension and reading speed are important goals. However, to be successful in college classes and on tests, this is not enough. College students need to implement strategies to help them _learn_ the new information. Identifying major and minor details in a reading is one helpful strategy. This helps you determine what is most important and what is less important—what is specific and general. A successful college student learns to interact with a reading by underlining and annotating. Translating underlining and annotations into notes will also help you learn reading material.

WHAT DO YOU ALREADY KNOW?

This brief questionnaire helps you assess your views on the work world, the theme of
the readings in this chapter. Fill in *A* for agree or *D* for disagree in the Before column.
When you finish this chapter, you'll come back and fill in the After column.

	BEFORE Agree or Disagree?	AFTER Agree or Disagree?
1. In hiring decisions, gender is not an issue.		
2. The best person gets the job.		
3. The law protects from discrimination at work.		
4. Minorities are now treated equally in hiring decisions.		

© Cengage Learning 2013

PRE-ASSESSMENT

This pre-assessment will help you measure what you already know and what you need
to learn about the reading skills and strategies explored in this chapter. Your results will
help you understand your strengths and weaknesses. Read the article, and then answer
the Comprehension Check questions that follow. You can also calculate your reading rate,
or how fast you read this article. Write down your exact starting time here:

   Start time: hour ____minutes____seconds____

Then, after you read, write down your exact end time. You'll read more about reading rate in
this chapter.

Secret Intelligence Service (M16)

1   Employees with global experience and cultural sensitivity are in high demand because
at least some aspect of almost every business today cuts across national boundaries.
As the following example shows, corporations aren't the only organizations seeking a
diverse workforce to cope with the challenges of globalization.

2   *James Bond need not apply.* Britain's secret spy agency, M16*, has embarked
on an intense campaign to recruit women and minorities, not the white males who

---

*Britain's Secret Intelligence Service is called M16. This government agency is like the Central Intelligence Agency, commonly known as the
CIA, in the United States.

have long been the face of M16. The agency's recruiting Web site encourages women, including mothers, to apply and assures them they won't be used as "seductresses." Applications from disabled candidates are also welcomed. But the biggest push is for ethnic minorities who speak languages such as Arabic, Persian, Mandarin, Urdu, and the Afghan languages of Dari and Pashto.

3   For intelligence agencies, diversity is considered *mission critical*. With terrorism being the key challenge, security agencies in the United States as well as Britain are seeking a multicultural workforce to act as receptionists, linguists, operational agents, technology officers, security guards, and so forth.

4   For Britain's M16, the push for more minority applicants is starting to pay off. In 2007, 40 percent of recruits from open recruiting were women and 11 percent were ethnic minorities. As Britain moves toward passage of a new "Equality Bill" that will strengthen discrimination laws and allow organizations to give preference to minorities, M16 is getting a head start. Pola Uddin, the first Muslim woman in the House of Lords, said it's about time James Bond got a taste of affirmative action.

5   Intelligence and security agencies recognize the importance of having people who understand and can fit in with the diverse and ever-changing global landscape. As the head of human resources for M16 put it ". . . [all] agencies have to show that they're making positive efforts [to diversify], but for us it means much more."

—DAFT. *The Leadership Experience,* 5E. © 2011 South-Western,
a part of Cengage Learning, Inc. By permission.

End time: _____ **hour** _____ **minutes** _____ **seconds**

Total reading time: _____ **minutes** _____ **seconds** (Subtract your end time from your starting time.)

Find the time on the chart that corresponds to your reading time to find your reading rate in words per minute.

TIME	WPM	TIME	WPM	TIME	WPM	TIME	WPM	TIME	WPM	TIME	WPM
1m	319	2m	160	3m	106	4m	80	5m	64	6m	53
1m 10s	273	2m 10s	147	3m 10s	101	4m 10s	77	5m 10s	62	6m 10s	52
1m 20s	239	2m 20s	137	3m 20s	96	4m 20s	74	5m 20s	60	6m 20s	50
1m 30s	213	2m 30s	128	3m 30s	91	4m 30s	71	5m 30s	58	6m 30s	49
1m 40s	191	2m 40s	120	3m 40s	87	4m 40s	68	5m 40s	56	6m 40s	48
1m 50s	174	2m 50s	113	3m 50s	83	4m 50s	66	5m 50s	55	6m 50s	47

(Continued)

COMPREHENSION CHECK

Circle the *best* answer to the questions based on information from the reading.

1   What is the best statement of topic for this reading?

A. Britain's secret intelligence agency, M16, traditionally hired white males.

B. Britain's secret intelligence agency, M16, and diversity

C. Spies and diversity

2   What is the main idea of this reading?

A. Britain's secret intelligence agency, M16, is diversifying its employees.

B. Applications from disabled candidates are also welcomed.

C. But the biggest push is for ethnic minorities who speak languages such as Arabic, Persian, Mandarin, Urdu, and the Afghan languages of Dari and Pashto.

3   What is the primary pattern of organization in this reading?

A. Classification

B. Comparison and contrast

C. Problem and solution

4   In paragraph 1, what do your infer the word *globalization* means?

A. Increasing diversity in today's workplace

B. Increasing the connectivity and interdependence in the world's economies

C. Increasing affirmative action by hiring more minorities

5   How many major supporting details are in paragraph 2?

A. 3

B. 4

C. 2

6   What transition word indicates an additional major supporting detail in paragraph 2?

A. Embarked

B. Encourages

C. Also

7   What is the main idea of paragraph 4?

A. Sentence 1

B. Sentence 2

C. The last sentence

8   How many major supporting details does the author present in paragraph 4?

A. 3

B. 4

C. 2

9 Why does the M16 want to hire more ethnic minorities who speak languages such as Arabic, Persian, Mandarin, Urdu, and the Afghan languages of Dari and Pashto?

    A. Because they want a multi-cultural workforce.

    B. Because terrorism is a key challenge.

    C. Because there are more women applicants from this language family.

10 Which of the following graphic organizers best represents the information in paragraph 2?

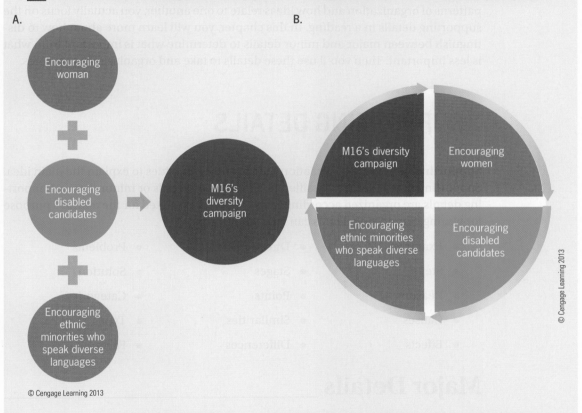

© Cengage Learning 2013

Based on how many questions you answered accurately in this Comprehension Check, do you need to increase your reading speed, slow down your reading speed, or maintain this reading speed? _____

FOCUS ON COMPREHENSION
Identifying and Organizing Supporting Details

In Chapter 5, you learned about the importance of identifying the relationships between ideas and the different kinds of patterns of organization. When you recognize patterns of organization and how ideas relate to one another, you actually focus on the supporting details in a reading. In this chapter, you will learn more about how to distinguish between major and minor details to determine what is important from what is less important. Then you'll use these details to take and organize effective notes.

SUPPORTING DETAILS

Supporting details are information that an author provides to explain the main idea. Supporting details can be classified as either major details or minor details. Supporting details are organized according to the pattern best suited for the author's purpose for writing. Supporting details can take many forms:

- Examples
- Steps
- Reasons
- Causes
- Effects

- Directions
- Stages
- Points
- Similarities
- Differences

- Problems
- Solutions
- Categories
- Types
- Facts

Major Details

Major details are the primary points that support the main idea of the paragraph, section, or of a whole reading. Look at the following example and see the major supporting details.

Changing Attitudes Toward Diversity

Attitudes toward diversity are changing partly because they have to as leaders respond to significant changes in our society, including demographic changes and globalization. In the United States, the minority population is now roughly 100.7 million, making about one in three U.S. residents a minority. Around 32 million people speak Spanish at home, and nearly half of these people say they don't speak English very well. White, American-born males now make up less than half the U.S. workforce, with many more women, people of color, and immigrants seeking employment opportunities.

—From DAFT. *The Leadership Experience,* 5E. © 2011 South-Western, a part of Cengage Learning, Inc. By permission.

Topic: Changing attitudes toward diversity

> **Main Idea:** Attitudes toward diversity are changing partly because they have to as leaders respond to significant changes in our society, including demographic changes and globalization.
>
> **Pattern of Organization:** Cause and effect
>
>> **Major Detail:** In the United States, the minority population is now roughly 100.7 million, making about one in three U.S. residents a minority.
>>
>> **Major Detail:** Around 32 million people speak Spanish at home, and nearly half of these people say they don't speak English very well.
>>
>> **Major Detail:** White, American-born males now make up less than half the U.S. workforce, with many more women, people of color, and immigrants seeking employment opportunities.

See how the details function to provide further information about the main idea? The main idea is a general statement about how attitudes toward diversity are changing. The supporting details provide specific examples of these changes.

Thinking It Through FINDING MAJOR DETAILS

Read this paragraph about globalization and identify the major details. Then answer the questions that follow.

The other factor contributing to increased acceptance of diversity is globalization. Leaders are emphasizing cross-cultural understanding so that people can work smoothly across borders . . . An unprecedented number of foreign-born CEOs now run major companies in the United States, Britain, and several other countries. Employees with global experience and cultural sensitivity are in high demand because at least some aspect of almost every business today cuts across national boundaries.

—From DAFT. *The Leadership Experience,* 5E. © 2011 South-Western, a part of Cengage Learning, Inc. By permission.

What is the topic? _____

What is the main idea? _____

What is the pattern of organization? _____

What are the major details?_____

_____

_____

(Continued)

FOCUS ON COMPREHENSION: Identifying and Organizing Supporting Details

Topic: Globalization
> **Main Idea:** Because an increased acceptance of diversity is a result of globalization, leaders are emphasizing cross-cultural understanding so that people can work smoothly across borders.
> **Pattern of Organization:** Cause and effect
>> **Major Detail:** An unprecedented number of foreign-born CEOs now run major companies in the United States, Britain, and several other countries.
>> **Major Detail:** Employees with global experience and cultural sensitivity are in high demand because at least some aspect of almost every business today cuts across national boundaries.

Both the first and second major supporting details function to support the main idea and that, in turn, supports the topic. The supporting details show specifics about how globalization has spurred leaders to promote cultural sensitivity and awareness.

On Your Own FINDING MAJOR DETAILS

In this paragraph, read to locate the major details. Answer the questions that follow to help guide you to find the major details. Feminization is a term that refers to the increasing number of women workers.

The feminization of the postindustrial workforce continues for several reasons. First, the decline in manufacturing and the rise in clerical and service occupations contributes to increased opportunities for women. Second, vast numbers of new jobs have been created in the service sector of the economy (retail, catering, clerical, leisure, and other personal services) and these are all traditionally "women's work." A third reason is the decline in male employment brought about early retirement.

—From GALLIANO. *Gender: Crossing Boundaries,* 1E. © 2003 Wadsworth,
a part of Cengage Learning, Inc. By permission.

Topic: _____

> **Main Idea:** _____

> _____

> **Pattern of Organization:** _____

>> **Major Detail:** _____

>> _____

>> **Major Detail:** _____

>> _____

>> **Major Detail:** _____

>> _____

Minor Details

Minor details are more specific points that support the major details, usually by providing examples of the major details (see Figure 6.1).

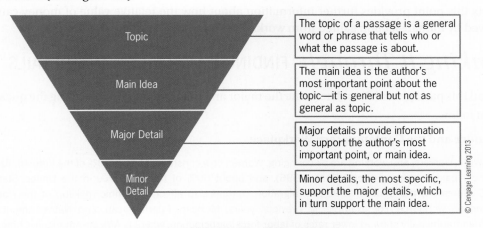

FIGURE 6.1 Relationships Between Ideas

Read this passage and see the major and minor details.

> Work can be one of the most satisfying aspects of life, because it expresses an important part of the self. Our occupation or vocation is often the vehicle for the expression of our creativity, talent, or acquired skills. The workplace is typically the arena for the development and expression of our achievement, strivings, and pursuit of excellence and productivity. Labor that is self-selected or that is aimed at some higher purpose is extremely fulfilling. Nor is there any doubt that money can help make life easier and more enjoyable. Although generous monetary compensation is a heavily endorsed cultural value in the West, the meaning of work can go way beyond that.
>
> —From GALLIANO. *Gender: Crossing Boundaries,* 1E. © 2003 Wadsworth,
> a part of Cengage Learning, Inc. By permission.

Topic: Work and satisfaction
Main idea: Work can be one of the most satisfying aspects of life, because it expresses an important part of the self.
Pattern of organization: Cause and effect
>   **Major Detail:** Our occupation or vocation is often the vehicle for the expression of our creativity, talent, or acquired skills.
>   **Major Detail:** The workplace is typically the arena for the development and expression of our achievement, strivings, and pursuit of excellence and productivity.
>   **Major Detail:** Labor that is self-selected or that is aimed at some higher purpose is extremely fulfilling.

FOCUS ON COMPREHENSION: Identifying and Organizing Supporting Details

Major Detail: Money can help make life easier and more enjoyable.

    Minor Detail: Although generous monetary compensation is a heavily endorsed cultural value in the West, the meaning of work can go way beyond that.

The fourth major detail concerns how money contributes to work satisfaction. The minor detail that supports this point provides further information about how the relative value of money can be over-shadowed by the satisfaction gained from work.

Thinking It Through FINDING MAJOR AND MINOR DETAILS

Read this passage and then determine the major and minor details by answering the questions that follow.

Gender and the Contemporary Workplace

Work, workers, and working are all changing. Women now constitute at least 40% of the industrialized world's paid workforce (World Bank, 1996), and about 60% of the workforce in the United States (U.S. Bureau of the Census, 1998). Immigration continues to affect the ethnic makeup of the North American workforce. For example, in previous years, Mexican, Puerto Rican, and Native American women traditionally showed lower rates of labor force participation, whereas African-American, Chinese, Japanese, and Filipino women showed rates higher than those of white women. However, all over North America, such ethnic differences are rapidly declining.

        —From GALLIANO. *Gender: Crossing Boundaries,* 1E. © 2003 Wadsworth,

        a part of Cengage Learning, Inc. By permission.

What is the topic? _____

What is the main idea? _____

What is the pattern of organization? _____

What are the major details? _____

_____

_____

What are the minor details? _____

_____

_____

Topic: Gender and the contemporary workplace

Main Idea: Work, workers, and working are all changing.

Pattern of Organization: Cause and effect

    Major Detail: Women now constitute at least 40% of the industrialized world's paid workforce and about 60% of the workforce in the United States.

> **Major Detail:** Immigration continues to affect the ethnic makeup of the North American workforce.
>> **Minor Detail:** Mexican, Puerto Rican, and Native American women traditionally showed lower rates of labor force participation.
>> **Minor Detail:** African-American, Chinese, Japanese, and Filipino women showed rates higher than those of white women.
>> **Minor Detail:** Ethnic differences are rapidly declining.

In this paragraph, the author uses two major points to support the main idea. The second major detail has three minor details that illustrate it. All three minor details provide examples of how immigration continues to affect the ethnic makeup of the North American workforce.

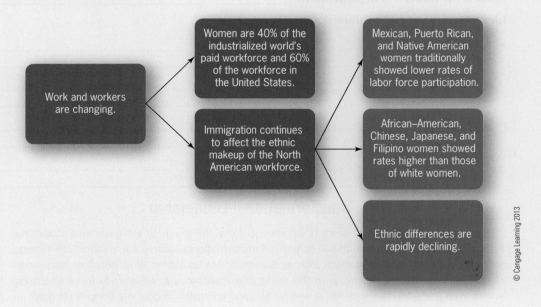

© Cengage Learning 2013

On Your Own FINDING MAJOR AND MINOR DETAILS

Read the following paragraphs to locate the major and minor details and answer the questions that follow.

1.
Types of Leaders

A group will often have more than one leader. Many groups have a designated **formal leader,** an assigned, appointed, or elected leader who is given legitimate power to influence others. During its

(Continued)

FOCUS ON COMPREHENSION: Identifying and Organizing Supporting Details

work life, a group may have only one formal leader, but several people may play leadership roles. **Informal leaders** are members of the group whose authority to influence stems from the power they gain through their interactions in the group. Informal leaders do not have legitimate power; rather, their influence comes from their expertise or the extent that other group members like and respect them.

—From VERDERBER/VERDERBER/SELNOW. *COMM* (with Access Bind-In Card), 1E.

© 2009 Wadsworth, a part of Cengage Learning, Inc. By permission.

What is the topic? _____

What is the main idea? _____

_____

What is the pattern of organization? _____

Identify the major and minor details:

- Major detail: _____

  _____

  - Minor detail: _____

    _____

- Major detail: _____

  _____

  - Minor detail: _____

    _____

2.
Transformational Leadership

This approach emphasizes being a visionary, helping the group to set goals and motivating, if not inspiring, the group to achieve its goals. Transformational leaders are creative, charismatic, and inspire others. Famous leaders such as Gandhi or Martin Luther King would be considered transformational leaders. To engage in this leadership approach, you will want to focus on the big picture, help the group to see things in a novel way, and energetically promote the group's goals.

—From VERDERBER/VERDERBER/SELNOW. *COMM* (with Access Bind-In Card), 1E.

© 2009 Wadsworth, a part of Cengage Learning, Inc. By permission.

What is the topic? _____

What is the main idea? _____

_____

What is the pattern of organization? _____

Identify the major and minor details:

- Major detail: _____

  _____

- Minor detail: _____
  _____

- Major detail: _____
  _____

3.   The causes of the glass ceiling* are varied. Some suggest that the glass ceiling is self-imposed by some women. For example, women may choose to work fewer hours than men in order to spend more time with their families. Women also measure success in the workplace differently than men. Men tend to measure success by high salaries and important job titles whereas women place a higher value on their relationships with colleagues and community service. Others suggest that ingrained stereotypes and socialization cause the glass ceiling. In some organizations, *the good old boy network* is still pervasive. When deciding who to promote in these organizations, women are often not even considered.

—"What is the Glass Ceiling?" by Jan Tucker, http://www.suite101.com/
content/the-glass-ceiling-a29187, August 19, 2007

*A metaphor that means that certain groups of people cannot rise in their jobs beyond a certain point—there is a symbolic ceiling to their career.

Topic: _____
Main idea: _____
_____

Pattern of organization: _____
Identify the major and minor details:

- Major detail: _____
  _____

  - Minor detail: _____
    _____

- Major detail: _____

  - Minor Detail: _____
    _____

- Major Detail: _____

  - Minor Detail: _____
    _____

  - Minor Detail: _____
    _____

FOCUS ON COMPREHENSION: Identifying and Organizing Supporting Details

TEXT MARKING AND ANNOTATING

Text marking, also referred to as *underlining,* gets readers interacting with a reading as part of an effective study strategy. After text marking, students take notes on the information they marked in the margins or on a separate piece of paper, which is called **annotation.** Both strategies are essential to successful comprehension and learning in college.

How to Mark a Text

While at first it may be a cumbersome method, marking your textbook provides the backbone of good study skills. It is not possible to underline points or mark the text without thinking about what you are doing, so this method almost guarantees concentration on the subject. Text marking promotes active reading and ensures that you make the most of the time you spend reading.

Text marking also helps you visually see how a reading is organized, which helps your brain to process it. Marking text is a process of sorting important from unimportant information in a reading. And, while sorting, you learn the information and prepare it for storage in your long-term memory. You selectively identify the most important information in the reading (you choose only certain things to mark with your pen or pencil), which is the groundwork for note taking. If you learn to use text-marking strategies, the follow-up strategies of taking notes, summarizing, outlining, mapping, and creating study guides will be much easier.

To mark text effectively, you must be able to locate the important information:

- Recognize the pattern of organization of a reading.

- See the relationships between ideas in a reading.

- Identify the main idea and supporting details.

These are all skills you have learned thus far, so you have a strong foundation to be successful at text marking. After you identify this information, go back and mark the text for them. Once your skills improve, you will be able to mark the text *as you read it the first time.*

There are endless text-marking methods and techniques available. But use what works best for you. Here are some suggestions on how to mark a text:

- Circle the topic, key terms, and definitions.

- Underline main ideas only.

- Enumerate (1, 2, 3) major details in the margin or, if there's space, above the major detail.

- Use lowercase alphabetical notations (a, b, c) for minor details in the margin or, if there's space, above the minor detail.

A variety of symbols and abbreviations can expand or add to your marking strategy. For example, if a passage is unclear, put a question mark (?) in the margin. If there is an interesting or surprising fact in a reading, put an exclamation mark (!) in the margin to draw your attention. If you come across an important definition, write "def" in the margin. Develop other techniques as you need them.

When you mark text, use a pen or pencil. Using only a highlighter can make it difficult to see the relationship between ideas because everything (main ideas and details) is the same color. Even if you use a different color for the main idea and supporting details, the act of interrupting your flow of concentration can disrupt your comprehension of the reading. Remember how limited your working memory capacity is and how quickly information can be bumped from this area. By trying this method of using just a pen or pencil, your concentration will not be disturbed.

Follow these steps to mark a text:

1. Preview the reading.
2. Read the passage in its entirety.
3. Determine the author's purpose.
4. Determine the topic of the reading.
5. Determine the pattern of organization.
6. Identify the main idea and supporting details.
7. Mark the text for the main idea and supporting details.
8. Annotate (make notes, paraphrasing the topic, main idea, and major and minor details) in the margins or on a separate piece of paper.

How to Annotate a Text _____

After you mark a text, you can **annotate** it—that is, write notes, paraphrasing the topic, main idea, and major and minor details in the margin or on a separate sheet of paper, based on your marking of the text.

Sifting through the ideas as you read is the hard part of the annotation process. You already have some practice doing this, though. Once you read a passage, you have thought about what the main idea is, the pattern of organization, and the supporting details. Now, organize this information in the margins or on a separate piece of paper right after you mark the text.

FOCUS ON COMPREHENSION: Identifying and Organizing Supporting Details

QUICK TIPS   THE *SOUL* METHOD OF MARKING AND ANNOTATING TEXT

The more you mark text, the more information you will learn and retain. SOUL is an acronym (an easy-to-remember term in which each letter represents a word) to help you remember the key points in text marking. SOUL stands for

Select. Make sure you are selective about choosing the key points.

Organize. Make sure you organize the key points based on the author's pattern of organization.

Understand. Make sure you understand what you're reading by paraphrasing the author's language.

Learn. Use your study notes to prepare for tests and learn the information.

Thinking It Through   TEXT MARKING AND ANNOTATING

Read this passage, noticing the text marking: The topic is circled, the main idea is underlined, and the major supporting details are numbered in red.

Career Success
By Joni Rose

Resilience

Do you get frustrated easily and give up? Everyone has career setbacks but it is how you respond to those setbacks that determines your ultimate career success. [1]If you wallow in self pity for weeks or months, it is time to seek professional help to get you out of your career funk. [2]Learn to accept setbacks as par for the course as you experiment with what works and what doesn't.

— "Career Success" by Joni Rose. © Joni Rose. By permission.

Here is this passage separated into the key parts:

Main idea: Everyone has career setbacks, but it is how you respond to those setbacks that determines your ultimate career success.

Pattern of organization: Comparison and contrast

    Major Detail: If you wallow in self pity for weeks or months, it is time to seek professional help to get you out of your career funk.

    Major Detail: Learn to accept setbacks as par for the course as you experiment with what works and what doesn't.

Now look at how this marked text can be annotated:

Career Success
By Joni Rose

(Resilience)

Do you get frustrated easily and give up? Everyone has career setbacks but it is how you respond to those setbacks that determines your ultimate career success. [1]If you wallow in self pity for weeks or months it is time to seek professional help to get you out of your career funk. [2]Learn to accept setbacks as par for the course as you experiment with what works and what doesn't.

—"Career Success" by Joni Rose.
© Joni Rose. By permission.

Resilience

Everyone has career setbacks but it is how you respond to those setbacks that determines your ultimate career success.

1. Seek professional help if you are in a career funk.

2. Accept setbacks as inevitable.

See how the notes in the margin depict the same information as the markings in the text itself? Annotation is writing down what you have marked in the text.

On Your Own TEXT MARKING AND ANNOTATING

Follow the process for marking the text and then annotating the important information in the margin. First, read the passage. Then, go back and mark the text. Afterward, transcribe the key points in the margin.

(Continued)

FOCUS ON COMPREHENSION: Identifying and Organizing Supporting Details

Career Success
By Joni Rose

Power of Choice

Successful people understand that it is their power of choice that determines their success. They are not victims. They don't blame others or other things for their success or failure. They seek out every opportunity to use their power of choice and never say "I don't have a choice". They understand that whatever they choose to do, there are inherent risks but they feel the fear and do it anyway. They also prepare themselves for possible failure with a plan B in mind and always look at failure as a learning experience.

—"Career Success" by Joni Rose.
© Joni Rose. By permission.

Topic: Power of choice

Main Idea:

1.
2.
3.
4.
5.

Now that you have some experience marking a text and then annotating it in the margins, develop some confidence by moving to longer passages. While a longer passage may seem harder to mark and annotate, if you take each paragraph step-by-step, then it is less overwhelming.

Thinking It Through MARKING AND ANNOTATING A LONGER TEXT

Here is a reading from an online magazine about Asian Americans and their representation in corporate America. Read and identify the pattern of organization, main idea, and the major and minor details. Go back and mark the reading for these elements. Then see how the key points have been transcribed in the margin.

1.   What is the topic?

2.   What is the author's purpose?

3.   What is the main idea?

4.   What is the pattern of organization?

Asian Americans are nearly twice as likely as Whites (55% vs. 29%) to graduate from college. For the past decade Asians have outnumbered Whites at UC Berkeley (40% vs. 36%), UCLA (41% vs. 37%), UC Irvine (56% vs. 27%) and UC Riverside (55% vs. 27%). Asians also collectively make up 28% of the enrollment at top 20 business schools. AA (Asian Americans) comprise 60% of Silicon Valley's professional and technical workforce.

Undoubtedly many factors contribute to Asian underrepresentation in the executive suites of American companies. The most frequently cited include the collective youth and inexperience of Asians in management positions, difficulty of fitting into the corporate cultures of old-line companies, propensity for leaving to work on startups, higher concentrations in technical fields and language deficiencies. Then of course there's the factor many suspect but few have been able to prove: racial stereotypes and prejudices.

—"Is the Glass Ceiling Cracking?"
Copyright 2000–2011 by Goldsea.com.
By permission.

I. Asian Americans and college
   A. Asian Americans are nearly twice as likely as whites to graduate from college.
      1. Asians out number whites at UC–Berkeley.
      2. Asians out number whites at UCLA.
      3. Asians out number whites at UC–Irvine.
      4. Asians out number whites at UC–Riverside.
      5. Asians collectively make up 28% of the enrollment at top 20 business schools.
      6. Asian Americans comprise 60% of Silicon Valley's professional and technical workforce.

II. Asian underrepresentation in American companies
   A. Many factors contribute to Asian underrepresentation in American companies.
      1. Inexperience in management positions
      2. Difficulty fitting in to corporate culture
      3. Leaving to work in new companies
      4. Higher numbers in technical fields
      5. Language issues
      6. Racial stereotypes

1. What is the topic of the reading? *This passage is about Asian Americans in college and underrepresentation in American companies.*
2. What is the author's purpose? *To inform the reader about the representation of Asian Americans in college and the workforce.*

(Continued)

FOCUS ON COMPREHENSION: Identifying and Organizing Supporting Details

3. What is the main idea of the reading? *Asian Americans, despite their educational advancement, are underrepresented in American businesses.*
4. What is the pattern of organization? *The author presents information about how Asian Americans are represented in colleges and the workforce and the struggles they face. The pattern is problem/solution. The problem is that although Asian Americans are competitively educated when compared with other groups, they are underrepresented in American corporate culture, implying that there is a glass ceiling preventing them from attaining their ambitions.*

On Your Own MARKING AND ANNOTATING A LONGER TEXT

Here is a passage from an online magazine, *Chicago now*, about Latinas in the workplace. Read and identify the pattern of organization, main idea, and the major and minor details. Then go back and mark the text for these elements. Do not worry about marking every point. Just mark and write in the margins the major details. Answer the following questions.

1. What is the topic? _____

2. What is the author's purpose? _____

3. What is the main idea? _____

_____

4. What is the pattern of organization? _____

Latinas Crack the Glass Ceiling
By Teresa Puente

Marlene Gonzalez, who worked in Corporate America, is one of the few Latinas to defy the statistical odds.

Only 63 percent of Latinas in the United States have completed high school, 4.4 percent have a bachelor's degree, 3.5 percent a master's degree and less than 2 percent have a doctorate.

And only 3.6 percent of Latinas work in management or professional occupations, Gonzalez said.

I. Problems facing Latinas in education and the workplace

  A. Statistical odds are against Latinas in corporate America.

    1.

    2.

    3.

    4.

    5.

Maria Pesqueira, President and CEO of Mujeres Latinas en Acción, a non-profit women's advocacy nonprofit in Chicago, said part of the problem is the high teen pregnancy rate among Latinas and overcrowding in high schools.

"How do we prevent them from dropping out?" Pesqueira asked.

More than 50 percent of Latinas have children before the age of 20.

"The teen pregnancy rate across the country among non-Latinas is going down and Latinas continue to go up. If we don't look at preventive programs, then we're not doing our part," Pesqueira said.

Cristina Lopez, president of the NHLI, said that Hispanic women have to help each other out.

"We need to get information out. We are educators in our community. If we know of resources, if we know of programs, we really need to let the community know so that they can take advantage of these resources," Lopez said.

Elvia Torres, who owns her own State Farm Agency, talked about the importance of mentoring. She hires high school and college students to work part-time in her office.

"I get phone calls from parents who say thank you so much for giving them an opportunity," she said.

Juanita Irizarry, a program officer with the Chicago Community Trust, said that she and colleagues have joined together to help sponsor individual Hispanic students to go to college. Some of them face financial barriers or barriers because they lack immigration papers.

"If we really care about these things, we have to put our money where our mouth is," Irizarry said.

The more women like these who succeed, the further we will go in breaking stereotypes.

—"Latinas Crack the Glass Ceiling" by Teresa Puente.
© 2009 Teresa Puente. By permission.

B. Teen pregnancy and overcrowding are issues in high schools.

1.

2.

C. Solutions for Latinas in education and the workplace involve helping each other out.

1.

2.

3.

4.

5.

FOCUS ON COMPREHENSION: Identifying and Organizing Supporting Details

NOTE TAKING FROM READINGS

Marking and annotating your readings is part of a system for studying and learning information. There are four steps to learning information in preparation for study (see Figure 6.2):

1. Read the passage, using all the active reading strategies you have learned so far.
2. Go back and mark the text.
3. Annotate by writing notes in the margin or on a separate piece of paper based on your marking of the text.
4. Rewrite your annotations and organize them further to make study notes.

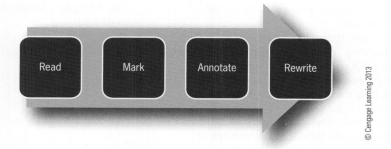

© Cengage Learning 2013

FIGURE 6.2 Learning Material from Readings Involves This Four-Step Process

You know that studying by repetition enables you to accurately and effectively retrieve new information from your long-term memory. Good note taking is an essential part of this learning process. You will transcribe, or rewrite, your text marking and annotations that show the main ideas and major and minor details into one of the following study formats:

- Outlines
- Summaries
- Double-column notes
- Graphic organizers

All of these formats help you understand and remember the main ideas and supporting details.

QUICK TIPS USING THE *SOUL* METHOD FOR TAKING NOTES

☑ Make sure you are SELECTIVE about choosing the key points (main ideas and supporting details).

☑ Make sure you ORGANIZE the key points based on the author's pattern of organization.

☑ Make sure you UNDERSTAND what you are writing (paraphrase the author's language).

☑ Use your study notes to prepare for tests and LEARN the information.

Outlines

Outlines are useful as a means of organizing information and showing the relationship between ideas. The most common type of outline is the **alphanumeric outline** (*alpha* = alphabet; *numeric* = numbers). The alphanumeric outline uses both letters of the alphabet (uppercase and lowercase) and numbers (Arabic and Roman numeral) indented as shown here.

Roman numerals (I, II, III, IV, V, VI, etc.)
    Capitalized letters (A, B, C, etc.)
        Arabic numerals (1, 2, 3, etc.)
            Lowercase letters (a, b, c, d, etc.)

The basic premise is that the more general a point, the closer it falls to the left of the outline. Similarly, the more detailed or minor a point, the more indented it is toward the right of the page. This structure demonstrates the relationship between topics, main ideas, and major and minor details.

I. Topic 1
    A. Main idea 1
        1. Major detail
        2. Major detail
            a. Minor detail
            b. Minor detail

    B. Main idea 2
        1. Major detail
            a. Minor detail
            b. Minor detail

FOCUS ON COMPREHENSION: Identifying and Organizing Supporting Details

    II. Topic 2
        A. Main idea 3
            1. Major detail
            2. Major detail

       To determine how much information to include in an outline (or any other note-taking method), you need to be aware of the purpose of the assignment. If the test will cover information from a whole chapter of a textbook, do you need to learn main ideas as well as major details? If the test will cover information from a section of a textbook or an article, do you need to learn minor details as well as the main ideas and major details? Be sure you understand your purpose for reading—what information will you be tested on to ensure you learned from your reading?

Thinking It Through CREATING AN OUTLINE

This example comes from a college textbook called *The Leadership Experience* by Richard L. Daft. Read the passage, the marks on the passage, and then read the explanation that follows. Then, look at the outline of this information. Notice how the main ideas are lined up toward the left of the page and the minor details are indented.

The Opportunity Gap
By Richard L. Daft

   A final challenge is the lack of opportunities for many minorities. In some cases, people fail to advance to higher levels in organizations because they haven't been able to acquire the necessary education and skills. For example, ①although educational opportunities for African-Americans have improved in recent years, black Americans still have only 79 percent of the status of white Americans in this area, according to a report by the National Urban League. ②Overall educational spending on black students is approximately 82 percent of the amount spent on white students, which contributes to greater ③struggles for black students and a ④higher dropout rate, especially among young men. ③Only about 60 percent of Hispanics complete high school, and ④both African-Americans and Hispanics lag behind whites in college attendance. ⑤Among Native Americans who complete high school, only 10 percent go to college, and of those only about half graduate. ⑥A 2008 report by the American Council on Education indicates that Hispanic and Native American young adults have even less education than their parents' generation.

> —From DAFT. *The Leadership Experience*, 5E. © 2011 South-Western,
> a part of Cengage Learning, Inc. By permission.

       There is a lot of information in this passage. The key is to break the information down into manageable chunks. What are three major topics in this paragraph? Think about the author's organization of this material. He compares the educational struggles of African American, Hispanic, and Native American students. These topics are useful to organize your outline. How many supporting details are given for each of the three categories of students? While your outline may not look exactly like the one here, your information should be similar. Each sentence in the paragraph is relocated to its proper position in the outline, according to its "rank" as the main idea, a major detail, or a minor detail.

I. Opportunity gap and minorities
  A. Main Idea: There are issues in attaining higher levels in organizations without the necessary education and skills among African American, Hispanic, and Native American students.
    1. Educational opportunities for African Americans have improved in recent years, but African Americans still have only 79 percent of the status of white Americans.
    2. Overall educational spending on black students is approximately 82 percent of the amount spent on white students.
      a. Struggles for African American students
      b. Higher dropout rate, especially among young men
    3. 60 percent of Hispanics complete high school.
    4. African Americans and Hispanics lag behind whites in college attendance.
    5. Among Native Americans who complete high school, only 10 percent go to college, and of those only about half graduate.
    6. A 2008 report by the American Council on Education indicates that Hispanic and Native American young adults have even less education than their parents' generation.

In this outline, major details are numbered and indented under the lettered heading, and minor details are lowercase lettered and indented even further. This information would be easier to learn than by just reading and rereading the paragraph because you can see in an outline how the ideas relate to one another—you can see the major details and how they are supported by the minor details.Remember that it is easier for your brain to learn when information is organized. Creating an outline is one way of organizing information to learn more effectively.

On Your Own CREATING AN OUTLINE

Create an outline of the following paragraph from the college textbook *The Leadership Experience*, by Richard L. Daft. First, mark the text. Then, fill in the outline template with the appropriate information from the paragraph.

(Continued)

FOCUS ON COMPREHENSION: Identifying and Organizing Supporting Details

Challenges Minorities Face
By Richard L. Daft

Creating an inclusive organizational environment where all individuals feel respected, valued, and able to develop their unique talents is difficult. Most people, including leaders, have a natural tendency toward **ethnocentrism**,which refers to the belief that one's own culture and subculture are inherently superior to other cultures. Moreover, studies by social psychologists suggest that there is a natural tendency among humans to identify themselves with a particular group and to feel antagonistic and discriminatory toward other groups. In high school, the jocks are aligned against the geeks, for instance. In hospital cafeterias, the surgeons sit in one area and the medical residents in another. In newspaper offices, the editorial folks are antagonistic toward the advertising people. The combination of this natural force toward separation, ethnocentric viewpoints, and a standard set of cultural assumptions and practices creates a number of challenges for minority employees and leaders.

—From DAFT. *The Leadership Experience*, 5E. © 2011 South-Western,
a part of Cengage Learning, Inc. By permission.

I. Challenges minorities face

A. Main Idea: _____

_____

_____

1. _____

_____

2. _____

_____

a. _____

b. _____

c. _____

Summaries _____

There are two main ways to represent an author's ideas in paragraph form. Paraphrasing, which you studied in Chapter 4, is one way. A paraphrase is the same length as the original and functions to clarify the whole passage by putting the author's ideas in your own words. Paraphrasing involves rewording the main idea as well as both major and minor details.

Another method of restating an author's ideas is by using a **summary.** Summaries, like outlines, focus on key points in a reading. Writing a summary shows that you understand the material because you paraphrase the author's ideas—you put an author's main idea and major details in your own words. All minor details, such as lists and examples, are left out of a summary. Be careful not to add information to the summary that the author has not stated. If you must take direct wording from a passage an author has written, be very sure to use quotation marks to signal that these are the author's words and not your own.

Summarizing allows your brain to process information in an organized format because you have to put an author's main idea and major details into your own words and use the same pattern of organization the author uses. Also, because you have to be clear on the main idea and major details, summarizing allows you to determine whether you *truly* understand what you have read. If you cannot summarize, check your notes and reread the passage, concentrating again on what's important. Creating a paraphrase of a reading can help you summarize: If you can rewrite a passage, you will be more certain that you understand it. Then, focus on just the major details and try your summary again.

A summary is written in paragraph format. A good rule is to make your summary about one fourth as long as the original reading. However, the length of a summary depends on the number of details in the original reading. If the original reading is dense with information, your summary will be longer than a quarter of the original piece. If the original reading contains a lot of minor details, your summary may be quite short.

QUICK TIPS SUMMARY ESSENTIALS

- A summary is a shortened passage, written in paragraph form that condenses the main idea and major details of a reading.

- A summary includes transitions, or signal words, in order to show the relationship between ideas.

- A summary of a reading must make sense on its own.

- A summary must reflect the pattern of organization the author used in the original passage as well as the author's purpose for writing.

- A summary does not contain minor ideas.

- A summary must not contain your idea ... only the ideas of the author."

FOCUS ON COMPREHENSION: Identifying and Organizing Supporting Details

HOW TO WRITE A SUMMARY

To write a summary, you need to apply everything you have learned so far about approaching a reading.

1. Find the topic of the reading.
2. Determine the author's purpose.
3. Determine the pattern of organization.
4. Determine the main idea.
5. Identify the major details.
6. Put the answers to 4 and 5 into your own words, paying attention to the pattern of organization.

Here is an example of a summary about challenges minorities face from the On Your Own exercises on outlines on page 422. Reread that paragraph, and then read the summary below. See how the same major details from your outline are included in the summary?

> There are several challenges that face minority students. First, most people tend toward ethnocentrism: the belief that one's own culture and subculture are inherently superior to other cultures. Second, humans tend to associate and identify with a group and discriminate against other groups.

Unlike the outline, the summary does not include the example of the high school, hospital, and newsroom peer groups because summaries do not contain minor details or lists.

Double-Column Notes _____

Double-column notes are an excellent note-taking method for reading as well as for taking class notes. **Double-column notes,** like outlining and summarizing, focus on main ideas. However, double-column notes allow you to quiz yourself when you study by writing down guide questions about the information you have to learn. Remember posing guide questions from Chapter 2? With double-column notes, you can use these guide questions to test your memory of key points and prepare for tests.

HOW TO TAKE DOUBLE-COLUMN NOTES

Divide your page as you see in Figure 6.3. In the right-hand section, take notes, however you prefer, though some kind of outline is usually best. In the left-hand section, write a question about each level of your outline, to use as a cue column. You can cover up the right-hand section and use the questions in the cue column to quiz yourself on the outlined material. At the bottom of the page, write the key points (main ideas and supporting details) or a summary of the page's notes to ensure that you understand what you took notes on.

Here is an example of double-column notes about challenges minorities face from the On Your Own exercises on outlines on page 422. See how the same major details that were in your outline appear in the double-column notes?

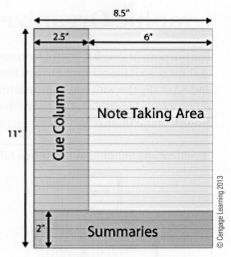

FIGURE 6.3 How to Set Up Your Double-Column Notes

What are the challenges for minority students?	I. Challenges for minority employees and leaders
	A. The combination of this natural force toward separation, ethnocentric viewpoints, and a standard set of cultural assumptions and practices creates a number of challenges for minority employees and leaders.
What is ethnocentrism?	1. Most people, including leaders, have a natural tendency toward ethnocentrism: the belief that one's own culture and subculture are inherently superior to other cultures.
What tendency do humans have that cause problems?	2. There is a natural tendency among humans to identify themselves with a particular group and to feel antagonistic and discriminatory toward other groups.
What are some examples of identifying with one particular group?	a. In high school, the jocks are aligned against the geeks. b. In hospital cafeterias, the surgeons sit in one area and the medical residents in another. c. In newspaper offices, the editorial folks are antagonistic toward the advertising people.

There are several challenges that face minority students. First, most people tend toward ethnocentrism: the belief that one's own culture and subculture are inherently superior to other cultures. Second, humans tend to associate and identify with a group and discriminate against other groups.

FOCUS ON COMPREHENSION: Identifying and Organizing Supporting Details

Graphic Organizers

The purpose of graphic organizer note-taking formats is the same as that of an outline: to show the relationships between ideas. There are many types of **graphic organizers,** and typically the way you choose which one to use depends on the pattern of organization of the reading. Recall from Chapter 5 where you learned that different types of graphics lend themselves to certain patterns of organization. Review Figure 6.4.

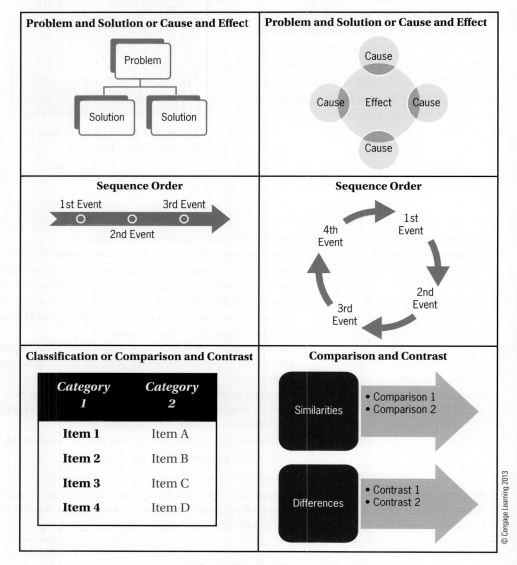

FIGURE 6.4 Types of Graphic Organizers

Here is an example of a graphic organizer about challenges minorities face from the On Your Own exercises on pages 422. Reread those paragraphs, and then look at Figure 6.5. Notice how the same major details included in the outline appear in the graphic organizers?

The outline, double-column notes, and graphic organizer about the challenges that minority students face are all different ways of depicting the same information. As you can see, there are many methods for taking notes, and each method has its benefits. The outline and summaries are good for longer reading passages, unlike a graphic organizer, which may become too cluttered. Graphic organizers are good for representing patterns of organization when you are studying the causes or effects of a topic or comparing and contrasting information. Double-column notes are good for studying since you can test yourself on the material by using the prompts in the left-hand margin while covering your information in the right-hand margin.

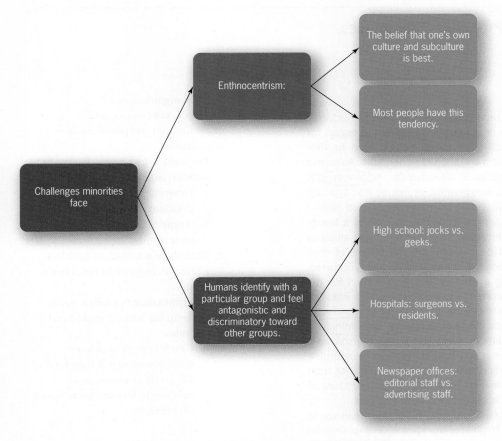

© Cengage Learning 2013

FIGURE 6.5 Challenges for Minority in a Graphic Organizer

FOCUS ON COMPREHENSION: Identifying and Organizing Supporting Details

On Your Own TAKING NOTES FROM A READING

Here is a paragraph from the text book *The Leadership Experience* by Richard Daft. Read the passage and look at the markings and annotations to: create an outline, write a summary, create double-column notes, and then create a graphic organizer. Answer the following questions to focus your comprehension.

1. What is the topic? _____

2. What is the pattern of organization? _____

3. What is the main idea? _____

_____

4. What are the major and minor details? _____

_____

Prejudice, Stereotypes, and Discrimination
by Richard Daft

One significant problem in many organizations is prejudice which is an adverse feeling or opinion formed without regard for the facts. Prejudiced people tend to view those who are different as deficient. An aspect of prejudice is stereotyping. A stereotype is a rigid, exaggerated, irrational, and typically negative belief or image associated with a particular group of people. When a leader and company act out prejudicial attitudes toward people who are the targets of their prejudice, discrimination has occurred. Paying a woman less than a man for the same work is gender discrimination. Refusing to hire someone because he or she has a different ethnicity is ethnic discrimination. For example, some years ago, the manager of the mergers and acquisitions department of a major bank encountered resistance from senior leaders because she wanted to hire an Indian applicant who wore a turban.

—From DAFT. *The Leadership Experience*, 5E.
© 2011 South-Western, a part of Cengage Learning, Inc. By permission.

I. Problems in organizations
  A. Prejudice, stereotypes, and discrimination are problems in organizations.
    1. Prejudice is an adverse feeling or opinion without using facts.
      a. Different people are viewed as deficient.
      b. A type of prejudice is stereotyping.
    2. Stereotype is a rigid, exaggerated, irrational, negative belief about a group.
    3. Discrimination is when a leader or company acts out prejudicial attitudes.
      a. Gender discrimination— paying women less than men
      b. Ethnic discrimination— refusing to hire someone based on ethnicity

Outline

_____

_____

_____

_____

_____

_____

_____

_____

Summary

_____

_____

_____

_____

_____

_____

_____

Double-Column Notes	

(Continued)

FOCUS ON COMPREHENSION: Identifying and Organizing Supporting Details

Graphic Organizer

QUICK TIPS TAKING GOOD NOTES IN COLLEGE CLASSES

- ☑ Listen actively and with concentration during lectures.

- ☑ Focus on main ideas and major details outlined in the lecture.

- ☑ Notice the pattern of organization the instructor uses for the lecture. For example, if the lecture concerns the causes of World War II, your notes should reflect a cause and effect pattern of organization.

- ☑ Write down information that the instructor emphasizes or repeats.

- ☑ Write down brief examples or page references in case you need to refresh your memory later.

- ☑ Practice formulating your own shorthand versions of common words. Example: Write the first several letters of a common word, and then abbreviate the ending that shows the part of speech: *attent'n* (*attention*), *eval'n* (*evaluation*), *speak'g* (*speaking*), *effect'v* (*effective*). You can develop your own methods of shorthand or learn other abbreviations.

- ☑ Write in phrases rather than sentences.

- ☑ Skip several lines after each topic so you can write in more information when you review later.

- ☑ Write topic-based questions in the left-hand margin, and rewrite, highlight, or clarify your notes as soon as possible after taking them to consolidate the information on the page and in your memory.

Practice Exercise 1: FINDING MAJOR DETAILS

For the following paragraphs, find the topic, main idea, pattern of organization, and major details.

1.
Functional Leadership

The functional perspective suggests that leadership involves acting in a way that helps the group achieve its goals. It might mean that the leader performs certain task or maintenance roles that are not

(Continued)

FOCUS ON COMPREHENSION: Identifying and Organizing Supporting Details

being handled by other members. Or it may involve the leader performing separate functions such as preparing the agenda, scheduling meetings, making assignments, and distributing minutes.

—From VERDERBER/VERDERBER/SELNOW. *COMM* (with Access Bind-In Card), 1E.
© 2009 Wadsworth, a part of Cengage Learning, Inc. By permission.

Topic: _____

Main idea: _____
_____

Pattern of organization: _____

Major details:

1. _____
_____

2. _____
_____

2. Leaders should be aware that there are a number of federal and state laws that prohibit various types of discrimination. Wal-Mart is facing a huge class-action lawsuit alleging that the retailer discourages the promotion of women to management positions and pays them less than men across all job positions. Numerous other companies, including Mitsubishi, EMC Corporation, FedEx Express, Allied Aviation Services, eBay, and Abercrombie & Fitch, have been hit by suits alleging the companies broke laws that prohibit discrimination on the basis of race, gender, age, physical disability, or other diverse characteristics.

—From DAFT. *The Leadership Experience,* 5E. © 2011 South-Western,
a part of Cengage Learning, Inc. By permission.

Topic: _____

Main idea: _____
_____

Pattern of organization: _____

Major details:

1. _____
_____
_____
_____

2. _____
_____
_____
_____

Practice Exercise 2: TAKING NOTES

Read the following paragraph, and then answer the questions and complete the exercises on outlining, summarizing, double-column note taking, and creating graphic organizers.

Blatant discrimination is not as widespread as in the past, but passive—and sometimes unconscious—bias is still a big problem in the workplace. Consider a report from the National Bureau of Economic Research (titled "Are Greg and Emily More Employable Than Lakisha and Jamal?"), which shows that employers sometimes unconsciously discriminate against job applicants based solely on the Afrocentric or African-American–sounding names on their resume. In interviews prior to the research, most human resource managers surveyed said they expected only a small gap and some expected to find a pattern of reverse discrimination. The results showed instead that white-sounding names got 50 percent more callbacks than African-American-sounding names, even when skills and experience were equal. Prejudicial attitudes are deeply rooted in our society as well as in our organizations. Sociologist William Biel proposes that people have innate biases and, left to their own devices, they will automatically discriminate. *Unconscious bias theory* suggests that white males, for example, will inevitably slight women and minorities because people's decisions are influenced by unconscious prejudice.

—From DAFT. *The Leadership Experience,* 5E. © 2011 South-Western,
a part of Cengage Learning, Inc. By permission.

Topic: _____

Main idea: _____
_____

Pattern of organization: _____

Complete this outline, filling in major and minor details.

1. _____
   _____

   a. _____
      _____

   b. _____
      _____

2. _____

   a. _____

   b. _____

(Continued)

FOCUS ON COMPREHENSION: Identifying and Organizing Supporting Details

Complete these double-column notes, including a summary in the bottom section.

Complete this graphic organizer.

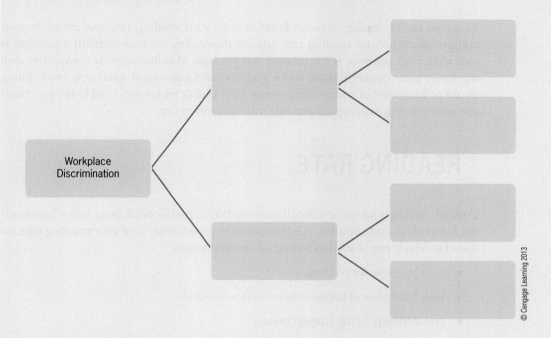

Workplace
Discrimination

© Cengage Learning 2013

FOCUS ON READING STUDY SKILLS

Reading Rate and Monitoring Comprehension

To be an active reader, become familiar with your reading rate and monitor your comprehension. Your reading rate adjusts depending on how difficult a passage is and what your purpose is for reading the passage. Monitoring your comprehension improves your concentration when you do not understand what you read. Being aware of your level of comprehension and the rate at which you read helps you manage your reading assignment and optimize your learning.

READING RATE

College reading is far more difficult than reading in high school. Because college reading is intensive and complex, it is important to consciously vary your **reading rate,** or speed at which you read, depending on several factors:

- Your purpose for reading

- Your background knowledge related to the topic

- The difficulty of the subject matter

  - The complexity and density of ideas

  - The level of complex vocabulary

  - The number and overlap of patterns of organization

- The level of comprehension the reading passage requires

For example, reading academic texts requires that you slow down your reading rate to absorb complex ideas. If you have a lot of background knowledge about the academic subject you are reading, you may be able to read faster and still absorb the new information. When you are reading a novel or magazine for entertainment, you can read it even more quickly because you do not necessarily have to learn the information the way you would for school (see Table 6.1).

Calculating Reading Rate _____

The readings in this chapter are followed by charts that you can use to get a sense of your reading rate. To calculate how many words per minute you read on your own, follow this equation:

total words read ÷ time it took you to read those words

Example: 1,140 words ÷ 10 minutes = 114 words per minute

To determine the number of words on a page, follow these steps:

1. Count the number of words in a line of text: ____ words
2. Count the number of words in a second line of text: ____ words
3. Count the number of words in a third line of text: ____ words
4. Add the number of words on all three lines of text together: ____ words
5. Divide the number of words on all three lines by 3:

____ words ÷ 3 = ____ words

6. Count the number of lines on a typical page: ____ lines
7. Count the number of pages in the reading: ____ pages
8. Multiply the number of words in #5 by the number of lines:

____ words × ____ lines = ____ words per page

9. Multiply words per page by the number of pages:

____ words per page × ____ pages = ____ total words

Your reading speed is only as good as your comprehension of the material. There's little point in reading too fast if your comprehension suffers.

TABLE 6.1 AVERAGE READING RATES DEPENDING ON YOUR PURPOSE FOR READING

PURPOSE FOR READING	AVERAGE WORDS PER MINUTE	PURPOSE FOR READING
Memorization	Fewer than 100 words per minute (wpm)	Intensive college study
Learning	100–200 wpm	College reading to take notes
Comprehension	200–400 wpm	College reading to understand information (not necessarily be able to recall all or most of it)
Skimming	400–700 wpm	To preview or survey a reading

FOCUS ON READING STUDY SKILLS: Reading Rate and Monitoring Comprehension

COMPREHENSION MONITORING

As an active reader, you know when you are having a comprehension problem. As you know from Chapter 1, being aware of what you are thinking about during thinking is called **metacognition**. If you are aware of reading comprehension problems and use strategies to deal with those problems, you are being metacognitively aware.

Monitoring comprehension helps you focus on your reading while being aware of your level of understanding. This awareness and your arsenal of strategies to fix any comprehension problems help you become a better learner (see Table 6.2). To effectively monitor your comprehension, expect to use before, during, and after reading strategies when reading to learn new information.

BEFORE	DURING	AFTER
• Activate background knowledge. • Set purpose for reading. • Preview. • Pose guide questions.	• Answer guide questions. • Mark text. • Annotate/take notes.	• Rewrite notes to solidify ideas and learn. • Use spaced practice to absorb ideas fully. • Predict test questions and practice answering them.

© Cengage Learning 2013

You should not expect to read everything in college at the same speed. Information that you are familiar with or find interesting, or that is clearly written and explained is easier to read. Read at a rate that allows you to concentrate and move along quickly to complete the assignment. If the topic of a reading is something you have little or no background knowledge about, slow down your reading rate and allow yourself extra time to grasp the major details and see the relationships between ideas. Study Table 6.2 of common comprehension problems and what you can do to fix them.

TABLE 6.2 HOW TO FIX PROBLEMS WITH COMPREHENSION

YOUR COMPREHENSION PROBLEM	PROBABLE CAUSE	HOW TO FIX YOUR PROBLEM
I don't understand the reading.	Difficult content	1. Slow down. 2. Turn headings into questions to focus your reading. 3. Use textual aids, such as chapter outlines or objectives and summaries, to provide an overview. 4. Read or skim previous chapters to understand context. 5. Read information on the same topic from an easier source to build up your background knowledge. Read a simplified text on the topic first to build up your background knowledge. 6. Write down specific questions to ask in class. 7. Ask a study partner to clarify or visit your college's support. 8. Ask your instructor for an overview of content. 9. Keep reading to see if your questions are clarified later in the text.
It seems that everything is important in the reading.	Idea density (there is a lot of information about the topic)	1. If you are reading science or technical material, everything, or much of it, may be important! 2. Outline or map the material after marking the text to separate main ideas from supporting ones. 3. Try to identify the pattern of organization to guide your understanding of what is important. 4. Look at the big picture. Instead of deciding that everything in a paragraph is important, consider the main idea of a section of the reading, rather than each paragraph. 5. Focus on key terms and how they relate to the organization (e.g., if the pattern is cause and effect, focus only on those two elements in the text).

(Continued)

FOCUS ON READING STUDY SKILLS: Reading Rate and Monitoring Comprehension

TABLE 6.2 HOW TO FIX PROBLEMS WITH COMPREHENSION

YOUR COMPREHENSION PROBLEM	PROBABLE CAUSE	HOW TO FIX YOUR PROBLEM
There are so many vocabulary terms I don't know in the reading.	Vocabulary level	1. Look for vocabulary clues (synonym, antonym, definition, and inference clues) to unlock the meaning of unfamiliar words. 2. Focus on word parts (prefixes, suffixes, and root words) to determine basic meaning and part of speech. 3. Use a dictionary, but pay attention to refocusing concentration repeatedly. 4. Use textual aids, such as the glossary, index, sidebars, and summaries, to see if you can find an overview of key words.
I don't know how to organize my notes or what to mark in the text.	Patterns of organization	1. Turn the topic or heading into a question: The answer to the question is the main idea. 2. Recall that structure is revealed in the answer to the question or main idea. 3. Focus on the relationships between ideas that reflect the organization of the subsection. 4. Use only the information in your notes that reflects the main pattern of organization. 5. Draw the information in a graphic organizer to clarify the relationship between ideas.
I can't concentrate on the reading.	Focus	1. Preview the reading to get an overview. 2. Pose and answer guide questions, and focus by finding the answers in the text. 3. Focus your mind by text marking. 4. Review your study environment, goals, and time management to make sure you are setting yourself up for success. 5. Read other engaging text about the topic to generate interest.

Practice Exercise 3: READING RATE WITH TEXT MARKING AND ANNOTATING

You will calculate your reading rate of this article. Write down your exact starting time here: **Start time: hour ____ minutes ____ seconds ____.** Then, after you read, write down your exact end time. Practice your text-marking and annotation skills on this reading as well.

Being Open to Opportunities

Peter M. Hess

1 How do you network with people you don't even know? This is a common question best answered by relating business networking to a form of social networking you've probably experienced— dating.

Imagine that someone you'd like to meet and get to know catches your eye. You see this person every day, but the individual seems oblivious to you. What can you do to make a connection?

You might begin by finding out something about the person—name, where the person lives or goes to school, other places the person frequents. You might determine if you have a mutual friend or acquaintance. You tap into any and all outside resources that will bring the two of you together in a social, academic, or work-related setting. As crazy as it may sound, this is networking.

Simple in theory, isn't it? In practice, networking isn't that difficult either. Networking is a skill learned as any skill would be, and the practice of networking starts by making a connection.

Networking is really only a series of connections that form a network of people working toward the same goal. When all the connections are made, the network is up and running. Picture a million people networking

(Continued)

FOCUS ON READING STUDY SKILLS: Reading Rate and Monitoring Comprehension

with each other. What do you think this can do for you and for them? Plenty.

The more people who know and respect you based on your professional conduct, the better your chances for successful networking. Successful networking results when you 1know yourself—your goals, your strengths, and your weaknesses— and when you remain open for opportunities, when you see the potential for a relationship that might not be obvious on the surface.

For example, perhaps you meet a computer programmer at a social engagement. If you aren't interested in computer programming, you might make the mistake of thinking that investing time in getting to know this person might not be of much value. But if you take the time to understand what this person does, whom the individual works for, where the person went to school, .you will probably discover information that might be useful in the future. Maybe the person works for a company that interests you. Perhaps the person has friends working for companies in which you are trying to gain access. Maybe the person knows the hard-to-reach human resource manager at one of your prime company targets.

Be an opportunist. Look beneath the surface and do some conversational probing in a nice and friendly manner. At a minimum, you'll get to know someone better. Quite possibly that brief conversation could lead you right through the door of your next employer.

—From HESS. *Career Success,* 2E. © 2008 South-Western, a part of Cengage Learning, Inc. By permission.

End time: hour ___minutes ___seconds ___

Total reading time: ____minutes ____seconds (Subtract your end time from your starting time.)

Find the time on the chart that corresponds to your reading time to find your reading rate in words per minute. Remember that the amount of background knowledge you have about the topic, the ease of vocabulary, the degree of your interest in the reading, as well as your purpose for reading, all affect your reading rate.

TIME	WPM	TIME	WPM	TIME	WPM	TIME	WPM	TIME	WPM	TIME	WPM
1m	435	2m	218	3m	145	4m	109	5m	87	6m	73
1m 10s	373	2m 10s	201	3m 10s	137	4m 10s	104	5m 10s	84	6m 10s	71
1m 20s	326	2m 20s	186	3m 20s	131	4m 20s	100	5m 20s	82	6m 20s	69
1m 30s	290	2m 30s	174	3m 30s	124	4m 30s	97	5m 30s	79	6m 30s	67
1m 40s	261	2m 40s	163	3m 40s	119	4m 40s	93	5m 40s	77	6m 40s	65
1m 50s	237	2m 50s	154	3m 50s	113	4m 50s	90	5m 50s	75	6m 50s	64

© Cengage Learning 2013

On a separate sheet of paper, complete the following activities.

1. Create an outline of this reading.
2. Write a summary of this reading.
3. Create double-column notes about this reading.
4. Create a graphic organizer of this reading.

FOCUS ON VOCABULARY
Improving Your College-Level Vocabulary

In college texts, you will encounter many words you do not know. In previous chapters and the textbook application, you've learned strategies for figuring out what an unknown word means—using vocabulary clues, word parts, and textbook aids, such as a key terms list. However, sometimes all those strategies will still leave you without a clear definition, so in those cases you need to be active in expanding your vocabulary by using a dictionary and learning more complex words through study.

USING A DICTIONARY

Every college student should own a good college dictionary. Using a dictionary is vital to building your college vocabulary. Online dictionaries are convenient and easy to access; however, if you don't know how to spell the word in question, it is difficult to use an online resource. With a print dictionary, however, if you come close to spelling the word correctly, you can often find it.

A dictionary provides the following information:

- Phonetic pronunciation

- A definition of a word

- What part of speech a word is—usually a noun, pronoun, verb, adjective, or adverb

- Ways a word can be used in different contexts

- The origin of a word—whether it is derived from Latin, Greek, old English, French, or another language

As valuable a reference tool as a dictionary is, it is usually a last resort for learning the meaning of an unfamiliar word because the disruption of looking a word up can cause to you to lose concentration, having negative effects on your comprehension and ability to transfer information to your long-term memory. You should exhaust all the vocabulary strategies you've learned before consulting a dictionary. The dictionary is a first resort, however, for spelling help (besides a spell-check program) and learning the part of speech or origin of a word.

Guide words at the top of each page in the dictionary indicate which alphabetical words listings are on those pages. For example, if a guide word on the top left of the page is *independence* and *individual* is on the top right of the page and the word you wanted to find was *indignant,* you are on the right page: *indignant* falls between *independence* and *individual* alphabetically.

Most dictionaries list entries in boldface print (see Figure 6.6). Following the word is its phonetic pronunciation and its part of speech. After this is the definition of the word and an example of how the word is used. Many dictionaries include the word's origin and how the parts of the word originally came to be, referred to as the **etymology** of the word. Abbreviations used for word origins can usually be found at the beginning of a dictionary (e.g., *L* = Latin; *OFr* = Old French; *Gr* = Greek; *OE* = Old English). Sometimes additional forms of the word are provided as well as synonyms.

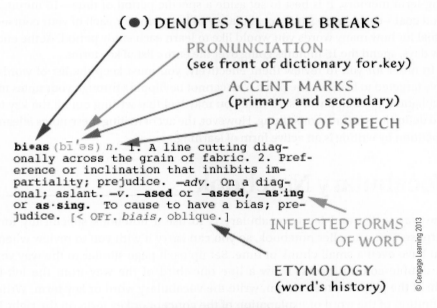

FIGURE 6.6 Definition Breakdown

TEXTBOOK GLOSSARIES

To ensure that you understand a key term or definition, you can also make use of a textbook's glossary, if one is included. A **glossary** is a list of all key terms and important concepts in a textbook. Glossary terms are often put in boldface and are sometimes in the margins of the chapters. Introductory college classes are often focused

FOCUS ON VOCABULARY: Improving Your College-Level Vocabulary

on the language of the discipline, so it's your responsibility to become fluent in the discipline's specialized vocabulary. If you use your textbook's glossary, you will be certain to have the correct definition for the term within that specific subject. (See the Textbook Application in this book, too.)

STRATEGIES FOR LEARNING KEY TERMS

Vocabulary and key terms must be reviewed repeatedly to be processed into your long-term memory. It is best to set aside a specific period of time—15 minutes is a good goal—each day to study vocabulary and key terms for each of your courses. Set a goal for how many words you would like to learn each study period. At the end of a few days, spend the 15 minutes going over the entire list of key terms.

In order for you to review them effectively, you must keep the list of words you have targeted to learn in one place. You cannot be flipping through your notes to find highlighted or circled words. At first, you may feel that writing out all the key terms and definitions is time-consuming. However, the act of writing these notes *is* learning; repetition by writing is an active form of learning.

Vocabulary Notebook

One way to list and learn vocabulary is to use a notebook specifically for this purpose. Use a smaller notebook, so you can carry it with you to review whenever you have even a small chunk of time. Set up each page similar to the way you set up double-column notes: Draw a line one-third of the way from the left-hand side of the page. In this column, write the vocabulary word or key term. Write the definition of the word or explanation of the concept or key term on the right-hand side of the page. Cover the right-hand side to test yourself on your recall of the word or term's meaning.

Vocabulary Cards

Index cards or flash cards are an effective tool to use for learning new vocabulary. Because cards are portable and can be secured with a rubber band, you can carry them with you for a quick review between classes, on public transportation, during breaks at work, and even when standing in line at a store.

To set up your vocabulary cards, on the unlined side of an index card, write the key term or word. On the reverse, lined side, write the word's definition, with an example. If the key term is a single word, include a sentence using the word that provides enough context to clearly point to the word's meaning. Some students also find that simple drawings or diagrams are helpful in solidifying definitions as they learn. Test yourself by trying to repeat the definition; then look at the reverse of the card to verify your answer. See Figure 6.7 for an example.

Definition   **Formal Leader**

An assigned, appointed, or elected leader who is given legitimate power to influence others.

—From VERDERBER/VERDERBER/SELNOW. *COMM* (with Access Bind-In Card), 1E.

© 2009 Wadsworth, a part of Cengage Learning, Inc. By permission.

FRONT OF INDEX CARD   **BACK OF INDEX CARD**

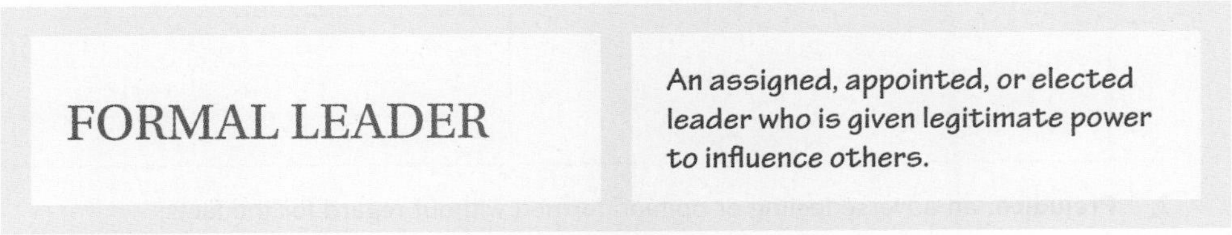

FORMAL LEADER   An assigned, appointed, or elected leader who is given legitimate power to influence others.

FIGURE 6.7 Vocabulary Card Example

Index cards come in several colors. Try choosing a specific color for each subject you are learning, and alternate these decks for study. For example, white index cards can be for biology, pink for psychology, green for history, and so on. Keep your cards arranged in alphabetical order so a term or word can be found easily. You should be systematic about reviewing each word in the deck at least every couple of weeks, and more frequently as a test nears. Once a test has passed, keep your cards for review for the cumulative, final exam. It is a morale booster to keep your vocabulary cards so you can admire the growing pile as you proceed from semester to semester. Remember, too, that college classes are cumulative in terms of content and skill development, so the key terms you learn for biology as a first-year student you will be expected to know for subsequent, related courses.

FOCUS ON VOCABULARY: Improving Your College-Level Vocabulary

On Your Own CREATING VOCABULARY CARDS

Complete vocabulary concept cards for each of the terms and their definitions below.

1. **Ethnocentrism:** the belief that one's own culture and subculture are inherently superior to other cultures.

> —From DAFT. *The Leadership Experience,* 5E. © 2011 South-Western,
> a part of Cengage Learning, Inc. By permission.

FRONT OF INDEX CARD	BACK OF INDEX CARD

2. **Prejudice:** an adverse feeling or opinion formed without regard for the facts.

> —From DAFT. *The Leadership Experience,* 5E. © 2011 South-Western,
> a part of Cengage Learning, Inc. By permission.

FRONT OF INDEX CARD	BACK OF INDEX CARD

3. **Stereotype:** a rigid, exaggerated, irrational, and typically negative belief or image associated with a particular group of people.

—From DAFT. *The Leadership Experience,* 5E. © 2011 South-Western, a part of Cengage Learning, Inc. By permission.

FRONT OF INDEX CARD	BACK OF INDEX CARD

4. **Informal leader:** a member of the group whose authority to influence stems from the power gained through their interactions in the group.

—From VERDERBER/VERDERBER/SELNOW. *COMM* (with Access Bind-In Card), 1E. © 2009 Wadsworth, a part of Cengage Learning, Inc. By permission.

FRONT OF INDEX CARD	BACK OF INDEX CARD

(Continued)

FOCUS ON VOCABULARY: Improving Your College-Level Vocabulary

5.   **Transformational leadership:** emphasizes being a visionary, helping the group to set goals and motivating, if not inspiring, the group to achieve its goals.

—From VERDERBER/VERDERBER/SELNOW. *COMM* (with Access Bind-In Card), 1E.

© 2009 Wadsworth, a part of Cengage Learning, Inc. By permission.

FRONT OF INDEX CARD	BACK OF INDEX CARD

APPLICATIONS

These applications will develop your skill of locating supporting details as well as strengthening your note taking strategies. Follow the instructions for each application and then answer the Comprehension Check questions. Each application serves to release more responsibility to the reader as these techniques become more automatic.

APPLICATION

This reading is from an article in the online *Huffington Post* written by Linda D. Hallman. She is the executive director of the AAUW, formerly known as the American Association of University Women, a national organization that takes positions on educational, social, economic, and political issues.

Read the passage through once. Then, go back and mark the text, annotating in the margin as you go or after you mark the text. You can also assess your reading rate. Write down your exact starting time here: **Start time: hour ___minutes ___seconds ___.** Then, after you read, write down your exact end time. Answer the Comprehension Check questions that follow the reading.

Happy (Un)equal Pay Day
By Linda D. Hallman

I. Women's and men's earnings
  A. Women have to work
    4 months extra to earn the
    same as a man in 1 year.
    1. Women earn 77 cents
      for every dollar a man
      earns.
    2. Pay equity isn't just a
      woman's issue; it's a
      family issue.

  B. The statistics
    1. Over a working lifetime,
      women lose $200,000.
    2. For poorer women, this
      means higher rates of
      a. Family poverty.
      b. Poorer health and
        nutrition.
      c. Fewer educational
        opportunities for the
        next generation.

1   It's Equal Pay Day again. On April 20, women's earnings finally catch up to men's earnings from the previous calendar year. Unfortunately, we have to work four extra months to get there.

2   A woman still earns, on average, just 77 cents for every dollar earned by a man. But pay equity isn't just a woman's issue. In the current economic downturn, with more women than ever serving as breadwinners, this is absolutely a family issue.

3   The statistics are disturbing. Over the course of her working life, gender-based pay disparity costs the average woman and her family more than $200,000, even more for women with professional degrees. At the lower end of the pay scale, wage inequality for women translates into higher rates of family poverty, poorer health and nutrition, and fewer educational opportunities for the next generation.

4   What does that mean in real terms? AAUW has collaborated with the National Partnership for Women & Families to provide some insight. For example, we found that in the nation's most populous state, California, a typical woman working full time is paid $40,521 per year, while a typical man in the same job would earn $47,758, creating an annual wage gap of $7,237.

5   *Without this wage gap, California's working women and their families could pay for a full year's worth of groceries, three extra months of mortgage and utilities payments, or more than 2,000 additional gallons of gas!*

6   So why does this problem persist? And more importantly, what can we do about it?

7   In part, the wage gap persists simply because women are still paid less than men for doing the same work. Women also don't move up the promotional ladder as quickly as men, even when our performance is superior.

8   There's another stumbling block. Simply put, how much money you make depends in large part on what you do for a living. According to a major new AAUW research report entitled "Why So Few? Women in Science, Technology, Engineering, and Mathematics," far fewer women than men are found in these higher-paying careers. With the single exception of the biological sciences, women today make up less than a third of the STEM* workforce. For engineers, the figure is just 11 percent.

9   All of us—parents, educators, and employers—have a role to play in breaking through the barriers. A large body of evidence shows that encouraging girls' achievement in science and math, creating college environments that support women in these fields, and counteracting our own implicit and explicit biases can increase our daughters' participation in these desirable high-wage careers.

10   Nonetheless, history clearly shows that when it comes to civil rights, only the government can enforce the rules and ensure a level playing field . . . for all Americans.

—Excerpt from "Happy (Un)equal Pay Day" By Linda D. Hallman, April 19, 2010 http://www.huffingtonpost.com/linda-hallman/happy-unequal-pay-day_b_543463.html © 2010 Linda D. Hallman. By permission.

End time: hour ____ minutes ____ seconds ____

Total reading time: minutes ____ seconds ____ (Subtract your end time from your starting time.)

C. What this means
   1. In California, a typical woman is paid $40,521 per year.
   2. A typical man in the same job earns $47,758.
   3. Without this gap, the woman could pay for
      a A full year of groceries.
      b. 3 months of mortgage and utilities.
      c. 2,000 gallons of gas.

D. Why the wage gap exists
   1. Women are paid less than men for doing the same work.
   2. Women don't get promoted as quickly as men.
   3. How much money you make depends on what you do.
      a. Few women are in science and tech fields.
      b. Women make up less than 1/3 of science workforce.
      c. 11% of engineers are women.

E. Solving the problem: We all need to break down barriers.
   1. Encourage girls in math and science.
   2. Create college environments that support women in these fields.
   3. Examine our own biases.

F. Government can enforce rules.

Find the time on the chart on the next page that corresponds to your reading time to find your reading rate in words per minute. Remember that the amount of background knowledge you have about the topic, the ease of vocabulary, the degree of your interest in the reading, as well as your purpose for reading, all affect your reading speed.

*Science, Technology, Engineering, Mathematics.

TIME	WPM	TIME	WPM	TIME	WPM	TIME	WPM	TIME	WPM	TIME	WPM
1m	465	2m	233	3m	155	4m	116	5m	93	6m	78
1m 10s	399	2m 10s	215	3m 10s	147	4m 10s	112	5m 10s	90	6m 10s	75
1m 20s	349	2m 20s	199	3m 20s	140	4m 20s	107	5m 20s	87	6m 20s	73
1m 30s	310	2m 30s	186	3m 30s	133	4m 30s	103	5m 30s	85	6m 30s	72
1m 40s	279	2m 40s	174	3m 40s	127	4m 40s	100	5m 40s	82	6m 40s	70
1m 50s	254	2m 50s	164	3m 50s	121	4m 50s	96	5m 50s	80	6m 50s	68

© Cengage Learning 2013

COMPREHENSION CHECK

TRUE/FALSE QUESTIONS

For the following statements, write a *T* if the statement is true or an *F* if the statement is false based on the reading.

___ 1. Women are paid the same as men for the same job with the same qualifications.

___ 2. Pay equality is just a woman's issue.

___ 3. Over the course of her working life, gender-based pay disparity costs the average woman and her family more than $200,000.

___ 4. Women make up half of the science, technology, engineering, and mathematics (STEM) workforce.

___ 5. There is nothing that can be done about this wage gap between men and women.

LITERAL COMPREHENSION—MULTIPLE CHOICE

Circle the best answer for the following questions.

Understanding Main Ideas

6. Why do women need to work four months extra in order to make the same amount of money as a man at the same job?

   a. Because women make around three-quarters of what a man makes per year

   b. Because women need to work harder to earn respect

   c. Because men get more vacation time from jobs

   d. Because women are harder workers than men

(Continued)

7. Why does the author think that this wage gap is a family issue?
    a. Because the family should support women in their careers
    b. Because increasing numbers of women head families, so their pay rate affects children
    c. Because women and men raise families together
    d. Because women with families take more time off work

8. The wage gap exists because
    a. Women are paid less than men for doing the same work.
    b. Women don't get promoted as quickly as men.
    c. How much money you make depends on what you do.
    d. All of the given answers.

9. What is the solution to this issue of the wage gap?
    a. Encourage girls to go into math and science.
    b. Rally for laws to enforce equal pay for women.
    c. Allow women to stay home with the family.
    d. Encourage girls into math and science, and create laws for equal pay.

Understanding Secondary Information and Locating Information

10. Which of the following consequences does *not* apply for poor women in the workforce?
    a. Family poverty
    b. More vacation time
    c. Poorer health and nutrition
    d. Fewer educational opportunities for the next generation

11. With regard to women in science fields, which of the following statistics is inaccurate?
    a. Few women are in science and tech fields.
    b. Women are particularly scarce in biological science fields.
    c. Women make up less than one third of the science workforce.
    d. Eleven percent of engineers are women.

12. How can we break down barriers to help solve this problem of unequal pay?
    a. Encourage girls in math and science.
    b. Create college environments that support women in math and science.
    c. Examine our own biases.
    d. All of the given answers.

13. According to the author, what is the proof that the government can be a source of justice for this situation?

a. The statistics

b. The numbers of women in Congress

c. History

d. There is no proof, only hope.

14. According to the reading, with the money lost from unequal pay in one year, a poor woman could pay for

a. A full year of groceries, 3 months of mortgage and utilities, and 2,000 gallons of gas

b. A full year of groceries plus 3 months of childcare

c. Four weeks of vacation pay

d. A full year of gasoline and 5 months of rent payments

15. According to the reading, children may suffer from this wage inequality because

a. There is less money for childcare.

b. There will be fewer educational opportunities in the future.

c. There will be fewer good jobs.

d. There will be tension in the home over this issue.

16. Is the earning gap more likely to be larger among poor women and men or professional women and men?

a. Poor women and men

b. Professional women and men

c. The impact is equal.

d. There is no evidence of either being more affected.

INFERENTIAL COMPREHENSION—MULTIPLE CHOICE

Circle the best answer for the following questions.

Making Inferences

17. Why do you think the author examines the impact on poor women of a loss of wages rather than for well-off women?

a. Because poor women are more influential with lawmakers

b. Because poor women deserve equal pay most

c. Because there's a bigger gap in pay among poor people than well-off people

d. Because the impact of this loss of earnings is more serious among the poor

18. Why do you think the pay gap is greater between professional men and women?

a. Because the greater the salary, the greater the difference

b. Because the higher up you climb, the more discrimination

(Continued)

    c. Because of the old boy's network

    d. Because professional women don't have as much experience on the job as professional men

Applying Information

19. Based on the information in this reading, in what field would the pay gap be most significant?

    a. Medical fields

    b. Real estate fields

    c. Educational fields

    d. Labor

Understanding Sentence Relationships

20. What is the pattern of organization of this reading?

    a. Cause and effect

    b. Definition/example

    c. Classification

    d. Specific order list

INCREASE YOUR COLLEGE-LEVEL VOCABULARY

Look up the following words from the reading in the dictionary. Find out the following information:

- A definition of a word
- What part of speech a word is—usually a noun, pronoun, verb, adjective, or adverb
- Ways a word can be used in different contexts

21. Equity (paragraph 2)

22. Disparity (paragraph 3)

23. Inequality (paragraph 3)

24. Populous (paragraph 4)

25. Implicit (paragraph 9)

26. Explicit (paragraph 9)

SHORT-ANSWER QUESTIONS

27. Do you have firsthand knowledge of discrimination in the workplace based on gender? If so, provide some details that outline the situation.

28. Write a summary of the main points of this reading.

29. Do you think that the pay gap situation is better or worse in other countries? Support your answer with specific examples.

APPLICATION ②

This application is an excerpt from *Career Success: Right Here, Right Now* by Peter M. Hess. Read the passage through once. Then, go back and mark the text, annotating in the margins as you go or after you mark the text. You can also assess your reading rate. Write down your exact starting time here: **Start time: hour ____minutes ____seconds ____**. Then, after you read, write down your exact end time. Answer the Comprehension Check questions that follow.

What Is Networking?
By Peter M. Hess

I. What is networking?
  A. Networking is the process of making, using, and retaining both professional and personal relationships with the goal of exchanging information or services among individuals, groups, or institutions that you develop personal resources through.
    1. Ability to pay attention
    2. Take action
    3. Become involved
    4. Show appreciation for others
  B. Think of every encounter you have with another person as a form of networking.
    1. Be on your best behavior.
    2. Be confident.
    3. Be prepared to speak about your goals.
    4. Be willing to listen to others.
    5. It's beneficial throughout your career.
II. Networking: informal or formal
  A Formal networking takes place in certain business environments.

What Is Networking?

Networking is the process of making, using, and retaining both professional and personal relationships with the goal of exchanging information or services among individuals, groups, or institutions. Through networking, you develop personal resources as a result of your ability to pay attention, take action, become involved, and show your appreciation for the positive gestures and actions of others.

Think of every encounter you have with another person as a form of networking. Be on your best behavior, be confident, be prepared to speak about your goals, and be willing to listen for ways you can assist other people in the achievement of their goals. You will find amazing benefits if you consistently practice networking strategies throughout the developmental stages of your career and beyond.

Informal Versus Formal Networking

Networking can be informal or formal. Formal networking takes place during informational interviews, when cold calling prospective employers, at career fairs, through internships, and while job shadowing. You can also find opportunities for formal networking at meetings of professionals in your field, at business-to-business exchange events sponsored by a local Chamber of Commerce, and during gatherings of your church or temple.

(Continued)

Informal networking can take place anywhere with anybody— your family and friends, those you know at school and at work, individuals with whom you share recreational or sporting activities, people you meet online, the butcher, the baker, the candle stick maker.

For example: Alexis E. is a writer with a long-term career objective of becoming a screenplay writer for Hollywood. She enhances her writing skills by taking credit-free courses in creative writing, nonfiction writing, and juvenile fiction writing at a local community college. Recently, Alexis signed up for a course in writing and publishing books.

"I thought it would be fun to learn about book publishing in case I want to turn one of my screenplays into a novel," Alexis said. On the first night of class, the instructor asked the students to introduce themselves and to tell why they had enrolled in the course. "I gave my little spiel," Alexis said, "and included the fact that my ultimate goal was screenplay writing and that I was looking for an agent. I knew it didn't fit with the scope of the course, but I threw it in anyway. As it turned out, one of the other students was originally from Los Angeles, where she had worked for an agent who handles screenplays. She gave me his name and number and said that I could mention that she had referred me. I contacted him, he remembered her, and he agreed to read one of my scripts. It's not easy to get an agent, and I wouldn't have been able to make that connection on my own."

Jose R. works part-time in the shipping department of a large department store while finishing his four-year business degree. His career objective is to break into retail sales. At the store's staff holiday party, Jose introduced himself to the manager of the menswear department and spent some time discussing industry issues and the particular challenges of running a specialty department. "We had a terrific conversation, and I told him about my wanting to start a career in sales," Jose said. "A few weeks later, I found a journal article at school that had some good ideas for handling one

1. Informational interviews
2. When cold-calling prospective employers
3. At career fairs
4. Through internships
5. While job shadowing
6. At professional meetings
7. At business exchange events
8. At places of worship
B. Informal networking can take place anywhere with anybody.
   1. Your friends and family
   2. People at work or school
   3. People at recreational events
   4. People online
C. Examples of networking
   1. Alexis E. the writer

   2. Jose R. in retail

of the problems he and I had discussed at the party. I made a copy of the article and some notes about how a few of the ideas could be implemented at the store. Then I dropped it off at his office."

The manager appreciated Jose's initiative and ideas. He called Jose to thank him and to mention that when the next sales associate opening occurred, he would let Jose know.

"I felt great because my wanting to help him made him willing to help me," Jose said.

—From HESS. *Career Success,* 2E. © 2008 South-Western, a part of Cengage Learning, Inc. By permission.

End time: hour _____ minutes _____ seconds _____

Total reading time: _____ minutes _____ seconds (Subtract your end time from your starting time.)

Find the time on the chart that corresponds to your reading time to find your reading rate in words per minute. Remember that the amount of background knowledge you have about the topic, the ease of vocabulary, the degree of your interest in the reading, and your purpose for reading affect your reading speed.

TIME	WPM	TIME	WPM	TIME	WPM	TIME	WPM	TIME	WPM	TIME	WPM
1m	637	2m	319	3m	212	4m	159	5m	127	6m	106
1m 10s	546	2m 10s	294	3m 10s	201	4m 10s	153	5m 10s	123	6m 10s	103
1m 20s	478	2m 20s	273	3m 20s	191	4m 20s	147	5m 20s	119	6m 20s	101
1m 30s	425	2m 30s	255	3m 30s	182	4m 30s	142	5m 30s	116	6m 30s	98
1m 40s	382	2m 40s	239	3m 40s	174	4m 40s	137	5m 40s	112	6m 40s	96
1m 50s	347	2m 50s	225	3m 50s	166	4m 50s	132	5m 50s	109	6m 50s	93

© Cengage Learning 2013

COMPREHENSION CHECK

TRUE/FALSE QUESTIONS

For the following statements, write a *T* if the statement is true or an *F* if the statement is false based on the reading.

(Continued)

___ 1. Not every encounter with people can be considered networking.

___ 2. Formal networking is more effective than informal networking.

___ 3. Networking allows you to develop personal resources.

___ 4. Networking can occur anywhere in your daily life.

___ 5. Networking is only done through work activities.

LITERAL COMPREHENSION—MULTIPLE CHOICE

Circle the best answer for the following questions.

Understanding Main Ideas

6. What is networking?

   a. Networking takes place during informational interviews, when cold calling prospective employers, at career fairs, through internships, and while job shadowing.

   b. Informal networking can take place anywhere with anybody.

   c. Networking is the process of making, using, and retaining both professional and personal relationships with the goal of exchanging information or services among individuals, groups, or institutions.

   d. Networking occurs with people you meet online.

7. What is the difference between formal and informal networking?

   a. Formal networking occurs in professional arenas whereas informal networking occurs in daily life.

   b. Formal networking involves the exchange of business cards whereas informal networking does not.

   c. Formal networking is more effective than informal networking.

   d. Both formal and informal networking can occur in both professional arenas and daily life.

8. Why should you network?

   a. To make friends and influence people

   b. To develop your personal resources

   c. To increase your salary

   d. To make social contacts

Understanding Secondary Information and Locating Information

9. Which of the following qualities does not help in networking?

   a. Your ability to pay attention

   b. Your ability to take action

    c. Your ability to become involved and your appreciation for others

    d. Your ability to outsmart your opponents

10. When should you practice networking?

    a. At the beginning of your career

    b. Throughout the developmental stages of your career and beyond

    c. When you are looking for a job

    d. When you want a bigger salary

11. How did Alexis meet her contact in screenwriting?

    a. Through work

    b. Through social activities

    c. At the supermarket

    d. At school

12. How did Jose meet his contact in retail?

    a. At work

    b. Through friends

    c. At a staff holiday party

    d. At his church

13. Which of the following would not constitute formal networking?

    a. Making contacts at a book club

    b. Making contacts at a staff party

    c. Making contacts at a conference

    d. Making contacts through clients

14. Networking is a tool to

    a. Get jobs.

    b. Make connections.

    c. Get leads for a career.

    d. All of the given answers.

INFERENTIAL COMPREHENSION—MULTIPLE CHOICE

Circle the best answer for the following questions.

Making Inferences

15. Why do you think the author includes the examples of Alexis and Jose?

    a. To illustrate the benefits of networking

    b. To show the differences and similarities between formal and informal networking

(Continued)

    c. To illustrate the benefits of networking as well as the differences and similarities between types of networking

    d. To show the reader exceptions to networking usage

16. Why do you think networking should be practiced throughout your career?

    a. You never know what will happen.

    b. You never know who you'll meet.

    c. Because you don't know what will happen or who you will meet

    d. Because it is expected in the corporate world

Applying Information

17. Based on the information in this reading, what type of networking did Alexis use?

    a. Formal

    b. Informal

    c. Both formal and informal

    d. She did not use networking.

18. Based on the information in this reading, what type of networking did Jose use?

    a. Formal

    b. Informal

    c. Both formal and informal

    d. He did not use networking.

Understanding Sentence Relationships

19. What is the overall pattern of organization of this reading?

    a. Cause and effect

    b. Definition/example

    c. Random order list

    d. Specific order list

20. What is the pattern of organization of the subsection "Informal Versus Formal Networking"?

    a. Compare and contrast

    b. Cause and effect

    c. Random order list

    d. Specific order list

INCREASE YOUR COLLEGE-LEVEL VOCABULARY

Complete this graphic organizer with information about networking, or create vocabulary cards for learning key terms.

21.

Networking	Formal Networking	Informal Networking
Defintion	Defintion	Defintion
_____	_____	_____
_____	_____	_____
_____	_____	_____
Examples	Examples	Examples
_____	_____	_____
_____	_____	_____
_____	_____	_____
_____	_____	_____

© Cengage Learning 2013

SHORT-ANSWER QUESTIONS

22. Which type of networking do you think is most effective?

23. Have you used either formal or informal networking? How did it work?

WRAPPING IT UP

STUDY OUTLINE

This is a list of key terms from this chapter for you to define in an organized format. In the following study outline, fill in the definitions and a brief explanation of the key terms in the Your Notes column. Use the strategy of spaced practice to review these key terms on a regular basis. Use this study guide to review this chapter's key topics.

KEY TERM	YOUR NOTES	
Supporting details		
Major details		
Minor details		
Text marking		
Annotation		
Annotate		
Alphanumeric outline		
Summary		
Double-column notes		
Graphic organizers		
Reading rate		
Metacognition		
Monitoring comprehension		
Etymology		
Glossary		

WHAT DID YOU LEARN?

At the beginning of this chapter, you assessed your views on workplace discrimination with the anticipation guide exercise. Now, go back to the beginning of the chapter and see if your views have changed after learning more about this topic.

GROUP ACTIVITY: ETHICS IN INTERVIEWS

Here is a scenario that concerns ethics in job interviews from a communications textbook called *Communicate!* Form a small group and discuss the questions following the scenario. Be prepared to justify your group's answers in class discussion or in writing, as your instructor assigns.

A Question of Ethics

Ken shifted in his chair as Ms. Goldsmith, his interviewer, looked over his résumé.

"I have to tell you that you have considerably more experience than the average applicant we usually get coming straight out of college," Ms. Goldsmith said. "Let's see, you've managed a hardware store, been a bookkeeper for a chain of three restaurants, and were the number-one salesman for six straight months at a cell phone store." "That's right," Ken said. "My family has always stressed the value of hard work, so I have worked a full-time job every summer since I entered junior high school, right through my last year of college. During the school year, I usually worked four to six hours a day after class."

"Very impressive," Ms. Goldsmith said. "And still you managed to get excellent grades and do a considerable amount of volunteer work in your spare time. What's your secret?"

"Secret?" said Ken nervously. "There's no secret—just a lot of hard work."

"Yes, I see that," said Ms. Goldsmith. "What I mean is that there are only 24 hours in a day and you obviously had a lot on your plate each day, especially for someone so young. How did you manage to do it?"

Ken thought for a moment before answering. "I only need five hours of sleep a day." He could feel Ms. Goldsmith's eyes scrutinizing his face. He hadn't exactly lied on his résumé—just exaggerated a little bit. He had, in fact, helped his father run the family hardware store for a number of years. He had helped his aunt, from time to time, keep track of her restaurant's receipts. He had also spent one summer selling cell phones for his cousin. Of course, his family always required him to do his school work first before they let him help at the store, so Ken often had little time to help at all, but there was no reason Ms. Goldsmith needed to know that.

"And you can provide references for these jobs?" Ms. Goldsmith asked.

WRAPPING IT UP

"I have them with me right here," said Ken, pulling a typed page from his briefcase and handing it across the desk.

—From VERDERBER/VERDERBER/SELLNOW. *Communicate!,* 13E. © 2011 Wadsworth,
a part of Cengage Learning, Inc. By permission.

1. Are the exaggerated claims Ken made in his résumé ethical? Do the ethics of his actions change at all if he has references (family members) who will vouch for his claims?
2. Many people justify exaggerating or even lying on their résumés by saying that everybody does it and then rationalizing that, if they don't do it too, they will be handicapping their chances to get a good job. If the consequences of acting ethically diminish your economic prospects, are you justified in bending the rules? Explain your answer. If you think bending the rules is acceptable in such circumstances, how far can you bend them before you cross the line into unacceptable behavior?

QUESTIONS FOR WRITING, DISCUSSION, OR REFLECTION

1. What do you feel is the most significant piece of information regarding workplace discrimination covered in this chapter? What are some ways you could use this information to improve your success in the job world?
2. Have you experienced discrimination on the job? What happened, and what was the outcome of this experience?
3. Research wage gaps. How much progress has been made since the 1970s?
4. Choose a textbook you use in another class and find a brief passage. Create an outline, summary, double-column notes, or graphic organizer of the passage.
5. Choose a textbook you use for another class and create vocabulary cards for each of the key terms in the reading assignment to prepare for a test on the subject.
6. Keep a log of your reading rates for different college reading assignments. Write a brief summary about how your reading rate varies depending on the type of information you read.

 # POST-ASSESSMENT

This assessment will help you understand your strengths and weaknesses in learning, understanding, and applying the skills and strategies discussed in this chapter. Preview the following article. Then read it all the way through and answer the Comprehension Check questions that follow. You can also calculate your reading rate, or how fast you read this article. Write down your exact starting time here:

Start time: hour _____ **minutes** _____ **seconds** _____. Then, after you read, write down your exact end time.

Denny's Restaurants

1   Once leaders examine and change themselves, they can lead change in the organization. Diversity presents many challenges, yet it also provides leaders with an exciting opportunity to build organizations as integrated communities in which all people feel encouraged, respected, and committed to common purposes and goals. Consider how leaders at Denny's Restaurants have improved diversity awareness to transform the company from an icon of racism to a paragon of diversity.

2   It was a spring morning in 1993 when six African-American Secret Service agents sat waiting for their food at Denny's for more than an hour while their white colleagues ate. Their meals arrived just before they had to leave. The highly publicized incident led to other revelations of discrimination against African-American customers and employees—and to a series of racial discrimination lawsuits. Thirteen years later, a Denny's executive received the "We Share the Dream Award" at the 18th annual Dr. Martin Luther King Jr. Awards Dinner. How did Denny's go from worst to first? It comes down to top leader commitment and some serious training to improve diversity awareness and behavior.

3   After settling the discrimination lawsuits in 1994, Denny's hired Rachelle Hood as its first chief diversity officer. Hood got the company to hire more than 100 diversity trainers and implemented training at every level. Every single person at Denny's—not just managers, dishwashers, and servers, but also media planners and leased security guards—attends diversity training with specific guidelines on how to apply diversity understanding and sensitivity to working in the restaurant business. In the "We Can" training program, for example, employees learn a three-step model: (1) *prevention*, such as how to behave in order to reduce the possibility of a guest or fellow employee feeling that he or she has been discriminated against; (2) *intervention*, which teaches people to "acknowledge, apologize, and act" when something goes wrong; and (3) *managing escalation*, in which employees learn how to genuinely listen, show empathy, and reduce the anger and frustration level. Denny's spends several million dollars a year on building awareness, and its diversity training system is one of the most comprehensive in the industry.

4   Hood cemented diversity awareness by working with managers to increase supplier diversity, developing marketing campaigns targeting minority customers, and tying managers' bonus pay to meeting diversity goals. In 1993, only one of the chain's franchises was minority-owned, the company had no minority suppliers, and the board was made up primarily of white males. Today, however, things are very different:

- More than 40 percent of Denny's franchises are owned by minorities.
- During a recent 10-year period, Denny's contracted nearly $1 billion for goods and services with minority suppliers, with African-Americans accounting for 48 percent of the business. That represents around 18 percent of the company's contracts, as compared to a national average of 3 to 4 percent.
- Forty-four percent of the board of directors is composed of women and people of color.
- Minority employees represent 41 percent of Denny's overall management and 59 percent of the workforce.   *(Continued)*

5   Thanks to these advancements, *Black Enterprise* magazine named Denny's one of the best corporations for African-Americans, and *Fortune* ranked Denny's in its list of "America's 50 Best Corporations for Minorities" two years in a row. Denny's turnaround is one of the best examples of how far and how fast a company can progress with strong leadership and an aggressive approach to culture change.

—From DAFT. *The Leadership Experience,* 5E. © 2011 South-Western,
a part of Cengage Learning, Inc. By permission.

End time: ____hour ____minutes ____seconds ____
Total reading time: _____minutes _____seconds (Subtract your end time from your starting time.)

Find the time on the chart that corresponds to your reading time to find your reading rate in words per minute.

TIME	WPM	TIME	WPM	TIME	WPM	TIME	WPM	TIME	WPM	TIME	WPM
1m	572	2m	286	3m	191	4m	143	5m	114	6m	95
1m 10s	490	2m 10s	264	3m 10s	181	4m 10s	137	5m 10s	111	6m 10s	93
1m 20s	429	2m 20s	245	3m 20s	172	4m 20s	132	5m 20s	107	6m 20s	90
1m 30s	381	2m 30s	229	3m 30s	163	4m 30s	127	5m 30s	104	6m 30s	88
1m 40s	343	2m 40s	215	3m 40s	156	4m 40s	123	5m 40s	101	6m 40s	86
1m 50s	312	2m 50s	202	3m 50s	149	4m 50s	118	5m 50s	98	6m 50s	84

© Cengage Learning 2013

COMPREHENSION CHECK

Circle the *best* answer to the questions based on information from the reading.

1   **What is the best statement of topic for this reading?**
    A. Denny's and diversity
    B. Denny's is an example of a business that overcame racism.
    C. Barriers to diversity

2   **What is the main idea of this reading?**
    A. Denny's has made improvements in diversity but still has a long way to go.

B. Denny's diversity turnaround is one of the best examples of how far and how fast a company can progress with strong leadership and an aggressive approach to culture change.

C. Thanks to these advancements, *Black Enterprise* magazine named Denny's one of the best corporations for African-Americans

3 **What type of main idea is the thesis of this reading?**

A. Explicit
B. Implied, method 1
C. Implied, method 3

4 **What is the primary pattern of organization in this reading?**

A. Definition and example
B. Comparison and contrast
C. Problem and solution

5 **What cause and effect transition word or phrase indicates a major supporting detail in paragraph 2?**

A. Publicized
B. Led to
C. Revelations

6 **What sentence is the main idea of paragraph 3?**

A. Sentence 1
B. Sentence 2
C. The last sentence

7 **In the "We Can" training program model cited in paragraph 3, how many steps are explained?**

A. 3
B. 4
C. 2

8 **In the "We Can" training program model, these steps follow what organizational pattern?**

A. Cause and effect
B. Compare and contrast
C. Sequence order

9 **What is the pattern of organization in paragraph 4?**

A. Compare and contrast
B. Simple order list
C. Classification

(Continued)

10   **Which of the following outlines best represents the information in paragraph 4?**

A.

    I. Hood cemented diversity awareness at Denny's

        A. Changes at Denny's

            1. In 1993, only one of the chain's franchises was minority-owned, the company had no minority suppliers, and the board was made up primarily of white males.

            2. Today, however, things are very different.

                a. More than 40 percent of Denny's franchises are owned by minorities.

                b. During a recent 10-year period, Denny's contracted nearly $1 billion for goods and services with minority suppliers, with African-Americans accounting for 48 percent of the business. That represents around 18 percent of the company's contracts, as compared to a national average of 3 to 4 percent.

                c. Forty-four percent of the board of directors is composed of women and people of color.

                d. Minority employees represent 41 percent of Denny's overall management and 59 percent of the workforce.

B.

    I. Hood cemented diversity awareness at Denny's

        A. Good changes at Denny's

            1. More than 40 percent of Denny's franchises are owned by minorities.

            2. During a recent 10-year period, Denny's contracted nearly $1 billion for goods and services with minority suppliers, with African-Americans accounting for 48 percent of the business. That represents around 18 percent of the company's contracts, as compared to a national average of 3 to 4 percent.

            3. Forty-four percent of the board of directors is composed of women and people of color.

            4. Minority employees represent 41 percent of Denny's overall management and 59 percent of the workforce.

        B. Negative changes at Denny's

            1. In 1993, only one of the chain's franchises was minority-owned, the company had no minority suppliers, and the board was made up primarily of white males.

Based on how many questions you answered accurately in this Comprehension Check, do you need to increase your reading speed, slow down your reading speed, or maintain this reading speed? _____

CRITICAL THINKING

Josie Lepe/San Jose Mercury News/MCT

CHAPTER 7 Critical Reading

THEME *Issues in the Modern World*

Relevant College Courses: Criminal Justice, Health Science, Ethics, Legal Studies

CRITICAL READING

THEME *Issues in the Modern World*

"In the modern world we have invented ways of speeding up invention, and people's lives change so fast that a person is born into one kind of world, grows up in another, and by the time his children are growing up, lives in still a different world."

— MARGARET MEAD, AMERICAN ANTHROPOLOGIST

OBJECTIVES

In this chapter, you will focus on:

COMPREHENSION SKILLS

Use the following critical reading strategies to read and understand arguments:

- Fact and opinion
- Types of support
- Author's credentials
- Intended audience

CRITICAL THINKING AND READING

READING STUDY SKILLS

Use critical thinking and reading strategies

VOCABULARY SKILLS

Recognize bias, tone, and loaded language

WHY DO YOU NEED TO KNOW THIS?

Problem:
Bridgette enrolled in community college right after graduating from high school last year. For many of her courses, she has to read essays where an author takes a point of view on a topical issue and argues one side. Although Bridgette has no trouble understanding what the author has written, she doesn't know how to determine which side wins in a written debate. Usually, she favors the argument that mirrors her point of view on the issue. She doesn't know what to look for to make an objective decision about which arguments are good and which are weak.

michaeljung/Shutterstock.com

WHAT ADVICE WOULD YOU OFFER TO BRIDGETTE?

_____

_____

_____

_____

Solution:
Bridgette can learn effective strategies to evaluate controversial texts. You know that reading textbooks in which the author's main purpose is to inform requires the comprehension skills you have acquired so far—but what about texts where the author's main purpose is to persuade? You will encounter many readings in your college courses where an author takes a position on an issue and then proceeds to defend that position. Understanding arguments heightens your skills of critical thinking, which involves analysis, synthesis, and evaluation. Learning how to map an argument helps you see the structure of a persuasive reading and react to the supporting arguments. Critical reading skills allow you to judge whether the argument is effective regardless of your personal opinion on the topic.

WHAT DO YOU ALREADY KNOW?

Jot down some facts you know about a few controversies in the media today. Do not edit your list—just brainstorm!

1 _____   6 _____

2 _____   7 _____

3 _____   8 _____

4 _____   9 _____

5 _____   10 _____

✓ PRE-ASSESSMENT

This pre-assessment will help you measure what you already know and what you need to learn about the reading skills and strategies explored in this chapter. Your results will help you understand your strengths and weaknesses. Read the article, and then answer the Comprehension Check questions that follow.

The Right to Privacy in a Mediated Society
By Rudolph F. Verderber, Kathleen S. Verderber, and Deanna D. Sellnow

1   For over a century, celebrities have complained that the media invades their privacy, but it was the death of Princess Diana in 1997 that focused worldwide attention on the extent to which celebrities are denied any right to privacy. From the paparazzi who literally hounded Princess Diana to her death, to the newspapers who publicized the college antics of the Bush twins, it appears that anyone the media takes an interest in can no longer expect even a basic right to privacy. Certainly, public figures expect to be scrutinized regarding their professional lives, but the current cult of celebrity has created a situation in which the media thinks little about also prying into their private lives. Not only that, but anyone connected to these public figures, including their families, is also subject to invasive media coverage.

2   For example, during the 2008 presidential campaign, the media covered the pregnancy of vice-presidential candidate Sarah Palin's 17-year-old unmarried daughter, Bristol, extensively. In addition, the father of Bristol's child and his parents were subjected to intense media scrutiny. Although Bristol's pregnancy didn't seem relevant to Palin's campaign, Reverend Debra Haffner (2008) argued in a *Huffington Post* column that when "family

matters relate directly to policy matters"—such as Palin's positions on sexuality education and teenage pregnancy—they are fair game. She maintained that calls for personal privacy could sometimes shroud political issues. But then-presidential candidate Barack Obama urged media to "back off these kinds of stories," saying, "People's families are off-limits, and people's children are especially off-limits. This shouldn't be a part of our politics. It has no relevance to Governor Palin's performance as a governor or her potential performance as a vice-president."

3   The debate over invasive media coverage was not clouded by politics in February 2009 when the celebrity Web site *TMZ.com* posted a photo of pop star Rihanna after she was physically assaulted by her then-boyfriend, R&B artist Chris Brown. The photo had been leaked by someone at the Los Angeles Police Department and, embarrassed, the department opened an internal investigation about the publication of the photo, saying it "takes seriously its duty to maintain the confidentiality of victims of domestic violence." However, *TMZ.com*'s executive producer, Harvey Levin, defended the publication of the photo, saying it helped put a face to the victims of domestic abuse. Even people who fight for the rights of victims of domestic abuse hesitantly supported the decision to publish the photo. Chicago author and advocate for battered women Susan Murphy-Milano speculated, "Maybe it is a good idea, if it's her, if young girls see this." She added that she hoped it would make young women think "Is the next picture going to be of her in a morgue?"

4   But what about Rihanna's right to privacy? *PR Week* points out that typical standards of journalism prevent reporters and editors from publishing names of victims. However, in the case of Rihanna, David Hauslaib, editorial director of *Jossip.com*, says, "We have this appetite for celebrity culture and it brings down any sort of safeguards we, as a media industry, have implemented to protect people." *The Gawker.com* further explored this debate about media ethics: "Critics say running the picture humiliates Rihanna at a time when she's already in emotional agony, that it pierces a zone of emotional and physical privacy already grossly violated in the apparent attack on her." Nonetheless, profit-seeking publishers know that publishing such a shocking image will increase their traffic hits, and thus they simply choose to run the risk of exploitation accusations.

5   In both these cases, proponents of breaking privacy boundaries argued that they did so for a greater good. In Palin's case, they maintained that the media coverage highlighted important political issues; in Rihanna's case, publishing her photo furthered awareness of the seriousness of domestic violence.

6   What do you think? Is the media justified in exposing the private moments of celebrities' lives, no matter how personal or painful, if doing so raises public awareness? Or is this sort of coverage just exploitive?

From VERDERBER/VERDERBER/SELLNOW. *Communicate!*, 13E. © 2011 Wadsworth, a part of Cengage Learning, Inc. By permission.

(Continued)

COMPREHENSION CHECK

Circle the best answer to the questions based on information from the reading.

1 What is the issue discussed in this passage?

A. Whether the public has a right to know about celebrities
B. Whether celebrities have a right to fight back
C. Whether media coverage of celebrities has gone too far in prying into their private lives

2 What is the author's point of view on this issue?

A. The public has a right to know about celebrities.
B. The media coverage of celebrities has gone too far in prying into their private lives.
C. The author presents both sides of the issue but does not take a position.

3 What are the two points of view on this issue, as discussed in the reading?

A. The media is justified in exposing the private moments of celebrities' lives, no matter how personal or painful, if doing so raises public awareness versus this sort of coverage is exploitive.
B. The media is justified in exposing private moments of celebrities' lives if it has to do with politics, versus this sort of coverage is unjustified with nonpolitical celebrities.
C. The media coverage is not justified in exposing public lives of celebrities, versus the media is justified in exposing public lives of celebrities.

4 What is the author's tone in this reading?

A. Angry
B. Humorous
C. Concerned

5 Is this statement from the reading a fact or an opinion?

For over a century, celebrities have complained that the media invades their privacy, but it was the death of Princess Diana in 1997 that focused worldwide attention on the extent to which celebrities are denied any right to privacy.

A. Fact
B. Opinion

6 Is this statement from the reading a fact or an opinion?

For example, during the 2008 presidential campaign, the media covered the pregnancy of vice-presidential candidate Sarah Palin's 17-year-old unmarried daughter, Bristol, extensively.

A. Fact
B. Opinion

7 **What type of support is used in this reading?**

A. Facts and statistics
B. Facts, reasons, and testimony
C. Examples and statistics

8 **Is the author biased?**

A. Yes
B. No

9 **Which word in this passage is an example of loaded language indicating bias?**

From the paparazzi who literally hounded Princess Diana to her death, to the newspapers who publicized the college antics of the Bush twins, it appears that anyone the media takes an interest in can no longer expect even a basic right to privacy.

A. Paparazzi
B. Media
C. Hounded

10 **Who is the intended audience?**

A. The press
B. The celebrities who are hounded
C. College students

FOCUS ON READING STUDY SKILLS

Critical Thinking and Critical Reading

Many students are surprised at the differences between high school and college academic expectations. Instead of just reading a few pages of a textbook and memorizing some facts each week for class, in college you are faced with chapters of dense, complex material per class each week. Instructors expect students to learn the information presented in class lectures and discussion *as well as* additional information presented in the textbook, whether or not it is discussed in class. This is why it is important to read and take notes from your textbook. Reading, marking the text, and taking notes for study equates to interacting with the material three times. Understanding and learning the material in college-level texts is vital; but what makes college reading different from high school reading is that college instructors expect you to think critically: to analyze, synthesize, and evaluate material you read.

CRITICAL THINKING

College courses require proficiency in **critical thinking.** Thinking critically means analyzing, evaluating, and synthesizing information. Before you can begin thinking critically, you need to comprehend, or understand, the material. You've learned how to do this in the previous chapters of this textbook. Comprehending involves recognizing the topic, main idea, the relationship between ideas, and supporting details.

To understand the different types of thinking for college success, spend a moment considering Figure 7.1, which illustrates Bloom's taxonomy, a six-level sequence of thinking skills that corresponds to levels of understanding. These levels

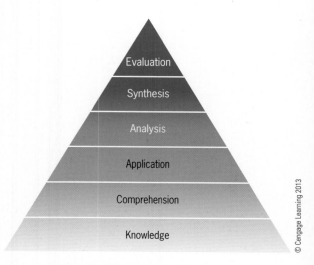

FIGURE 7.1 Bloom's Taxonomy

of understanding are related to how you interpret and use information that you read, from simple comprehension to more complex levels of reasoning. In college, instructors expect that you can already perform on the first three levels—that you can comprehend and apply what you read for class. In college courses, you will practice your critical thinking skills on the higher three levels. The levels of Bloom's taxonomy are explained in Table 7.1.

TABLE 7.1 BLOOM'S TAXONOMY

BLOOM'S CATEGORY	EXAMPLE	KEY WORDS THAT SUGGEST LEVEL OF THINKING REQUIRED
Knowledge: Understand and recall information	Answering questions that are explicit in the text	*define, describe, identify, state*
Comprehension: Understanding a problem or content, interpreting it, and being able to paraphrase it	Paraphrasing a passage, finding a main idea, summarizing a reading	*comprehend, explain, restate, interpret, paraphrase, summarize, outline, discuss*
Application: Applying or using a new concept or idea in another context	Applying a skill to a new reading (like On Your Own exercises from this book)	*apply, construct, demonstrate, relate*
Analysis: Separating information into parts to see how they fit together	Seeing the relationship between ideas, drawing conclusions, applying the most useful reading strategy to the task at hand	*analyze, compare, contrast*
Synthesis: Putting parts together to form a whole, focusing on creating something new and forming a new conclusion	Putting together two or more readings on a topic and integrating ideas	*combine or synthesize material, compose, reconstruct, rewrite*

© Cengage Learning 2013

(Continued)

FOCUS ON READING STUDY SKILLS: Critical Thinking and Critical Reading

TABLE 7.1 BLOOM'S TAXONOMY

BLOOM'S CATEGORY	EXAMPLE	KEY WORDS THAT SUGGEST LEVEL OF THINKING REQUIRED
Evaluation: Making a judgment about the value of a reading or point of view.	Looking at the strengths and weaknesses in an argument	*judge or evaluate, conclude, criticize, interpret, justify, support*

CRITICAL READING

A **critical reader** goes beyond understanding what is written on a literal level (beyond comprehension of topic, main idea, and supporting details) and makes a judgment about the strengths and weaknesses of a piece of writing. Only after you fully understand what the author has written can you begin to think about the author's ideas critically. Reading critically does not mean picking apart an idea to find fault, as the word *criticize* is often understood in everyday speech. Rather, critical reading involves applying the higher levels of Bloom's critical thinking skills to interact with the reading and seeing how it relates to your background knowledge.

- During reading:
  - **Analyzing** information requires that you see the relationship between ideas and understand how these ideas interrelate with the topic, or the whole reading.

- After reading:
  - **Synthesizing** information requires that you fully understand *related* ideas, or can see the relationship between ideas from more than one source, and can then draw conclusions and derive judgments by putting together information from these different sources to come up with a conclusion on your own.

  - **Evaluating** information requires that you fully understand the idea and can judge strengths, weaknesses, issues, or consequences of the idea.

On Your Own SOLVING CRITICAL THINKING PUZZLES

One way to sharpen your mind is to decode puzzles. This type of critical thinking exercises your mind. Some of these puzzles are lateral thinking puzzles that require you to think outside the box and come up with solutions that are creative or unusual. These puzzles also make you think about your own assumptions in solving problems. An *assumption* is a belief that is taken for granted. By uncovering your assumptions, you can analyze your own bias about certain topics. (You'll learn more about bias later in this chapter.) Try the following puzzles and see if your ability to solve them improves with practice.

1. What letter comes next in the series? ZXCVBN_____

2. Which number comes next in the series? –1, 1, 0, 1, 1, 2, 3, 5, 8, _____

3. If you are in St. Louis and it is noon, it is 1 P.M. in New York and 6 P.M. in Paris. What time is it for the following:

   a. Time in St. Louis if it is noon in Paris?

   b. Time in Paris if it is 5 P.M. in New York?

   c. Time in New York if it is 11:30 P.M. in Paris?

4. At an art gallery, a woman is looking at a portrait. You overhear her say, "I have no brothers or sisters, but that woman's mother is my mother's daughter." Who is the portrait of?

5. A chef has two containers—one is a five gallon container and the other is a three gallon container. The chef needs to measure exactly one gallon of liquid for his recipe. How can he do this without wasting any liquid?

Answers

1. M (letters on the first line of a keyboard)
2. 13 (each number is the sum of the previous 2)
3. 7 A.M.; 10 P.M.; 6:30 P.M.
4. Her daughter
5. The chef should fill the three gallon jug and empty it into the 5 gallon jug. Then, he should fill the 3 gallon jug again and pour the contents into the 5 gallon jug. Whatever liquid is left in the 3 gallon jug must equal 1 gallon.

FOCUS ON VOCABULARY
Recognizing Bias, Tone, and Loaded Language

In controversial writing—writing in which an author has a specific point of view about an issue—an author's primary purpose is to persuade the reader to agree with his or her point of view. If an author has a distinct point of view about an issue, then he or she has an opinion about that issue. In neutral or objective writing, the author's purpose is to inform and convey facts with little or no underlying opinion. An author has two elements at his or her disposal to persuade the reader to accept his or her point of view about an issue: word choice and style of writing.

BIAS AND TONE

In controversial writing, **bias,** or the side an author takes on an issue, is directly related to the **tone,** or underlying attitude, an author has about a subject (see Table 7.2 and Figure 7.1). An author's choice of words, or diction, is extremely important. After all, an author only has words to persuade a reader. An author will be very deliberate in selecting particular vocabulary and arranging words

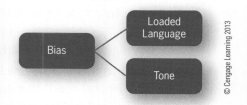

© Cengage Learning 2013

FIGURE 7.2 An Author's Bias Dictates Both His or Her Tone and Choice of Words

TABLE 7.2 LOOKING AT LANGUAGE CRITICALLY

BIAS	LOADED LANGUAGE	TONE
The author's side on an issue as revealed by choice of words and tone	A word or phrase is loaded if it carries connotation—either positive or negative associations—beyond its dictionary meaning.	The author's underlying attitude or emotion toward the subject as revealed by words or writing style

© Cengage Learning 2013

to convey his or her message. Most authors are acutely aware of the connotations of the words and phrases they choose. **Connotation** refers to what a word or phrase suggests on an emotional level.

> We should outlaw all paparazzi since they cause more trouble than they're worth.

In this example, the author has a bias. Is she for or against the paparazzi? The author is against the paparazzi. You know that because of the firm language: *we should outlaw all paparazzi*. The position is stated clearly and strongly, using the word *should*. What is the author's tone? The author feels strongly that the paparazzi should be outlawed (not just restricted or contained), so the author's tone is angry, concerned, disgusted, or any other adjective that conveys strong disapproval. Tone, then, can be described with any adjective. This means that you and another person may not use exactly the same word to describe tone, just like no two people would express an implied main idea in exactly the same words. As long as your choice of words conveys the same general sentiment and you can support your answer, you would both be right.

Loaded Language

Heavily biased words and phrases are referred to as **loaded language,** or words and phrases that an author chooses to convey a point of view and that reveal bias. A word or phrase is considered loaded if it suggests strong feelings—whether negative or positive—beyond its strict dictionary definition. A reader who is not aware of loaded language can misconstrue an author's point. Persuasive writing is manipulative, which is not always a negative. After all, it is the author's job to persuade. He or she will use whatever means are available to do so.

Loaded language reveals a great deal about an author's tone. You can tell if an author is angry, sad, frustrated, excited, arrogant, disturbed by, or disgusted with a subject from her or his choice of words. Also, you can make an inference about the author's opinion on the given issue from the word choice used. The author's word choice and style of writing may also reveal the audience for whom her or his writing is intended. Consider this example about BP's chief executive being fired after the company's oil disaster in the Gulf of Mexico. See if you can

FOCUS ON VOCABULARY: Recognizing Bias, Tone, and Loaded Language

determine the author's tone, as well as which words in particular have connotations that reveal any bias about the issue. What do you think is the author's opinion on the issue?

> Few tears will be shed for ousted BP chief executive Tony Hayward, who famously attended a yacht race while his company's blown-out oil well decorated the Gulf of Mexico with crude, and who whined to reporters during the crisis that he wanted "my life back."

> —Editors, *USA Today*, "Our view on Big Oil: BP replaces CEO, but what about its safety policies?" http://www.usatoday.com/news/opinion/editorials/2010-07-28 editorial28_ST_N.htm, © 2010 *USA Today*. Reprinted with Permission.

Phrases like *few tears will be shed, blown-out oil well decorated the Gulf of Mexico with crude,* and *who whined to reporters*, all suggest that the author disapproves of the BP chief executive. This language is loaded because it suggests a strong opinion on the part of the author. The choice of words reveals that the author is biased. The author's tone is angry, disgusted, disapproving, or condemning. Contrast this example with an unbiased statement:

> When the Deepwater Horizon oil rig sank to the bottom of the Gulf of Mexico on April 22, 11 men were missing and a gushing well was emptying into the sea. It happened to be Earth Day.

> —"Energy's costs finally meet the eyes" by Meera Subramanian, *USA Today,* May 12, 2010. © 2010 *USA Today*. Reprinted with Permission.

In this passage, the author does not use loaded language but presents information in a straightforward manner, communicating facts. Her tone is serious and factual.

Neither bias nor loaded language always suggests something negative. They do suggest taking a side on an issue, however. Depending on your point of view, you may either agree or disagree with an author's point of view or bias. For example, consider this statement:

> The college years are the best time in your life.

The word *best* suggests that the author takes a position on the issue about the impact of the college years in your life. The word *best* suggests a bias toward the point of view that these years are positive. The author is still biased, but in a positive way.

On Your Own   RECOGNIZING BIAS

Consider this first paragraph from the pre-assessment, "The Right to Privacy in a Mediated Society," by Verderber, Verderber, and Sellnow. Circle all the words that indicate bias. Discuss with a partner or in class how the words you chose that indicate bias slant the argument.

> For over a century, celebrities have complained that the media invades their privacy, but it was the death of Princess Diana in 1997 that focused worldwide attention on the extent to which celebrities are denied any right to privacy. From the paparazzi who literally hounded Princess Diana to her death, to the newspapers who publicized the college antics of the Bush twins, it appears that anyone the media takes an interest in can no longer expect even a basic right to privacy. Certainly, public figures expect to be scrutinized regarding their professional lives, but the current cult of celebrity has created a situation in which the media thinks little about also prying into their private lives. Not only that, but anyone connected to these public figures, including their families, is also subject to invasive media coverage.
>
> —From VERDERBER/VERDERBER/SELLNOW. *Communicate!*, 13E. © 2011 Wadsworth,
> a part of Cengage Learning, Inc. By permission.

On Your Own   RECOGNIZING BIAS, TONE, AND LOADED LANGUAGE

Consider the following passages that concern alternative energy and explore both sides of the issue concerning the firing of BP's chief executive, Tony Hayward, who was replaced by Robert Dudley. Carl-Henric Svanberg is the chairman of the board of BP—usually the chairman, along with other board members, can hire or fire the chief executive. These opinions were published in *USA Today*.

As you read these passages, ask yourself, Is the author biased? What is the author's tone? What loaded language reveals that tone? Circle loaded words or phrases that suggest tone, and then identify what the tone of the passage is. Be prepared to discuss your ideas with the class.

1. He'll [Tony Heyward, former BP chief executive] get his wish in October, when he'll be succeeded by fellow BP executive Robert Dudley, whose to-do list has at least four urgent items: Make sure the well is finally capped, put a less obnoxious face on the world's second

(Continued)

FOCUS ON VOCABULARY: Recognizing Bias, Tone, and Loaded Language

largest private oil company, dig the company out of its costly hole and—most important—change a culture that apparently puts safety a distant second to cutting costs.

—Editors, *USA Today,* "Our view on Big Oil: BP replaces CEO, but what about its safety policies?"

http://www.usatoday.com/news/opinion/editorials/2010-07-28 editorial28_ST_N.htm,

© 2010 *USA Today.* Reprinted with Permission.

Biased? _____

Tone: _____

2. The trouble is that BP has been through this sort of crisis before, eventually dumped a CEO, and little changed. Even now, neither Hayward nor Dudley seems to understand (or will admit) that their company has a problem. Hayward spoke Tuesday as if the April 20 blowout that killed 11 men was just a fluke: "Sometimes you step off the pavement and get hit by a bus," he said. Yeah, but in this case, it was as if BP was running, texting and talking on a cellphone when it blundered into the street.

—Editors, *USA Today,* "Our view on Big Oil: BP replaces CEO, but what about its safety policies?"

http://www.usatoday.com/news/opinion/editorials/2010-07-28 editorial28_ST_N.htm,

© 2010 *USA Today.* Reprinted with Permission.

Biased? _____

Tone: _____

3. A week later, Interior Secretary Ken Salazar announced federal approval for the nation's first offshore wind farm in Nantucket Sound near Hyannis, Mass., which will turn an aquatic area the size of Manhattan into an oceanic-industrial complex with 130 massive turbines reaching 440 feet into the sky.

—"Energy's costs finally meet the eyes" by Meera Subramanian, *USA Today,* May 12, 2010.

© 2010 *USA Today.* Reprinted with Permission.

Biased? _____

Tone: _____

4. Dudley seems just as clueless as the man he's replacing. "I don't accept, and have not witnessed, this cutting of corners and the sacrifice of safety to drive results," he said, according to *The New York Times.* You have to wonder whether this guy has been asleep for the past five years.

—Editors, *USA Today,* "Our view on Big Oil: BP replaces CEO, but what about its safety policies?"

http://www.usatoday.com/news/opinion/editorials/2010-07-28 editorial28_ST_N.htm,

© 2010 *USA Today.* Reprinted with Permission.

Biased? _____

Tone: _____

5. The BP board is deeply saddened to lose a CEO whose success over some three years in driving the performance of the company was so widely and deservedly admired.

    —Other views on Big Oil: Board is 'deeply saddened' Statement by BP chairman Carl-Henric Svanberg,
    http://www.usatoday.com/news/opinion/forum/2010-05-13-column13_ST_N.htm,
    © 2010 *USA Today*. Reprinted with Permission.

    Biased? _____

    Tone: _____

6. Weeks ago, some of the migratory birds that are now whistling their mating songs in the idylls of Cape Cod might have passed over Chandeleur Islands off Louisiana, where the oil slick first made contact with land last Thursday.

    —"Energy's costs finally meet the eyes" by Meera Subramanian, *USA Today*, May 12, 2010.
    © 2010 *USA Today*. Reprinted with Permission.

    Biased? _____

    Tone: _____

7. The tragedy of the Macondo well explosion and subsequent environmental damage has been a watershed incident. BP remains a strong business with fine assets, excellent people and a vital role to play in meeting the world's energy needs.

    —Other views on Big Oil: Board is 'deeply saddened' Statement by BP chairman Carl-Henric Svanberg,
    http://www.usatoday.com/news/opinion/forum/2010-05-13-column13_ST_N.htm,
    © 2010 *USA Today*. Reprinted with Permission.

    Biased? _____

    Tone: _____

8. We are highly fortunate to have a successor of the caliber of Bob Dudley who has spent his working life in the oil industry both in the U.S. and overseas and has proved himself a robust operator in the toughest circumstances.

    —Other views on Big Oil: Board is 'deeply saddened' Statement by BP chairman Carl-Henric Svanberg,
    http://www.usatoday.com/news/opinion/forum/2010-05-13-column13_ST_N.htm,
    © 2010 *USA Today*. Reprinted with Permission.

    Biased? _____

    Tone: _____

FOCUS ON COMPREHENSION
Reading Arguments

In this chapter, you will learn techniques to read more complex readings that you will encounter in college reading—arguments—and to make judgments about a reading. To do this, you must use everything you have learned so far in this textbook. To work toward reading critically, you learned to employ the following steps to understand a reading, operating on the levels of knowledge, comprehension, and application of information, according to Bloom's taxonomy:

1. Determine the topic.
2. Determine the pattern of organization.
3. Determine the author's main idea, or thesis.
4. Determine the supporting details that back up the main idea.

Now you will apply this method to arguments—a text in which a point of view about an issue is presented—and apply critical thinking skills using analysis, synthesis, and evaluation.

UNDERSTANDING ARGUMENTS

When an author takes a position or expresses an opinion on a topic, the author's purpose is to persuade (see Figure 7.3 for the differences between persuasive writing and informative writing). This is also known as an **argument.** An argument is defined as a discussion or debate involving different points of view. Some of the terms and concepts you have learned in this book are referred to differently when talking about arguments. For example, a topic is called an **issue** in arguments. Similarly, the main idea is referred to as the author's **point of view.** Supporting details are called **supporting arguments.**

QUICK TIPS ARGUMENT TERMS

	INFORMATIVE WRITING	ARGUMENTS
Author's Purpose	To inform	To persuade
Subject	Topic	Issue
Main Point	Main idea or thesis	Point of view
Body of Writing	Supporting details	Supporting arguments

© Cengage Learning 2013

As noted, an issue is the subject of an argument. It is useful to use the phrase *whether or not . . .* when formulating the issue of an argument, so that the author's point of view is easier to identify. For example, if the issue is *whether or not* gun control laws should be strengthened, an author's point of view is either (1) "Yes, gun control laws should be strengthened" or (2) "No, gun control laws should not be strengthened."

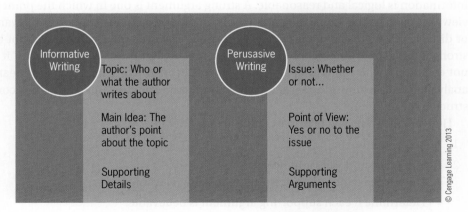

FIGURE 7.3 Persuasive Versus Informative Writing

FOCUS ON COMPREHENSION: Reading Arguments

EVALUATING ARGUMENTS

When you watch a sports match, you probably have a favorite team. However, the fact that you favor one team over the other may not influence your opinion about which team played the best game. And, if you're a serious sports fan, you could see errors in your favorite team's game that made them unsuccessful. Although you may not endorse the other team, you probably could see why they won. This sports analogy can be applied to critical reading. Just because you agree with an author's point of view doesn't mean you have to agree that his or her argument was well constructed.

To think critically, you must evaluate arguments. A critical reader makes an informed judgment about the strengths and weaknesses of an argument—this is evaluation. One way to determine if an argument is good or bad is to think about whether you agree with the author's point of view on the issue. While this may influence your decision, a critical reader also makes a judgment about an argument that is based on logic and reasoning.

Although it may seem simple to construct a good argument—one in which the point of view is clear and the support is both relevant and complete—it is not as easy as it appears. To be a critical reader, you need to dissect an argument to make sure the information is logical and reasonable. A strong argument is one in which the point of view is proven by the supporting arguments; in other words, the support is relevant, or directly relates to the point of view expressed. However, an argument will not be strong if the supporting arguments are not complete, if it is not believable, or if it is not consistent with the author's point of view. Deconstructing an argument means analyzing it to see how the parts fit together and understanding how the author constructed the argument.

Here are the steps you take to evaluate an argument:

1. Map the argument.
2. Identify the supporting arguments.
   - Determine if the supporting arguments are relevant.
   - Determine if each supporting argument is believable.
3. Check the credentials of the author.
4. Determine the intended audience of the argument.

Mapping Arguments _____

The first step in evaluating an argument is to identify the components of the argument, or to **map the argument**. You have experience outlining readings from Chapter 6—remember how you mark text for topic, main idea, and supporting details? When you map an argument, the idea is the same, but the slightly different language for arguments is used. Because you have practice seeing the relationships between ideas, mapping arguments will be straightforward. Mapping involves the following:

- Identifying the issue
- Identifying the author's point of view on the issue
- Identifying the supporting arguments
- Identifying the type of supporting argument

To map an argument, follow this template:

1. **Issue:** Whether or not . . . [summarize the issue (topic) of the argument]
2. **Author's Point of View:** The author's opinion (main idea) about the issue

   Supporting argument 1:

   Supporting argument 2:

   Supporting argument 3:

   Supporting argument 4:

   Supporting argument 5:

   Supporting argument 6:

There may or may not be six arguments to back up an author's point of view, as in this example. It is up to the reader to determine how many supporting arguments the author makes to support his or her point of view.

FACT AND OPINION

To begin understanding the kinds of supporting arguments an author can use, you need to understand the difference between fact and opinion. A **fact** is something that can be proven; an **opinion** is one person's belief, or something that cannot be proven. Facts are straightforward, provable, and documented pieces of information—facts exist, are known to exist, or can be verified to exist. Statistics, or factual results in the

FOCUS ON COMPREHENSION: Reading Arguments

form of numbers, often support an author's point of view. Statistics are facts, but how they are interpreted is often a matter of opinion, because they are often used to convince a reader of a point of view. Although these numbers or results could be verified (i.e., they can be traced to a study or report), do not always assume statistics prove the main idea without question. For example, statistics used out of their original context can be misleading. Often statistics from another source could be used for an equally verifiable counterargument.

Opinions, on the other hand, are someone's *interpretation* of facts. Opinion statements cannot be verified or proven. You may well agree with someone's opinion; you may even see the opinion as obvious and true. But an opinion can be debated. In other words, someone can argue the opposite point of view, or counterargue, and still be right.

For example, a writer could cite examples of statistics and facts about the negative health effects of smoking tobacco, but add that because of these facts, we should make smoking illegal. The facts are used to bolster the opinion. Others could argue that the facts about the negative impact of smoking may suggest we increase the smoking age rather than ban the drug altogether. In either case, facts are used to support the authors' opinions.

Opinions involve a value judgment, and they are often signaled by words or phrases like *in my opinion, the truth is, I think, we should, we must,* or *we ought to.* A **value judgment** is a decision about what is right and what is wrong based on an individual's opinion and values. All of these phrases indicate an opinion, regardless of how convincing that opinion is. Also, anything that has not yet happened must be an opinion because it cannot be verified, even if it seems very likely. For example, projections about population growth in 2050 are opinions, even if they are based on reasonable deductions derived from already available facts and are mathematically probable. But *probable* is not a fact—it's an opinion.

QUICK TIPS DIFFERENCES BETWEEN FACTS AND OPINIONS

Facts	Opinions
✔ Can be proven or verified	✔ Are someone's interpretation of facts
✔ May be statistics, but the *interpretation* of statistics is an opinion	✔ Involve a value judgment
	✔ Are signaled by words and phrases like *the truth is, I think, we ought to, we should,* etc.

Thinking It Through   RECOGNIZING FACT AND OPINION

The following passages come from an article in *The New York Times*, "Tell-all Generation Learns Not To," by Laura M. Holson. The article concerns the issue of publishing personal and sometimes incriminating information about yourself on social networking sites. Consider each passage and think about whether the information is fact (it could be proven to be true) or opinion (not able to be proven).

> The conventional wisdom suggests that everyone under 30 is comfortable revealing every facet of their lives online, from their favorite pizza to most frequent sexual partners. But many members of the tell-all generation are rethinking what it means to live out loud.

In this example, the author presents an opinion. While it may be true that many are rethinking what it means to "let it all hang out" online, this is not proven or verified with facts.

> While participation in social networks is still strong, a survey released last month by the University of California, Berkeley, found that more than half the young adults questioned had become more concerned about privacy than they were five years ago—mirroring the number of people their parent's age or older with that worry.

In this example, the author provides facts to support her point that young adults are concerned about their privacy on social networks. The survey results can be verified and shown to be true. You can read the original study from the University of California to verify the data.

> Younger teenagers were not included in these studies, and they may not have the same privacy concerns.

In this example, part of the statement is a fact and part is an opinion. Can you determine which part is factual and can be verified? The first part of the sentence is a fact. This can be proven by looking at the age of the participants in the study. However, the second part of the passage cannot be proven: *they may not have the same privacy concerns*. This is the author's opinion; the author's use of the word *may* signals an opinion, not a fact. There is no way of proving whether or not the younger teenagers who were not included in the study have privacy concerns.

On Your Own   RECOGNIZING FACT AND OPINION

Read these additional excerpts on the next page from the article "Tell-all Generation Learns Not To" and identify whether they are facts or opinions. Put an *F* next to the statements that are facts and an *O* next to the statements that are opinions.

(Continued)

FOCUS ON COMPREHENSION: Reading Arguments

____ 1. In a new study to be released this month, the Pew Internet Project has found that people in their 20s exert more control over their digital reputations than older adults, more vigorously deleting unwanted posts and limiting information about themselves.

____ 2. "Social networking requires vigilance, not only in what you post, but what your friends post about you," said Mary Madden, a senior research specialist who oversaw the study by Pew, which examines online behavior. "Now you are responsible for everything."

____ 3. The erosion of privacy has become a pressing issue among active users of social networks.

____ 4. Last week, Facebook scrambled to fix a security breach that allowed users to see their friends' supposedly private information, including personal chats.

____ 5. Sam Jackson, a junior at Yale who started a blog when he was 15 and who has been an intern at Google, said he had learned not to trust any social network to keep his information private.

____ 6. Mistrust of the intentions of social sites appears to be pervasive.

____ 7. In its telephone survey of 1,000 people, the Berkeley Center for Law and Technology at the University of California found that 88 percent of the 18- to 24-year-olds it surveyed last July said there should be a law that requires websites to delete stored information.

____ 8. And 62 percent said they wanted a law that gave people the right to know everything a website knows about them.

____ 9. That mistrust is translating into action.

___ 10. In the Pew study, to be released shortly, researchers interviewed 2,253 adults late last summer and found that people ages 18 to 29 were more apt to monitor privacy settings than older adults are, and they more often delete comments or remove their names from photos so they cannot be identified.

TYPES OF SUPPORTING ARGUMENTS

Understanding the different ways an author can present both facts and opinions to support his or her point of view will help you become a more informed critical reader. An author can use these types of supporting arguments to support his or her point of view on an issue (see also Table 7.3).

1. **Facts.** As you learned, facts are supporting points that can be verified, or proven. Make sure the facts that are used to reinforce the point are directly related to the point. Statistics are a type of fact. Furthermore, the *interpretation* of

statistics blurs the line between fact and opinion. Although textbooks appear to contain factual, objective information, be aware that the author may be biased if all opposing points of view on the subject are not mentioned.

> **Example:** Many thousands of Americans die each year from smoking.

2. **Reasons.** Reasons are opinions based on facts. Reasons are logical arguments, although they are not usually verifiable (provable). In other words, a counterargument could use equally valid reasons to support the opposing point of view.

> **Example:** Because many thousands of Americans die each year from smoking, health education must be a priority at schools.

3. **Examples.** Examples illustrate or clarify the author's point of view. These may be logical and reasonable, but they cannot be verified like facts or statistics. Examples often support reasons. Examples are usually found in a series of specific statements or descriptions that support an overall point.

> **Example:** There are several health concerns for Americans. For example, many thousands of Americans die each year from tobacco-related diseases. In addition, obesity is a growing concern that leads to a variety of health conditions, such as diabetes and heart disease.

4. **Testimony.** This type of support is used when an author cites an expert witness or someone seen to be an authoritative source to comment on, and back up, the point of view. Testimony can also be a quote from someone involved in an issue. Testimony may be based on facts to some extent, but it is someone's opinion based on facts. Testimony can also derive from eyewitness accounts that are not always accurate. While eyewitness testimony can carry substantial weight, particularly if the testimony was reported to an official source, this does not mean that the report is accurate or indisputable. The eyewitness could have misconstrued the event or misrepresented the information. An example of testimony is a court of law, in which a person testifies by answering the questions of a prosecutor or defense attorney, or an expert witness passes judgment relevant to the trial proceedings.

> **Example:** "Americans will be more likely to change their behavior if they have a meaningful reward—something more than just reaching a certain weight or dress size. The real reward is invigorating, energizing, joyous health. It is a level of health that allows people to embrace each day and live their lives to the fullest without disease or disability."
>
> —VADM Regina M. Benjamin, M.D., M.B.A., Surgeon General, January 28, 2011.

FOCUS ON COMPREHENSION: Reading Arguments

5. **Counterarguments.** A writer can use a counterargument (as do lawyers in court) to first outline what the opposing side argues and then prove the opposing side wrong or point out errors in reasoning. This is a very effective method of debate because it undercuts the arguments of the opposing side. To counterargue, an author can use facts, reasons, examples, or testimony. Notice the underlined part of this passage where the author counterargues McKinsey & Co.'s view that if we invest in energy efficiency, we will make back our investment within 10 years. The author counterargues that we need to find a solution beyond energy efficiency and come up with different renewable energy sources.

> **Example:** McKinsey & Co., one of the world's top consulting firms, reported last year that Americans will save twice what we invest in energy efficiency within 10 years. <u>But even if we are able to climb this slippery slope toward self-sacrifice, humans everywhere will continue to sop up energy from various sources. If the same mind power and engineering feats now being directed to capping the Gulf's unruly well could be channeled into a proactive renewable energy initiative worthy of the Manhattan Project or the Apollo Program, that would be a start. But no matter where our energy comes from in the future, ignorance is no longer an option.</u>
>
> —"Energy's costs finally meet the eyes" by Meera Subramanian, *USA Today*, May 12, 2010. © 2010 *USA Today*. Reprinted with Permission.

TABLE 7.3 IDENTIFYING TYPES OF SUPPORTING ARGUMENTS

FACTS	REASONS	EXAMPLES	TESTIMONY	COUNTERARGUMENT
• Numbers • Statistics • Verifiable events	• Informed opinion • Logical arguments • Reasoned conclusions • Based on facts, but not verifiable	• Lists in support • Names • Dates • Events • Specific cases • Facts or opinions that backup a reason or a fact	• Expert witnesses • Expert opinion • Verifiable, but is someone's expert opinion	• Laying out the other side's points and finding fault with them • Can use facts, reasons, examples, and testimony

Thinking It Through IDENTIFYING SUPPORTING ARGUMENTS

In the following example, note how the author first reports a misconception on the side of those who are in favor of the death penalty, and then goes on to argue why those in favor of the death penalty are wrong. The author argues *against* the death penalty but says what those *in favor of* the death penalty say and argues that they are wrong. What are the different types of supporting arguments that are used to persuade the reader?

> Those who argue for the death penalty cite that it costs tax payers less to execute an inmate than to incarcerate the inmate for life. Frankly, this argument is, at best, misguided and, at worst, wrong since it costs far more to finance the legal appeals process for a prisoner on death row whose life ends in execution than it does to finance a life sentence (counterargument). Using conservative rough projections, the Commission estimates the annual costs of the present (death penalty) system to be $137 million per year* (fact). The average cost of defending a trial in a federal death case is $620,932, about 8 times that of a federal murder case in which the death penalty is not sought (fact)*. All aspects of the criminal justice system have costs. Examples of costs society bears are the costs of apprehending offenders, trials, law enforcement and punishment (example). We need to look at our societal costs and consider which to eliminate so we spend our hard-earned tax dollars in the best way possible (reason). The most significant cost is the death penalty. According to Richard C. Dieter, Executive Director, Death Penalty Information Center, "Millions are spent to achieve a single death sentence that, even if imposed, is unlikely to be carried out. Thus money that the police desperately need for more effective law enforcement may be wasted on the death penalty. (testimony)"**

This example includes both fact and opinion:

Fact: It costs far more to finance the legal appeals process for a prisoner on death row whose life ends in execution than it does to finance a life sentence.

Opinion: This argument is, at best, misguided and, at worst, wrong. . . .

The author provides some specific facts to support the claim that life-in-prison sentences cost taxpayers less money and is thus a reason we need to consider this issue. Examples of other costs associated with the justice system are provided as well. In addition, testimony is used to further support the point of view.

Here the author expresses one side of the issue and then proceeds to counterargue it:

Counterargument: Those who argue for the death penalty cite that it costs tax payers less to execute an inmate than to incarcerate the inmate for life. Frankly, this argument is, at best, misguided and, at worst, wrong since it costs far more to finance the legal appeals process for a prisoner on death row whose life ends in execution than it does to finance a life sentence.

---

*From www.deathpenaltyinfo.org.
**From *Testimony Before the Pennsylvania Senate Government Management and Cost Study Commission.*

(Continued)

FOCUS ON COMPREHENSION: Reading Arguments

In this next example, the author provides statistics to back up the claim that death penalty costs are very high for the American taxpayer:

Facts: Using conservative rough projections, the Commission estimates the annual costs of the present (death penalty) system to be $137 million per year. The average cost of defending a trial in a federal death case is $620,932, about 8 times that of a federal murder case in which the death penalty is not sought.

Reason: We need to look at our societal costs and consider which to eliminate so we spend our hard-earned tax dollars in the best way possible.

Here, the author presents the facts about the costs of death penalty cases, and follows them with an opinion based on those facts.

The author also provides examples of costs to society that derive from death penalty cases:

Example: Examples of costs society bears are the costs of apprehending offenders, trials, law enforcement and punishment.

This is a quote from an expert that supports the author's point:

Testimony: The most significant cost is the death penalty. According to Richard C. Dieter, Executive Director, Death Penalty Information Center, "Millions are spent to achieve a single death sentence that, even if imposed, is unlikely to be carried out. Thus money that the police desperately need for more effective law enforcement may be wasted on the death penalty.

Information cited from http://www.deathpenaltyinfo.org/costs-death-penalty, Quote from Testimony before the Pennsylvania Senate Government Management and Cost Study Commission, June 7, 2010 by Richard C. Dieter, Executive Director Death Penalty Information Center, http://www.deathpenaltyinfo.org/documents/PACostTestimony.pdf, ©2010 Death Penalty Information Center.

On Your Own IDENTIFYING SUPPORTING ARGUMENTS

For the following passages, identify the type of support used. Put an *F* next to the passage if it's primarily fact, an *R* if it's primarily a reason, an *E* if it's primarily an example, a *T* if it's primarily testimony, and a *C* if it's primarily counterargument.

____ 1. In March 2005, the United States Supreme Court ruled that the death penalty for those who had committed their crimes at under 18 years of age was cruel and unusual punishment and hence barred by the Constitution.

____ 2. Juveniles were eligible for the death penalty for crimes such as rape, robbery, burglary, and murder.

____ 3. For the past 15 years, the federal constitutionality of the American juvenile death penalty was a reasonably well-settled issue.

___ 4. In *Thompson v. Oklahoma*, 487 U.S. 815 (1988), the United States Supreme Court held that executions of offenders age 15 and younger at the time of their crimes are prohibited by the Eighth Amendment to the United States Constitution.

___ 5. Opponents of the death penalty may feel that a juvenile knows right from wrong; science has suggested, however, that the adolescent brain is not fully developed and that the area of the brain associated with rational decision making is still in development.

As a critical reader, you do not want to accept what an author writes at face value. Table 7.4 lists some initial questions you can ask yourself regarding an author's point of view and supporting arguments to begin to delve beneath the surface of what is said and formulate your own opinion about an argument.

Information cited from http://www.deathpenaltyinfo.org/costs-death-penalty, Quote from Testimony before the Pennsylvania Senate Government Management and Cost Study Commission, June 7, 2010 by Richard C. Dieter, Executive Director Death Penalty Information Center, http://www.deathpenaltyinfo.org/documents/PACostTestimony.pdf, ©2010 Death Penalty Information Center.

TABLE 7.4 EVALUATING SUPPORTING ARGUMENTS

IS THE SUPPORT EFFECTIVE? ASK THESE QUESTIONS				
FACTS	REASONS	EXAMPLES	TESTIMONY	COUNTERARGUMENT
Are the facts verifiable? Are the statistics interpreted and, therefore, part opinion?	Are the arguments logical? Are the conclusions reasonable?	Are the lists or other examples directly relevant to the point being proven?	Are the experts qualified to pass judgment?	Are the opponents' points clearly and convincingly disproven?

© Cengage Learning 2013

Determining If Supporting Arguments Are Relevant

Evaluating an argument involves first mapping an argument so you know what the major supporting points are. Then, the next step is deciding if the supporting arguments are relevant to the author's point of view. **Relevant** means directly relating to the author's point of view. Whether a supporting argument is relevant has to do with whether there are errors in the author's reasoning that make you question if the supporting argument directly relates to the point of view. If you are a fan of courtroom drama in novels, movies, or television, you may have read or seen how lawyers approach the judge when the other side presents evidence that is not relevant,

FOCUS ON COMPREHENSION: Reading Arguments

shouting, "Irrelevant, Your Honor!" Based on whether the newly submitted evidence relates directly to the issue at hand, the judge may choose to allow or not allow that evidence to be heard. To determine if an author's argument is relevant, ask yourself, Do the supporting arguments directly relate to the author's point of view?

Thinking It Through   DETERMINING IF SUPPORT IS RELEVANT

The following are examples of both relevant and irrelevant arguments. Notice how the examples of irrelevant supporting arguments do not support the point of view, while relevant ones do.

> The candidate for the Senate loves to go fishing when he is back on his ranch in his hometown. Isn't he what America needs?

Issue: Whether or not the candidate for the Senate is good for the position.

Author's point of view: Yes, the candidate is good for the position.

Supporting argument: The candidate loves to go fishing and attend his hometown meetings when he can.

The fact that the candidate for the Senate loves to attend hometown meetings and fish is not relevant to his position in the government. But the author manipulates you by making you think the candidate is just a regular guy and, therefore, will do a good job for you. The support for the author's point of view is not relevant to the argument.

> The candidate for Senate has a documented history of representing his constituents as well as ten years' experience working in government in Washington.

Issue: Whether or not the candidate for the Senate is good for the position.

Author's point of view: Yes, the candidate is good for the position.

Supporting argument: The candidate has a documented history of representing his constituents as well as 10 years' experience working in government in Washington.

The fact that the candidate for the Senate has a 10-year track record of representing his constituents directly supports the point of view that he is a good candidate for the job of senator.

> Anthony Cisneros has proven to be an excellent choice for governor. Everyone's voting for him and we all know he will be the best person for the job.

Issue: Whether or not Anthony Cisneros should be governor

Author's point of view: Yes, Anthony Cisneros should be elected governor.

Supporting argument: Everybody's voting for him.

The opinion of this statement is that because everyone's voting for Anthony Cisneros for governor, you should, too. But does the information that everyone's voting for him really support the point of view? No facts are provided to sustain the point of view that he would be good for the job. The supporting argument is irrelevant.

> Maria Vasquez is the best choice for governor. She has distinguished herself in the state legislature for over ten years and has a law degree that allows her to truly understand the intricacies of how politics works.

Issue: Whether or not Maria Vasquez should be governor

Author's point of view: Yes, Maria Vasquez should be elected governor.

Supporting argument: She has worked in the legislature (distinguished herself—which implies she's done a good job) for over 10 years.

Supporting argument: She has a law degree that enables her to understand politics.

In this example, the supporting facts directly back up the author's point of view. The facts that Maria Vasquez has experience in the legislature and has a law degree both directly pertain to the author's point of view. These supporting arguments are relevant.

On Your Own DETERMINING IF SUPPORT IS RELEVANT

For the following examples, map the parts of the argument to identify the supporting arguments; then decide if the supporting arguments are relevant or irrelevant and explain why.

1. How can we trust the eyewitness who claims that Jeff Harris is not guilty of the crime for which he is accused? This witness is a known gambler; and, therefore, her testimony is irrelevant.

   Issue: _____

   Author's point of view: _____

   Supporting argument: _____

   _____

   Relevant or Irrelevant? _____

   Explnation: _____

   _____

   _____

2. Jasmine thinks that parents should carefully monitor their children's TV viewing. The next thing you know, those kids won't be able to play outside, either.

(Continued)

FOCUS ON COMPREHENSION: Reading Arguments

Issue: _____

Author's point of view: _____

Supporting argument: _____

_____

    Relevant or irrelevant? _____

Explanation: _____

_____

_____

3.   Mark is against allowing his nieces and nephew to watch violence on television. For one thing, studies have demonstrated that children exposed to violent images have less impulse control than those who are not.

Issue: _____

Author's point of view: _____

Supporting argument: _____

_____

    Relevant or Irrelevant? _____

Explanation: _____

_____

_____

4.   Our founding fathers would never have tolerated the absence of prayer in public schools. They created a nation "under God," so we must abide by their original intentions and make school prayer a law.

Issue: _____

Author's point of view: _____

Supporting arguments: _____

_____

    Relevant or irrelevant? _____

Explanation: _____

_____

_____

5.   Smokers have rights. We have the right to freedom and the right to the pursuit of happiness like everyone else. Those who seek to take away your rights are taking away your liberty. That is un-American.

Issue: _____

Author's point of view: _____

Supporting arguments: _____

_____

Relevant or irrelevant? _____

Explanation: _____

_____

_____

Determining If an Argument Is Strong

To determine if a whole argument is strong, you need to check not only that the supporting arguments relate directly to the author's point of view, but also that they are believable or convincing. If the supporting arguments are relevant and believable, the argument is strong. If the support is not relevant and believable, the argument is not strong (see Figures 7.4 and 7.5).

Sometimes support for an argument is not believable, which leads the reader to question whether the whole argument is sound or believable. If you do not believe what the author is arguing, then the point of view is in question. Consider the example on the next page.

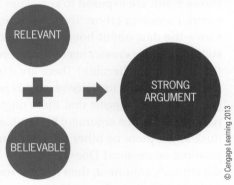

FIGURE 7.4 An Argument Is Strong if the Support Is Relevant and Believable

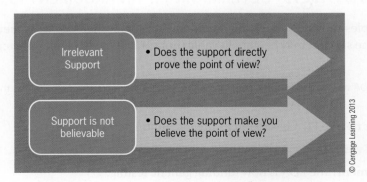

FIGURE 7.5 Relevant and Believable Supporting Arguments

FOCUS ON COMPREHENSION: Reading Arguments

Watching violence creates aggressive behavior in young people, so we should forbid exposure to these media. Studies have shown that teenagers who watch more than one hour of TV per day are far more likely to grow up to commit violent crimes. Some studies indicate that youths who watch up to three hours of TV violence per day were four times more likely to grow up to commit violent crimes than teens who watch less violence while growing up.

> **Point of view:** Watching violence creates aggressive behavior in young people, so we should forbid exposure to these media.
>
> **Supporting Argument 1:** Exposure to more than 1 hour of violent TV a day while growing up increases the chances of a teen committing violent crime when an adult.
>
> **Supporting Argument 2:** Teens who watch 3 hours per day are four times more likely to commit crimes as adults

The author provides a point of view that watching violent movies increases violent behavior in young people, so we should forbid exposure to these influences. In support of this point, the author provides data about how many hours of television shows youth are exposed to correlates to the chances of that teenager growing up to commit a violent crime. The supporting arguments do relate to the author's point of view—the data about hours of watching violence does back up the idea that exposure to violence creates aggression in young people. So the support is relevant. But is the argument believable? There are data that show an increase in aggression resulting from exposure to violence, so this part is reasonable enough. However, the author goes further to suggest that there ought to be no exposure to violence at all. Is this reasonable? Is this argument believable? How are we as a society supposed to enforce this? Might there be other related influences in young people's lives that could also promote aggression? Does the author have a sound argument? If you can question the author's argument, then it is not sound. Remember, the burden of proof is on the author to convince the reader.

Thinking It Through   DETERMINING IF AN ARGUMENT IS STRONG

The following examples provide supporting arguments for the author's point of view that is relevant. However, the support may be unbelievable (not sufficient to convince the reader).

Example 1: The FDA has begun to fund genetic testing for Huntington's disease. Clearly, the FDA has found a cure.

Issue: Whether or not the FDA has found a cure for Huntington's disease

Author's point of view: The FDA has found a cure for Huntington's disease.

Supporting argument: The FDA is now funding genetic testing.

In this example, the author uses the funding of genetic testing as proof that a cure has been found for Huntington's disease, but evidence is not provided to support this claim.

Example 2: Video games must be closely monitored and even censored because of the violence they encourage. The perpetrators of the crime were both adolescents who were known to play video games frequently. Clearly, gaming unleashed their savage impulses as they became desensitized to violence.

Issue: Whether or not video games should be monitored and censored because they encourage violence

Author's point of view: Yes, video games should be monitored and censored.

Supporting arguments: (1) Perpetrators of the crime were adolescents who played video games. (2) Gaming made them savage and desensitized to violence.

In this example, the crime committed by the adolescents was attributed to the video games. The author jumps to a conclusion without proof. The supporting arguments are not believable.

Example 3: We should ban the use of memory-blocking drugs. Ethically, blocking someone's memory equals altering the person's mind. Some argue that memory-blocking pharmaceuticals are useful and humane for people who have suffered post-traumatic stress disorder or who have suffered from the aftermath of a violent crime or similar trauma.

Issue: Whether or not the memory-blocking drugs should be banned

Author's point of view: Yes, the memory-blocking drugs should be banned.

Supporting arguments: (1) Blocking memory alters a person's mind. (2) Some people argue that memory-blocking pharmaceuticals are useful.

The author merely restates the point of view without providing any evidence to support the claim that the drug should be banned. In addition, she contradicts her point of view by including inconsistent reasoning—the point that some people argue that memory-blocking drugs are useful *contradicts* the point of view.

On Your Own DETERMINING IF AN ARGUMENT IS STRONG

For the following examples, map the argument and then decide if the argument is strong. If the support is not relevant or believable, explain why it does not directly back up the point of view.

1. Rap music became popular at the same time things started to go wrong in our cities. Crime rates skyrocketed and drug abuse doubled. If we got rid of rap, our cities would be better and safer.

    Issue: _____

(Continued)

FOCUS ON COMPREHENSION: Reading Arguments

Point of view: _____

Supporting arguments: _____

_____

Explanation: _____

_____

_____

2.   The death penalty is very costly to our society. The Commission estimates the annual costs of the present (death penalty) system to be $137 million per year.

Issue: _____

Point of view: _____

Supporting arguments: _____

_____

Explanation: _____

_____

_____

3.   Yolanda is great at racing cars on Mario Cart. She must be a good driver on our city streets, too. I bet she could drive a motorcycle.

Issue: _____

Point of view: _____

Supporting arguments: _____

_____

Explanation: _____

_____

_____

4.   The social turmoil and decadence in today's society will be our downfall. We have a corrupt government, and money is squandered by the rich.

Issue: _____

Point of view: _____

Supporting arguments: _____

_____

Explanation: _____

_____

_____

5. The death penalty should be abolished in the United States because it's so costly. The average cost of defending a trial in a federal death case is $620,932, about eight times that of a federal murder case in which the death penalty is not sought.

Issue: _____

Point of view: _____

Supporting arguments: _____

_____

Explanation: _____

_____

_____

Author's Credentials _____

To evaluate an argument, you also need to pay attention to who the author is because it can influence your judgment about the argument. Whether or not an author's background, experience, and expertise—the **author's credentials**—lend authority to his or her point of view is an important consideration. The word *credentials* comes from the Latin root, *cred,* which means "believable." As a critical reader, you want to consider if the author is qualified to render a decision on the issue. If the author has authority by virtue of his or her background, experience, or expertise, then this authority lends some weight to the author's point of view and supporting arguments. If the author does not have the background, experience, or expertise to pass judgment on the issue, then this weakens the author's argument. For example, an author with a medical degree would hold more credibility when arguing a medical issue than an author who is simply a medical correspondent for a newspaper.

Intended Audience _____

It is important to consider whom the author has in mind as his or her readers. You can determine the author's **intended audience** by looking at the choice of language and style of writing (level of vocabulary, tone, bias, and loaded language),

FOCUS ON COMPREHENSION: Reading Arguments

as well as the type of publication in which the writing is found and typical readership of that publication (see Figure 7.6). For example, if the reading is from a college-level textbook, the probable intended audience is college students. If the publication is a general U.S. newspaper, the probable audience is the general public. If the publication is an academic journal, the probable audience is those educated in that discipline.

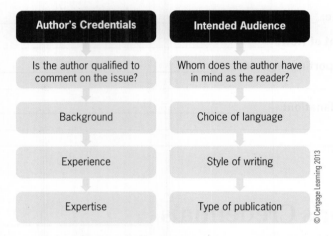

FIGURE 7.6 Determining an Author's Credentials and Intended Audience

Thinking It Through EVALUATING AN ARGUMENT

In this example, you will walk through the complete process for evaluating an argument. Follow along with these steps and see how this argument, which appeared in the legal issues textbook *Law, Politics, and Society*, has been dissected to determine if it is strong.

1. Map the argument.

2. Identify the supporting arguments and what type of support it is: fact, reason, example, testimony, or counterargument.

3. Determine if the supporting arguments are relevant.

4. Determine if the argument is strong.

5. Check the credentials of the author.

6. Determine the intended audience of the argument.

Can Capital Punishment Be an Effective Deterrent?
By Suzanne Samuels

Yes: [1]Many people claim that the fact that the United States continues to have one of the highest per capita rates of homicide in the world is proof that the death penalty does not function effectively as a deterrent. [2]Individual and general deterrence can only work if punishment is swift, certain, and severe, and the practice of capital punishment in the United States meets none of these requirements. Many advocates of capital punishment argue that it could serve as an effective deterrent, if only it were altered to ensure that punishment was both swift and certain. [a]At present, it takes nearly one decade to move through all of the appeals in a capital punishment case. [b]These appeals and this long delay are costly to the state and interfere with the closure that the victim's family needs to move forward. [3]What is needed are more laws like the 1996 Effective Death Penalty and Anti-Terrorist Bill, which requires that appeals in federal death penalty cases be initiated within one year of the sentence. [4]Many states have also passed laws limiting appeals in death penalty cases. [5]These changes in the law increase the chances that capital punishment will be both swift and certain, and thus will function as an effective deterrent in the future.

> **Evaluating the argument:** Has the author proven that the death penalty would be a deterrent if punishment were swift and certain?
>
> **Issue:** Whether or not capital punishment is an effective deterrent
>
> **Point of view:** Capital punishment could be an effective deterrent if punishment were swift and certain.

Supporting arguments:

1. Reason: High homicide rates prove the death penalty does not deter people from committing crime. This statement is not proven by any supporting evidence. There may be other reasons that homicide rates are high—for example, poverty and drug abuse, among others.

2. Reason: People will only be deterred if punishment is swift, certain, and severe.

   a. Fact: It takes decades to move through appeals. Does the fact that it takes decades to move through the appeals process prove that a swift and certain punishment for homicide will work as a deterrent? No, this supporting argument, instead, would back up a statement of the time involved in going through the appeals process only (that it takes decades).

   b. Fact: Appeals cost the state and don't allow "closure." While this may be true, it does not support the point that a swift and certain punishment would deter homicide.

3. Reason: We need more laws like Effective Death Penalty and Anti-Terrorist bill (punishment initiated within 1 year). If the author can prove that swift appeals will ensure that the death penalty is a deterrent to crime, then this point would be effective. However, the author has not yet convinced us that this measure would act as a deterrent.

4. Fact: Many states have passed laws limiting appeals. The author does not provide any evidence that these bills have proven to be effective. It may be a fact that many states

(Continued)

FOCUS ON COMPREHENSION: Reading Arguments

are passing such laws, but how can anyone prove that acts of terrorism (or homicide) are reduced as a result?

5. Reason: These changes increase the likelihood that punishment will be swift and certain and will act as a deterrent. While these legal rulings and bills may increase the likelihood that punishment will be swift and certain, the author has not proven that such bills would act as a deterrent to those contemplating homicide. Furthermore, this argument simply restates the author's point of view.

So, is the argument relevant and strong? No, the author has not proven that swift and certain capital punishment would deter crimes. Since the punishment for capital crimes is neither swift nor certain now, the author cannot hope to prove this conclusion because it hasn't happened. In addition, too many variables are not taken into consideration, such as wrongful convictions, the effects of good versus poor legal representation, and the possibility that rich people can buy better defense.

Author's credentials: This is written by Susan Samuels, who wrote a textbook about legal issues. You can assume she is an authority on legal issues.

Author's intended audience: Since this is from a textbook for college students, the intended audience is college students who are studying criminal justice.

From SAMUELS. *Law, Politics, and Society.* © 2006 Wadsworth, a part of Cengage Learning, Inc. By permission.

On Your Own EVALUATING AN ARGUMENT

Now you will evaluate another argument that appeared in a legal issues textbook, *Law, Politics, and Society*. Follow these steps to dissect this argument to determine if it is strong:

1. Map the argument.
2. Identify the supporting arguments and what type of support it is: fact, reason, example, testimony, or counterargument.
3. Determine if the supporting arguments are relevant.
4. Determine if the argument is strong.
5. Check the credentials of the author.
6. Determine the intended audience of the argument.

Can Capital Punishment Be an Effective Deterrent?
By Suzanne Samuels

No: One of the most often cited arguments in favor of capital punishment is that it deters criminals from committing homicide. In fact, there is little evidence that the threat of capital punishment serves as an effective general deterrent. The "yes" side argues in favor of amending death penalty law to limit appeals and expedite executions, but these changes will increase the chances that an innocent person will be executed. And it is not entirely clear that the public speaks with one voice on this issue—in reality, debate about capital punishment continues to rage in many states, with many opponents calling for an end to its practice. The governors in two states, Maryland and Illinois, have imposed moratoriums on executions, halting them while the states conduct investigations into the prevalence of wrongful convictions and racial bias in the application of capital punishment. We should be skeptical about policy arguments that justify and in fact seek to expedite the use of capital punishment at a time when many abuses and wrongful convictions are beginning to see the light of day.

Issue: _____

Point of view: _____

Supporting arguments:

1. **Counterargument:** _____
_____

2. **Counterargument:** _____
_____

3. **Reason:** _____
_____

4. **Fact:** _____
_____

5. **Reason:** _____
_____

Author's credentials: _____
_____

Author's intended audience: _____
_____

Evaluating the argument: Has the author really proven that the death penalty is an effective deterrent? _____
_____
_____

Practice Exercise 1: RECOGNIZING FACT AND OPINION

For the following statements, identify each as a fact (*F*), opinion (*O*), or a statement that includes both fact and opinion (*F/O*).

(Continued)

FOCUS ON COMPREHENSION: Reading Arguments

____ 1. Elliot Schrage, who oversees Facebook's global communications and public policy strategy, said it was a good thing that young people are thinking about what they put online.

____ 2. But at the same time, companies like Facebook have a financial incentive to get friends to share as much as possible.

____ 3. That's because the more personal the information that Facebook collects, the more valuable the site is to advertisers, who can mine it to serve up more targeted ads.

____ 4. Two weeks ago, Sen. Charles Schumer, D-N.Y., petitioned the Federal Trade Commission to review the privacy policies of social networks to make sure consumers are not being deliberately confused or misled.

____ 5. The action was sparked by a recent change to Facebook's settings that forced its more than 400 million users to choose to "opt out" of sharing private information with third-party websites instead of "opt in," a move which confounded many of them.

____ 6. Andrew Klemperer, a 20-year-old at Georgetown University, said it was a classmate who warned him about the implications of the recent Facebook change—through a status update on (where else?) Facebook.

____ 7. Now he is more diligent in monitoring privacy settings and apt to warn others, too.

____ 8. Helen Nissenbaum, a professor of culture, media and communication at New York University and author of "Privacy in Context," a book about information sharing in the digital age, said teenagers were naturally protective of their privacy as they navigate the path to adulthood, and the frequency with which companies change privacy rules has taught them to be wary.

—Holson, "Tell-all Generation Learns Not To"

Practice Exercise 2: EVALUATING ARGUMENTS

This passage is from *Law, Politics, and Society,* a textbook about criminal justice by Susan Samuels. There is a reference to a Supreme Court case that pertains to diversity in law. *Grutter v. Bollinger* (2003) is a case in which the United States Supreme Court upheld the affirmative action admissions policy of the University of Michigan Law School. Evaluate the argument, following these steps:

1. Map the argument.

2. Identify the supporting arguments and what type of support it is: fact, reason, example, testimony, or counterargument.

3. Determine if the supporting arguments are relevant.

4. Determine if the argument is strong.

5. Check the credentials of the author.

6. Determine the intended audience of the argument.

Is the Lack of Diversity Among Lawyers an Issue That Should Be Aggressively Addressed?

By Susan Samuels

Yes: There is a striking lack of representation among people of color and women in both law schools and in the most prestigious positions in government and private practice. For example, while women are admitted to law schools in roughly the same number as men, people of color continue to be grossly underrepresented. And there are relatively few attorneys of color or women attorneys who are partners in our nation's major law firms or in leadership positions in government practice. Without better representation at the bar, women and people of color cannot fully exercise their influence. This is significant, because they are not fully able to represent their interests or to represent the interests of women or people of color in the judicial or legislative processes. In *Gruter,* a majority of the U.S. Supreme Court justices recognized the importance of all kinds of diversity, including ethnic and racial diversity, in law school classes and on the bar. They noted that law students and lawyers who are exposed to the viewpoints of those who look different have an advantage in litigation, especially given the fact that the U.S. population, and thus its judges and juries, are becoming increasingly diverse. In sum, diversity is good for both lawyers and the larger community.

Practice Exercise 3: EVALUATING ARGUMENTS

This passage is from *Law, Politics, and Society*, a textbook about criminal justice by Susan Samuels. Evaluate the argument, following these steps:

1. Map the argument.

2. Identify in brackets the supporting arguments and what type of support it is: fact, reason, example, testimony, or counterargument.

3. Determine if the supporting arguments are relevant.

(Continued)

FOCUS ON COMPREHENSION: Reading Arguments

4. Determine if the argument is strong.

5. Check the credentials of the author.

6. Determine the intended audience of the argument.

Is the Lack of Diversity Among Lawyers an Issue That Should Be Aggressively Addressed?
By Susan Samuels

No: The American bar is becoming more diverse. Women enter law school at the same rate, or in some places, at higher rates, than their male counterparts. And since 1993, women attorneys and attorneys of color have increased their numbers in large law firms and in partnership positions. The gains are modest but unmistakable. While diversity is an important goal, it makes little sense to pursue this goal at the expense of other, equally important values, among these, being judged on the basis of merit rather than on the color of one's skin or one's gender.

Our culture prizes hard work and motivation, and people have a right to be evaluated on the basis of their achievements. In at least some law schools, there is an assumption that all people of color have been admitted through an affirmative action program and that none of these individuals are qualified. Ultimately, this assumption generates a sense of inferiority and continuing questions about the qualifications of women and people of color pervades both the law school community and the larger community of law firms and legal employers. In this way, affirmative action runs counter to the high value our culture places on individual merit and harms both the individual and the larger society.

APPLICATIONS

These applications will develop your skills of determining important points in an argument, assessing fact and opinion, types of support, and evaluating arguments. Also, you will identify loaded language, tone, and bias in a reading. Follow the instructions for each application, and then answer the Comprehension Check questions. Each application serves to release more responsibility to the reader as these techniques become more automatic.

APPLICATION

This article was first published in *USA Today*, a popular national newspaper. The issue concerns the national crime rankings that list cities in order of crime. In recent years, Detroit, St. Louis, Baltimore, and Camden, New Jersey, have vied for the questionable position as most dangerous city in the United States. The author is a professor of criminology and criminal justice at the University of Missouri–St. Louis. Evaluate the argument, following these steps.

1. Map the argument, underlining the author's point of view and numbering the major supporting arguments.
2. Mark the supporting arguments and what type of support it is: fact, reason, example, testimony, or counterargument.
3. Determine if the supporting arguments are relevant. _____
4. Determine if the argument is strong. _____
5. Check the credentials of the author. _____
6. Determine the intended audience of the argument. _____
_____

After you have done this, answer the Comprehension Check questions that follow.

Why City Crime Rankings Offer a Misleading Picture
By Richard Rosenfeld

1   In a <u>dubious</u> tradition of the season, Americans are being told which of their cities is the "safest" and "most dangerous," according to the latest FBI crime statistics. And once again, cities such as Detroit, St. Louis, Camden, N.J., and others are facing an avalanche of bad publicity.

2   This annual rite would be laughable were it not for the uncritical media attention it <u>garners</u> and the real harm it inflicts on the <u>tarnished</u> cities. This year, the harm stands to grow. Despite pleas from the FBI, the U.S. Conference of Mayors and criminologists, CQ Press published the annual rankings again on Nov. 18. That's unfortunate, because ranking cities by their crime rates is meaningless, damaging and irresponsible.

(Continued)

Here's why:

3   Knowing the city in which a person lives reveals next to nothing about his or her crime risk, especially when compared with genuine risk factors such as age and lifestyle. The young and people who spend their evenings outside of the home are at far greater risk than the elderly and homebodies.

4   The neighborhood you live in also matters. In all cities, serious crime is disproportionately concentrated in a handful of high-risk neighborhoods. Differences in crime rates are far greater within cities than between them. And the rankings give equal weight to crimes of vastly different seriousness and measurement error. People don't want their car stolen, but most people would prefer losing their car to losing their life in a homicide.

5   Cities differ in the degree to which their citizens report crimes. We do not know how much of the difference between any two cities' crime ranks is real and how much reflects measurement error.

"City" vs. "Suburb"

6   Cities also differ in other ways that have nothing to do with their crime risk but can greatly affect their ranking. Pure geographic <u>happenstance</u>—the location of the boundary line separating "city" and "suburb"—is one. Some central cities are geographically small and do not include as many middle-class areas as do larger central cities. If they did, the added population would lower their crime rate.

7   St. Louis, where I live, is less than 62 square miles in a metropolitan area of 3,322 square miles and contains only 13% of the area population. Washington is only 61 square miles in a metropolitan area of 6,509 square miles and contains only 12% of the metro population. In contrast, well over half of the residents in the Memphis metro area live in the central city, which covers about 280 square miles.

Crime Equation

8   A city's crime rate equals the number of crime victims (the numerator) divided by the city population (the denominator). So if a Bethesda, Md., resident is a victim of crime in Washington, he is added to the numerator but not the denominator in calculating Washington's crime rate. This circumstance artificially inflates the crime rate in communities where the central city's population is dwarfed by that of the suburban areas.

9   For all these reasons, if crime rates are to be compared at all, the comparisons should be among metropolitan areas, not central cities. Doing so can change the picture dramatically. St. Louis, second in crime among central cities according to the new city rankings, places 120th in crime among the nation's metropolitan areas.

10   The FBI, which compiles the police data that are misused in crime rankings, has long understood the <u>distortions</u> inherent in comparisons of city crime rates. This year, the FBI has on its website a "Caution Against Ranking." It states: "These rough rankings . . . lead to simplistic and/or incomplete analyses that often create misleading perceptions adversely affecting communities and their residents."

11   The FBI is right. Crime rankings tell us little about how safe we are, but the rankings themselves can hurt. Businesses think twice about relocating to "dangerous" cities. Organizations think twice about holding conventions there. Families think twice about visiting. Suburban residents needlessly fear the city. Crime rankings make no one safer. They should be ignored.

Issue: _____

Point of view: _____

From Richard Rosenfeld, *USA Today* Blog—November 29, 2007, page 11 http://www.usatoday.com/printedition/news/20071129/opcom-wednesday.art.htm, © 2007 *USA Today*. Reprinted with Permission.

COMPREHENSION CHECK

TRUE/FALSE QUESTIONS

For the following statements, write a *T* if the statement is true or an *F* if the statement is false based on the reading.

____ 1. The author feels that publishing city crime rankings is damaging.

____ 2. The author feels that city crime rankings spoil the reputation of certain cities.

____ 3. The author thinks that crime ratings are accurate.

____ 4. The author thinks that crime rankings are misleading.

____ 5. The author blames the American public for the misperception of crime rankings.

LITERAL COMPREHENSION—MULTIPLE CHOICE

Circle the best answer for the following questions.

Understanding Main Ideas

6. What is the author's issue?
    a. Whether or not city crime rankings offer a misleading picture
    b. Whether or not crime rankings are promoted by the FBI
    c. Whether or not crime ranking should not be ignored
    d. Whether or not the FBI is right about crime rankings

7. The author's point of view is
    a. Yes, city crime rankings offer a misleading picture.
    b. Yes, crime rankings are promoted by the FBI.
    c. No, crime ranking should not be ignored.
    d. Yes, the FBI is right about crime rankings.

(Continued)

Understanding Secondary Information and Locating Information

8. Which of the following is not a supporting argument in this reading?

   a. Knowing the city in which a person lives reveals next to nothing about his or her crime risk, especially when compared with genuine risk factors such as age and lifestyle.

   b. The neighborhood you live in also matters in understanding crime ratings.

   c. St. Louis is one of the most dangerous cities in the country, if not the most dangerous.

   d. The FBI, which compiles the police data that are misused in crime rankings, has long understood the distortions inherent in comparisons of city crime rates.

9. Is the following supporting argument a fact or an opinion?

   Cities differ in the degree to which their citizens report crimes.

   a. Fact

   b. Opinion

   c. Both fact and opinion

   d. Neither fact nor opinion

10. Is the following statement a fact or an opinion?

   A city's crime rate equals the number of crime victims (the numerator) divided by the city population (the denominator).

   a. Fact

   b. Opinion

   c. Both fact and opinion

   d. Neither fact nor opinion

11. Is this statement a fact or an opinion?

   For all these reasons, if crime rates are to be compared at all, the comparisons should be among metropolitan areas, not central cities.

   a. Fact

   b. Opinion

   c. Both fact and opinion

   d. Neither fact nor opinion

INFERENTIAL COMPREHENSION—MULTIPLE CHOICE

Circle the best answer for the following questions.

Making Inferences

12. What is the tone in this reading?
    a. Sentimental
    b. Annoyed
    c. Hopeless
    d. Sad

13. Is the author biased?
    a. Yes
    b. No
    c. Hard to tell
    d. Both biased and unbiased

14. Who is the intended audience?
    a. The general public
    b. The FBI
    c. CQ Press
    d. College students/criminal justice students

15. Which of the following words is not an example of loaded language from paragraphs 1 and 2?
    a. Dubious
    b. Tarnished
    c. Garners
    d. Meaningless

16. This reading has support that is mainly
    a. Facts and reasons.
    b. Reasons and counterarguments.
    c. Testimony and facts.
    d. Counterarguments and examples.

(Continued)

INCREASE YOUR COLLEGE-LEVEL VOCABULARY

Determine the meaning of these words from context or look them up in a dictionary. The words are underlined in the text. Next to the words, write the definition and whether or not the word is an example of loaded language.

1. Dubious: _____

2. Garners: _____

3. Tarnished: _____

4. Happenstance: _____

5. Distortions: _____

SHORT-ANSWER QUESTIONS

17. What is the author's purpose in writing this piece? How do you know? Be specific.

18. Describe the author's intended audience? How do you know? Be specific.

19. What is the author's tone in the passage? Provide examples directly from the text of language that demonstrate tone.

20. Locate your city or a city with which you are familiar in Table 7.5. What is your experience with that city? Is it as dangerous as it is supposed to be? Explain your answer.

TABLE 7.5 2010 CITY CRIME RATE RANKINGS*

RANK CITY	SCORE
1. St. Louis, MO	381.62
2. Camden, NJ	374.33
3. Detroit, MI	356.44
4. Flint, MI	310.31
5. Oakland, CA	308.29
6. Richmond, CA	287.15

TABLE 7.5 2010 CITY CRIME RATE RANKINGS*

RANK CITY	SCORE
7. Cleveland, OH	260.60
8. Compton, CA	260.13
9. Gary, IN	250.48
10. Birmingham, AL	244.83
12. Memphis, TN	236.32
13. New Orleans, LA	226.95
14. Jackson, MS	218.91
15. Little Rock, AR	213.99
16. Baton Rouge, LA	205.59
17. Buffalo, NY	202.43
18. New Haven, CT	196.86
19. Hartford, CT	192.15
20. Dayton, OH	191.14
21. Kansas City, MO	186.01

Source: CQ Press using reported data from the FBI, "Crime in the United States 2009." Copyright © 2010 CQ Press, a division of SAGE Publications, Inc. The study assigns a crime score to each city, with zero representing the national average.

*Includes murder, rape, robbery, aggravated assault, burglary, and motor vehicle theft.

21. Do you think crime rankings provide any useful function? State your point of view, and support it with three relevant arguments.
22. Would you choose against living in or visiting a city because of its high crime ranking? Explain your answer.
23. Are you surprised by any of the rankings? Choose three rankings, and explain your answer.

APPLICATION ②

This passage is from *Law, Politics, and Society,* a textbook about criminal justice by Susan Samuels. Samuels presents a pro (yes) and con (no) written debate about whether or not the Department of Homeland Security terror alert codes make us safer (see Figure 7.7). Evaluate each argument, following these steps:

1. Map the argument, underlining the author's point of view and numbering the major supporting arguments.
2. Mark the supporting arguments and what type of support it is: fact, reason, example, testimony, or counter argument.
3. Determine if the supporting arguments are relevant. _____
4. Determine if the argument is strong. _____

   _____
5. Check the credentials of the author. _____
6. Determine the intended audience of the argument. _____

After you have done this, answer the Comprehension Check questions that follow.

FIGURE 7.7 The Homeland Security Advisory System

Do the Department of Homeland Security Terror Alert Codes Make Us Safer?

By Susan Samuels

Pro

Yes: The Color-Coded Threat Level System provides much-needed information to the public and to law enforcement and safety personnel about existing security threats. The Department of Homeland Security maintains this system, which grades the risk from low to severe, with corresponding color codes. Law enforcement and public safety officers all over the United States can use this code to gauge the terror threat and can know exactly when they should activate different plans to combat terrorism or respond to a specific threat. The goal of this system is to make security alerts uniform and to fully apprise public officials about ongoing terrorist activities. This color-coded system is intended to be used with the Homeland Security Threat Advisory, which provides specific warnings to officials who need this information to combat known threats to national security. In short, this system makes us safer by providing standardized information about terror threats to the people who need it most—law enforcement and safety officers on the front lines in the battle against terrorism.

Issue: _____

_____

Point of view: _____

_____

COMPREHENSION CHECK

TRUE/FALSE QUESTIONS

For the following statements, write a *T* if the statement is true or an *F* if the statement is false based on the reading.

____ 1. The color-coded threat level system grades the risk from low to severe, with corresponding color codes.

____ 2. The general public can use this code to gauge the terror threat.

____ 3. The Color-Coded Threat Level System provides much-needed information to the public and to law enforcement and safety personnel.

____ 4. The goal of this system is to make security alerts uniform and to fully apprise the public about ongoing terrorist activities.

____ 5. The author is against using the Color-Coded Threat Level System.

(Continued)

LITERAL COMPREHENSION—MULTIPLE CHOICE

Circle the best answer for the following questions.

Understanding Main Ideas

6. The issue is
   a. Whether or not the public needs the color-coded threat level system to gauge the terror threat.
   b. Whether or not law enforcement needs the color-coded threat level system to gauge the terror threat.
   c. Whether or not the Department of Homeland Security terror alert codes make us safer.
   d. Whether or not the color-coded threat level system needs upgrading.

7. The author's point of view is
   a. Yes, the public needs the color-coded threat level system to gauge the terror threat.
   b. Yes, law enforcement needs the color-coded threat level system to gauge the terror threat.
   c. Yes, the Department of Homeland Security terror alert codes make us safer.
   d. No, the color-coded threat level system does not need upgrading.

Understanding Secondary Information and Locating Information

8. Which of the following is not a supporting argument in this reading?
   a. The Department of Homeland Security maintains this system, which grades the risk from low to severe, with corresponding color codes.
   b. Law enforcement and public safety officers all over the United States can use this code to gauge the terror threat and can know exactly when they should activate different plans to combat terrorism or respond to a specific threat.
   c. The goal of this system is to make security alerts uniform and to fully apprise public officials about ongoing terrorist activities.
   d. This system makes us safer by providing standardized information about terror threats to the people who need it most—law enforcement and safety officers on the front lines in the battle against terrorism.

9. Is the following supporting argument a fact or an opinion?

   The Department of Homeland Security maintains this system, which grades the risk from low to severe, with corresponding color codes.

a. Fact

b. Opinion

c. Both fact and opinion

d. Neither fact nor opinion

10. Is the following statement a fact or an opinion?

This system makes us safer by providing standardized information about terror threats to the people who need it most—law enforcement and safety officers on the front lines in the battle against terrorism.

a. Fact

b. Opinion

c. Both fact and opinion

d. Neither fact nor opinion

INFERENTIAL COMPREHENSION—MULTIPLE CHOICE

Circle the best answer for the following questions.

Making Inferences

11. What is the tone in this reading?

a. Serious

b. Annoyed

c. Frustrated

d. Angry

12. Is the author biased?

a. Yes

b. No

c. Hard to tell

d. Both biased and unbiased

13. Who is the intended audience?

a. The general public

b. Homeland Security officers

c. Those in government

d. College students/criminal justice students

(Continued)

14. Assuming this is a weak argument, which of the following reasons would apply?

    a. Arguments 3 and 4 say the same thing in different words as argument 2.

    b. The author is not a credible source.

    c. The tone is too serious.

    d. The point of view is not relevant.

15. This reading has support that is mainly

    a. Fact.

    b. Reasons.

    c. Testimony.

    d. Counterargument.

Do the Department of Homeland Security Terror Alert Codes Make Us Safer?

By Susan Samuels

Con

No: This system does not make us safer—it provides little in the way of information to either the public or to law enforcement and safety personnel. The five levels, ranging in color from green (low risk of terrorist activity) to red (severe risk of terrorist activity) are not specific enough to apprise the public of actual threats. For example, what is the real difference between a guarded risk of attack and a significant risk of attack? And how is the public to really understand these differences? We have been on and off the yellow/orange alerts (elevated risk of attack/high risk of attack), but no one has ever clarified why we moved between levels. In fact, we moved to the lower level directly *after* the presidential election in November 2004, prompting some to say that the higher alert might have been used for political reasons—that is, to keep the threat of terror high on the public's agenda and thus convince the public of the need to reelect the president. Perhaps even more troubling than this lack of clarity is the fact that these terror alerts may themselves make the public more afraid and thus more vulnerable to being terrorized. In the absence of clear evidence about why the alert has been raised, the American public may feel as if there is information that they simply are not getting that underscores some real and serious threat to them specifically. The accompanying fear actually serves the terrorists' goals very well—it makes us fear that we are not safe in our country and that the next attack is imminent. It is hard to go about your business when you are waiting for the next attack, and the alerts increase this sense of vulnerability without providing any real information about the actual threat.

Issue: _____

_____

Point of view: _____

_____

_____

From SAMUELS. *Law, Politics, and Society.* © 2006 Wadsworth, a part of Cengage Learning, Inc. By permission.

COMPREHENSION CHECK

TRUE/FALSE QUESTIONS

For the following statements, write a *T* if the statement is true or an *F* if the statement is false based on the reading.

____ 1. The five levels, ranging in color from green (low risk of terrorist activity) to red (severe risk of terrorist activity) are not specific enough to apprise the public of actual threats.

____ 2. We have been on and off the yellow/orange alerts (elevated risk of attack/high risk of attack), but no one has ever clarified why we moved between levels.

____ 3. We moved to the lower level directly *before* the presidential election in November 2004.

____ 4. Some people feel that the fact that the alert level moved to a lower level after the presidential election (and was higher during the election) was to keep the threat of terror high on the public's agenda and thus convince the public of the need to reelect President Bush.

____ 5. The author is opposed to the idea that Homeland Security terror alert codes make us safer.

LITERAL COMPREHENSION—MULTIPLE CHOICE

Circle the best answer for the following questions.

Understanding Main Ideas

6. The issue is

   a. Whether or not the public needs the color-coded threat level system to gauge the terror threat.

   b. Whether or not law enforcement needs the color-coded threat level system to gauge the terror threat.

   c. Whether or not the Department of Homeland Security terror alert codes make us safer.

   d. Whether or not the color-coded threat level system needs upgrading.

(Continued)

7. The author's point of view is
   a. No, the public needs the color-coded threat level system to gauge the terror threat.
   b. No, law enforcement needs the color-coded threat level system to gauge the terror threat.
   c. No, the Department of Homeland Security terror alert codes do not make us safer.
   d. Yes, the color-coded threat level system does need upgrading.

Understanding Secondary Information and Locating Information

8. Which of the following is not a supporting argument in this reading?
   a. The five levels, ranging in color from green (low risk of terrorist activity) to red (severe risk of terrorist activity), are not specific enough to apprise the public of actual threats.
   b. We have been on and off the yellow/orange alerts (elevated risk of attack/high risk of attack), but no one has ever clarified why we moved between levels.
   c. Perhaps even more troubling than this lack of clarity is the fact that these terror alerts may themselves make the public more afraid and thus more vulnerable to being terrorized.
   d. This system does not make us safer—it provides little in the way of information to either the public or law enforcement and safety personnel.

9. Is the following supporting argument a fact or an opinion?

   The five levels, ranging in color from green (low risk of terrorist activity) to red (severe risk of terrorist activity) are not specific enough to apprise the public of actual threats.

   a. Fact
   b. Opinion
   c. Both fact and opinion
   d. Neither fact nor opinion

10. Is the following statement a fact or an opinion?

   Perhaps even more troubling than this lack of clarity is the fact that these terror alerts may themselves make the public more afraid and thus more vulnerable to being terrorized.

   a. Fact
   b. Opinion
   c. Both fact and opinion
   d. Neither fact nor opinion

11. **Is this statement fact or opinion?**

> It is hard to go about your business when you are waiting for the next attack, and the alerts increase this sense of vulnerability without providing any real information about the actual threat.

a. Fact

b. Opinion

c. Both fact and opinion

d. Neither fact nor opinion

INFERENTIAL COMPREHENSION—MULTIPLE CHOICE

Circle the best answer for the following questions.

Making Inferences

12. What is the tone in this reading?

a. Serious

b. Annoyed

c. Frustrated

d. Angry

13. Is the author biased?

a. Yes

b. No

c. Hard to tell

d. Both biased and unbiased

14. Who is the intended audience?

a. The general public

b. Homeland Security officers

c. Those in government

d. College students/criminal justice students

15. This reading has support that is mainly

a. Fact.

b. Reasons.

c. Testimony.

d. Counterargument.

(Continued)

INCREASE YOUR COLLEGE-LEVEL VOCABULARY

For the following phrases or sentences from the readings in Application 2, determine if the language used indicates a biased point of view. Next, determine the author's tone based on her choice of language.

PHRASE/SENTENCE	BIASED	TONE
16. much-needed information		
17. The Department of Homeland Security maintains this system, which grades the risk from low to severe, with corresponding color codes.		
18. The goal of this system is to make security alerts uniform and to fully apprise public officials about ongoing terrorist activities.		
18. Perhaps even more troubling than this lack of clarity is the fact that these terror alerts may themselves make the public more afraid and thus more vulnerable to being terrorized.		
20. The five levels, ranging in color from green (low risk of terrorist activity) to red (severe risk of terrorist activity), are not specific enough to apprise the public of actual threats.		
21. It is hard to go about your business when you are waiting for the next attack.		

SHORT-ANSWER QUESTIONS

22. Which of the arguments on the effectiveness of Homeland Security codes do you think is most convincing? Provide examples for your opinion.

23. Which of the arguments is the strongest? Provide specific reasons for your point of view.

24. Choose two arguments from one of the readings, and write a passage counterarguing them. Make sure to specifically address the errors in reasoning.

25. Invent a system of alerting the public and officials about terrorism that is different from the color code system. Outline your system, and explain why it would be effective.

WRAPPING IT UP

STUDY OUTLINE

In the following study outline, fill in the definitions and a brief explanation of the key terms in the Your Notes column. Use the strategy of spaced practice to review these key terms on a regular basis. Use this study guide to review this chapter's key topics.

KEY TERM	YOUR NOTES
Critical thinking	
Critical reader	
Analyzing	
Synthesizing	
Evaluating	
Bias	
Tone	
Connotation	
Loaded language	

(Continued)

WRAPPING IT UP

KEY TERM	YOUR NOTES
Argument	
Issue	
Point of view	
Supporting arguments	
Map the argument	
Fact	
Opinion	
Value judgment	
Reasons	
Examples	
Testimony	

KEY TERM	YOUR NOTES
Counterargument	
Relevant	
Author's credentials	
Intended audience	

WHAT DID YOU LEARN?

Jot down some facts you learned about controversial issues in the media today.

1 _____

2 _____

3 _____

4 _____

5 _____

6 _____

7 _____

8 _____

9 _____

10 _____

WRAPPING IT UP

GROUP ACTIVITY: DEBATING CONTROVERSIAL ISSUES

Choose one of the issues in this chapter, or decide on another one. Divide into teams and have one team argue in favor (pro) of the issue. Have the second team argue against (con) on the issue. Make sure to observe these rules for debating:

1. Work as a team to prove your point of view.
2. Allow each individual a chance to make his or her point in the debate.
3. Always practice respectful interpersonal communication.
4. Write down points you want to make to counterargue an opponent rather than interrupt him or her.
5. Have fun—debates can become impassioned; and while you want to be enthusiastic about your opinion or point of view, you also need to keep it in perspective as a critical thinking exercise.

QUESTIONS FOR WRITING, DISCUSSION, OR REFLECTION

1. Research a controversial issue of your choice. Take a position and construct a strong argument to support your point of view.
2. Choose a textbook you use for another class or a magazine or news editorial. Find five examples of loaded language. Explain how these examples demonstrate an author's tone and bias.
3. Take a position on one of the issues in this chapter and outline your major arguments.

POST-ASSESSMENT

This assessment will help you understand your strengths and weaknesses in learning, understanding, and applying the skills and strategies discussed in this chapter. Preview the following article. Then read it all the way through and answer the Comprehension Check questions that follow.

Coloring the News: Is the Information Provided by the Media Biased?
By Rudolph F. Verderber, Kathleen S. Verderber,
and Deanna D. Sellnow

1   When you watch a newscast or read an online news article, do you expect the information you receive to be objective and reported without any kind of bias? Or do you assume that all news is biased in some way? Or do you assume bias only from certain sources, such as FOX News or MSNBC, which have both been accused of, respectively, a conservative and a liberal bias.

2   What makes us think that the news we receive is biased or unbiased? One of the factors is presentation. One journalist who personifies a professional, unbiased delivery—even almost thirty years after his final broadcast as a news anchor—is Walter Cronkite. Cronkite anchored and reported for the *CBS Evening News* from 1962 to 1981 and was so admired and respected that he was named "the most trusted man in America" in a 1972 poll. He delivered the news in a calm, straight forward manner no matter what he was reporting, betraying emotion only rarely, such as when he announced the death of President John F. Kennedy. He also took pains to ensure that he would be clearly understood by listeners, training himself to speak 124 words per minute, which is 40 words per minute slower than the average American speaks. And he always made it very clear when he was veering from reporting the news to expressing an opinion. A tireless advocate of objective journalism, he once said, "[The journalist's] job is only to hold up the mirror—to tell and show the public what has happened."

3   Contrast this image of responsible, reliable reporting with the information we receive from many cable TV news programs today. In an effort to fulfill cable TV's demand for 24-hour-a-day programming, even respected news organizations such as CNN must present not only the "hard news" but also news analysis, sensational graphics, and chitchat among program hosts. As a result, the news many people watch blurs the lines between opinion, entertainment, and the straight forward presentation of facts. In addition, some cable news anchors and show hosts have become the subject of controversy for their on-air rants, partisan attacks, and melodramatic grandstanding, including Bill O'Reilly, Keith Olbermann, and Geraldo Rivera—all of whom are reporters who were trained in the principles of fair reporting.

4   Another factor that makes us suspect the information in news reports is biased is how events are covered. News coverage during presidential campaigns tends to generate a lot

(Continued)

of interest and analysis. During the 2008 presidential race, some charged the media was showing bias in support of Democratic candidate Barack Obama. *The Washington Post's* Deborah Howell (2008) reported that during the first week of June 2008, Obama dominated political stories by 142 to Republican candidate John McCain's 96, a 3-to-1 advantage. Although she acknowledged that numbers weren't everything and that Obama generated a lot of coverage because he was the first African American nominee and initially less well-known than McCain, she argued that readers deserved comparable coverage of both candidates.

5   Nonetheless, there is little consensus in the debate over media bias. People disagree not only about the issue of bias itself, but also about how to determine if there is bias, or if such a determination is even possible. For example, expert statistical analysis of media bias, such as *A Measure of Media Bias* by Tim Groseclose and Jeffrey Milyo, has been disputed by other experts who believed there were faults in this study's research methods. And *Scientific American's* Vivian B. Martin (2008) writes, "Most media scholars do not think the issue of bias can be settled by a formula."

6   Whatever your thoughts about media bias, you'll be a better-informed consumer if you learn how to evaluate news source bias critically. Fairness and Accuracy in Reporting (FAIR) provides a helpful list of factors that can contribute to bias in news reporting:

- Corporate ownership
- Advertiser influence
- Official agendas
- Telecommunications policy
- The public relations industry
- Pressure groups
- The narrow range of debate
- Censorship
- Sensationalism

7   FAIR also recommends asking the following critical questions when evaluating news information:

- Who are the sources?
- Is there a lack of diversity?
- From whose point of view is the news reported?
- Are there double standards?
- What are the unchallenged assumptions?
- Is the language loaded?
- Is there a lack of context?
- Do the headlines and stories match?
- Are stories on important issues featured prominently?

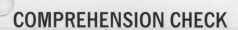

COMPREHENSION CHECK

Circle the best answer to the questions based on information from the reading.

1 **What is the issue discussed in this passage?**

A. Whether or not the information provided by the media is accurate

B. Whether or not the information provided by the media is biased

C. Whether or not the information provided by the media is relevant

2 **What is the author's point of view on this issue?**

A. Yes, the information provided by the media is accurate.

B. Yes, the information provided by the media is biased.

C. The author presents both sides of the issue but does not take a position.

3 **Which of the following is not a major supporting argument regarding how to tell if the media is biased?**

A. One of the factors is presentation. Look at how the news is reported.

B. Today, the news many people watch blurs the lines between opinion, entertainment, and the straight forward presentation of facts.

C. The *Washington Post's* Deborah Howell (2008) reported that during the first week of June 2008, Obama dominated political stories by 142 to Republican candidate John McCain's 96, a 3-to-1 advantage.

4 **What is the author's tone in this reading?**

A. Angry

B. Objective

C. Humorous

5 **Is this statement from the reading a fact or an opinion?**

One journalist who personifies a professional, unbiased delivery—even almost thirty years after his final broadcast as a news anchor—is Walter Cronkite.

A. Fact

B. Opinion

(Continued)

6 **Is this statement from the reading a fact or an opinion?**

[E]xpert statistical analysis of media bias, such as *A Measure of Media Bias* by Tim Groseclose and Jeffrey Milyo, has been disputed by other experts who believed there were faults in this study's research methods.

A. Fact
B. Opinion

7 **What type of support is used in this reading?**

A. Facts and statistics
B. Facts, reasons, and testimony
C. Examples and statistics

8 **Are the authors credible?**

A. Yes
B. No

9 **Who is the intended audience?**

A. The press
B. The celebrities who are hounded
C. College students

10 **What word in the following sentence indicates biased language?**

A tireless advocate of objective journalism, he once said, "[The journalist's] job is only to hold up the mirror—to tell and show the public what has happened."

A. Objective
B. Journalism
C. Tireless
D. Mirror

OBJECTIVES

This application includes a full textbook chapter from a communications textbook, *Communicate!* by Rudolph F. Verderber, Kathleen S. Verderber, and Deanna D. Sellnow. In this application, you will focus on transferring your reading and study skills to a college-level textbook chapter by:

- **Applying what you've learned to the chapter**
  - Eight Steps to Approaching Textbook Reading
- **Understanding Test-Taking Strategies: Taking Subjective Tests**
  - Question-Answer Relationships
  - Taking Short Answer and Essay Tests
  - Overcoming Test Anxiety

APPLYING WHAT YOU HAVE LEARNED TO A FULL-LENGTH TEXTBOOK CHAPTER

"Chapter 3: Communicating Verbally" from *Communicate!* by Rudolph F. Verderber, Kathleen S. Verderber, and Deanna D. Sellnow

In all the chapters of this book, you have learned about successful college reading and note taking. Now, you will practice transferring these skills to a real college textbook chapter, unedited and uncut. This may seem a daunting task, but you will find the content of this chapter to be interesting and not as hard as you may think. The trick is to look at the sections in the text logically and to use what you have learned.

This chapter has two major subsections. Here is an outline of major headings and subheadings. Carefully review this outline because it will form the basis for your questioning and note taking as you make your way through the chapter.

The Nature and Purposes of Language

   Purposes of Language

   The Relationship Between Language and Meaning

   Cultural and Gender Influences on Language Use

Improving Language Skills

   Use Clear Language

   Use Language That Makes Your Messages Memorable

   Use Linguistic Sensitivity

EIGHT STEPS TO APPROACHING THIS TEXTBOOK READING

This application describes eight steps to approaching a textbook chapter. However, the purpose of this application is to make you a better college reader and student. So, you must *transfer* these steps to your other college textbook reading assignments. Remember to apply the reading process (before, during, and after reading strategies) you learned in Chapter 1. Make sure to read for topic, main ideas, and supporting details as reflected in the author's pattern of organization. The first Textbook Application worked through eight steps for reading a college textbook chapter. Now you will expand on that process by adding further skills and strategies you have learned. There are still eight steps, but these steps are expanded and developed to make your reading and comprehension of textbook chapters even better. Once you're ready, follow these steps in approaching this Textbook Application chapter:

Step 1: Survey the chapter, paying special attention to the textbook features. To survey a reading, do the following:

1. Read the title and ask yourself, "What is the reading about?" This helps you determine the topic of the chapter.

2. Ask yourself, "What do I already know about this topic?" Jot down some main points, or discuss them with a partner. This step is important because you are activating your prior knowledge to prepare your memory to accept new information on the topic. So, don't skip this part!

3. Predict what you think the reading will cover.

4. Flip through the reading and read headings, captions, and look at the diagrams or pictures.

5. Turn the title and headings into questions to hone in on content and organization, or use the chapter objectives at the beginning and turn them into question form to guide your reading.

6. Scan for words you don't know and circle them.

7. Repeat step 3. What do you *now* think the reading will cover?

Step 2: Read the chapter objectives at the beginning of the chapter carefully— these are the key areas you will learn about. Additionally, notice the major headings and subheadings and their relationship to the objectives.

Step 3: Turn these objectives into questions to focus your reading. The objectives will correspond with the headings and subheadings in the chapter. Here is a list of headings and subheadings of "Communicating Verbally." Convert the headings into questions.

THE HEADINGS AND SUBHEADINGS	THE HEADINGS AND SUBHEADINGS TURNED INTO QUESTION FORMAT
The Nature and Purposes of Language	
Purposes of Language	
The Relationship Between Language and Meaning	
Cultural and Gender Influences on Language Use	
Improving Language Skills	
Use Clear Language	
Use Language That Makes Your Messages Memorable	
Use Linguistic Sensitivity	

Step 4: Read each section first, looking for the answers to the questions you created from the headings, or looking for the answers to the objectives posed as questions.

Step 5: As you read, answer the questions posed by your objective questions or guide questions in your notebook. Read each section first, and then mark the text. Review Chapter 6 about text marking and annotation as well as note taking strategies if you need to. Remember, circle concepts or definitions, underline main ideas, enumerate major supporting details, and lowercase-alphabetize minor supporting details.

As you read, take notes, writing down major points for each major section and minor section, based on your text marking. (Answer the questions you created when you turned headings and subheadings into questions so you hone in on major points.) You can use an outline, double-column note, or web format for your notes, based on the degree of detail the passage contains and based on the pattern of organization of that section.

Step 6: When you surveyed the reading, you circled words that are unknown to you. However, in addition, circle any vocabulary that is unfamiliar as you read, and use context clues or word part clues or marginal definitions to help you make a guess as to the word's meaning.

Create vocabulary flash cards for each definition, as you learned in Chapter 6. Also, to understand language in the reading itself, make sure to apply all the vocabulary strategies you have learned in this text: use context clues; use word part clues; look for transition words and phrases; use the dictionary if necessary; and consider tone, bias, and loaded language.

Step 7: Rewrite notes.

1. Using the notes you created when you marked the text from Step 5 and referring to the textbook chapter again, identify the following on a separate piece of paper for each subsection:

   - What is the nature and what are the purposes of language?

   - What are the purposes of language?

   - What is the relationship between language and meaning?

   - What are cultural and gender influences on language use?

   - How do you improve language skills?

   - How do you use clear language?

   - How do you use language that makes your messages memorable?

   - How do you use linguistic sensitivity?

2. Refer to the Learning Objectives at the beginning of the chapter. Can you answer these questions? Questions such as these are great hints as to the types of essay questions you may be asked on a test!

   a. What are the purposes of language?

   b. What is the relationship between language and meaning?

   c. How do culture and gender affect language use?

   d. How can you make your language more clear?

   e. How can you make your messages more memorable?

   f. What can you do to ensure your listener will understand the words you choose?

   g. How can you phrase messages to demonstrate linguistic sensitivity?

Step 8: Take a test. Based on your careful reading and note taking of the chapter, prepare to take a short-answer and essay test on the information. You'll learn more about test taking after you've read the textbook chapter. Make sure to study the section on short-answer and essay test taking to hone your skills.

Communicating Verbally

Questions you'll be able to answer after reading this chapter:

- What are the purposes of language?
- What is the relationship between language and meaning?
- How do culture and gender affect language use?
- How can you make your language more clear?
- How can you make your messages more memorable?
- What can you do to ensure your listener will understand the words you choose?
- How can you phrase messages to demonstrate linguistic sensitivity?

Donna approached her friend Mary and said, "Ed and I are having a really tough time."

"I'm sorry to hear that," replied Mary. "What's happening?"

"Well, you know, it's just the way he acts."

"Is he being abusive?"

"Uh, no—it's not that. I just can't seem to figure him out."

"Well, is it what he says?"

"No, it's more what he doesn't say."

"What do you mean 'what he doesn't say'?"

"You know, he comes home and I ask him where he's been."

"And . . . ?"

"He says he was working overtime."

"And you don't believe him?"

"No, I believe him. It's just that he's working so much, I'm starting to feel lonely."

"Have you talked with him about this?"

"No, I don't know how to say it, and I don't think he'd understand me."

Given what Donna has said and the way she has said it, would you understand? Sometimes, for a variety of reasons, the way we form our messages makes it difficult for others to understand. Sometimes the problem is what we say; other times it's how we say it.

As Thomas Holtgraves (2002), a leading scholar in language use, reminds us, "Language is one of those things that we often take for granted" (p. 8). Yet we could all improve our use of language. In this chapter, we discuss the nature of and purposes for language and improving our verbal language skills.

The Nature and Purposes of Language

Language is both a body of symbols (most commonly words) and the systems for their use in messages that are common to the people of the same speech community.

A **speech community**, also called a language community, is a group of people who speak the same language. There are between 3,000 and 4,000 speech communities in the world. Around 60 percent of the world's speech communities have fewer than 10,000 speakers. The five largest speech communities, in order, are Mandarin Chinese, Spanish, English, Arabic, and Hindi (World Almanac, 2007).

Words are symbols used by a speech community to represent objects, ideas, and feelings. [1]Although the word used to represent a particular object or idea varies from language to language, for a word to be a symbol all the members of the speech community must recognize it as standing for the same object, idea, or feeling. [2]Different speech communities use different word symbols for the same phenomenon. For example, the season for planting is called *spring* in English-speaking communities but *printemps* in French-speaking communities.

Speech communities also vary in how they put words together to form messages. The structure a message takes depends on the rules of grammar and syntax that have evolved in a particular speech community. For example, in English a sentence must have at least a subject (a noun or pronoun) and a predicate (a

language

a body of symbols (most commonly words) and the systems for their use in messages that are common to the people of the same speech community.

speech community

a group of people who speak the same language (also called a language community).

words

symbols used by a speech community to represent objects, ideas, and feelings.

verb). To make a statement in English, the subject is placed before the predicate. In Mandarin Chinese, however, an idea is usually expressed with a verb and a complement (which is rarely a noun and usually another verb or an adjective).

Language affects how people think and what they pay attention to. This concept is called the Sapir–Whorf hypothesis, named after two theorists, Edward Sapir and Benjamin Lee Whorf (Littlejohn & Foss, 2008). [2]Language allows us to perceive certain aspects of the world by naming them and allows us to ignore other parts of the world by not naming them. For instance, if you work in a job such as fashion or interior design that deals with many different words for color distinctions, you will be able to perceive finer differences in color. Knowing various words for shades of white, such as ecru, eggshell, cream, ivory, pearl, bone china white, and antique white, actually helps you see differences in shades of white. [3]Similarly, there are concepts that people do not fully perceive until a word is coined to describe them. Think of words added to American English vocabulary in the last few years such as google, texting, couch potato, or mouse potato. The behaviors to which those words refer certainly existed before the terms were coined. But as a society, we did not collectively perceive these behaviors until language allowed us to name them.

Ulrich Niehoff/imagebroker/Alamy

Today we know what a *couch potato* is, but that was not the case 30 years ago.

Purposes of Language

Although language communities vary in the words they use and in their grammar and syntax systems, all languages serve the same purposes.

1. We use language to designate, label, define, and limit. So, when we identify music as "punk," we are differentiating it from other music labeled rap, rock, pop, indie, country, or R&B.
2. We use language to evaluate. Through language we convey positive or negative attitudes toward our subject. For instance, if you see Hal taking more time than others to make a decision, you could describe Hal positively as "thoughtful" or negatively as "dawdling." Or you might describe a comedy like the movie *Superbad* positively as "hilarious" or negatively as "vulgar." Kenneth Burke (1968), a prominent language theorist, describes this as the power of language to emphasize hierarchy and control. Because language allows us to compare things, we tend to judge them as better or worse, which leads to social hierarchy or a pecking order. Certainly, programs like *What Not to Wear* and *Flip This House* use language to suggest how to judge certain looks as better or worse.
3. We use language to discuss things outside our immediate experience. Language lets us talk about ourselves, learn from others' experiences,

What are the purposes of language?

Sapir–Whorf hypothesis
a theory claiming that language influences perception.

share a common heritage, talk about past and future events, and communicate about people and things that are not present. Through language, we can discuss where we hope to be in five years, where we plan to go for spring break, or learn about the history that shapes the world we live in. If you ever watch television programs on the discovery channel, you are learning from things outside your own experiences.

4. We use language to talk about language. We also use language to communicate about how we are communicating. For instance, if your friend said she would see you "this afternoon," but she didn't arrive until 5 o'clock, and you ask her where she's been, the two of you are likely to discuss your communication and the different interpretations you each bring to the phrase "this afternoon." You might also relate to this if you've ever had a professor tell you an assignment is due "next week," and then asks for it first thing Monday morning with a comment that she "will not accept late papers."

The Relationship Between Language and Meaning

On the surface, the relationship between language and meaning seems perfectly clear: We select the correct words, structure them using the rules of syntax and grammar agreed upon by our speech community, and people will interpret our meanings correctly. In fact, the relationship between language and meaning is not nearly so simple for five reasons.

What is the relationship between language and meaning?

First, the meaning of words is in people, not in the words themselves. If Juan says to Julia that the restaurant is expensive, each of them probably has a different meaning of the word *expensive*. Maybe Juan thinks one meal will cost $40, whereas for Julia, *expensive* might mean a $20 meal. All words, especially abstract ones, have multiple meanings depending on who is using them and who is hearing them. What does *expensive* mean to you?

a   2Second, words have two levels of meaning: denotation and connotation. Denotation is the direct, explicit meaning a speech community formally gives a word—it is the meaning found in a dictionary. Different dictionaries may define words in slightly different ways. For instance, the *Encarta World English Dictionary* defines *bawdy* as "ribald in a frank, humorous, often crude way," and the *Cambridge American English Dictionary* defines *bawdy* as "containing humorous remarks about sex." Similar? Yes, but not the same. Not only that, but many words have multiple definitions. For instance, the *Random House Dictionary of the English Language* lists 23 definitions for the word *great*. Connotation, the   b feelings or evaluations we associate with a word, may be even more important to our understanding of meaning than denotation. C. K. Ogden and I. A. Richards (1923) were among the first scholars to consider the misunderstandings resulting from the failure of communicators to realize that their subjective reactions to words are based on their life experiences. For instance, when Tina says, "We bought an SUV; I think it's the biggest one Chevy makes," Kim might think "Why in the world would anyone want one of those gas guzzlers that take up so much space to park?" and Lexia might say, "Oh, I envy you. I'd love to own a vehicle that has so much power and sits so high on the road." Word denotation and

denotation
the direct, explicit meaning a speech community formally gives a word.

connotation
the feelings or evaluations we associate with a word.

connotation are important because the only message that counts is the message that is understood, regardless of whether it is the one you intended.

³Third, meaning may vary depending on its syntactic context (the position of a word in a sentence and the other words around it). For instance, in the same sentence a person might say, "I love to vacation in the mountains, where it's really cool in mornings and you're likely to see some really cool animals." Most listeners would understand that "mornings are really cool" refers to temperature and "see some really cool animals" refers to animals that are uncommon or special.

⁴Fourth, the language of any speech community will change over time. Language changes in many ways, including the creation of new words, the abandonment of old words, changes in word meanings in segments of society, and the influx of words from the mixing of cultures. For instance, the latest edition of *Merriam-Webster's Collegiate Dictionary* contains 10,000 new words and usages. New words are created to express new ideas. For example, younger generations, businesspeople, and scientists, among others, will invent new words or assign different meanings to words to better express the changing realities of their world. For example, *bling* is used to describe flashy jewelry, *marathoning* is the practice of watching an entire season of a TV series in one sitting, a *desktop* is the visual surface we see on our computer screen, and *greenwashing* is the practice of making a misleading claim about the environmental benefits of a product, service, technology, or company practice. In the past 20 years, entire vocabularies have been invented to allow us to communicate about new technologies. So we *google* to get information, use the *wi-fi* on our *laptop*, and listen to a *podcast* while writing a *blog*. Words used by older generations may fade as they no longer describe current realities or are replaced by new words. We once used a *mimeograph*, but now we use a *copy machine*. In addition, some members of the speech community will invent new meanings for old words to differentiate themselves from other subgroups of the language community. For instance, in some parts of the country, young people use the word *bad* to mean "intense," as in "That movie was really bad," or *sick* to mean "cool" as in "That bike is really sick," or the word *kickin'* to mean "really great" as in "That concert was really kickin'."

⁵Fifth, as a society absorbs immigrants who speak different languages and becomes more multicultural, the language of the dominant group gradually absorbs some words from the languages of the immigrants. In English we use and understand what were once foreign words, such as *petite, siesta, kindergarten*, and *ciao*. Similarly, the slang used by a subgroup may also eventually be appropriated by the larger speech community. For example, the African American slang terms for "girlfriend," *shorty* or *boo*, are now used and understood by a more diverse group of American speakers.

Cultural and Gender Influences on Language Use

Culture and gender both influence how words are used and interpreted. Cultures vary in how much meaning is embedded in the language itself and how much meaning is interpreted from the context in which the communication occurs. In low-context cultures, like the United States and most

syntactic context
the position of a word in a sentence and the other words around it.

low-context cultures
cultures in which messages are direct, specific, and detailed.

People in high-context cultures rely on contextual cues to understand a speaker's meaning.

northern European countries, messages are typically quite direct and language is very specific. [1]Speakers say exactly what they mean, and the verbal messages are very explicit, with lots of details provided. [2]In low-context cultures, what the speaker intends the message to mean is not heavily influenced by the setting or context; rather, it is embedded in the verbal message. In high-context cultures, like Latin American, Asian, and American Indian, what a speaker intends for you to understand from the verbal message depends heavily on the setting or context in which it is sent. [1] So verbal messages in high-context cultures may be indirect, using more general and ambiguous language. [2]Receivers in high-context cultures, then, rely on contextual cues to help them understand the speaker's meaning (Samovar, Porter, & McDaniel, 2009).

When people from low-context cultures interact with others from high-context cultures, misunderstandings often occur. Imagine that Isaac from a German company and Zhao from a Chinese company are trying to conduct business.

How do culture and gender influence language use?

ISAAC: "Let's get right down to it. We're hoping that you can provide 100,000 parts per month according to our six manufacturing specifications spelled out in the engineering contract I sent you. If quality control finds more than a 2-percent error, we will have to terminate the contract. Can you agree to these terms?"

ZHAO: "We are very pleased to be doing business with you. We produce the highest quality products and will be honored to meet your needs."

ISAAC: "But can you supply that exact quantity? Can you meet all of our engineering specifications? Will you consistently have less than a 2-percent error?"

ZHAO: "We are an excellent, trustworthy company that will send you the highest quality parts."

high-context cultures
cultures in which messages are indirect, general, and ambiguous.

feminine styles of language
use words of empathy and support, emphasize concrete and personal language, and show politeness and tentativeness in speaking.

Isaac is probably frustrated with what he perceives as general, evasive language used by Zhao, and Zhao may be offended by the direct questions, specific language, and perceived threat in Isaac's message. Global migration, business, and travel are increasing the interactions that occur between people accustomed to high- or low-context expectations. As this happens, the likelihood of misunderstanding increases. To be a competent communicator, you will need to be aware of, compensate for, or adapt to the cultural expectations of your conversational partner.

Societal expectations for masculinity and femininity also influence language use. [1]According to Wood (2007), feminine styles of language typically use words of empathy and support, emphasize concrete and personal language, and show politeness and tentativeness in speaking.[2] Masculine styles of language often use words of status and problem solving, emphasize abstract and general language, and show assertiveness and control in speaking.

[1]Feminine language often includes empathic phrases like "I can understand how you feel" or "I've had a similar experience, so I can sense what you are going through." [2]Likewise, feminine language often includes language of support such as "I'm so sorry that you are having difficulty" or "Please let me know if I can help you in any way." [3]Feminine language often goes into detail by giving specific examples and personal disclosures. To appear feminine is to speak politely by focusing on others and by not being too forceful with language. Words and phrases like "I may be wrong but . . ."; "It's just my opinion"; "maybe"; "perhaps"; and "I don't want to step on anyone's toes here" are associated with feminine styles of speaking.

[1]By contrast, masculine styles of speaking often emphasize status through phrases like "I know that . . ." and "My experience tells me" and communicates problem solving or advice giving through such language as "I would . . ."; "You should . . ."; and "The way you should handle this is . . .". Masculine styles of communication may [2]favor theoretical or general discussions and avoid giving personal information about oneself. [3]To appear masculine, one's language must be forceful, direct, and in control through such phrases as "definitely," "I have no doubt," "It is clear to me," and "I am sure that . . . ".

Women and men can use both masculine and feminine language, although, generally, dominant American society expects women to use feminine language and men to use masculine language. One style is not inherently better than another, but each may be better suited to certain communication situations.

Improving Language Skills

Regardless of whether we are conversing with a friend, working on a task force, or giving a speech, we should strive to use language in our messages that accurately conveys our meanings. We can improve our messages by choosing words that make our meaning clear, choosing language that makes our messages memorable, and choosing language that demonstrates linguistic sensitivity.

Use Clear Language

We ought to choose words that help listeners assign meaning that is similar to what we intended. Compare these two descriptions of a near miss in a car: *"Some nut almost got me a while ago"* versus *"An hour ago, an older man in a banged-up Honda Civic ran the light at Calhoun and Clifton and almost hit me broadside while I was in the intersection waiting to turn left at the cross street."* In the second message, the language is much more specific, so both parties would be likely to have a more similar perception of the situation than would be possible with the first message.

Often as we try to express our thoughts, the first words that come to mind are general in nature. **Specific words** clear up confusion caused by general words

masculine styles of language
use words of status and problem solving, emphasize abstract and general language, and show assertiveness and control in speaking.

specific words
words that clarify meaning by narrowing what is understood from a general category to a particular item or group within that category.

How can you make
your language
more clear?

by narrowing what is understood from a general category to a particular group within that category. Specific words are more concrete and precise than general words. What can we do to speak more specifically?

For one, we can select a word that most accurately captures the sense of what we are saying. At first I might say, "Waylon was angry during our work session today." Then I might think, "Was he really showing anger?" So I say, "To be more accurate, he wasn't really angry. Perhaps he was more frustrated or impatient with what he sees as a lack of progress by our group." What is the difference between the two statements in terms of words? By carefully choosing words, you can show shades of meaning. Others may respond quite differently to your description of a group member showing anger, frustration, or impatience. The interpretation others get of Waylon's behavior depends on the word or words you select. Specific language is achieved when words are concrete or precise or when details or examples are used.

Concrete words are words that appeal to our senses. Consider the word *speak*. This is an abstract word—that is, we can speak in many different ways. So instead of saying that Jill *speaks in a peculiar way*, we might be more specific by saying that Jill *mumbles, whispers, blusters*, or *drones*. Each of these words creates a clearer sense of the sound of her voice.

We speak more specifically when we use **precise words**, narrowing a larger category to a smaller group within that category. For instance, if Nevah says that Ruben is a "blue-collar worker," she has named a general category; you might picture an unlimited number of occupations that fall within this broad category. If, instead, she is more precise and says he's a "construction worker," the number of possible images you can picture is reduced; now you can only select your image from the specific subcategory of construction worker. So your meaning is likely to be closer to the one she intended. To be even more precise, she may identify Ruben as a "bulldozer operator"; this further limits your choice of images and is likely to align with the one she intended you to have.

Clarity also can be achieved by adding detail or examples. For instance, Linda says, "Rashad is very loyal." The meaning of loyal ("faithful to an idea, person, company, and so on") is abstract, so to avoid ambiguity and confusion, Linda might add, "He defended Gerry when Sara was gossiping about her." By following up her use of the abstract concept of loyalty with a concrete example, Linda makes it easier for her listeners to ground their idea of this personal quality in a concrete or real experience. We can also clarify our messages by providing details. The statement "He lives in a really big house" can be clarified by adding details: "He lives in a 14-room Tudor mansion on a six-acre estate."

We can also increase clarity by dating information. **Dating information** are details that specify the time or period that a fact was true or known to be true. Because nearly everything changes with time, not dating our statements can lead some people to conclude that what we are saying is current when it is not. For instance, Parker says, "I'm going to be transferred to Henderson City." Laura replies, "Good luck—they've had some real trouble with their schools." On the basis of Laura's statement, Parker may worry about the effect his move will have on his children. What he doesn't know is that Laura's information about this

concrete words
words that appeal to the senses and help us see, hear, smell, taste, or touch.

precise words
words that narrow a larger category to a smaller group within that category.

dating information
specifying the time or time period that a fact was true or known to be true.

problem in Henderson City is over five years old. Henderson City still may have problems, or the situation may have changed. Had Laura replied, "Five years ago, I know they had some real trouble with their schools. I'm not sure what the situation is now, but you may want to check," Parker would look at the information differently.

Here are two additional examples:

Undated: Professor Powell is really enthusiastic when she lectures.
Dated: Professor Powell is really enthusiastic when she lectures—at least she was *last semester* in communication theory.

Undated: You think Mary's depressed? I'm surprised. She seemed her regular, high-spirited self when I talked with her.
Dated: You think Mary's depressed? I'm surprised. She seemed her regular, high-spirited self when I talked with her *last month*.

To date information, before you make a statement (1) consider when the information was true and (2) verbally acknowledge the date or period when the information was true. When you date your statements, you increase the clarity of your messages and enhance your credibility.

Finally, we can increase clarity through indexing generalizations. **Indexing generalizations** is the mental and verbal practice of acknowledging individual differences when voicing generalizations. Although we might assume that someone who buys a Mercedes is rich, that may not be true for all Mercedes buyers. Thus, just because Brent has bought a top-of-the-line, very expensive Mercedes, Brent is not necessarily rich. If we said, "Brent bought a Mercedes; he must be rich," we should add, "Of course not all people who buy Mercedes are rich."

Let's consider another example:

Generalization: Your Toyota should go 50,000 miles before you need a brake job; Jerry's did.
Indexed Statement: Your Toyota may well go 50,000 miles before you need a brake job; Jerry's did, *but of course, all Toyotas aren't the same.*

To index, consider whether what you are about to say applies a generalization to a specific person, place, or thing. If so, qualify it appropriately so that your assertion does not go beyond the evidence that supports it.

To ensure that our listeners decode our messages as we intend them, we can use words that are specific, concrete, and precise. We can also provide details and examples, as well as date our information and index our generalizations. Ultimately, our goal is to be understood. Practicing these strategies will help us achieve that goal.

indexing generalizations
the mental and verbal practice of acknowledging the presence of individual differences when voicing generalizations.

Use Language That Makes Your Messages Memorable

Because your listeners cannot simply re-read what you have said, effective verbal messages use vivid wording and appropriate emphasis to help listeners understand and remember the message.

How can you make your messages more memorable?

Vivid wording is full of life, vigorous, bright, and intense. For example, a novice football announcer might say, "Jackson made a great catch," but a more experienced commentator's vivid account would be "Jackson leaped into the air with double-coverage, made a spectacular one-handed catch, and landed somehow with both feet planted firmly in the end zone." The words *spectacular, leaped, one-handed catch*, and *planted firmly* paint an intense verbal picture of the action. Vivid messages begin with vivid thoughts. You are much more likely to *express* yourself vividly when you have physically or psychologically *sensed* the meanings you are trying to convey.

Vividness can be achieved quickly through using similes and metaphors. A **simile** is a direct comparison of dissimilar things and is usually expressed with the words *like* or *as*. Clichés such as "She walks like a duck" and "She sings like a nightingale" are both similes. A **metaphor** is a comparison that establishes a figurative identity between objects being compared. Instead of saying that one thing is like another, a metaphor says that one thing *is* another. Thus, a problem car is a "lemon" and an aggressive driver is a "road hog." As you think about and try to develop similes and metaphors, stay away from trite clichés. Although we use similes and metaphors frequently in conversations, they are an especially powerful way to develop vividness when we are giving a speech. Try developing and practicing one or two different original metaphors or similes when you rehearse a speech to see which works best.

Finally, although your goal is to be vivid, be sure to use words that are understood by all your listeners. Novice speakers can mistakenly believe they will be more impressive if they use a large vocabulary, but using big words can be off-putting to the audience and make the speaker seem pompous, affected, or

vivid wording
wording that is full of life, vigorous, bright, and intense.

simile
a direct comparison of dissimilar things.

metaphor
a comparison that establishes a figurative identity between objects being compared.

Using Specific Language

Communication Skill

Skill	Use	Procedure	Example
Clarify meaning by narrowing what is understood from a general category to a particular group within that category, by appealing to the senses, by choosing words that symbolize exact thoughts and feelings, or by using concrete details or examples.	To help the listener picture thoughts analogous to the speaker's.	1. Assess whether the word or phrase to be used is less specific (or concrete or precise) than it could be. 2. Pause to consider alternatives. 3. Select a more specific (or concrete or precise) word, or give an example or add details.	Instead of saying, "Bring the stuff for the audit," say, "Bring the records and receipts from the last year for the audit." Or instead of saying, "Make sure you improve your grades," say, "This term, we want to see a B in Spanish and at least a C in algebra."

Clarifying General Statements

Skill Building

Rewrite each of these statements to make it more specific by making general and abstract words more concrete and precise. Add details and examples.

1. My neighbor has a lot of animals that she keeps in her yard.
2. When I was a little girl, we lived in a big house in the Midwest.
3. My husband works for a large newspaper.
4. She got up late and had to rush to get to school. But she was late anyway.
5. Where'd you find that thing?
6. I really liked going to that concert. The music was great.
7. I really respect her.
8. My boyfriend looks like a hippie.
9. She was wearing a very trendy outfit.
10. We need to have more freedom to choose our courses.

stilted. When you have a choice between a common vivid word or image and one that is more obscure, choose the more common.

Emphasis is the importance you give to certain words or ideas. Emphasis tells listeners what they should seriously pay attention to. Ideas are emphasized through proportion of time, repetition, and transitions. Ideas to which you devote more time are perceived by listeners to be more important, whereas ideas that are quickly mentioned are perceived to be less important. Emphasizing by repeating means saying important words or ideas more than once. You can either repeat the exact words, "A ring-shaped coral island almost or completely surrounding a lagoon is called *an atoll*—an atoll," or you can restate the idea using different words, "The test will contain about four essay questions; that is, all the questions on the test will be the kind that require you to discuss material in some detail." Emphasizing through transitions means using words that show the relationship between your ideas. For example, some transitions summarize *(therefore, and so, so, finally, all in all, on the whole, in short, thus, as a result)*, some clarify *(in fact, for example, that is to say, more specifically)*, some forecast *(also, and, likewise, again, in addition, moreover, similarly, further)*, and some indicate changes in direction or provide contrasts *(but, however, on the other hand, still, although, while, no doubt)*.

Use Linguistic Sensitivity

Linguistic sensitivity means choosing language and symbols that demonstrate respect for your listener(s). Through appropriate language, we communicate our respect for those who are different from us. To do so, we need to avoid language our listeners might not understand, as well as language that might offend them. Linguistic sensitivity can be achieved by using vocabulary our listeners understand, using jargon sparingly, using slang that is appropriate to our listeners and the situation, using inclusive language and using language that is not offensive.

1. Adapt your vocabulary to the level of your listener. If you have made a conscious effort to expand your vocabulary, are an avid reader, or have spent time conversing with others who use a large and varied selection

How can you phrase your messages to demonstrate linguistic sensitivity?

emphasis
the importance given to certain words or ideas.

linguistic sensitivity
language choices that demonstrate respect for listener(s).

of words, then you probably have a large vocabulary. As a speaker, the larger your vocabulary, the more choices you have from which to select the words you want. Having a larger vocabulary, however, can present challenges when communicating with people whose vocabulary is more limited. One strategy for assessing another's vocabulary level is to listen to the types and complexity of words the other person uses and to take your signal from your communication partner. When you have determined that your vocabulary exceeds that of your partner, you can use simpler synonyms for your words or use word phrases composed of more familiar terms. Adjusting your vocabulary to others does not mean talking down to them. Rather, it demonstrates respect and effective communication to select words that others understand.

2. Use jargon sparingly. **Jargon** refers to technical terms whose meanings are understood only by a select group of people based on their shared activity or interests. We may form a special speech community, which develops a common language (jargon) based on a hobby or occupation. Medical practitioners speak a language of their own, which people in the medical field understand and those outside of the medical field do not. The same is true of lawyers, engineers, educators, and virtually all occupations. For instance, lawyers may speak of briefs and cases, but the general public might associate such terms with underwear (briefs) and packages of beer or soda (cases). If you are an avid computer user, you may know many terms that non-computer users do not. Likewise, there are special terms associated with sports, theatre, wine tasting, science fiction, and so on. The key to effective use of jargon is to use it only with people who you know will understand it or to explain the terms the first time you use them. Without explanation, jargon is basically a type of foreign language. Have you ever tried to listen to a professor who uses jargon of his or her field without defining it? If so, how did it affect your learning of the material?

3. Use slang appropriate to the listeners and to the situation. **Slang** is informal vocabulary developed and used by particular groups in society. Slang performs an important social function. Slang bonds those in an inner circle who use the same words to emphasize a shared experience. But slang simultaneously excludes others who don't share the terminology. The simultaneous inclusion of some and exclusion of others is what makes slang popular with youth and marginalized people in all cultures. Slang may emerge from teenagers, urban life, college life, gangs, or other contexts. A young adult, for instance, might say, "My bad" for "I made a mistake." *Sweet* could be translated as "That's great, fine, or excellent." Using slang appropriately means using it in situations where people understand the slang and avoiding it with people who do not share the slang terminology.

There is a new type of slang developing with digital and Internet technology. Experts in computer-mediated communication (Thurlow, Lengel, & Tomic, 2004) explain that with texting, for example, many of the rules of grammar, style, and spelling are broken. Many people adopt a phonetic type of spelling, which increasingly is understandable to this speech

jargon
technical terms whose meanings are understood only by select groups.

slang
informal vocabulary used by particular groups in society.

community but may not be understandable to others. Texters know, for example, that *lol* is short for "laugh out loud," *brb* stands for "be right back," and *jk* means "just kidding." Some communication experts who emphasize traditional styles of communication regard this new language of texters as incorrect, deficient, or inferior. Although this shorthand is convenient in cyberspace, using it in other settings could be problematic.

4. **Use inclusive language. Generic language** uses words that apply only to one sex, race, or other group as though they represent everyone. This usage is a problem because it excludes a portion of the population it ostensibly includes. For example, English grammar traditionally used the masculine pronoun *he* to stand for all humans regardless of gender. According to this rule, we would say, "When a person shops, he should have a clear idea of what he wants to buy." Despite traditional usage, it is hard to picture people of both sexes when we hear the masculine pronoun *he*.

Jeffrey Blankfort/Jeroboam

Why do you suppose someone felt compelled to add *woman* to this sign?

   The following techniques can help you be more inclusive: First, use plurals. For instance, instead of saying, "Because a doctor has high status, his views may be believed regardless of the topic," you could say, "Because doctors have high status, their views may be believed regardless of the topic."   Second, use both male and female pronouns: "Because a doctor has high status, his or her views may be believed regardless of the topic." Stewart, Cooper, Stewart, and Friedley (1998) cite research showing that when speakers refer to people using "he and she," and to a lesser extent "they," listeners often visualize *both* women and men (p. 68). Thus, when speakers avoid generic language, it's more likely that listeners will perceive a message that is more gender balanced.   Third, avoid using words that are gender specific. For most sex-biased expressions, you can use or create suitable alternatives. For instance, use *police officer* instead of *policeman* and substitute *synthetic* for *man-made*. Instead of saying *mankind*, change the wording—for example, change "All of mankind benefits" to "Everyone benefits."

5. **Use nonoffensive language.** Finally, you can demonstrate linguistic sensitivity by choosing words that do not offend your listeners. Do you swear when you are with your friends but clean up your act when you are with your grandparents? If so, you are self-monitoring your language so that you don't offend your grandma. Just as you modify your speech when you are with your grandmother, so too you should avoid language that is offensive to those you are talking with.

generic language
using words that may apply only to one sex, race, or other group as though they represent everyone.

Speech Assignment: **Communicate on Your Feet**

What Does It Mean?

The Assignment

Following your instructor's instructions, work alone, partner with some-one in the class, or form a small group. Make up a nonsensical word and then develop a short speech clarifying its meaning using the tools you have learned in this chapter. If you work with a partner or in a small group, identify a representative to present the speech to the class. After each speech has been presented, ask a volunteer from the audience to paraphrase the meaning of the word.

Guidelines

1. Be sure to include an attention catcher, listener relevance link, speaker credibility, and thesis with preview in your introduction. Be sure to include transitions between each main point. And be sure to restate the thesis with summary of main points and clincher in your conclusion.
2. Be sure to incorporate the concepts for clarifying meaning in ways that are vivid and linguistically sensitive in your speech.

A Question of Ethics

What Would You Do?

One day Heather, Terry, Paul, and Martha stopped at the Student Union Grill before their next class. After they had talked about their class for a few minutes, the conversation shifted to students who were taking the class.

"By the way," Paul said, "do any of you know Fatty?"

"Who?" the group responded in unison.

"The really fat guy who was sitting a couple of seats from me. We've been in a couple of classes together—he's a pretty nice guy."

"What's his name?" Heather asked.

"Carl—but he'll always be Fatty to me."

"Do you call him that to his face?" Terry asked.

"Aw, I'd never say anything like that to him—I wouldn't want to hurt his feelings."

"Well," Martha chimed in, "I'd sure hate to think that you'd call me 'skinny' or 'the bitch' when I wasn't around."

"Come on—what's with you guys?" Paul retorted. "You trying to tell me that you never talk about another person that way when they aren't around?"

"Well," said Terry, "maybe a couple of times—but I've never talked like that about someone I really like."

"Someone you like?" queried Heather. "Why does that make a difference? Do you mean it's OK to trash-talk someone so long as you don't like the person?"

1. Sort out the ethical issues in this case. How ethical is it to call a person you supposedly like by an unflattering name that you would never use if that person were in your presence?

2 From an ethical standpoint, is whether you like a person what determines when such name-calling is OK?

Summary

Language is a body of symbols and the systems for their use in messages that are common to the people of the same language community. Language allows us to perceive the world around us. Through language we designate, label, and define; we evaluate; discuss things outside our immediate experience; and talk about language.

The relationship between language and meaning is complex because the meaning of words varies with people, people interpret words differently based on both denotative and connotative meanings, the context in which words are used affects meaning, and word meanings change over time.

Culture and gender influence how words are used and how we interpret others' words. In low-context cultures, messages are direct and language is specific. In high-context cultures, messages are indirect, general, and ambiguous. Societal expectations of masculinity and femininity influence language.

We can increase language skills by using specific, concrete, and precise language; by providing details and examples, dating information, and indexing generalizations; and by developing verbal vividness and emphasis. We can speak more appropriately by choosing vocabulary the listener understands, using jargon sparingly, using slang situationally, and demonstrating linguistic sensitivity.

Key Terms

concrete words (550)
connotation (546)
dating information (550)
denotation (546)

emphasis (553)
feminine styles of language (548)
generic language (555)
high-context cultures (548)
indexing generalizations (551)

jargon (554)
language (544)
linguistic sensitivity (553)
low-context cultures (547)
masculine styles of language (549)

Skill Learning Activities

3.1: Identifying Specific Language (550)

Pick an article or essay from your favorite magazine (either the print or online version). Read through the piece, highlighting instances in which the writer uses concrete words and precise words. Also identify places in which the writer employs abstractions or generalizations that could be made more specific if they were expressed with either concrete or precise words.

3.2: Dating and Indexing Messages (551)

Read the examples below and practice adjusting messages so that they are dated or indexed. After writing your first draft, check to make sure that your revision is more concrete, precise, and provides examples and details. Now read your response aloud. Does it sound natural? If not, revise it until it does.

1. Oh, Jamie's an accounting major, so I'm sure she keeps her checkbook balanced.
2. Forget taking statistics; it's an impossible course.
3. Never trying talking to Jim in the morning; he's always grouchy.
4. Don't bother to buy that book for class. You'll never use it.
5. I can't believe you bought a dog. I mean, all they do is shed.

3.3: Similes and Metaphors (552)

Over the next three days, as you read books, newspapers, and magazine articles and listen to people around you talk, make notes of both the trite and original similes and metaphors you hear. Choose three that you thought were particularly vivid. Write a paragraph in which you briefly describe how and why they impressed you.

Web Resources

3.1: Merriam-Webster Online (550)

Merriam-Webster's online dictionary and thesaurus is an excellent resource that can help you not only at school but also in the workplace.

3.2: Slang Dictionary (554)

The Online Slang Dictionary is a collaborative project that features slang contributed by people from all around the world.

FOCUS ON TEST-TAKING STRATEGIES
Taking Subjective Tests

Objective tests, as you learned in Textbook Application 1, require you to choose a correct answer, insert a missing term or match definitions and concepts. They are called **objective tests** because there is a right and a wrong best answer. **Subjective tests** are different in that these tests require you to write your response and, often, take a position on an issue and interpret information that you have read. Preparing for subjective tests requires you to understand first and foremost what you are being asked and what type of written response suits the type of question you need to answer.

QUESTION-ANSWER RELATIONSHIPS

Question-Answer Relationships, or **QAR,** is a strategy that helps you understand what type of question is being asked and, therefore, how to answer it. In other words, using QAR gives you insight into what critical thinking level the question roughly corresponds to. You learned about the different levels of comprehension and critical thinking in Chapter 7. QAR, however, is simpler than the six levels of Bloom's taxonomy because this strategy breaks question types into four levels. This reading and learning strategy is very helpful when you interact with written text. By identifying the particular type of question you are being asked, you can gain insight into how to answer it.

This strategy works well for reading comprehension questions as well as for answering test questions. Questions fall into one of these four categories. If you identify the category, you will be able to answer the question more accurately.

1. **Right There.** This type of question is literal. You are being asked to locate information in the text that is explicitly stated and can be found in a particular spot.

   According to the passage, in what year was the author born?

2. **Think and Search.** Like Right There, this type of question compels you to find a literal or directly stated answer and locate information in the passage. However, unlike a Right There question, Think and Search requires you find the answer in at least two areas of the passage.

   Describe two or more techniques the author suggests to reduce the effects of stress.

3. **Author and You.** This type of question requires you to comprehend the passage and to locate information. However, you must also use your own experience or opinion along with that of the author.

FOCUS ON TEST-TAKING STRATEGIES: Taking Subjective Tests

Do you agree or disagree with the thesis of the article?

4. **On Your Own.** This type of question refers exclusively to your own opinion about a topic or your own experience and background knowledge.

How do you think the U.S. prison system could be improved?

In your opinion, what stresses do teenagers in the United States have to confront today?

With a partner or individually, find an example of each of the four types of questions in the QAR strategy in Chapters 1–7.

SHORT-ANSWER QUESTIONS

To respond to short-answer questions, first you need to determine what you're being asked. Use QAR strategies as well as understanding the types of questions you can be asked (see Types of Essay Questions later). For short-answer questions, the instructor wants you to fully answer the question in a paragraph or a few complete sentences. Only relate main ideas and major details unless the question asks you to provide examples.

Example: What is a speech community?

Short Answer: A speech community, also called a language community, is a group of people who speak the same language. There are between 3,000 and 4,000 speech communities in the world. Around 60 percent of the world's speech communities have fewer than 10,000 speakers. The five largest speech communities, in order, are Mandarin Chinese, Spanish, English, Arabic, and Hindi.

ESSAY QUESTIONS

Essay questions are often used to test your understanding of and opinion about an issue or reading. You will use your critical thinking skills to demonstrate how you have evaluated a reading when writing a good response to an essay question. When you write a response to an essay question, make sure your writing is coherent (makes sense) and logical. It is a good idea to make an outline of all the key points you wish to make, *before* you write, including your examples as supporting details to backup your main idea. A good guideline is to spend at least half as much time *planning* your essay as you do writing it, so that you carefully consider what you will say and how you will say it. A poorly planned essay usually lacks organization. Just as it is important to recognize the pattern of organization when you read an essay, it is equally important to use a pattern of organization when you write an essay. When you have completed drafting your essay, read it over carefully several times. Make any revisions you believe are necessary, and then proofread your work to locate and correct spelling, punctuation, and grammatical errors.

There are three major parts to taking a short-answer or an essay test: preparing for the test, taking the test, and before submitting the test.

Part 1. Preparing for the Essay or Short-Answer Test

1. Look over your notes for the class.

2. Refine your notes on the reading on which the test is based.

3. Anticipate questions that might be asked; look at discussion questions following the readings for ideas on what might be asked. Look at the headings, if any, or consider the topic of the reading or subsections, and use your skills for posing guide questions to anticipate test questions.

4. Prepare notes on possible questions and draft or outline your answers.

Part 2. Taking the Test

1. Read the questions carefully before responding.

2. Underline important parts of the questions so you make sure to address each part in your answer. Identify the type of question you are required to answer using the Question-Answer Relationship strategy.

3. Make a detailed outline of what you are going to say, including all examples. Your detailed outline will include the main idea, and major and minor supporting details. Remember to structure your notes to reflect the author's main pattern of organization in the reading.

4. Plan your time carefully according to the point value of the question. For example, if an essay is worth 20 points and a short-answer question is worth 5 points, plan to spend the majority of your time outlining, drafting, and proofreading your essay.

5. If you are not sure how to structure your essay, turn the question you are answering into a thesis statement by providing your opinion on the topic.

6. Provide at least three supporting points for your answer. This would be three supporting details for a short-answer question (as in the example

FOCUS ON TEST-TAKING STRATEGIES: Taking Subjective Tests

given earlier on speech communities) and three major points for each of three body paragraphs in an essay. Each body paragraph should contain several examples to support your topic sentence. If you are writing a persuasive essay, provide at least three supporting arguments to backup your point of view.

Part 3. Before Submitting the Test

1. Read your essay over to make sure the structure is clear and to catch any mistakes in spelling, punctuation, and grammar.
2. Double-check that you have included your name and the question to which you are responding!

Types of Essay Questions

This technique—learning how to identify exactly what you are being asked to write about—is helpful in writing essays or even short-answer questions. Most essay questions require that you have a firm grasp of the readings on which the essays are based. In addition, you will need to add your opinion or ideas in interpreting the readings.

Here are 10 common words used in formulating essay questions, along with a brief explanation of what you should do in responding to the question. If you understand the question, you will be able to use the appropriate pattern of organization in your response.

1. **Summarize:** Provide main points only.
2. **Outline:** Provide main points only.
3. **Compare/contrast:** What are the similarities and/or differences?
4. **Trace:** What is the sequence of events in time order?
5. **Explain:** Why? State your point and provide explanatory examples or reasons.
6. **Evaluate (or critique):** What are the arguments for or against and what are the strengths and/or weaknesses of each?
7. **Interpret:** What does the idea mean? How does it fit in with other, related information?
8. **Describe:** What are the important characteristics?
9. **Classify:** In what category does the subject belong? Explain why.
10. **Define:** What does the concept or key term mean? Provide examples of the idea.

OVERCOMING TEST ANXIETY

Test anxiety is a feeling we can all relate to. Who hasn't gotten nervous before a test? We all have. Most of the time, you get nervous for the following reasons:

1. You are not feeling well.
2. You are not prepared.
3. The test is really important, like a final exam or a placement test.

Let's face it, testing is a part of school and it's a part of life. Testing is here to stay, so you need to use strategies to reduce anxiety in order to do your best. Check out the following tips:

Before the Test

1. If you have a documented learning disability, make sure to research testing accommodations at your school early and completely.
2. Get a good night's sleep.
3. Review information just before you go to sleep because there's some evidence that your mind processes this information while you sleep.
4. Eat a good breakfast so a growling stomach does not distract you during the test.
5. Wear comfortable clothing, again to avoid any distractions.
6. Do not cram—used spaced practice and overlearn material (see Chapter 1).
7. Review major points right before the test—short-term memory can hold information for a brief amount of time, so there are limits to this tactic.
8. Use acronyms (each letter in a made-up word represents a word—e.g., NATO is North Atlantic Treaty Organization; AIDS is Acquired Immune Deficiency Syndrome) and rhymes to learn complicated information (My Very Educated Mother Just Served Us Nine Pies—each first letter of each word stands for the name of one of the planets in order from the Sun: Mercury, Venus, Earth, Mars, Jupiter, Saturn, Uranus, Neptune, Pluto)

During the Test

1. Breathe deeply, tense and untense muscles, and think of a calm, pleasant scene to reduce stress and anxiety.
2. Read the entire test over.
3. Answer questions you know the answer to (take care if you are using a Scantron test answer sheet to mark your answers in the correct space).

FOCUS ON TEST-TAKING STRATEGIES: Taking Subjective Tests

4. Do not change answers unless you are positive the new answer is correct (see Objective Test Taking in Textbook Application 1).

5. Note the time allotted for the test. For essay tests, you should plan to prepare your answer for at least half the allotted time.

6. Spend the most time on questions that are worth the most points.

7. Put difficult questions into your own words (paraphrase them).

8. Determine exactly what you are being asked to do (see essay test prompts and QAR).

9. Always read over your test answers or essays.

After the Test

1. Review your notes again to catch missing points only to the extent that it may help you learn the information for another test.

2. Do not fret over the test once it's done. Learn from your mistakes. Look over the questions on which you lost points. Read the instructor's comments, and see the instructor for further explanation if you have questions.

3. Take a deep breath, reward yourself, and move on to the next assignment.

If you apply these strategies consistently, your anxiety should diminish and your performance on tests should improve. If this isn't the case, talk with your instructor, advisor, or counselor about alternative measures.

On Your Own TAKING SUBJECTIVE TESTS

As your instructor assigns, answer a selection of the following questions. Your instructor may require you to complete your answers with or without notes on the chapter. Refer to the hints about taking short-answer and essay questions. Also, consider the Question-Answer Relationship suggested in each question you answer. Check your answer for spelling and syntax before you submit it.

SHORT-ANSWER QUESTIONS	ESSAY QUESTIONS
1. Summarize what is meant by a *speech community*.	1. Summarize the relationship between language and meaning.
2. Outline the Sapir-Whorf hypothesis.	2. Outline cultural influences on language.
3. Compare/contrast feminine and masculine styles of language.	3. Compare/contrast high-context and low-context methods of cultural communication.
4. Trace the uses of words.	4. Trace the relationship between language and meaning.
5. Explain the characteristics of clear language.	5. Explain how to make your messages memorable using specific examples.
6. Evaluate (or critique) the ethical concerns in "A Question of Ethics."	6. Evaluate (or critique) the varied use of language in *The Language of the Frontier.*
7. Interpret the message of the photo of the men working sign on page 555.	7. Interpret the main idea of *The Language of the Frontier.* Provide evidence from the feature to support your answer.
8. Describe *linguistic sensitivity*.	8. Describe how you can use language to make your message memorable in a workplace situation.
9. Classify the types of cultures in terms of communication.	9. Classify three major immigrant populations in the United States, and theorize which type of communication culture they would traditionally belong to.
10. Define *words*.	10. Define what makes a good communicator. Be sure to use language from the chapter to illustrate your definition.

CREDITS

This page constitutes an extension of the copyright page. We have made every effort to trace the ownership of all copyrighted material and to secure permission from copyright holders. In the event of any question arising as to the use of any material, we will be pleased to make the necessary corrections in future printings. Thanks are due to the following authors, publishers, and agents for permission to use the material indicated.

CHAPTER 1

Pages 22–24 and 57: From HALES. *An Invitation to Health, Brief Edition (with Personal Health Self Assessments),* © 2010 Brooks/Cole, a part of Cengage Learning, Inc. Reproduced with permission. www.cengage.com/permissions. Pages 27–29 and 46–48: From MASTER STUDENT. Book Block for Ellis' *BAMS: The Essential Guide to Becoming a Master Student,* 1E. © 2010 Wadsworth, a part of Cengage Learning, Inc. Reproduced by permission. www.cengage.com/permissions. Pages 36 and 37: From SHEPARD. Cengage Advantage Books: *Sociology,* 10E. © 2010 Wadsworth, a part of Cengage Learning, Inc. Reproduced by permission. www.cengage.com/permissions. Pages 38–40: "Procrastination: Ten Things To Know" by Hara Estroff Marano, *Psychology Today Psyched for Success,* 23 August 2003; Article ID: 2711; http://www.psychologytoday.com/articles/index.php?term=pto-20030823-000001&print=1.

CHAPTER 2

Pages 62–63, 71, 73–79, 83–85, and 122–123: From HALES. *An Invitation to Health, Brief Edition (with Personal Health Self Assessments),* © 2010 Brooks/Cole, a part of Cengage Learning, Inc. Reproduced with permission. www.cengage.com/permissions. Pages 67–69, 72–73, and 94: From KAIL/CAVANAUGH. *Human Development,* 5E. © 2010 Wadsworth, a part of Cengage Learning, Inc. Reproduced by permission. www.cengage.com/permissions. Pages 67 and 68: "Tips for Staying Healthy" from Center for Young Women's Health Staff. ©2011 Center for Young Women's Health, Children's Hospital Boston. All rights reserved. Used with permission. www.youngwomenshealth.org. Pages 70 and 82: The American Psychological Association, http://www.apa.org/helpcenter/stress.aspx. The American Psychological Practice Directorate gratefully acknowledges the assistance of Sara Weiss, Ph.D., and Nancy Molitor, Ph.D., in developing this fact sheet. © 2010 American Psychological Association. Page 72: Jeannette Curtis, "Stress Management: Managing Your Time," accessed from http://www.webmd.com/balance

/stress-management/stress-management-managing-your-time. Used with permission. Page 83: From the American Institute of Stress. Used with permission. Page 83: From the National Institutes of Health, http://www.nlm.nih.gov/medlineplus/stress.html. Pages 102–105: From "10 Healthy Habits That May Help You Live to 100", by Deborah Kotz, *U.S. News and World Report, February* 2009. Copyright 2009 by *U.S. News & World Report*. Reproduced with permission. Pages 111 and 112: From MASTER STUDENT. Book Block for Ellis' *BAMS: The Essential Guide to Becoming a Master Student*, 1E. © 2010 Wadsworth, a part of Cengage Learning, Inc. Reproduced by permission. www.cengage.com/permissions.

CHAPTER 3

Pages 128 and 129: "Money = Happiness" by John M Grohol, PSYD http://psychcentral.com/blog/archives/2008/09/05/money-happiness/. Used with permission. Pages 132, 146, and 158: From Wired.com, Jonah Lehrer, "Why Money Makes You Unhappy". http://www.wired.com /wiredscience/2010/07 /happiness-and-money-2/ Copyright © 2010 Condé Nast Publications. All rights reserved. Originally published in Wired.com. Reprinted by permission. Page 133: "How to Regularly Balance Your Checkbook" from http://www.ehow.com/how_2597_regularly-balance-checkbook.html. Pages 134 and 137: "Does financial-literacy education work?" Laura Levine from Billitteri, T. J. (2009, September 4). Financial literacy. *CQ Researcher, 19,* 717–740. Retrieved October 6, 2010, from CQ Researcher Online, http://library.cqpress.com.ezproxy.stlcc.edu/cqresearcher/cqresrre2009090406, Copyright © 2009 CQ Press, a division of SAGE Publications, Inc. Pages 136, 147, 157, 196, and 197: From Duncan Greenberg, "Billionaire Clusters", *Forbes* Magazine, April 2, 2009. Reprinted by Permission of Forbes Media LLC © 2011. Page 137: Reprinted by permission of Harold Ober Associates Incorporated. Extract by Langston Hughes from *Freedomways* magazine, Summer 1963, Vol. 3, #3. Copyright © 1963. Copyright renewed 1991 by Arnold Rampersad and Ramona Bass. Page 138: Consumer Reports, "Mark Your Calendars: What's on Sale When." Copyright 2011 by Consumers Union of U.S., Inc. Yonkers, NY 10703-1057, a nonprofit organization. Reprinted with permission from the January 2011 issue of Consumer Reports for educational purposes only. No commercial use or reproduction permitted. www.ConsumerReports.org. Page 139: "How to Write a Check" from http://www.ehow.com/how_567_write-check.html. Page 139: Francesca Levy, "The World's Happiest Countries, Forbes.com © 2010 Forbes.com. Pages 146–148 and 158–159: From *Money,* 8/1/2006, © 2006 *Money*. All rights reserved. Used by permission and, protected by the Copyright Laws of the United States. The printing, copying, redistribution, or retransmission of this Content without express written permission is prohibited. Pages 149 and 156–158: From KAIL /CAVANAUGH. *Human Development*, 5E. © 2010 Wadsworth, a part of Cengage Learning, Inc. Reproduced by permission. www.cengage.com/permissions. Pages 150–152, 154–155, and 187–189: From SHEPARD. Cengage Advantage Books: Sociology, 10E. © 2010 Wadsworth, a part of Cengage Learning, Inc. Reproduced by permission. www.cengage.com/permissions. Page 159: From GALLIANO. Gender: Crossing Boundaries, 1E. © 2003 Wadsworth, a part of Cengage Learning, Inc. Reproduced by permission. www .cengage.com/permissions. Pages 179–182: From Newsweek, 10/15/2007, © 2007 The Newsweek/Daily Beast Company LLC. All rights reserved. Used by permission and protected by the Copyright Laws of the United States. The printing, copying, redistribution, or retransmission of the Material without express written permission is prohibited. Page 187: World Bank, World Development indicators, online database (http://publications.worldbank.org/WDV, accessed May 25, 2007)/ It also appears on the 2007 World Population Data Sheet. (Washington, DC: Population Reference Bureau), 2007.

CHAPTER 4

Pages 202 and 265: Adapted from "Our Genes/Our Choices," Fred Friendly Seminars, Inc., © 2010 http://www.pbs.org/inthebalance/archives/ourgenes/what_do_you_know.html. Pages 203–204 and 225: "Do Our Genes Make Us Popular?" by Jordan Lite http://www.scientificamerican.com/blog/60-second-science/post.cfm?id=do-our-genes-make-us-popular—or-no-2009-01-26 Reproduced with permission. Copyright © 2009 Scientific American, Inc. All rights reserved. Page 206: By permission from *Merriam-Webster's Collegiate® Dictionary*, 11th Edition. © 2011 by Merriam-Webster, Incorporated (www.merriam-webster.com). Page 207, 210–212, and 231: "How do genes influence behavior?" by Joseph McInerney http://www.ornl.gov/sci/techresources/Human_Genome/elsi/behaviors.html by the U.S. Department of Energy and the National Institutes of Health. Pages 209 and 210: "What is behavioral genetics?" by Joseph McInerney http://www.ornl.gov/sci/techresources/Human_Genome/elsi/behaviors.html by the U.S. Department of Energy and the National Institutes of Health. Page 217: "1990 Human Genome Project" from "Introduction: Understanding Heredity" by Lexi Krock, NOVA/PBS; http://www.pbs.org/wgbh/nova/genome/her_gen.html © 2010. From FRONTLINE/Tehran Bureau/WGBH Boston. Copyright © updated April 2001, WGBH Educational Foundation. Pages 217, 238, and 239: Genome Facts, NOVA/PBS; http://www.pbs.org/wgbh/nova/genome/facts.html © 2010. From FRONTLINE/Tehran Bureau/WGBH Boston. Copyright © updated April 2001, WGBH Educational Foundation. Page 220, 221, 224, 226, 227, 242, and 256–258, From KAIL/CAVANAUGH. *Human Development*, 5E. © 2010 Wadsworth, a part of Cengage Learning, Inc. Reproduced by permission. www.cengage.com/permissions. Pages 222 and 229: "Nature versus Nurture: Twin and Adoption Studies" http://www.nurture-or-nature.com/articles/twin-and-adoption-studies/index.php, © 2011 Tree.com, Inc. Pages 222 and 229: "Gene Environment Interaction" http://www.nurture-or-nature.com/articles/gene-enviroment-interaction/index.php, © 2011 Tree.com, Inc. Pages 222 and 241: "Biological Determinism" http://www.nurture-or-nature.com/articles/biological-determinism/index.php © 2011 Tree.com, Inc. Page 223: "Testing DNA Knowledge" http://www.healthtree.com/articles/genetic-testing/what-is-dna/, © 2011 Tree.com, Inc. Page 223, 227, and 232: Looking for Trouble, by Greg Fish, *Business Week* http://www.businessweek.com/debateroom/archives/2008/01/genetic_tests_i.html, © 2008 Bloomberg Businessweek. Used with permission. Page 226: "How is behavioral genetics studied?" by Joseph McInerney http://www.ornl.gov/sci/techresources/Human_Genome/elsi/behaviors.html by the U.S. Department of Energy and the National Institutes of Health. Pages 230 and 231: "DNA testing", http://www.healthtree.com/articles/genetic-testing/dna-test/, © 2011 Tree.com, Inc. Pages 231, 239, and 240: "Researching Your Ancestry Through DNA Testing", http://www.nurture-or-nature.com/articles/researching-ancestry/index.php, © 2011 Tree.com, Inc. Pages 232 and 241: "Testing DNA: Paternity, Ancestry and Prenatal DNA Testing", http://www.tree.com/health/genetic-testing-dna-test.aspx ©2011 Tree.com, Inc. Page 234 and 235: From: Genetic Consultation, from US National Library of Medicine. http://ghr.nlm.nih.gov/handbook/consult?show=all. Page 236–238: From the National Institutes of Health, http://history.nih.gov/exhibits/genetics/sect1f.htm. Pages 241 and 242: "What implications does behavioral genetics research have for society?" by Joseph McInerney http://www.ornl.gov/sci/techresources/Human_Genome/elsi/behavior.shtml by the U.S. Department of Energy and the National Institutes of Health. Pages 249–251: From Newsweek, 9/24/2009, © 2009 The Newsweek/Daily Beast Company LLC. All rights reserved. Used by permission and protected by the Copyright Laws of the United States. The printing, copying, redistribution, or retransmission of the Material without express

Page 267: "Self-Confidence: Nature or Nurture?" by Ray B. Williams http://www.psychologytoday.com/node/30794. Used with kind permission of Ray Williams. Pages 305–307: Adapted from Table 5.1 in Success Types for Medical Students, J. W. Pelley and B. K. Dalley (Texas Tech Univ. Extended Learning, 1997). Used by permission of John W. Pelley. Page 309: Based on J. K. DiTiberio & A. L. Hammer. (1993). Introduction to Type in College. Palo Alto, CA: Consulting Psychologists Press.

CHAPTER 5

Page 322: From *Power Sleep* by James B. Maas, Ph.D. and M L Wherry. Copyright © 1998 by James B. Maas, Ph.D. Used by permission of Villard Books, a division of Random House, Inc. and with kind permission of the author. Pages 322–324: "What Happens When You Sleep?" http://www.sleepfoundation .org/article/how-sleep-works/what-happens-when-you-sleep. Page 324: http://www.luciddreamex-plorers.com/dreamscience/ Used with kind permission from Richard Hilton. Pages 338 and 361: "Sleep-walking", National Sleep Foundation http://www.sleepfoundation.org/article/sleep-related-problems /sleepwalking. Pages 339, 340, 341, 345, and 349: From *Newsweek*, 4/27/2009, © 2009 The Newsweek /Daily Beast Company LLC. All rights reserved. Used by permission and protected by the Copyright Laws of the United States. The printing, copying, redistribution, or retransmission of the Material with-out express written permission is prohibited. Pages 342 and 347: "Narcolepsy and Sleep", National Sleep Foundation http://www.sleepfoundation.org/article/sleep-related-problems/narcolepsy-and-sleep. Pages 342, 352, and 354: From *Newsweek*, 8/9/2004, © 2004 The Newsweek/Daily Beast Company LLC. All rights reserved. Used by permission and protected by the Copyright Laws of the United States. The printing, copying, redistribution, or retransmission of the Material without express written permission is prohibited. Page 343: "Good habits for good sleep," from "Tips...to get a good sleep" by Gretchen Rubin, March 24, 2010 http://shine.yahoo.com/channel/health/tips-to-get-good-sleep-1229593/. Page 344: "Sleep Talking", National Sleep Foundation http://www.sleepfoundation.org/article/sleep-related-problems/sleep-talking. Page 346 and 365: "REM Behavior Disorder and Sleep", National Sleep Foundation http://www.sleepfoundation.org/article/sleep-related-problems/rem-behavior-disorder-and-sleep. Pages 346 and 347: "Restless Legs Syndrome (RLS) and Sleep", National Sleep Foundation http://www.sleepfoundation.org/article/sleep-related-problems/restless-legs-syndrome-rls-and-sleep. Page 347: "Nightmares and Sleep", National Sleep Foundation http://www.sleepfoundation .org/article/sleep-related-problems/nightmares-and-sleep. Pages 351–354, 357, and 363: "How to Get a Good Night's Sleep", http://www.k-state.org/counseling/topics/life/sleep.html, Originally written in 1989 by David G. Danskin, Ph.D., University Counseling Services; adapted and modified in 1997 by Dorinda Lambert, Ph.D. for use on the Internet. Page 351, 354, 363, and 364: Weir, Kirsten. "Who needs sleep? Maybe you do. Here's what you need to know about slumber, from A to Zzzzzzz's. (YOUR BODY)." Current Health 2, (Oct 2005): 16(4). Special Permission granted by Weekly Reader, published and copy-righted by Weekly Reader Corporation. All rights reserved. Page 353: "Animals' Sleep: Is There a Human Connection?", National Sleep Foundation, http://www.sleepfoundation.org/article/how-sleep-works /animals-sleep-there-human-connection. Page 354, 355, 358, and 364: From the National Institutes of Health, http://science-education.nih.gov/supplements/nih3/sleep/guide/info-sleep.htm. Pages 358, 361, 363: "Solutions for Sleep Deprivation College Students and Sleep Deprivation", http://www.sleep-deprivation.com/articles/causes-of-sleep-deprivation/students-and-sleep.php, © 2011 Tree.com, Inc.

Page 360: "4 Reasons To Sleep More: Why You Need More Sleep Tonight", http://www.fitnessmagazine. com/health/spirit/get-to-sleep-guide/5-steps-to-a-good-nights-sleep/?page=7 © Laurel Naversen Geraghty. Used with kind permission of the author. Page 369: From When Dreaming is Believing: The (Motivated) Interpretation of Dreams. Morewedge, Carey K.; Norton, Michael I. *Journal of Personality and Social Psychology,* 2009, Vol. 96, No. 2, 249–264. © 2009 American Psychological Association. Reproduced with permission. The use of APA information does not imply endorsement by APA. Page 371: From NAIRNE. *Psychology,* 5E. © 2009 Wadsworth, a part of Cengage Learning, Inc. Reproduced by permission. www.cengage.com/permissions. Pages 375 and 376: "Nightmares: What Do They Mean? Are They Just Scary Inventions of Our Minds?" by Kassidy Emmerson 2010 © Associated Content, All rights reserved. Pages 382–385: From PASTORINO/DOYLE-PORTILLO. *ACP WHAT IS PSYCHOLOGY,* 2E. © 2008 Wadsworth, a part of Cengage Learning, Inc. Reproduced by permission. www.cengage. com/permissions. Page 385: From Ontogenetic Development of Human Sleep-Dream Cycle, by H. P. Roffwarg, J. N. Muzino and W. C. Dement, Science, 1966, 152:604–609. Copyright 1966 by the AAAS. Reprinted by permission. Page 391: From "Day persons, night persons, and variability in hypnotic susceptibility" by B. Wallace in *Journal of Personality and Social Psychology,* 1993, 64, 827–833 (Appendix, p.833). Copyright © 1993 by the American Psychological Association. Adapted with permission. Page 393: By *Mail On Sunday* Reporter http://www.dailymail.co.uk/health/article-1289813/How-bad-dreams-lead-high-anxiety.html# © Associated Newspapers Ltd. Used with permission.

CHAPTER 6

Pages 398, 399, 402, 403, 420, 422, 428, 432, 433, 448, 449, 467, and 468: From DAFT. *The Leadership Experience,* 5E. © 2011 South-Western, a part of Cengage Learning, Inc. Reproduced by permission. www. cengage.com/permissions. Pages 404–406: From GALLIANO. *Gender: Crossing Boundaries,* 1E. © 2003 Wadsworth, a part of Cengage Learning, Inc. Reproduced by permission. www.cengage.com/permissions. Pages 408, 432, 447, 449, and 450: From VERDERBER/VERDERBER/SELNOW. *COMM* (with Access Bind-In Card), 1E. © 2009 Wadsworth, a part of Cengage Learning, Inc. Reproduced by permission. www.cengage.com/permissions. Pages 412–414: "Career Success" by Joni Rose from http:// www.suite101.com/content/career-success-a11173 © Joni Rose. Used with permission. Page 415: Underlining example "Is the Glass Ceiling Cracking?" From http://www.goldsea.com/Air/Issues/Ceiling/ ceiling.html, April 1, 2008. Copyright 2000–2011 by Goldsea.com. Reprinted by permission. Pages 416 and 417: Latinas crack the glass ceiling by Teresa Puente, http://www.chicagonow.com/blogs/chicanisima/2009/08/latinas-crack-the-glass-ceiling.html. © 2009 Teresa Puente. Used by kind permission of the author. Pages 441–442 and 457–459: From HESS. *Career Success,* 2E. © 2008 South-Western, a part of Cengage Learning, Inc. Reproduced with permission. www.cengage.com/permissions. Pages 451 and 452: Excerpt from "Happy (Un)equal Pay Day" By Linda D. Hallman, April 19, 2010 http://www .huffingtonpost.com/linda-hallman/happy-unequal-pay-day_b_543463.html © 2010 Linda D. Hallman. Used with permission. Page 466: From VERDERBER/VERDERBER/SELLNOW. *Communicate!,* 13E. © 2011 Wadsworth, a part of Cengage Learning, Inc. Reproduced by permission. www.cengage.com/ permissions.

CHAPTER 7

INDEX

NOTE

NOTE

NOTE

NOTE

NOTE

NOTE

NOTE

NOTE

NOTE